W9-BNK-508

This is an annual. That is to say, it is substantially revised each year, the new edition appearing in April of that year. Those wishing to submit additions, corrections, or suggestions for the 1986 edition, should submit them prior to August 1, 1985, using the forms provided in the back of this book. (Letters reaching us after that date will have to wait for the 1987 edition.)

What Color Is
Your Parachute?

Other Books by
Richard N. Bolles

*The Three Boxes of Life, and How
To Get Out of Them*

Where Do I Go From Here With My Life?
(co-authored with John C. Crystal)

1985 Edition

What Color Is Your Parachute?

A Practical Manual for Job-Hunters & Career Changers

by

Richard Nelson Bolles

Ten Speed Press

The map drawings for
The New Quick Job-Hunting Map (Appendix A)
are by STEVEN M. JOHNSON,
author of *What The World Needs Now*

Copyright © 1985, 1984, 1983, 1982, 1981, 1980, 1979, 1978, 1977, 1976, 1975, 1972, 1970
by Richard Nelson Bolles. All rights reserved. No part of this book may be reproduced
in any form, except for brief reviews, without the written permission of the publisher.
Library of Congress Catalog Card No. 81-50471
ISBN 0-89815-143-0   paper
ISBN 0-89815-144-9   cloth

© Copyright 1981. United Features Syndicate, Inc. Used by permission.

Published by Ten Speed Press, P.O. Box 7123, Berkeley, California 94707.

Type set by Joanne Shwed, Mary Fran McCluskey, and Design & Type, San Francisco
Printed by Consolidated Printers, Inc., Berkeley, California

Preface

OR: WHY THIS BOOK WAS WRITTEN

There are two kinds of job-hunters. Successful ones. And unsuccessful ones.

It is tempting to think that the successful ones were just lucky. And the unsuccessful ones just unlucky.

For we are all, after all, at the mercies of large forces in the job-market, over which we have no control—is that not true?

Well, yes and no.

When surveys are done of successful vs. unsuccessful job-hunters, it turns out that there is a difference *in the way they conduct their job-hunt.*

In other words, *you* help to determine whether you will be successful in your job-hunt or not, by how *you* conduct your job-hunt.

I thought I ought to report to the nation—I did not dream "the world," though now this book has been translated into five other languages—*what* successful job-hunters do, so that we might have more of them. Over eight million people are out of work currently, in this country. That's a tragedy.

It turns out that the major issue in job-hunting seems to be that of Power.

Typically, unsuccessful job-hunters or career changers are crushed by their discovery of how much power is in the hands of Those Out There: their past employer, their would-be future employers, large inhumane corporations, an unconcerned government, an apparently unfeeling universe.

Successful job-hunters or career changers seem to (instinctively, or with coaching) start out by asking, "Okay, those people out there have a lot of power, but WHAT IS WITHIN MY POWER? What do I have control over? What is up to me?" That's what this book is all about.

I do not want to be misunderstood as claiming that there is some kind of magical formula which, if you follow it religiously, will absolutely guarantee that you will find the job you want, or be able to make a dramatic career change successfully, without going back to school. There is no such formula. You can do everything right, follow every instruction in this book faithfully, and still not find a job. Anyone who claims otherwise is obviously a fool or a charlatan.

What I do want to be understood as claiming is that you can *vastly* improve your chances, at job-hunting or career changing, IF you take seriously what IS within your own power, and work hard at THAT, instead of (as is the fashion, in this country of ours) "bitchin' and moanin'" about what is NOT within your power.

Having faced the job-hunt, and even career change, myself a number of times, I have done my own share of complaining, in my day. It is immensely enjoyable, as I can testify; but it doesn't get you a job.

As countless thousands of job-hunters know, from the depths of their being, the key to successful job-hunting involves the HARD WORK of sitting down and doing homework on yourself. Not a little, but a lot. That's what this book is all about.

There is no magical formula. But there ARE jobs out there. Between 1,000,000 and 3,000,000 a year. Someone is going to get those jobs. It is not necessarily going to be the person who can best do the job. That might be true in the kingdom of Heaven; but we are still here on Earth. The person who gets the job will be the person who knows the most about how to get hired.

We know from research that the enthusiastic job-hunter is infinitely more likely to be the one who finds a job than the matter-of-fact job-hunter (or career changer) who is merely "plodding through the paces." The more time you spend on identifying your greatest enthusiasms, the more you increase your chances of finding one of the jobs THAT ARE OUT THERE.

Your greatest asset in going about your job-hunt or career change is your own self-confidence BORN OF SELF KNOWLEDGE. The better you know your talents, gifts, skills — and in priority — the better your chances of finding a job.

The particular strategies in this book are not of recent origin. They were born during the era of the Great Depression. And they were born among blue-collar workers.

At that time, most workers were male. That is no longer the case, as we are all well aware. Given the massive influx of women into the job market during the past decade or so, no book on job-hunting or career changing these days can be insensitive to the issue of sexism in language. It was in 1960 that I myself first protested language with the omnipresent male pronouns, even when referring to women. However, twenty-four years later we are still, as a society, without any real consensus as to how to deal with the problem. Casey Miller and Kate Swift, in their excellent book *The Handbook of Non-sexist Writing,* have cogently argued — from history — that even as the solely plural "you" became in time a pronoun that could be both plural and singular, so the normally plural "they" must (in our time) begin to be used with singular ante-cedents, as well as plural. As they so well put it, in former times agreement in number was more important than agreement in gender, but now agreement in gender is more important than agreement in number. They further argue that this has already begun to become rather common usage ("Anyone using this beach after 5 p.m. does so at their own risk." — rather than "at his or her own risk.") In any event, following their wise advice, I have in this book consistently used "they" and "their" with singular antecedents.

In addition to my indebtedness to these two thoughtful authors, I want to express my indebtedness to others. I have throughout this book been scrupulous about giving credit for ideas wherever credit is due. Hence you will find the names of idea-inventors scattered throughout the book: John Holland, Bernard Haldane, Sidney Fine, and others. I am indebted to them all, as is every job-hunter or career changer who uses their ideas. But I would like particularly to single out John C. Crystal. When I first began, back in 1969, the research of suc-cessful job-hunting strategies, of which this book is the out-come, John took the time — as no one else did — to explain to me in great detail and at great length, over a period of several months, what was wrong with the whole job-hunting process in our society, and what could be done about it. He suggested the organizing principles which became the cornerstones (and titles) of chapters 5, 6 and 7 in this book. Later we collaborated in the writing of another book, *Where Do I Go From Here With My Life?*, which is a description of the life/work planning process that he developed over the years, out of many tributaries. We are friends to this day, and I am ever in his debt.

I also want to express my great debt of gratitude to the layout pixie and genius who has designed this book every year since 1972, Bev Anderson. Readers over the years have admired her handiwork; you ought therefore to know her name. She is a jewel.

So is my publisher, Phil Wood. He and I have not only been business associates, but friends as well, for over ten years now. I can say of him (and his associate, George Young and my proofreader, Jackie Wan) what few authors can say about their publisher: they are wonderful. Phil lets me write without editors, he lets me choose my own title, supervise the layout of each edition, and in general make the book to be exactly what I want it to be. In a word, kindness and gentleness and mutual respect are the attributes of our relationship. And they have been from the start, even when *Parachute* was in its most humble beginnings, bereft of any sign that it would ever become what it has become: the best-selling job-hunting and career changing book of all time. I would like his rare spirit to be recognized; hence this testimony.

My office staff in Walnut Creek, Suzette D'Martine and Joy DeLara, deserve a special word of appreciation, also, for all they do to help me deal with the ten thousand letters we receive each year. I cannot answer them all, but what I cannot, they can—and do. I hope they have a reward in Heaven, as well as here on Earth.

As for those letters, which so many of you send in, I cannot thank you enough. I *know* that the ideas contained in this book *work*; we got them from successful job-hunters. But it is wonderful to receive so many heart-warming letters from many of the two million people who have used this book, thus far. I enjoy hearing that you were able to figure out what you wanted to do with your life, and find it.

Readers have continually asked me, over the years, to share some of these letters, comments, and success stories. I have resisted doing that, because I think it sounds so much like a medicine man offering testimonials for his patent medicine.

But there is a sweetness in the letters and comments we receive, which warms the heart of the reader, so this year I am relenting, and sharing four letters with you who asked.

The first one:

"My English degree was useless in 1975: no teaching jobs, little experience. I wound up in a warehouse of low tech. Four years later, I was browsing books in a bookstore trying to find Christmas presents for mom and everyone else, when this strange title, *What Color Is Your Parachute?* grabbed my wallet and purchased itself, despite my ill feelings toward career manuals. I tell you no lie, the technique really worked. It wasn't exactly easy, but after six months of spare-time effort and two months of door knocking, street beating and network building, I made the break into software technical writing, with hardware sprinkled in for body. Take heart, dear lovers of the liberal arts. Though the slings and arrows cut your guts to ribbons, maintain your pride. You can grasp any technology you need to learn, be it programming, electronics or any other discipline, for you have learned how to learn, how to listen, how to communicate and, above all, how to think. Motivate yourself; please don't be the fool I was for four underpaid and stagnant years." (Ray Kampa, Nederland, Colorado)

The second:

"I cannot state too strongly what an enormous difference *Parachute* has made to my attitude in searching for a new job. The impossible has been made manageable and achievable." (Michael Robinson, New York City)

The third:

"I arrived in Portland in early September with an M.A. in Japanese linguistics, a vague idea of what I wanted to do, and a determination to use *Parachute* — which I bought two years ago and hadn't done much more than read through. I liked the philosophy right away and thought I'd give it an honest try. The upshot is that I know more about Portland after six weeks than I knew about Ithaca, N.Y., after ten years. I'm investigating international banking (!) which had not even occurred to me as a possibility. Three things from *Parachute* have been particularly helpful.

1. *Don't box yourself in or let anyone else do it to you.* I started out investigating a narrow field, and things got interesting when I stopped doing that.

2. *Don't believe anything you hear once.* I interview 5-10 people just to get a 'sense of the body' before I *begin* to believe things like 'American women have no chance in Asian business.' (That's the one *I* hear—most often from American men projecting their own feelings.)

3. *Beware of* under*employment.* The person who is ready to help me break into banking—if I decide I want to—was talking about skills and a level of responsibility I had exercised as a teacher, but at a level of salary which most teachers never see. If I take the plunge, I will be well-compensated for my period of *un*employment. (No surprise to you, right?) It's still not easy for me to call total strangers, but the results have been worth it. Thank you for writing such a useful book." (Liz Hengeveld, Portland)

And the last:

"I bought the '83 edition of *Parachute* in October of '83 at the suggestion of a close friend. I am 24 years old and was in a dead end 'underemployed' job. I worked in a shirt factory. I felt I was wasting my life in this job—but I didn't know how to get out, or what I wanted to do, or what I would be good at. Your book answered all of these questions and more. I believe that every senior in high school and college, at the beginning of their last year, should receive *Parachute*—I have recommended it to so many of my friends. Today is Sunday—tomorrow I start work as a Special Police Officer in our city's police department. So, for the first time in my life I actually am looking forward to going to work. By the way, I *did* follow the advice in *Parachute* and I did all my HOMEWORK. It is true—you can't wait for your ship to come in. You have to row out and GET IT. Dreams *do* come true. THANK YOU!! P.S. I am the first female ever hired by the Shamokin Police Department!" (Cathy Jo May, Shamokin, Pennsylvania)

I am *very* touched by such letters, and I thank each and every one of the ten thousand of you who write me, each year. I'm sorry I can't quote *all* your wonderful letters.

I close this preface with some statistics.

In our society, job-hunting (and career changing) is a repetitive activity. You have to (or you want to) go job-hunting NOW. But you will be doing it again, in all likelihood. The average job in America lasts 3.8 years. The average worker in our society works for ten different employers during their lifetime. The figures are probably not substantially different in other parts of the Western world.

Since job-hunting (and career changing) is such a repetitive activity in most of our lives, it is important that you do not depend upon someone else—your high school guidance teacher, your college career planning office, an employment agency, or an executive job-hunting place—to do the job-hunt FOR YOU. They can be helpful coaches, but no more than that. It is essential that, as much as you can, you learn to do the job-hunt for yourself. That way, as often as you have to go about it, after this, you will know how to do it effectively and successfully.

There is an ancient saying, which says it well: "Give me a fish, and I will eat for today; teach me to fish, and I will eat for the rest of my life." (Lao Tzu)

This book is an attempt to teach you how to fish with respect to the most difficult task that any of us faces in this life: the job-hunt, and career change.

It is difficult, because so much "rides upon it." Not just getting some bread. Not just finding something you can enjoy doing. What is riding upon it, when all is said and done, is the whole question of Who You Are.

To go about the job-hunt truly effectively requires not only that you find a job, but that you find a job which FITS YOU. Fits who you are, and why you are here in this world, and what it is that you have to contribute to this broken, hungry and nuclear-anxious world. If as a result of reading this book carefully, and thoughtfully following the steps it recommends, you discover in the end that your hunt was not only a job-hunt but also, in some sense, a spiritual journey into the very heart of you, no one will be surprised — least of all me.

Peace, and shalom, my friend.

Dick Bolles
P.O. Box 379
January 1, 1985   Walnut Creek, CA 94597

Contents

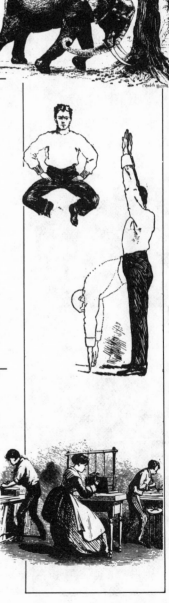

Your job-hunt is tax deductible. What to do about shyness. How much to trust your informants. Five questions to ask about an organization. How to choose a new geographical place to work. Six Practical Aids to help your research. What books to look at in the library. How to find contacts. Can someone else do all this for you? Informational interviewing: its virtues and its defects. The difference between Curiosity and Trickery. The seven rules to observe when doing Informational Interviewing or Research. How to survey a faraway place. Inspiration vs. perspiration.

CHAPTER SEVEN / PAGE 145

YOU MUST IDENTIFY THE PERSON WHO HAS THE POWER TO HIRE YOU AND SHOW THEM HOW YOUR SKILLS CAN HELP THEM WITH THEIR PROBLEMS

The difference between research interviews and job interviews. Trying to make up your mind what kind of job you want. Trying to find out who has such jobs. How many want the job that you want? The nature of the job market. The nature and importance of the monthly unemployment figure. How many vacancies are there? Four reasons why there aren't as many people competing with you as you think. Jobs not yet born. Why you *must* use *The New Quick Job-Hunting Map*, before you go out on interviews. Rules for identifying an organization's problems. How to read an organization's mind. The four uses of resumes. Why resumes work. Why resumes don't work. Your potential contacts in a faraway place. Why you probably should not approach a company's personnel department for a hiring interview. When it is okay to approach a personnel department. How to deal with handicaps during the job-hunt. Why all generalizations about employers are wrong. Typical questions an employer asks. The fear behind employers' questions. The four topics you need to cover in an interview. What signs the employer is looking for, during the interview. The crucial thank you note. If you get invited back for a second interview. Salary negotiation: its principles. What various occupations paid in 1984. How earnings vary within occupations. Promotions and raises. How to improve your luck. What is success?

APPENDIX A / PAGE 217

The New Quick Job-Hunting Map

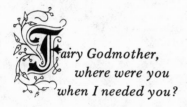

Fairy Godmother,
where were you
when I needed you?

Cinderella

CHAPTER ONE

A Job-Hunting
We Will Go

Okay, this is it.
You've been idly thinking about it, off and on, for
some time now, wondering what it would be like.
To be earning your bread in the marketplace.
Or maybe you're already out there,
And the problem is choosing another job — or career —
The old one having run out of gas, as it were.
Anyhow, the moment of truth has arrived.
For one reason or another, you've got to get at it —
Go out, and look for a job, for the first time or the twentieth.
You've heard of course, all the horror stories.
Of ex-executives working as taxi-drivers
Of former college profs with two masters degrees
working as countermen in a delicatessen.
Of women Ph.D.s who can only get a job as a secretary.
Of laid-off auto-workers waiting for the call (back to work)
that never comes.
And you wonder what lies in store for *you*.

Of course, it may be that the problem is all solved.
Maybe some friend or relative has button-holed you
and said, "Why not come and work for me?"
So, your job-hunt ends before it begins.
Or, it may be that you came into your present
career after a full life doing something else, and
You know you're welcome back there, anytime;
Anytime, they said.
And, assuming they meant it,
no problem, right?
So long as that's what you still want to do.
Or maybe you've decided this is the time to
adopt a simpler way of living,
And, so far, it's going well.
But for the vast majority of us,
that isn't how it goes.
We have to find a job, we do,
And no one's making it any easier.
We feel like Don Quixote, mounted, lance in hand; and
the job-hunt is our windmill.

Those who have gone this way before us
   all tell us the very same thing:
      This is how we all go about it, when our job-hunting time has come:
       We procrastinate,
         That's what we do.
           Busy winding things up, we say.
             Or, just waiting until we feel a little less 'burnt-out' and
             more 'up' for the task ahead, we say.
              Actually, if the truth were known,
               we're hoping for that miracle,
                you know the one:
                 that if we just sit tight a little longer,
                 we won't have to go job-hunting at all, because
                 the job will come hunting for us.
                 Right in our front door, it will come.
                 To show us we are destiny's favorites,
                 Or to prove that God truly loves us.
                But, it doesn't, of course, and
             eventually, we realize, with more than a touch of franticness,
           that time and money
         are beginning to run out.

        Time to begin our job-hunt (or career change) in deadly earnest.
       And all of our familiar friends immediately
      are at our elbow, giving advice—
     solicited or unsolicited, as to what it is we should do.
    "Jean or Joe, I've always thought you would make a great teacher."
   So we ask who they know
   in the academic world,
   and, armed with that name,
   we go a-calling. Calling, and
    sitting, cooling our heels
     in the ante-room of the Dean's office,
      until we are ushered in, at last:
       "And what can I do for you, Mr. or Ms.?"
        We tell them, of course, that we're job-hunting.
         "And one of my friends thought that you…"
         Oops. We watch the face change,

And we (who *do* know something about body language),
  Wait to hear their words catch up with their body.
    "You feel I'm 'over-qualified'? I see.
      Two hundred applications, you say, already in hand
        For five vacancies? I see.
          No, of course I understand."
            Strike-out. Back to the drawingboard. More advice, from
              well-meaning family or friends:
                "Jean or Joe, have you tried the employment agencies?"
                "Good thinking. Which ones should I try?
                The ones that deal with professionals? Where are they?
                Okay. Good. Down I'll go."
                And down we do go.
                Down, down, down, to those agencies.
              The ante-room again.
            And those other hopeful, haunted faces.
          A new twist, however: our first bout
        with The Application Form.
      "Previous jobs held.
    List in reverse chronological order."
  Filling all the questions out. Followed by
  That interminable wait.
And then, at last, the interviewer,
 She of the over-cheerful countenance, and mien—
She talks to us. "Now, let's see, Mr. or Ms.,
What kind of a job are you looking for?"
"Well," we say,
"What do you think I could do?"
She studies, again, the application form;
"It seems to me," she says, "that with your background
—it is a *bit* unusual—
You might do very well in sales."
  "Oh, sales," we say. "Why yes," says she, "in fact
    I think that I could place you almost immediately.
      We'll be in touch with you. Is this your phone?"
        We nod, and shake her hand, and that is the
          Last time
            We ever hear from her.
              Words are apparently not always to be believed;
                Sometimes they are used just to soften rejection.
                  Strike out, number two.

Now, our original ballooning hopes that we would quickly land a job
are running into some frigid air,
   So we decide to confess at last
      Our need of help — to some of our more successful friends
         in the business world (if we have such)
         Who *surely* know what we should do, at this point.
            The windmill is tiring us. What would they suggest
               that Don (or Donna) Quixote should do?
                  "Well," say they (beaming warmly), "what kind of a job
                  are you looking for?"
                  Ah, *that*, again! "Well, you know me well, what do you think
                  I can do? I'll try almost anything,"
               we say, now that it's four minutes to midnight, as it were.
            "You know, with all the *kinds* of things I've done —"
         we say; "I mean, I've done this and that, and here and there,
   It all adds up to a kind of puzzling kaleidoscope; but you see things
That I don't see, so there must be *something* you can suggest!"

"Have you tried the want-ads?" asks our friend.
"Or have you gone to see Bill, and Ed, and John, and Frances and Marty?
Ah, no? Well tell them I sent you."
So, off we go — now newly armed, with new advice.
We study the want-ads. Gad, what misery is hidden in
Those little boxes. Misery in jobs which are built
As little boxes, for the large spirits of men and women.
But, nevertheless we dutifully send our resume, such as it is,
To every box that looks as though
It might not be a box.
And wait for the avalanche of replies, from bright-eyed people
Who, seeing our resume, will surely know
Our worth; even if, at this point, our worth seems increasingly
Questionable in our own eyes.
Avalanche? Not even a rolling stone. (Sorry about that, Bob.) Not a pebble.

Well, time to go see all those people that our friend said we
ought to go see.
You know: Bill, and Ed, and John, and Frances and Marty.
They seem slightly perplexed, as to why we've come,
And in the dark about exactly
Just exactly what it is they are supposed to do for us.
We try to take them off the hook; "I thought, friend of my friend,
Your company might need — of course, my experience *has*
Been limited, but I am willing, and I thought perhaps
that you..."

The interview drags on, downhill now, all the way
As our host finishes out the courtesy debt,
Not to us but to the friend that sent us; and
then it is time for us to go.
Boy, do we go! over hill and valley and dale,
Talking to everyone who will listen,
Listening to everyone who will talk
With us; and thinking that surely there must be
Someone who knows how to crack this terribly frustrating
job-market;

This job-hunt process seems the loneliest task of our lives.
And we idly wonder: is it this difficult for other people?
Well, friend, the answer is *YES*.

Are other people *this* discouraged, and desperate
And frustrated, and so low in self-esteem after
A spell of job-hunting?
The answer, again—unhappily—is
YES.

YES.

YES.

*W*ell, yes, you do have
great big teeth; but, never mind
that. You were great to at
least grant me this interview.

Little Red Riding Hood

CHAPTER TWO

Rejection
Shock

OUR NEANDERTHAL
JOB-HUNTING PROCESS

Sure, the preceding account of the job-hunt is rather bleak. But it has happened, is happening, and will continue to happen to countless millions of job-hunters in just the fashion described (or even worse). Including you and me.

Is it because we are different from other job-hunters? No. This happens to about 95% of all the people in this country who get involved in the job-hunt, at one time or other in their lives.

Let us put the matter simply and candidly: The whole process of the job-hunt in this country is Neanderthal. (Say it again, Sam.)

In spite of the fact that nearly every adult American man and, presently, two out of every three women aged 16-64 have been or will be involved in the job-hunt at some time in their lives, we are condemned to go about the job-hunt as though we were the first person in this country to have to do it.

Year after year, our 'system' condemns man after man and woman after woman to go down the same path, face the same problems, make the same mistakes, endure the same frustrations, go through the same loneliness, and end up either still unemployed after an inordinately long period of time, or —

what is much more likely — underemployed, in the wrong field, at the wrong job, or well below the peak of our abilities. Neanderthal, indeed!

And when we turn to the "experts" in this field to say, "Show me a better way," we are chagrined to discover that the genuine experts (who *do* exist) are few and far between, and awfully difficult to find; while most of those whom the world accounts as experts (so-called "personnel people" or "human resource developers") are — in their quiet, meditative moments, and in their heart of hearts — *just as baffled by this job-hunt, and just as aware that they haven't yet come up with the answer to it, as we are.*

"Let's put it this way — if you can find a village without an idiot, you've got yourself a job."

From *The Saturday Review*, 8/8/77. Reprinted by special permission.

This is never more clear than when *they themselves* are out of a job, and have to join the multitude in "pounding the pavements." You would think that they would absolutely be in their element, and know just precisely what to do. Yet the average executive (even the personnel executive) who yesterday was screening, interviewing and hiring any number of people, is

just as much at a loss as anyone else *to know how to go about
the job-hunt systematically, methodically, and successfully.*

Very often, the best plan they can suggest to themselves is
the best plan they could suggest, in the past, to others: "The
numbers game." That's right, the numbers game. It sometimes
has a somewhat more sophisticated title (like, say, *systematic
job search),* but in most cases this is what it comes down to, and
this is what a number of experts are honest enough to call it.

THE NUMBERS GAME

In its original evolution, someone must have worked it all
out, *backwards.* It wouldn't have been all that difficult. The
logic would have gone like this:

For the job-hunter to get a job they really like, they need to
have two or three job offers to choose among.

In order to get those two or three offers, the job-hunter probably ought to have *at least* six interviews at different companies.

In order to get those six interviews he or she must mount a
direct mail campaign, sending out *x* resumes to prospective
employers, with covering letters, or whatever other kind of mail
will titillate prospective employers and their screening committees (personnel department, executive secretaries, et al.) like:
telegrams, special delivery letters, or whatever. So, how many is
"x"? Well surveys have indicated that each 100 resumes sent out
will get either 1-2^1, or 2-3^2 or 3-4^3 invitations for the job-hunter
to come in for an interview, — the figure depending on which
expert you are talking to, listening to or reading.

Consequently, the conclusion of this game is that you should
send out at least 500 resumes, with some experts saying 1,000
or 1,200, and others saying that there is no limit: send out 10-
15 each day, say they, keeping a card-file on them, recording
each outcome — responses, completed interviews and so forth.

In a nutshell, that is The Numbers Game — the best that the
personnel system in this country has been able to come up with
(except for a creative minority — more about them later).

You like?

1. Executive Register, 72 Park Street, New Canaan, Conn. 06840, cited this figure.
2. Albee, Lou, *Job Hunting After Forty,* cites this figure (on his page 137).
3. Uris, Auren, *Action Guide for Executive Job Seekers and Employers,* cites this
figure (on his page 140).

Most of the job-hunting books you can pick up at your local bookstore for five or ten bucks will sell you this game.

Most of the job counselors you can go to (paying fees up to $3,000 or higher) will sell you little more than this game — with maybe a little psychological testing and video-taped interview-role-playing thrown in.

Most of the personnel people in whose offices you may sit, will counsel you for nothing, . . . but *in this game.*

There may be a few variations here and there: and sometimes this old game is hidden under an exquisitely clever new vocabulary, so it sounds like a very different system. But if you are listening carefully to what they are saying, you will suddenly awake to realize it is, in the end, The Little Ol' Game We've All Come To Love and Know So Well: Numbers.

HOW WELL DOES IT WORK?

Now, let's face facts: no matter how much of a gamble it sounds, for *some* people this numbers game works <u>exceedingly well</u>. They luck in. They end up with just the job they wanted, and they are ecstatically happy about the whole thing . . . especially if they were engaged in only aimless job-hunting behavior prior to stumbling upon this plan. This works just beautifully, by contrast — *for some people.*

For other people, this numbers game works <u>passably well</u>. They end up with a job of sorts, and a salary, even though in retrospect it is not really the kind of work they had been hoping for, and the salary is quite a bit below what they really needed or wanted. But . . . a job is a job is a job. (Parenthetically, the one thing that the job-hunt 'system' in this country does, and does exceedingly well, is scaring people to the point where they are more willing to lower their self-esteem and hence their expectations as to what they will settle for.) So the numbers game works passably, as far as some people are concerned.

But for the vast majority of people who use this 'system' (some 80-95% of them, we guess) it <u>just</u> <u>doesn't</u> <u>work</u> <u>at</u> <u>all</u> — and particularly for those who are trying to break into a new career. With some notable exceptions, second-careerists have the most difficulty with this system.

Thus, some job-hunters have sent out 400, 500, 600, 700, 800 resumes or more, without getting <u>one</u> <u>single</u> <u>invitation</u> to come in for an interview. Only the polite acknowledgement ("thank you for yours of the sixteenth. We regret . . . ") or the polite turndown ("we will however keep your resume on file (in the wastebasket!) and should anything . . . ", or — in many cases, no answer at all.

PEOPLE-IN-THE-FORM-OF-PAPER

Nor, from the *company's* point of view, is it difficult to see why. Some companies receive as many as 250,000 resumes in a year. And even small companies may receive as many as ten to fifteen a week. The employment world floats on a sea of resumes, as some experts have observed.[1] Hence, in dealing with resumes at employers' headquarters, the key word for the personnel department (and executive secretaries) is not selection, but *elimination.* (Of course, if you're agriculturally minded — or Biblically minded — you may prefer: *winnowing the crop.*) Here, to a particular organization, flows in this endless stack of People-in-the-Form-of-Paper, day after day. If you're working there, and they hand that stack to you, what do you do with it? Well, of course. You go through it, to see if you can get the stack down to more manageable size. You look to see who you can eliminate.

Who gets nominated for this dubious honor? Well, $140 a week file-clerks who are applying for a President's job. And $140,000 a year Presidents who are willing to settle for file-clerks' jobs. And resumes so poorly written you can't tell anything about the men or women behind them. And resumes so slickly written (usually by a hired professional) that you can't tell anything about the man or woman behind them. And . . . people applying for a job for which they look as though they

---

1. Snelling, Robert, *The Opportunity Explosion,* p. 129.

do not have the necessary qualifying experience or credentials. Indeed, the resumes that have the greatest difficulty in getting through this Screening Process are those belonging to Zig Zag people, would-be career-changers who've accumulated a lot of experience in their old Zig profession, and now are trying to Zag. Their resumes, unless they are done extremely cleverly, find this Screening Out Process is a killer.

Well, all in all, how likely is *your* resume to survive the Process? A study of a number of different companies has revealed that they send out only one invitation to an interview for every 245 resumes that they receive *on an average*. But this average represents a range between companies which consent to one interview for every 36 resumes they receive, and companies which send out only one invitation to an interview for every 1,188 resumes they receive.[1] In terms of the first process that resumes are subjected to, therefore, the Screening Out Process searches for reasons to eliminate 35 out of every 36 resumes if we are lucky; or for reasons to eliminate on up to 1,187 out of every 1,188 resumes received if we're dealing with a tough company or market.

You are of course free to doubt these statistics and decide they are simply unbelievable. Or, you may want to make your resume *the one that gets through*. Or, you may want to know a better system altogether than the Numbers Game. We will try to point out aids for all three groups: the Doubters, the System-beaters, and the Alternatives-seekers.

REJECTION SHOCK

But, first of all, every job-hunter must *understand* our country's beloved job-hunting *system*. What it is. How it works. What its limitations are. What its out-and-out defects are.

Why? Well, first of all, to save yourself from Rejection Shock. Rejection Shock occurs when you set out to look for a job, confidently follow all the instructions that you are given about the Numbers Game (via books, articles, friends or paid professionals) only to discover that none of this works *for you* and after a lengthy period of time you are still unemployed. You then go into personal psychological Shock, characterized by a slow or

---

1. Deutsch, Shea & Evans, Inc. quoted on page 73 in *Electronic Design 16.*

rapid erosion of your self-esteem, a conviction that there is something wrong *with you*, leading in turn to lower expectations, depression, desperation and/or apathy. This assumes, consequently, all the proportions of a major crisis in your life, your personal relations and your family, leading to loneliness, irritability, and withdrawal, where divorce is often a consequence and even suicide is not unthinkable.[1] *(One major executive career counselor did a survey of 15,000 clients, and discovered that 75% of them were either facing, in the midst of, or just out of, a marital divorce.)*[2]

Rejection Shock also occurs when you set out to look for a job, confidently follow all the instructions you are given about the Numbers Game, only to discover that this only *partially* works for you, and after a lengthy period of time (often) you have gotten a job in which you are *under-employed*. You are in the wrong field, or at the wrong job, or well below the peak of your abilities. You go into Shock, consequently, because though you have a job you feel under-valued, ill-at-ease, underpaid and poorly-used, *and* you think you must be content with this under-employment *because you think that something is fundamentally wrong with you.* In the midst of Shock, as you are, it never occurs to you that perhaps something is fundamentally wrong with *the whole job-hunting 'system' in this country.*

A NATIONAL TRAGEDY

It should be every job-hunter's high purpose to avoid not only the obvious devil of Un-employment, but also the less-obvious devil of Under-employment, with every resource that is at your command. And, more than that, to determine to help

1. See Albee, Lou, *Job Hunting After Forty.*
2. In a study conducted by J. Frederick Marcy and Associates.

others to understand the Neanderthal 'system' in this country, so that they too may be spared the blight of these two devils.

Insiders estimate that even in Good Times 80% of our working people are Under-employed.[1] One doesn't want to even think what the figure might be during Hard Times. Certainly, in any case, this is a national tragedy. But people submit to it because they regard Under-employment as preferable to Un-employment. They prefer pounding a typewriter to pounding the pavements.

And in this instinctive fear, they are quite right. Insiders again and again announce statistics which reveal that those who regard the job-hunt as an occasion for leaping to a better job are taking a big gamble, and especially so if they are either on in years (polite euphemism) or unemployed, or both. Witness these statistics with regard to men in particular:

Of the several thousand middle-aged men who lose their jobs this month, one year from now 80% will be unemployed, under-employed (at lesser salary than before), or eking out a private income, even in Good Times, estimates one insider.[2]

Three million people are trying to get better jobs (at over $30,000 a year), and of these, 75% will not succeed in finding them — estimates another insider.[3]

A year from now, 20% of those middle-aged men who lose their jobs will still be unemployed.[4]

The cause of all this *(in large measure)*: failure to understand the job-hunting system in this country.

The result: Rejection Shock.

And, if it happens to You: Tragedy.

1. California State University at Fullerton, in its *CP & PC News*, reported a sixteen year study of 350,000 job applicants, which concluded that 80% were in the wrong jobs. As did Herbert Greenberg, president of Marketing Survey and Research Corporation (*The Futurist*, August, 1978).
2. Albee, *op. cit.*, p. 3.
3. John C. Crystal.
4. Albee, *op. cit.*, p. 3.

HOW TO USE THE NUMBERS GAME,
INSTEAD OF BEING USED BY IT

A second reason why every job-hunter ought to understand the numbers game, in all its parts, is you may want to use *some* parts of it to *supplement* your main program outlined in chapters 4 through 7.

A study of *The Job Hunt* by Harold L. Sheppard and A. Harvey Belitsky[1] revealed that the greater the number of auxiliary avenues used by the job-hunter, the greater the job-finding success. It makes sense, therefore, to know *all* the avenues that are open to you, how they work and what their limitations are, so that you can choose *which* avenue or avenues you want to use, and *how* you want to use them. You will then be in the driver's seat about these matters, as you should be.

The parts of this game most commonly alluded to are:

- mailing out your resume
- contacting executive search firms
- answering newspaper ads
- placing newspaper ads
- going to private employment (or placement) agencies
- going to the federal/state employment agency
- contacting college placement firms
- using executive registers or other forms of clearinghouses
- making personal contacts through friends, personal referrals and so forth.

We will look at the virtues, and defects, of each of these now, in rapid succession; to see why they usually don't work — and how you might get around their limitations. I will quote some statistics as I go along, in order to *illustrate* the aforementioned defects.[2] So, on with our exciting story.

---

1. In their book, *The Job Hunt: Job-Seeking Behavior of Unemployed Workers in a Local Economy.*
2. You will note that some of these statistics are not, ahem, *current* — to put it gently. That's because the most recent study about this-or-that part of the numbers game was done some years ago, and after seeing the depressing findings, no one has thought it useful to repeat that study since that time. And, believe me — the numbers game *hasn't* changed that much, since the studies cited.

HEADHUNTERS,
OTHERWISE KNOWN AS
EXECUTIVE SEARCH FIRMS

If you play the numbers game, and especially if you pay someone to guide you through it, you will be told to send your resume to Executive Search firms. And what, pray tell, are *they?* Well, they are recruiting firms that are retained by employers. The very existence of this thriving industry testifies to the fact that employers are as baffled by our country's Neanderthal job-hunting 'system' as we are. Employers don't know how to find decent employees, any more than we know how to find decent employers. So, what do employers want executive recruiting firms to do? They want these firms to *hire away* from other firms or employers, executives, salespeople, technicians, or whatever, who are already employed, and rising. From this, you will realize these head-hunting firms are aware of, and trying to fill, known vacancies. That's why, in any decent scatter-gun sending out of your resume, you are advised — by any number of experts — to be sure and include Executive Search firms. Not surprisingly, there are even a number of enterprising souls who make a living by selling lists of such firms.

You can get lists of such firms from:

1. The American Management Association, Inc., 135 W. 50th St., New York, NY 10020, has a list entitled *Executive Employment Guide,* $3.

2. The Association of Executive Recruiting Consultants, 151 Railroad Ave., Greenwich, CT 06830, has its own list of sixty top recruiters. $2.

3. Kenneth Cole publishes *The Recruiting and Search Report,* (Box 895, Naperville, IL 60566) 312-355-8133. $14 for two lists. Has worked hard to locate all known recruiters in the U.S. and their specialties. Current data base includes 10,000 recruiting firms.

4. Directory of Executive Recruiters, published by Consultant News, Templeton Road, Fitzwilliam, NH 03447. Published yearly, $18 or so. Lists several hundred firms and the industries served.

EXECUTIVE RECRUITERS

<u>Name</u>: Executive recruitment consultants, executive recruiters, executive search firms, executive development specialists, management consultants.

<u>Nicknames</u>: head-hunters, body snatchers, flesh peddlers, talent scouts.

<u>Number</u>: estimates vary, from 2,300 to 10,000.

<u>Volume of business</u>: they had combined billings of more than $300 million a year in 1980.[1]

<u>Number of vacancies handled by a firm</u>: each staff member can only handle 6-8 searches at a time (as a rule)[2]; so, multiply number of staff that a firm has (if known) times six. Majority of firms are one-two staff (hence, are handling 5-10 current openings); a few are four to five staff (20-25 openings are being searched for); and the largest have staffs handling 80-100 openings.

The question is: do you *want* these lists, i.e., are they going to do you any good?

Well, let's say you regard yourself as an executive, and so you decide to send recruiters your resume (unsolicited — they didn't ask you to send it, you just sent it). The average Executive Search firm may get as many as 100 to 300 such resumes a week. Or "broadcast letters." And, as we see above, the majority of such firms may be handling five to ten *current openings,* for which they are looking for executives who are presently employed and rising.

Well okay, that Executive Recruiter is sitting there with 100 to 300 resumes in his or her hands, at the end of that week — yours (and mine) among them. You know what's about to happen to that stack of People-in-the-Form-of-Paper. That old Elimination, Winnowing, or Screening Process again. Your chances of surviving? Well, the first to get eliminated will be those who—

1. *Business Week,* May 5, 1980.
2. Butler, L.A., *Move In and Move Up,* pp. 160-61.

a) are not presently executives, or b) are not presently employed as such, or c) are not presently rising in their firm.[1]

That's why even in a good business year, many experts say to the unemployed: *Forget it!* I do think it is necessary, however, to point out that things are changing in the Executive Recruiting field. For one thing, some firms now call themselves Executive Recruiters when yesterday they would have been called Employment Agencies. These new Recruiters do indeed represent employers; but they are hungry for the names of job-hunters, and in many cases will interview a job-hunter who comes into the office unannounced or mails them a resume. I have known so-called Recruiters who truly extended themselves on behalf of very inexperienced job-hunters. So, were I job-hunting this year, I think I would get one of the aforementioned Directories, look up the firms that specialize in my particular kind of job or field, and go take a crack at them. I wouldn't have done that when *Parachute* first came out. But times do change!

ANSWERING
NEWSPAPER ADS

Experts will advise you, for the sake of thoroughness, to study the job advertisements in your newspaper *daily* and to study *all of them, from A to Z* — because ads are alphabetized by job title; and there are some very strange and unpredictable job titles floating around. Then you are advised that if you see an ad for which you might qualify, even three quarters, send off:

    a) your resume, OR
    b) your resume and a covering letter, OR
    c) just a covering letter.

In short, what they're telling you is that you're playing the Numbers Game, when you answer ads. And the odds are stacked against you just about as badly as when you send out your resume scatter-gun fashion. How badly? (Better sit down.) A study conducted in two sample cities revealed (and I quote)

1. If you want to know more about the executive recruiting world, and what it is that the job-hunter can learn from recruiters, see your library or bookstore for the excellent *Secrets of a Corporate Headhunter* by John Wareham (Atheneum, New York, 1980).

"that 85% of the employers in San Francisco, and 75% in Salt Lake City, did not hire any employees through want ads" in a typical year. Yes, that said *any* employees, *during the whole year.*[1] Well, then why are ads *run*? For the fascinating answer to that, read "Blind Ad Man's Bluff" in David Noer's *How to Beat The Employment Game.*[2]

NEWSPAPER ADS

<u>Where Found</u>:

1. In the business section of the Sunday *New York Times* and the education section; also in Sunday editions of the *Chicago Tribune* and the *Los Angeles Times.*

2. In the business section (often found with the sports section) of your daily paper; also daily *Wall Street Journal* (especially Tuesday and Wednesday's editions).

3. In the classified section of your daily paper (and Sunday's, too).

<u>Jobs Advertised</u>: usually those which have a clear-cut title, well-defined specifications, and for which either many job-hunters can qualify, or very few.

<u>Number of Resumes received by Employer as Result of the Ad</u>: 20-1,000, commonly.

<u>Time It Takes Resumes to Come In</u>: 48-96 hours. Third day is usually the peak day, after ad is placed.

<u>Number of Resumes NOT Screened Out</u>: Only 2-5 out of every 100 (normally) survive. In other words, 95-98 out of every 100 answers *are* screened out.

1. Olympus Research Corporation, *A Study To Test the Feasibility of Determining Whether Classified Ads in Daily Newspapers are An Accurate Reflection of Local Labor Markets and of Significance to Employers and Job Seekers.* 1973. From: Olympus Research Corporation, 1290 24th Avenue, San Francisco, CA 94122.
2. Ten Speed Press, Box 7123, Berkeley, CA 94707. $4.95. Or at your local library.

THINGS TO BEWARE OF IN NEWSPAPER ADS

BLIND ADS (no company name, just a box number). These, according to some insiders, are particularly unrewarding to the job-hunter's time.

FAKE ADS (positions advertised which don't exist)— usually run by placement firms or others, in order to fatten their "resume bank" for future clout with employers.

PHONE NUMBERS in ads: don't use them except to set up an appointment. Period. ("I can't talk right now. I'm calling from the office.") Beware of saying more. Avoid getting screened out prematurely over the telephone.

THOSE PHRASES which need lots of translating, like: "Energetic self-starter wanted" (= You'll be working on commission)
"Good organizational skills" (= You'll be handling the filing)
"Make an investment in your future" (= This is a franchise or pyramid scheme)
"Much client contact" (= You handle the phone, or make 'cold calls' on clients)
"Planning and coordinating" (= You book the boss's travel arrangements)
"Opportunity of a lifetime" (= No where else will you find such a low salary and so much work)
"Management training position" (= You'll be a salesperson with a wide territory)
"Varied, interesting travel" (= You'll be a salesperson with a wide territory)

Of course, you may be one who still likes to cover all bets, and if so, you will want to know how *your* resume can be the one that gets through the Screening Process. (Let's be honest: answering ads *has* paid off, for *some* job-hunters.)

Most of the experts say, *if* you're going to play this game:

1. All you're trying to do, in answering the ad, is to avoid getting screened out, and to be invited in for an interview. Period. So, quote the ad's specifications, and tailor your resume or case history letter (if you prefer *that* to a resume) — so that *you* fit their specifications as closely as possible.

2. Omit all else from your response (so there is no further excuse for Screening you out). Volunteer *nothing* else. Period.

3. *If* the ad requested salary requirements, some experts say ignore the request; others say, state a salary range (of as much as three to ten thousand dollars variation) adding the words "depending on the nature and scope of duties and responsibilities," or words to that effect. If the ad does not mention salary requirements, *don't you either.* Why give an excuse for getting your response Screened Out?

PLACING ADS YOURSELF

Sometimes job-hunters try to make their availability known, by placing ads themselves in newspapers or journals.

PLACING ADS

Name of Ads (Commonly): Positions wanted (by the job-hunter, that is).

Found in: *Wall Street Journal*, professional journals and in trade association publications.

Effectiveness: Very effective in getting responses from employment agencies, peddlers, salesmen, and vultures who prey on job-hunters. Practically worthless in getting responses from prospective employers, who rarely read these ads. But it *has* worked for some.

Recommendation: If you take odds seriously, you'd better forget it. Unless, just to cover all bets, you want to place some ads in professional journals appropriate to your field. Study other people's formats first, though.

Cost: Varies.

ASKING PRIVATE EMPLOYMENT
AGENCIES FOR HELP

PRIVATE EMPLOYMENT AGENCIES

Number: Nobody Knows, since new ones are born, and old ones die, every week. There are probably at least 8,000 private employment or placement agencies in the U.S. Maybe a lot more.

Specialization: Many specialize in executives, financial, data processing, or other specialties.

Fees: Employer; or job-hunter may pay *but only when and if hired.* Fees vary from state to state. Tax deductible. In New York, for example, a fee cannot exceed 60% of one month's salary, i.e., a $15,000 a year job will cost you $750. The fee may be paid in weekly installments of 10% (e.g., $75 on a $750 total). In 80% of executives' cases, it is the employer who pays the fee.

Contract: The application form filled out by the job-hunter at an agency *is* the contract.

Exclusive handling: Don't give it, even if they ask for it. If you find a job independently of them, you may still have to pay them a fee.

Nature of business: Primarily a volume business, requiring rapid turnover of clientele, with genuine attention given only to the most-marketable job-hunters, in what one insider has called "a short-term matching game."

Effectiveness: Some time back, a spokesman for the Federal Trade Commission announced that the average placement rate for employment agencies was only 5% of those who walked in the door. (That means a 95% failure rate, right?)

PRIVATE EMPLOYMENT AGENCIES continued

<u>Loyalty</u>: Agency's loyalty in the very nature of things must lie with those who pay the bills (which in most cases is the employer), and those who represent repeat business (again, employers).

<u>Evaluation</u>: An agency, with its dependency on rapid-turnover volume business, usually has no time to deal with *any* problems (like, career-transitions). *Possible exception for you to investigate:* a new, or suddenly expanding agency, which needs job-hunters badly if it is ever to get employers' business.

**ASKING THE
FEDERAL-STATE
EMPLOYMENT SERVICE
FOR HELP**

UNITED STATES EMPLOYMENT SERVICE

Number: 2,600 offices in the country. USES (often called "Job Service") has been greatly reduced in staff and budget recently.

Services: Most state offices of USES not only serve entry level workers, but also have services for professionals. Washington, D.C. had most innovative one. Middle management (and up) job-hunters still tend to avoid it.

Nationwide Network: In any city (as a rule) you can inquire about job opportunities in other states or cities, for a particular field. Also see Job Bank (page 31).

Openings: Nine million non-agricultural job vacancies were listed with USES in 1979. Today, who knows?

UNITED STATES
EMPLOYMENT SERVICE

<u>Placements</u>: Of the 15+ million registering with USES
in 1979, approximately 30% were placed in jobs.
Almost half of these were blue-collar jobs, and
another quarter were white-collar jobs. A survey
of one area raised some question about the quality of placement, moreover, when it was discovered that 57% of those placed in that geographical area by USES were not working at their jobs
anymore, just 30 days later.[1] (That would reduce
the placement rate to 17%, *at best*; an 83% failure rate. It's probably closer to 13.7% placement,
hence an 86.3% failure rate.)

---

1. The San Francisco Bay Area, for the period January 1966 thru April 1967, as
reported in *Placement and Counseling In a Changing Labor Market: Public and Private
Employment Agencies and Schools.* Report of the San Francisco Bay Area Placement
and Counseling Survey, by Margaret Thal-Larsen. HR Institute of Industrial Relations,
UC Berkeley, August, 1970.

COLLEGE
PLACEMENT
CENTERS

COLLEGE PLACEMENT OFFICES

Where Located: Most of the 3,280 institutions of higher education in this country have some kind of placement function, however informal.

Helpfulness: Some are very good, because they understand that job-hunting will be a repetitive activity throughout the lives of their students; hence they try to teach an empowering process of self-directed job-hunting. Other offices, however, still think they have done their job if they have helped "each student find a job upon graduation," through the use of recruiters, bulletin board listings, and the like; i.e., if they help their students with this one job-hunt this one time.

Directory: A directory of these offices is published, and is available for perusal in most Placement Offices. It is called the *Directory of Career Planning and Placement Offices,* and is published by the College Placement Council, Inc., Box 2263, Bethlehem, PA 18001. This directory is not a complete listing of all such offices in the country. The Career Planning and Placement Office (c/o Office of Counseling and Testing) at Western Nevada Community College, for example, has asked us to point out that they exist, even though they are not in this directory. (7000 Sullivan Lane, Reno, NV 89505. 702-673-4666.)

If you are not only a college graduate but also a hopeless romantic, you will have a vision of blissful cooperation existing between all of these placement offices across the country. So that if you are a graduate of an East Coast college, let us say, and subsequently you move to California, and want help with career planning, you should in theory be able to walk into the placement office on any California campus, and be helped by that office (a non-altruistic service based on the likelihood that a graduate of that California campus is, at the same moment, walking into the placement office of your East Coast college – and thus, to coin a phrase, "one hand is washing another"). Some places do do this. But, alas and alack, dear graduate, in most cases it doesn't work like that. You will be told, sometimes with genuine regret, that *by official policy*, this particular placement office on this particular campus is only allowed to aid its own students and alumni. One Slight Ray of Hope: on a number of campuses, there are career counselors who think this policy is absolutely asinine, so if you walk into the Career Planning office on that campus, *are lucky enough to get one of Those Counselors,* and you don't mention whether or not you went to that college – the counselor will never ask, and will proceed to help you just as though you were a real person.

This restriction (to their own students and graduates) is less likely to be found at Community Colleges than it is at four-year institutions. So if you run into a dead end, try a Community College near you.

SUBSCRIBING TO
REGISTERS OR
CLEARINGHOUSES
OF VACANCIES

REGISTERS OR CLEARING-HOUSE OPERATIONS

These are attempts to set up "job exchanges" or a kind of bulletin board where employer and job-hunter can meet. The private clearinghouses commonly handle both employer and job-hunter listings, charging each.

<u>Types</u>: federal and private; general and specialized fields; listing either future projected openings, or present ones; listing employers' vacancies, or job-hunters' resumes (in brief), or both.

<u>Cost to Job-Hunter</u>: ranges from free, to $75 or more.

<u>Effectiveness</u>: A register may have as many as 13,000 clients registered with it (if it is a private opera-

tion), and (let us say) 500 openings at one time, from employer clients. Some registers will let employer know of every client who is eligible; others will pick out the few best ones. You must figure out what the odds for you as job-hunter are. A newer register *may* do more for you than an older one.

This is a very popular idea, and new entrants in the field are appearing constantly. On the following cards, we list some examples:

REGISTERS ETC.
continued

General Clearinghouse Listing Present Vacancies: The
State Employment Offices in 48 states, covering
more than 300 separate labor market areas, have
set up a computerized (in most cities) *job bank*
to provide daily listings of job openings in that
city. If every employer cooperated and listed
every opening they had, each day, it would be a
great concept. Unhappily, employers prefer to
fill many jobs above $11,000 in more personal,
informal ways. So the Job Bank remains a rather
limited resource for such jobs. *Can be a helpful
research instrument,* however. A summary of the
job orders placed by employers at Job Banks

during the previous month used to be published
under the title of "Occupations In Demand At
Job Service Offices." It is apparently no longer
available.

A Clearinghouse of Newspaper Ads: The idea of someone reading on your behalf the classified sections
of a lot of newspapers in this country, and publishing a summary thereof on a weekly basis (or
so), is not a new idea — but it is apparently
growing increasingly popular. Problem: how old
the ads may be by the time you the subscriber
read them. That answer will turn out to be the

REGISTERS ETC.
continued

sum of the following times: a) the time it took for the hometown paper, in which the ad first appeared, to be sent to the town in which the clearinghouse operates; plus b) the time the clearinghouse held on to the ad, — especially if it just missed "last week's" edition of the clearinghouse Report; plus c) the time it took, after insertion in the Report, before the Report came 'off the press'; plus d) the time it took for the clearinghouse's Report to get across the country to you (discount this last, if you live in the clearinghouse's backyard; otherwise give this Large Weight, especially if it is not sent First Class/Airmail — or have you forgotten about our

beloved Postal Service?); plus e) the time it takes to get your response from your town to the town in which the ad appeared. You'll recall from page 21 that most classified ads receive more than enough responses within 96 hours of the ad's first appearing; how likely an employer is to wait for you to send in your response many days, or even weeks, later, is something you must evaluate for yourself — and weigh that against the cost of the service. If you want it, there are several places offering this service. Among the most reliable: the *Wall Street Journal* publishes a weekly compilation of "career-advancement positions" from its four regional

REGISTERS, ETC.
continued

editions. $3 an issue. Available on some news-stands, or order from: National Business Employ-ment Weekly, 420 Lexington Ave., New York, NY 10170. 212-808-6792.

Register for Teachers: The NESC Jobs Newsletters are published by the National Education Service Center, 221A East Main Street, Riverton, WY 82501. 307-856-0170. Between April and August, this weekly series of Newsletters lists between 1,000 and 2,000 new listings each week. Each week's edition contains only new listings, none repeated. The newsletters are published year round, with fewer listings in the months August to April. One month's trial subscription is $35 , with subscription refunded if first issue is re-turned within a week of receiving it, due to its

not being helpful to you. You select one or more of fourteen different job categories, and receive listings of jobs in those categories only.

Register for Government Jobs: *Federal Career Oppor-tunities,* published bi-weekly by Federal Re-search Service, Inc., 370 Maple Avenue West, Box 1059, Vienna, VA 22180. 703-281-0200. Each issue is 64 pages, and lists 3,200+ currently available federal jobs, in both the U.S. and over-seas. Subscription: $34 for six issues.

Registers in the Church: Intercristo is a national Christian organization that lists over 35,000 jobs, covering 4,600 vocational categories, available within about 2,000 Christian organizations in the U.S. or overseas. Their service, called Intermatch, costs the job-hunter $35. In 1984, 12,000 people used Intercristo; one out of every fifteen job-hunters who used this service found a job thereby. Their address is 19303 Fremont Ave. N., Seattle, WA 98133, and their toll-free phone number is 800-426-1342. Dick Staub, Executive Director.

Register for the Blind: Job Opportunities for the Blind, 1800 Johnson St., Baltimore, MD 21230. 301-659-9314, or 1-800-638-7518. Exists to inform blind applicants about positions that are open with public and private employers throughout the country. Maintains a computerized listing. Also, they have cassette instructions on *everything* for the blind job-seeker. Operated by the National Federation of the Blind in partnership with the U.S. Department of Labor.

OTHER REGISTERS OR CLEARINGHOUSES:

Is a thing a register or not? If job listings exist all by themselves, they tend to be legitimately called "registers." If they exist within the framework of a journal or magazine which also contains other material, they tend to be called "ads." There is a list of such journals; see Feingold, S. Norman, and Hansard-Winkler, Glenda Ann, *900,000 Plus Jobs Annually: Published sources of employment listings.* Garrett Park Press, Garrett Park, MD 20896. $8.95, prepaid. Lists more than 900 journals which carry employment want ads. The following list straddles both sides:[1]

---

1. My thanks to my friend, John William Zehring, former Director of Career Planning and Placement at Earlham College, for help with this list.

For Social Occupations: Volunteers for Educational and Social Services, 3001 S. Congress Ave., Austin, TX 78704 publishes a list of jobs available. The Family Service Association of America, 44 E. 23rd St., New York, NY 10010 publishes *Social Casework,* a journal which includes listings of jobs with social agencies.

For Internships and Jobs with Nonprofit Organizations: *Community Jobs,* published by the Community Careers Resource Center, 1520 16th St., N.W., Washington, D.C. 20036. Phone 202-387-7702. Subscription: $12/yr. for individuals.

For Jobs Overseas: *International Employment Hotline.* Monthly issues profile international employment opportunities. International Employment Hotline, P.O. Box 6170, McLean, VA 22106. $13.50 for three months for subscribers living in U.S. or Canada; $21.50 for three months, for those living elsewhere.

For Jobs In Criminal Justice: The *NELS Monthly Bulletin*, National Employment Listing Service, Criminal Justice Center, Sam Houston State Univ., Huntsville, TX 77341, 713-294-1692. $25 for 12 monthly issues. A non-profit service providing information on current job opportunities in the criminal justice and social services fields.

For Jobs with Youth or Children: The Child Care Personnel Clearinghouse, Box 548, Hampton, VA 23669 publishes a bi-annual list called *Help Kids.* You *must* enclose $1 for postage and handling, in order to get it, however.

For Jobs with Museums or Other Cultural Opportunities: *NCES* (Northeast Cultural Employment Services) *JOBSLETTER.* Published by N.C.E.S., Box 1080, Portland, ME 04104. Payment must accompany subscription ($38 for 10 issues, $75 for 24 issues). Published weekly.

For Jobs Outdoors: Environmental Opportunities, Box 670, Walpole, NH 03608, publishes a monthly listing of environmental jobs, internships and positions wanted notices under the same name. Cost is $20 for six months; $36 for one year. Latest copy: $3.50. Each issue contains 24-40 full time positions in a variety of disciplines. The Natural Science for Youth Foundation, 16 Holmes St., Mystic, CT 06355 publishes a bi-monthly job-listing, called *Opportunities*; the list costs $15.

Colorado Outward Bound School, 945 Pennsylvania St., Denver, CO 80203 publishes a nationwide "Jobs Clearing House" list.

One final word about registers: the very term "register" can be misleading. The vision: one central place where you can go, and find listed every vacancy in a particular field of endeavor. *But, sorry, Virginia; there ain't no such animal.* All you'll find by going to any of these places is *A Selected List* of some of the vacancies. A smorgasbord, if you will.

So far as finding *jobs for people* are concerned, these clearinghouses and agencies (like employment agencies) really end up finding *people for jobs.* (Think about it!) Heart of gold though they *may* have, these agencies serve employers better than they serve the job-hunter.

And yet there are always *ways* of using such registers to gain valuable information for the job-hunter and to suggest places where you may wish to *start* researching your ideal job (more in chapter 5). So, at the least, you *may* want to consult the Federal job bank (if there is one in your city), and perhaps a relatively inexpensive Register (if there is one in your particular field), as *auxiliaries* to the main thrust of your job-search.

OTHER IDEAS

Your Resume in a Book: Some organizations circulate small booklets which are essentially mass distribution of people's resumes in concise form. Forty-Plus Clubs do this, through their *Executive Manpower Directory.* So do some of the executive registry places. Evaluation as to its worth to you as job-hunter: well, it's a gamble, just like everything else in this Numbers Game system. A real gamble, if you are trying to start a new career. You have to boil your resume down to a very few words, normally. And then decide if you stand out. If not, forget it. If yes, well . . . maybe.

OTHER IDEAS

<u>Off-Beat Methods</u>: Mailing strange boxes to company presidents, with strange messages (or your resume) inside; using sandwich board signs and parading up and down in front of a company; sit-ins at a president's office, when you are simply determined to work for *that* company, association, or whatever. You name it — and if it's kooky, *it's been tried*. Sometimes it has paid off. Kookiness is generally ill-advised, however. $64,000 question every employer must weigh: if you're like this *before* you're hired, what will they have to live with *afterward*?

To summarize the effectiveness of all the preceding methods in a table (you do like tables, don't you?), we may look at the results of a survey the Bureau of the Census made. The survey, made in 1972 and published in the *Occupational Outlook Quarterly* in the winter of 1976, was of ten million job-seekers. Unhappily, this ten-year-old study is valid still:

USE AND EFFECTIVENESS OF
JOB SEARCH METHODS

Method	Usage*	Effective-ness Rate**
Applied directly to employer	66.0%	47.7%
Asked friends about jobs where they work	50.8	22.1
Asked friends about jobs elsewhere	41.8	11.9
Asked relatives about jobs where they work	28.4	19.3
Asked relatives about jobs elsewhere	27.3	7.4
Answered local newspaper ads	45.9	23.9
Answered nonlocal newspaper ads	11.7	10.0
Private employment agency	21.0	24.2
State employment service	33.5	13.7
School placement office	12.5	21.4
Civil Service test	15.3	12.5
Asked teacher or professor	10.4	12.1
Went to place where employers come to pick up people	1.4	8.2
Placed ad in local newspaper	1.6	12.9
Placed ad in nonlocal newspaper	.5	***
Answered ads in professional or trade journals	4.9	7.3
Union hiring hall	6.0	22.2
Contacted local organization	5.6	12.7
Placed ads in professional or trade journals	.6	***
Other	11.8	39.7

   * Percent of total jobseekers using the method.
  ** A percentage obtained by dividing the number of jobseekers who found work using the method, by the total number of jobseekers who used the method, whether successfully or not.
*** Base less than 75,000

Well, anyway, Mr. or Ms. Job-hunter, this just about covers the favorite job-hunting system of this country *at its best*. (Except personal contacts, which we give special treatment — chapter 6.) The Numbers Game.

If it works for you, right off, *great!* But if it doesn't, you may be interested in *the other plan* — you know, the one they had saved up for you, in case all of this didn't work? Small problem: with most of the personnel experts in our country, *there is no other plan.*

And that is that.

The Inquiring Reporter
asked the young woman why
she wanted to be a mortician.
Because, she said, *I enjoy
working with people.*

The San Francisco Chronicle

CHAPTER THREE

The True Nature
of The World
# of Work

YOU *CAN* DO IT!

So far, 'midst all of the facts and figures, two facts have stood out — like Mt. Everest — above all others:

1. In this country and all other countries within Western culture, our whole job-hunting 'system' is no system at all, but just a big fat gamble. If you find a job, it has more to do with 'pure luck' than anything else.

2. The job-hunting gamble poses particular difficulties for anyone who is trying to change careers — as four out of five of us will do, before our lifetime is over. (Remember, even a home-maker who decides to find a job 'downtown' is by definition changing careers: from 'homemaker' to 'whatever.')

MAYBE EIGHT TIMES

If we only had to go job-hunting once in our lives, this would be bad enough. But the average worker has to deal with the job-hunt *eight* times during his or her lifetime.

Nor can we always choose when those times will be. You may be *employed* today, and *job-hunting* tomorrow. 'Luck' enters in at every moment of your life in the world of work, and at any moment that luck may turn bad.

Everyone ought to be taught, from high school on, the true nature of the world of work. Unhappily, we are taught no such thing in high school. We have to learn the following truths about the world of work on our own, often from bitter experience:

1. You will get hired sometimes, for reasons which may have nothing to do with how qualified you are, or aren't. On some unconscious level, you just strike a spark.

2. You will not get hired sometimes, for reasons which may have nothing to do with how qualified you are, or aren't. On some unconscious level, you just don't strike a spark.

3. You will get promoted sometimes, for reasons which may have nothing to do with how well you are doing there.

4. You will not get promoted sometimes, for reasons which may have nothing to do with how well you are doing there.

5. Your employer may treat you well, in accordance with their stated values.

6. Your employer may treat you very badly, in total contradiction of their stated values.

7. Your employer may go on forever, and you may have a job for life, if you want it.

8. Your employer may go out of business, without warning and at a moment's notice, dumping you out on the street.

9. Your employer may stay in business, but you may be abandoned, terminated, fired or otherwise put out on the street, without warning, and at a moment's notice.

10. If you are terminated suddenly, your employer may do everything in the world to help you find other employment.

11. If you are terminated suddenly, your employer may feel that they do not owe you anything. You will feel as though you had been unceremoniously deposited on the rubbage heap.

12. Other employees may promise they will fight to save your job, but you need to be prepared for the fact that when the chips are down, they may actually do nothing to help you.

These are not pleasant facts, but they are *the facts*. Learn them now, and you will not feel the soul-chilling disillusionment that comes to men and women when they are 45 and learn for the first time that this is the way things are.

You need to stay cheerfully optimistic about the human race in the world of work, hoping always for the best, while at the same time being realistically prepared for the worst. In other words, dear reader, no matter how happily employed you may presently be, *you need to be always prepared and ready to go job-hunting*.

Some of you, of course, have only now picked up this book, when all these things have already come to pass, in your own life. You know too well their truth. Now you have but one course open to you that will do you any good: and that is, to leave the past behind, let go of your righteous anger at how different the world of work is from what you thought it would be, AND GET ON WITH YOUR LIFE.

According to a study published by Future Directions for a Learning Society, more than 40 million Americans are in some stage of career transition or job-change, in any given year. This is hardly surprising. The need for career-change is ever upon us.

Some careers have a built-in limit, such as baseball players, football players, boxers, runners, and the like. When that limit is reached, you *have to* change careers. Other careers could go on forever, in theory, but they have a high "burnout" rate. This is true of teachers, traveling salespeople, counselors, psychiatrists, personnel people, those who serve and care for other people, and so on. The initial enthusiasm and energy vanish, for some people, sooner than they had anticipated when they went into that profession, all starry-eyed. When you've gotten 'burned out,' you *want* to change careers. Some jobs get phased out by our society, as we move from a manufacturing to an information society. The buffalo-skinners, buggy whip makers, and blacksmiths of yesteryear, have their equivalents in our own day and age. If occupations are not becoming exactly extinct, currently, they are at the very least seeing a sizeable decline in their numbers. If you are a steelworker, a copper miner, a farmer, an airline worker, or a middle manager, you *know* what I mean. Sooner or later, you may *need* to change careers.

Career-change is also an issue for those who are forcibly retired before they are ready to retire — who still want to work. And for those who serve in the military, and are discharged at an early age. And for those who serve in the home, and then decide they want to or need to go to work. They face a career-change by definition.

Given the present course of history, it seems that career planning is something that *almost all* of us are going to face sooner or later. Many a job-hunt is of necessity a career-hunt.

The job-hunt lies before you. Perhaps even a career-change. And what are you to do? Must you go out and play the numbers game, as outlined in the last chapter? As Peggy Lee says, "Is that all there is?"

Well, of course not. Would I write this book, just to tell you *that* bad news? There is a more excellent way than playing the numbers game. *That's* what this book is about.

SOME JOB-HUNTERS GET REALLY GOOD AT IT

If you go out (as we did) and talk to SUCCESSFUL job-hunters and career-changers, as opposed to UNSUCCESSFUL ones, you discover one striking fact. The difference between the two is not due to some factor out there in the world, but to a difference in their behavior — their job-hunting behavior. What was that behavior? Well, SOME of them found just the job they wanted by playing 'the numbers game.' But MOST of them did not. Most of the successful job-hunters and career-changers, who succeeded against all odds, conducted their job-hunt or career-change using an entirely different 'system' or 'process.'

We will talk about *what* they did, in a moment. But first it is worth noticing the assumptions out of which their actions flowed. In the case of successful job-hunters, — particularly those who succeeded against all odds — their job-hunt was based on four basic assumptions, which are the absolute opposite of the assumptions of 'the numbers game':

1. <u>Successful job-hunters assume that no one else will do the job-hunt for you; a successful outcome is entirely dependent on how much time you give to it.</u> You therefore must make the job-hunt a full-time job: which means devoting at least thirty-five hours a week to the job-hunt or career-change.

'The numbers game' assumes by contrast, as we have seen, that someone else is out working for you (employment agencies, newspaper ads, or your resume, as it floats hither and yon) while you are relaxing at home, waiting for the offers to materialize. The consequence of this assumption is traced out in behavior: two-thirds of all job-hunters (playing 'the numbers game', of course) spend less than five hours a week on their job-hunt. Now, *of course* some people find a job, even though they give so little time to it. Luck is luck. But so many more *don't*. And the reason is right here.

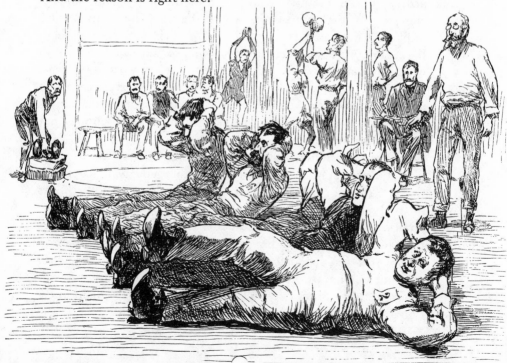

By devoting thirty-five hours a week to the job-hunt, successful job-hunters or career-changers are devoting SEVEN TIMES as much time to their job-hunt, as most job-hunters do. It's *hardly* surprising that they thereby speed up the time the job-hunt takes by a factor of seven, and increase their chances of finding a job, by a factor of seven.

2. Successful job-hunters assume that before setting out on your job-hunt or career-change, you MUST do as many hours of homework on yourself as possible, so that you know:

a) exactly what your strongest, highest, and most favorite skills are; and

b) exactly where you would most like to be able to use them — type of activity, product, or service; type of organization; size of organization; its goals or aims; location; etc.

They assume you must be as definite as you can be, about what you are looking for.

'The numbers game,' by contrast, assumes you should remain as loose and vague as possible about what you are looking for, so that you will be free to take advantage of whatever vacancies may come your way. "Good grief," say successful job-hunters and career-counselors; "this is why we have so many people in this country who are not unemployed but *under*employed — working at jobs where they are miserably underutilized, where they are bored out of their minds, and where they can't wait for weekends to come, so that they can go do what they really enjoy doing. According to various surveys, somewhere between 20% to 60% of all workers are engaged in jobs where they feel their full talents are not being used. This is the inevitable consequence of 'trying to hang loose' about what you are looking for."

Successful job-hunters realize that even if you are 40 years old, if there are 22 years remaining that you want to work, that's 22 times 50 weeks times 40 hours, or 44,000 hours of work ahead of you. Spending 20 to 30 hours or more doing homework on yourself before you start your job-hunt, in order to make that 44,000 hours more worthwhile is just common sense. NOT to spend 20 to 30 hours or more doing homework on yourself, before you start out on your job-hunt, and thus risking 44,000 miserable hours on the job, is just plain vocational suicide.

And of course, if you are, say, 22 years old, you've got almost twice as many hours in the world of work ahead of you, and therefore almost twice as much at stake.

This homework about which we speak has, incidentally, been given a name. It is called "career planning" or "life/work planning." It is also called "just plain common sense."

3. Successful job-hunters assume that you must first decide whether an organization is of any interest to you, before that organization decides whether you are of any interest to them. It is important for you to take the initiative, and go look at any job you think you might be interested in, and any organization you think you might be interested in, before you get down to the business of seeking job interviews to get you hired.

'The numbers game' assumes, by contrast, that you cannot take the initiative. You must wait to go to a given employer, until he or she has signaled that they have a vacancy — by means of newspaper ads, or notification to an employment agency, or responding positively to their resume. You sit by the telephone, waiting. As a consequence of this assumption, it is hardly surprising that surveys have revealed the average job-hunter contacts only six potential employers a month.

Successful job-hunters, spending seven times as many hours per month on their job-hunt, and determined to go look at any organization that they are even curious about, may contact seven times as many employers, or forty-two a month. Even though the visits are not yet seeking a job, until they have made up their mind which organizations they like best, the contacts are still of crucial importance to their ultimate job-hunting success.

4. Successful job-hunters assume that in essence the job-hunt is an information hunt, and that once you know what you are looking for, you must use as many different avenues as possible to turn up that information. You must never 'put all your eggs in one basket.'

'The numbers game,' by contrast, tends to motivate job-hunters to concentrate on only one or two methods of job-hunting. Indeed, faced with thirteen different possible avenues of job-hunting as we saw in the last chapter, surveys reveal the average unsuccessful job-hunter is only using 1.6 different methods of those thirteen.

Well, you see from all this that the numbers game is *not* the only way to job-hunt. There is another way, a better way.

THERE IS HOPE

If you are going job-hunting tomorrow, and you haven't time to finish this book today, there are still fifteen things we can tell you that will immediately improve your chances of finding a job tomorrow. And improve them dramatically:

1. You will improve your chances of finding a job if you give more time to your job-hunt: preferably thirty-five hours a week.

2. You will improve your chances of finding a job if you take the initiative, and go face-to-face with employers. That is the most effective method of job-hunting, as every survey has revealed. It is more effective than sending resumes, sending letters, answering ads, or anything else.

3. You will improve your chances of finding a job if you visit small businesses instead of large ones. Two-thirds of all the new jobs created in a typical eight-year period (1969-1976) were discovered to have been created by businesses with twenty or less employees.

4. You will improve your chances of finding a job if you take time to do some homework on yourself, identifying your skills in great detail — and in priority.

TRAVELS WITH FARLEY by Phil Frank (c) 1982 Field Enterprises, Inc. Courtesy of Field Newspaper Syndicate

5. You will improve your chances of finding a job if you take the time to learn about the places you visit, before you knock on their doors. Asking your friends what they know, visiting the library to study the many business information

sources there, taking the time to 'research' the organization will put you way ahead of those who know nothing about the place — and show it.

6. You will improve your chances of finding a job if you are gently persistent, without becoming aggressively obnoxious. Persistent about *how much* you hunt: nine to five, five days a week. Persistent about *how* you hunt: going back to the same places — if they really interest you — that you visited three weeks ago. A vacancy may have developed in the meantime. You just never know.

7. If nothing turns up in your old line of work, you will improve your chances of finding a job if you take the label off of yourself. You are not "a steelworker." You are not "an auto worker." You are not "a teacher," or "housewife" or "manager." You will improve your chances of finding a job if, instead, you think of yourself and describe yourself in terms of your skills. "I am a person who is good with his hands." "I am good at solving problems." "I am good at motivating people to work closely with each other." And so on.

8. If nothing turns up in your old line of work, you will improve your chances of finding a job if you discover some alternative names for the work you do — or some alternative jobs where you could use the same skills — rather than zeroing in on a job that has just one name.

9. If nothing turns up in your old line of work, you will improve your chances of finding a job if you 'go after' many different organizations, instead of just one or two. And many different *types* of organizations.

10. You will improve your chances of finding a job if you use as many different avenues of job-hunting as possible, never putting all your eggs into just one basket or one method — such as just sending out resumes, or just answering ads.

11. You will improve your chances of finding a job if you figure out what makes you different and better than the other people who do what you do. Are you more painstaking? Do you give more attention to detail? Do you produce higher quality work? Are you more persistent about solving problems? Are you more patient with people? If you know what makes you stand quietly apart from the herd, and can communicate this clearly during interviews, you greatly increase your chances of being the one chosen, when a vacancy arises.

12. You will improve your chances of finding a job if you get as many other eyes and ears out looking on your behalf, as possible. This means you have to: a) know exactly what kind of work you are looking for; and b) cultivate *everyone* you meet, friend or stranger, getting their name and phone, asking for their help.

13. You will improve your chances of finding a job if you look as sharp as you possibly can, at all times while you are unemployed and job-hunting. This means staying well-dressed, well-groomed, and walking erect — showing to every onlooker by all these outward signs how much of an asset you would be to any organization that hires you.

14. You will improve your chances of finding a job if you send short written thank-you notes each night to *everyone* you talked to that day about your job-hunt — friends, contacts, strangers, receptionists, secretaries, employers. Everyone. Thanking them for their help, and telling them how much you will appreciate their letting you know if they hear of anything along the lines of the work you are looking for.

15. You will improve your chances of finding a job if, beyond all actions, you have the right attitude: that no one *owes* you a job, not your former employer, not the union, not the government, not the employment service, not the town or city you live in. You have to *win* the job, by convincing some employer doing work that interests you, that you would be the best possible person he or she could hire — in terms of competency, stick-to-it-iveness, dedication and productivity.

Now you see, what you have here is a bunch of *techniques* for job-hunting. Techniques that are within *your* control, and ability. Techniques that reduce the odds against you. That change your luck.

If we were to diagram all this (you hate diagrams? go on to the next page), it would look something like this.

Here is the normal job-hunt as practiced throughout Western Civilization, "the numbers game":

		Technique (what you do)		Luck
USING THE NUMBERS GAME TECHNIQUES (Newspaper ads, resumes, etc.)	First month of job-hunt	‖‖		
	Second month of job-hunt	‖‖		
	Third month of job-hunt	‖‖		
	Fourth month of job-hunt	‖‖		

A *little* of it depends on *what you do,* i.e., the techniques you use. But *most of it* is pure LUCK. That's *why* it's called "the numbers game." It's like "playing the numbers" in Las Vegas or Atlantic City. There, if your luck is good, you hit the jackpot. If your luck is bad, you lose your shirt — or blouse.

Here, if your luck is good, you find a job. If your luck is bad, you have to go on welfare.

When you stop playing "the numbers game" *even a little* in your job-hunt, and add more *techniques* to what you are doing, you *reduce* the amount of *luck* you need for your job-hunt to succeed.

You change the diagram of your job-hunt to look more like this:

		Technique		Luck
USING THE 15 CREATIVE JOB-HUNTING TECHNIQUES (as described on pages 48-50)	First month of job-hunt	‖‖‖‖‖‖‖‖		
	Second month of job-hunt	‖‖‖‖‖‖‖‖		
	Third month of job-hunt	‖‖‖‖‖‖‖‖		
	Fourth month of job-hunt	‖‖‖‖‖‖‖‖		

Now, you see where all this is going. *Obviously,* if we could come up with even better techniques of job-hunting for you, you could take *control* of more and more of your job-hunt and its outcome, instead of leaving it to pure *luck*. And that *is* the point of techniques: they give you more *control,* or power.

Naturally, there is a thriving industry — and has been, for decades — of people trying to come up with more, and better, techniques for you as job-hunter. They sit up all night trying to find more techniques for you. These unsung heroes and heroines are called by various names: career counselors, vocational experts, manpower planners, and so on.

Some have come up with brilliant ideas. Others have come up with ideas that are not so hotsy-totsy. Let's look at some of them, beginning with the ones that are not so swell.

OCCUPATIONAL FORECASTS

You know how this began. You can hear the boys in the back room, talking: "I know how we can help John Q. or Jane Q. Jobhunter. We'll tell them the jobs they *should* go into. Let's identify the ones where the demand will far exceed the supply. It won't require job-hunters to have any skills at job-hunting. They can just say, 'Here I am, take me.' And employers will leap to take them. We'll remove all the luck element, entirely. This will be a sure thing."

Uh huh. That's how occupational forecasts got started, folks. Now, *of course* you believe them. And you want me to tell you what the latest hot scoop is from the occupational forecasters. So that you can go run to get those jobs where you're *sure* to get hired.

Okay, I'll tell you what the popular wisdom is, among manpower experts these days; *and then,* at no extra charge, I'll tell you what I think is wrong with that wisdom. The popular wisdom is that the ten fastest growing places — geography-wise, and hence job-wise, are (in order): Fort Lauderdale, Tucson, Houston, Phoenix, Austin, San Diego, Oxnard (California), Columbia (South Carolina), Tampa, and Albuquerque. In other words, with few exceptions, the Sunbelt.

The jobs which are going to have the greatest demand from employers (again, according to the popular wisdom) are: computer technology, especially computer programmers; data processing (another way of saying the same thing), especially in software; robotics, dealing especially with the use of robots in industry; productivity experts; genetic engineering or bioengineering; machine-tool workers; tool-and-die workers; and — surprise — secretaries (a vanishing breed in some sections of the country).

The biggest changes forecast for the coming decade are (1) those connected with the computerizing of small businesses (and large) as we move more and more rapidly toward "the electronic society"; (2) the growth in home offices — linked by computer to a central work office; (3) the growth in consequent "employment by contract" — with home-officed persons contracting their services perhaps to more than one company; (4) the growth of self-employment comprised of several contract jobs rather than just one — with some individuals holding down not two jobs but three, four, or five part-time jobs, all of which together add up to one full-time job; (5) the growth of totally new industries based on research and development currently being done in the energy field; and (6) the growth of hospices, home medical care, and other alternatives to hospitals. Workers looking ahead at these changes, and moving into these fields before they surge, will probably find the greatest opportunities — according to popular wisdom.

Now if something on the above list immediately piques your interest, and sends off rockets in your head and heart, wonderful! But if, on the other hand, your response in your gut is: "None of the above," what can we say to you? Here's where my criticism of the popular wisdom begins.

Well, first of all, the forecasts of job-experts are often wrong. We can begin with that. And boy, have they been wrong! Back in 1970, few if any 'experts' saw the energy crisis coming, with all its consequent effects upon the job-market. They have been just as in error over trends they thought were coming, but which never materialized.

Secondly, new trends and new jobs are the "glamor" parts of the world of work; but these depend upon the less glamorous sections of the world of work for their survival and growth. What St. Paul said in another connection is equally applicable here: "There are many members, but one body. And the eye cannot say to the hand, 'I have no need of you'; or again the head to the feet, 'I have no need of you.' On the contrary, it is much truer that the members of the body which seem to be weaker are necessary." (I Corinthians 12:20-22) All the talk about the glamor trends in the world of work during the 1980s should not obscure the fact that we still need good auto mechanics to fix our cars, and good doctors to assist us in maintaining our body's health, and good mailpersons to get our bills to us.

Thirdly, by the time forecasts get published, and by the time you prepare for the specialty of interest, there often is a lot more competition for that sort of job than you had been led to believe there would be. So, you're not delivered from the need to compete, any more than you would be for some of the less glamorous jobs.

This puts you right back where you were, before you read the Occupational Forecasts. That is, facing lots of competition for any job you decide to go after. And, therefore, needing better *techniques* than occupational forecasts.

©Copyright 1982 United Feature Syndicate, Inc. Used by special permission.

RETRAINING

When forecasts don't help, *this* is the next favorite technique of the manpower experts.

You can hear the boys in the back room being hailed by someone outside. "Hey, Joe, the forecasts didn't work. And I've got a bunch of job-hunters out here who can't find any jobs in their old line of work. What should I do with them?" Silence from the back room, for a spell. And then a voice, shouting for joy: "Hey, I've got a great idea. Let's send them back to college for 'retraining.' By the time they get out, maybe the job market will have changed for the better." "Great idea, Joe. But what do we train them *in*?" Silence from the back room. Then the same voice, again, shouting for joy: "We'll use the list left over from our occupational forecasts. I knew we'd find a use for that list, sooner or later!"

That's how it began. Maybe. But now you hear this technique being advanced, on all fronts. *Every time* someone is out of a job, decides maybe they need a new career, and asks, "What shall I do?" you can count on it, that the experts they turn to will say, in one unanimous voice: "Go get retrained. Go back to school."

Retraining *always* seems to be *the* recommended technique for changing careers. There is, of course, a reason for this. *By now, we have all been brainwashed into thinking that there are only two things that will get us a job: credentials that are convincing, or experience that is convincing. We all figure we've got to have one or the other.*

Let's examine this idea to see why. And to see what's wrong with it.

1. CONVINCING EXPERIENCE. If you want to be a machinist, and you've done machinist's work for ten years, you have *convincing experience.* In other words, if you've done a particular thing long enough, most people don't care *how* you picked it up, way back when. It is sufficient that you have proved yourself, by doing it. This doesn't hold so well, of course, when you want to change careers. Your new career may demand no skills that you don't already have. But you used them *in a different setting,* and in the service of *different special knowledges* than would now be required. Consequently, many employers will feel you have no experience that is convincing enough for them to put you in this new career at their place.

2. NEW CREDENTIALS. What are you to do? Well, of course. *If* there is only one other thing that will get you a job, namely *credentials,* you're going to have to go back to school and get credentials for your new career. A shiny new degree *in that new field.*

To be sure, sometimes this idea is absolutely on target. There *are* certain fields where you *must* have all the training you can possibly get. Law and medicine come immediately to mind. Architecture. And some others. If that is the sort of thing you want to do, as your next career, you most certainly *are* going to have to go back to school.

But, hey. Not *every* time we want to change a career. Not for *every* career, no matter what.

And not even — sometimes — for the careers you would think. You need to beware of *General Rules*. A general rule, for example, is that if you want to be a full professor at a University, you *must* possess a doctoral degree. That's the general rule. But, there are exceptions. There are people who are full professors, yet they possess *no* such credential as a doctorate. We're lucky if they even have a master's degree. They had acquired such knowledge of a particular field by *doing it* out there in the world, that some University was dying to get its hands on them. "But, sir — I know this man can teach this subject, and all that, but *he has no doctorate*. We can't hire him. The University rules say so." "Rubbish, Frobishoff, get me the University lawyer. We'll figure some way around this. *I want this man.*" It is a foregone conclusion he will get him, too.

It is also a foregone conclusion that there are at least ten people with a Ph.D. *dying* to teach at the University in question, who can't get hired there — even as our man, without the doctorate, *is* getting hired there.

So, the Achilles heel of this favorite *technique* of manpower experts, is that *getting retrained is no guarantee that you will get hired*. Conversely, if you lack the retraining, *that's* no guarantee that you *won't* get hired. If . . . . .

If you will go out, tomorrow, and start looking not for the Rules, but for those who are *exceptions* to the Rule. And if you will interview them to ask how they did it, *in many cases* you too can get hired without retraining. And in a shiny new career.

The fallacy of Retraining, as a job-hunting or career-changing technique, is ultimately this: there are not just two ways to get a job — Experience or Credentials. There are three ways.

The third way, to which little attention has ever been paid by the supposed experts in manpower planning, is: *make the employer want you* so badly that he or she *doesn't care* about a silly old thing like credentials. How? By:

3. A DEMONSTRATION OF YOUR SKILLS. Right before the prospective employer's eyes. Well, great idea. But, *how* do you do that? It depends on the skill you are claiming. Does it have to do with Information or Data? The whole job-hunt deals with information and data. By the way in which you research the company or organization, before you ever call on them, you can demonstrate you have the skill you claim.

Does the skill you are claiming, have to do with People? By the way you deal with people during your job-hunt, from the receptionist to the executive there at that organization, you can demonstrate that you have the skill you are claiming.

Does the skill you are claiming, have to do with things that you make or repair? You can take in with you some pictures or even a sample of your work, to the job interview.

Let's face it. This is not a universal formula, guaranteed to work. *Some* employers will not be the least impressed by any demonstration you give them. That may even happen *as a rule*. But you are not looking for *the rule*. You are looking for *the exception*.

All employers divide into those who will only hire you if you've had many years experience in this particular career, and: those who are willing to take a chance on you. *You are looking for those who are willing to take a chance on you.* They are more likely to be found in small companies or organizations, than in large. By small, I mean organizations with 100 employees or less. It is therefore with such companies that you should spend the greatest amount of your time and research.

PROBLEM-SOLVERS GET HIRED

The major issue you are facing, in the minds of employers, is not what skills your have, but to what end and purpose do you set them? Do you use your skills to merely while away the time? Or do you like to use your skills to solve problems?

No matter how much organizations may seem to be different, on the surface, underneath they have this common denominator: they all deal with some kind of problem. Universities, businesses, nonprofit organizations, volunteer organizations, charities, hospitals, foundations, Mom and Pop stores, all require people who are good at solving problems. Indeed, organizations *must* have such people, if they are to survive. It doesn't matter *what title* is hung on a person, in order to justify hiring them. They are being hired because in this organization faced with problems, the hiring officer is betting that the new employee(s) will be *part of the solution, rather than part of the problem.*

Now, the $64,000 question. *How* do you demonstrate to a prospective employer, the fact that you are going to be a problem-solver if he or she hires you? Answer: by the way in which you conducted your job-hunt.

The manner in which you do your job-hunt, and the manner in which you would do the job you are seeking, are not assumed by the employer to be two unrelated subjects. They are one and the same. A slipshod, half-hearted *job-hunt,* is the best warning an employer has, that you will do a slipshod, half-hearted *job* . . . were they foolish enough to hire you. On the other hand, a thorough, professionally-conducted *job-hunt* is the best evidence an employer could ask for, that you will do a thorough, professional *job* for them.

The employer wants assurances that if they hire you, you are going to be part of the solution and not part of the problem at that place. Their best clue about which way that is going to go, is to look at the way in which you are doing your job-hunt.

The very word "job-hunt" is merely a clever disguise for "problem." *Are* you facing a problem right now? Yop. Finding a job. Or a new career. How are you going about *solving* that problem? That's what the employer wants to know.

If you come in to the employer's office, having done your homework first — knowing *a lot* about yourself, and knowing *a lot* about this organization, any employer *that you would want to work for, anyway* — will be impressed. You will stand out from other job-hunters or career-changers, *as one who is better at solving problems* than the others. Because, obviously, you went about solving *this* problem — the job-hunt — in such a thorough and professional way.

That's *much* more impressive than a credential from a school — in most cases.

That's why you're holding this book in your hand. So you can conduct your job-hunt or career-change in as thorough and professional a manner as possible. The job-hunting life you save, will be *your own.*

Star light, star bright,
    I wish I may, I wish I might,
find this job I want,
            Tonight!

CHAPTER FOUR

You Can
Do It!

Techniques.

That's what we learned in the previous chapter: we need techniques. Techniques to help us go about career-change and job-hunting in the most professional manner possible. And in the most effective manner possible — cutting our dependency on *luck,* down to a minimum.

The minute we start looking for career-changing or job-hunting techniques, however, we are tempted to think that what is called for is a library. For, after all, does not everyone have special problems? Does not everyone need a special book, just for them? Do you not need a special book, just for you?

If we followed this line of reasoning, we see immediately that we would need *at least* twenty-four different books of techniques; viz.,

---

I.   Manuals on Job Dissatisfaction

   A. A Manual for Executives Who Want To Change Careers
   B. A Manual for Executives Who Want To Know How To Restructure or Improve Their Present Job
   C. A Manual for Workers Who Want To Change Careers
   D. A Manual for Workers Who Want To Start Their Own Business, At Home or Elsewhere
   E. A Manual for Blue-Collar Workers Who Want To Know How To Restructure or Improve Their Present Job
   F. A Manual for (So-Called) 'Housewives' Who Want To Find Volunteer Activities Outside To Supplement Their Activities in the Home
   G. A Manual for 'Housewives' Who Want To Find Part-Time Work, or An Internship
   H. A Manual for 'Housewives' Who Want To Enter The Labor Market (or World of Work) Full-Time

II. Manuals on Ways Around the Traditional Job-Hunting Method, When It Doesn't Work, No Matter How Hard We Try

   A. A Manual for the Teenager Who Cannot Find Work
   B. A Manual for the High-School Graduate Who Cannot Find Work
   C. A Manual for the Liberal Arts College-Graduate Who Cannot Find A Job in His or Her Field

D. A Manual for Members of Minority Groups in This Country Who Cannot Find A Job in Their Field

E. A Manual for Members of Minority Groups in This Country, Who Cannot Find The Kind of Job They Want, Because of Prejudice

F. A Manual for 'Housewives' Who Have No Credentials Or Experience in the World of Work (As They Suppose)

G. A Manual for Ex-Offenders Who Cannot Find Work Because of Employer-Prejudice About Their History

H. A Manual for Ex-Addicts Who Cannot Find Work Because of Employer-Prejudice About Their History

I. A Manual for Psychiatric Outpatients, Who Cannot Find Work Because of Employer-Prejudice About Their History

J. A Manual for the Handicapped Who Cannot Find Work Because of Employer-Prejudice About Their Abilities

K. A Manual for Alcoholics Who Cannot Find Work Because of Low-Motivation

L. A Manual for Middle-Aged Job-Hunters Who Cannot Find Work Because of Employer-Prejudice About Their Age

M. A Manual for Short Male Job-Hunters Who Cannot Find Executive Jobs Because of Employer-Prejudice About Their Height

N. A Manual for Retired Persons Who Cannot Find Work Because of Employer-Prejudice About Their Age

O. A Manual for Female Job-Hunters Who Cannot Find The Proper Wage That Their Expertise and Position Entitle Them To, Because of Employer-Prejudice About Their Femaleness

P. A Manual for Welfare-Recipients Who Cannot Find Work Because of (Supposedly) Few "Marketable Skills"

You will think of others, I am sure.

Fortunately, each different kind of job-hunter or career-changer does NOT need a separate book of techniques. For the essence of truly effective job-hunting or career-change is *the same for everyone.*

THE THREE BASIC STEPS OF
EFFECTIVE JOB-HUNTING AND
CAREER-CHANGE

Behind the idea that we need so many different books is that assumption that most job-hunters are not handicapped; but some are. And that's why we need special books. For those job-hunters who are handicapped.

There's one problem with this assumption.

Everyone who is going job-hunting or planning a career-change is handicapped. We start with that basic fact.

It isn't that some job-hunters and career-changers are handicapped while others aren't. All of us are handicapped. The only issue is: *what* is our handicap, — and, *how obvious* is it? Our handicap may be shyness. It may be lack of experience. It may be one of the many things that *some* employers are prejudiced about. It may be our age. It may be our color. It may be our sex. It may be our personal history. It may be that we were fired from our last job. It may be that we didn't have as much education as we wished. It may be that our body or senses are impaired, in some way. But *every* job-hunter is handicapped, in some way.

We all need the same thing.

A method that *works,* for the handicapped.

Over the years, such a method has been devised. There's nothing very *surprising* about it. Many job-hunters have figured it out, all by themselves. A bunch of pioneering career-counselors have refined and polished it up, over the years. But in many ways their 'system' is just a systematic definition of how successful job-hunters conduct their job-hunt, when left on their own. Job-hunters are the unsung heroes and heroines of this 'process,' — which we may call "the creative method of job-hunting and career-change." For it is they who invented it. It is they who used it, and proved that it worked.

Down through the past few decades it has always been true: career-counselors are trained by their clients: the job-hunters and career-changers who come to them, asking for their help. Career-counselors pretend they are leading their clients — students, executives, displaced homemakers, blue-collar workers, or whoever — to the oasis of the Ideal Job. But in actuality, *any* career-counselor who is on the ball, is *always* watching out of the corner of their eye to see what *a good job-hunter* does, by instinct. Then of course, the following week, the career-counselor claims he — or she — invented that bright idea.

Over the years, then, *good* career-counselors (a very elite group) have distilled the basic behaviors of *successful* job-hunters and career-changers down to an irreducible minimum of *three* techniques:

Whether you are going about a career-change or just a job-hunt, and irrespective of what handicap you have, to be successful, YOU MUST DEFINE, IN DETAIL:

1. WHAT is it you want to do?
2. WHERE do you want to do it?
3. HOW do you identify the person who has the power to hire you, and show them how your skills can help them with their problems?

WHAT? WHERE? HOW? The three unavoidable pieces of homework that you must do, for your job-hunt to be truly effective and professional.

The job-hunt or a career-change is *the problem,* for you.

How do you *solve* that problem? By thorough homework on the subject of What?, Where? and How?—and this is true, no matter what road you are taking, within the land of Job-Hunt.

Whether you are hunting for a job while still employed, or hunting for a job while unemployed, you need to know *what* your favorite and strongest skills are, *where* you most want to be able to use those skills, and *how* to find such a job or career.

Whether you want to continue in your present career (at a new place), or start a new career, you need to know *what* your favorite and strongest skills are, *where* you most want to be able to use those skills, and *how* to find such a job or career.

Whether you are looking for part-time work, or full-time work, you need to know *what* your favorite and strongest skills are, *where* you most want to be able to use those skills, and *how* to find such a job or career.

If you want to go back to school for legitimate retraining, you need to know *what* are the skills you already have, *where* you need further training or knowledge, and *how* you will then find a place to use this new training.

If you are thinking about doing volunteer work or an internship, you need to know *what* skills you have to offer, *where* you would most like to be able to use them, and *how* to find such volunteer work or internship.

If you want to work for yourself, whether in one career or in a composite career, you need to know *what* skills you have — so that you can hire the other skills still needed — , *where* you can best use those skills, and *how* you go about finding your clients, your market, your customers, and sell yourself to them.

In our earlier diagrams of the job-hunt as popularly conceived, we divided the hunt into time zones — the first month, the second month, the third, and the fourth. The average job-hunt today takes 16.4 weeks, or almost exactly four months. So, *if* you're going to think of the job-hunt in terms of monthly periods, that seems fair. Four months is, however, only the average. Experienced outplacement people say that as a rule of thumb, one may expect the job-hunt will take one month *for every ten thousand dollars of salary that you are going after.* If you seek $40,000 or less, then four months is a reasonable time to allot to your job-hunt. But if you are an executive in mid-career, seeking a salary of $70,000, then seven months is a more reasonable expectation, at a minimum.

Rather than thinking of the job-hunt in terms of months,

however, it is more useful to think of it in terms of the three *phases* that you must work your way through . . . however long it takes.

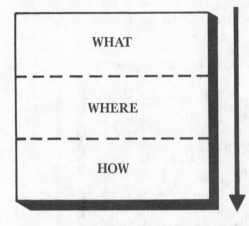

WHAT

WHERE

HOW

FIRST YOU MUST
DEFINE WHAT
ARE YOUR FAVORITE
SKILLS

THEN, WHERE
YOU WANT TO USE
THEM

THEN, HOW
DO YOU FIND
SUCH A JOB

In your case, maybe the first *phase* — figuring out WHAT — will only take you a weekend. A *full* weekend. *If* you use the New *Quick Job-Hunting Map* in the back of this book. Maybe the second phase — figuring out WHERE — will take you two months. If you go talk to a lot of people. And maybe the third phase — figuring out HOW to find such a job, and get hired there — will take you a month and a half. It would then all come out to about four months, as before. But, the time is unequally divided among the three phases.

The important point, however, is that you need to work through all three phases — professionally, completely, and thoroughly — no matter how long it does or does not take.

Some of our readers have done it all in two or three weeks. But you probably don't want to hear about *that*. I know when I'm out job-hunting, *I* certainly don't. People who can do in a minute what it takes me hours or days to do, always depress me. But, it's nice to know it *can* be done, in a short time. *If* luck is with you.

Ah yes, *luck*. It's time we looked again at an overview of the job-hunt. We saw earlier that the job-hunt is largely a matter of sheer luck, when you're playing "the numbers game." We saw that the part luck played *decreases* as you apply more *techniques* to your job-hunt or career-change.

Now, we have come to *as much* technique as we know of. How does that affect the overall picture of our job-hunt, and particularly the part that *luck* plays?

Well, we can't *eliminate* the role that *luck* plays in your job-hunt, but we can say that if you do all this homework, you will at least have chased it into a corner:

The Job-Hunt, and Career-Change

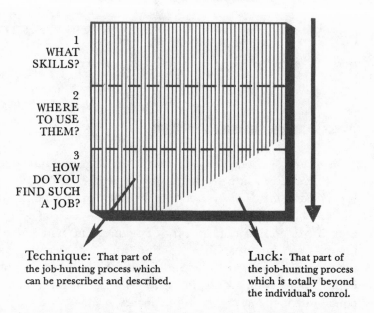

**1
WHAT
SKILLS?**

**2
WHERE
TO USE
THEM?**

**3
HOW
DO YOU
FIND SUCH
A JOB?**

Technique: That part of
the job-hunting process which
can be prescribed and described.

Luck: That part of
the job-hunting process
which is totally beyond
the individual's conrol.

That is to say, when you are figuring out WHAT are your strongest and most favorite skills, *luck* doesn't play any real part at all. And then, when you are figuring out WHERE you want to use those skills, luck doesn't really enter in, either. It's a matter of your faithfully following the techniques outlined in chapter 6. It is only when you get down to the actual hunt for the person who has the power to hire you, that *luck* becomes an important factor in your job-hunt.

You can *affect* your luck for the better, as we shall see in chapter 7. But the point I want to make for now, is that there is no way to completely eliminate the part that *luck* plays, your use of all the *techniques* described in chapters 5, 6, 7 and in the New *Quick Job-Hunting Map* will at least *reduce* the role of *luck,* in your job-hunt, to its irreducible minimum.

The remainder of this book will be devoted to describing those techniques *in detail.* Chapter 5 is devoted to WHAT. Chapter 6 to WHERE. Chapter 7 to HOW. And the New *Quick Job-Hunting Map* to putting all three together.

RESOURCES FOR YOU
TO DRAW ON

You will naturally want to know what or who there is to help you, as you go through this process of the job-hunt or career-change. Here are the types of resources you can draw on:

I. *Yourself.* Doing the homework for yourself, tackling the Map in Appendix A, reading and re-reading chapters 5, 6, and 7, is to be preferred above all other resources, for any number of reasons. First of all, knowledge which you gain for yourself is more ingrained than knowledge that is simply handed to you by others. Secondly, the job-hunt process rightly understood is itself a preparation for, and training in, skills you will need to exercise once you get the job; to deprive yourself of the opportunity to get valuable practice in these skills during the job-hunting process, is to make it just that much more difficult for yourself on the job. Thirdly, even if you pay money (and a whole lot of it) to one kind of professional agency or another, there is no guarantee that they will do the process any better than, or even as well as, you would do it yourself.

MORAL
Every investment of your money is a gamble unless you have first tried to do it on your own, know what you did find out, what you did not find out, and therefore what kind of help you now need from others.

II. *Books and Other Visual or Audio Materials.* If there's a particular phase where you get bogged down, a particular technique that confuses you, a particular obstacle you want help in getting around, then check out Appendix B — where such things are listed, by subject. I would urge you, however, to read all the

way through chapters 5, 6 and 7 *first,* to get an overview. I get
letters from readers which say, "I've only read part of your
book so far, but I want to know what you have to suggest about
... " And, of course, they refer to a subject that *is* covered in
the chapters they haven't yet read. So, do *read* before you write.
And if, after you read this book, there's something that's per-
plexing you, *do* check out the different subjects and books that
are listed in Appendix B. That's why they are there.

III. *Free professional help.* When people get bogged down in
their job-hunt, they often rush off to pay some career counselor
to help them. Well, that's okay; but sometimes, if you'll just
stop to analyze exactly what you need at that particular moment, you might discover there is professional help for you that
is available *at no cost.* Examples of where such free help is to be
found:

- the reference librarian, at your local library or college
  library;
- career counseling offices at your nearby community
  college;
- job-clinics at your local Chamber of Commerce, Federal/
  State Employment agency, Advertising Council, and the
  like;
- local federally-funded "job clubs," for specific populations,
  such as WIN recipients, etc. Your local Federal/State
  employment office often knows their locations and times

of meeting; funding comes, in most cases, from the Joint
Training and Partnership Act of the Federal Government;
- self-directed job-support groups that meet in local
  churches or synagogues, in many communities.

There is a section in Appendix C at the back of this book
that lists a few of these, and tells you how to find others. In
some cases, the help isn't, strictly speaking, totally free. But the
dues charged are so small, that for all intents and purposes we
may classify them as free.

The likelihood that such help is available in your community
increases if you are from certain *disadvantaged* groups, as low
income, or welfare recipients, or youth, or displaced workers, or
those laid off permanently. Ask around.

IV. *Professional help for a fee.* Now here, a lot depends on
what kind of help you need or want. Is it aptitude/skills testing?
The grand-daddy of all such firms is Johnson O'Connor, nee
Human Engineering Laboratory, located in some of our principal
cities in the U.S. You can write them at 347 Beacon St., Boston,
MA 02116 for a list of their offices. There are other such firms
around the country, many of them staffed by former employees
of Johnson O'Connor — such as Ability Potentials, Inc. in College
Park, Maryland. Many colleges and universities will give you
vocational testing, for somewhat more modest fees. You do
need to ask whether it is *aptitude* testing or merely *interests*
testing. I have more to say about that in the next chapter. The
distinction is important.

If you want help with the overall process of job-hunting,
Appendix C in the back of this book has a Sampler that lists
some of the career counseling offices to be found around the
country. Your yellow pages will also have a list of these in your
area, under the headings of "Aptitude and Employment Testing," "Career Counseling," "Executive Consultants," "Management Consultants," "Personnel Consultants," and "Vocational
Consultants." You will have to pick your way with great care
through those woods. Just when you think you've gotten safely
to grandmother's house, you may find there is a wolf there.
Appendix C has an introductory section which I would urge
you read no less than three times before you ever venture forth
to press your money and your job-hunt into somebody else's
hands.

Some professional groups have their own counseling centers. For example, if you are a clergyperson, you will want to look at the church career development centers which have sprung up all over the country. A list of them is to be found under "The Special Problems of Clergy," section 15 in Appendix B, page 292.

V. *Your Family or Friends.* I believe as a general rule — there *are* exceptions — you ought to try never to go through the job-hunt *all by yourself alone.* Co-opt *somebody* — your partner or mate, a grown-up son or daughter who lives nearby, your best friend, someone you know well from your church or synagogue — to be your weekly *support person.*

PRACTICAL EXERCISE (SO YOU DON'T GO IT ALONE)

Choose a support-person for your job-hunt. Ask them if they're willing to help you. Assuming they say Yes, put down in both your appointment books a regular weekly date when they will *guarantee* to meet with you, check you out on what you've done *already,* and be very stern with you if you've done little or nothing since your previous week's meeting. The more a gentle but firm taskmaster this confidante is, the better. Tell them that it is at least a 20,000 hour, $500,000 project. Or whatever. It's also responsible, concerned, committed *Stewardship.*

Where did we get 20,000 hours? Well, a forty-hour a week job, done for fifty weeks a year, adds up to 2,000 hours annually. So, how long are you going to be doing this new job or new career that you are looking for? How many years do you plan to stay in the world of work? Ten years? That means 20,000 hours. Longer than that? Even more hours. So, it's *at least* a 20,000-hour project.

Why $500,000? Well, figure it out for yourself. Say, you hope to start this new job or new career of yours at $20,000 a year. Even if you are forty years old, you still have thirty good years of work left in you. So, let us say that over that period of thirty years you get enough raises to make your annual salary somewhere between $25,000 and $30,000. Multiply this by thirty years, and you get a total earnings of something in the neighborhood of more than half a million dollars. If you've got more years ahead of you, or a higher potential salarywise, you're talking about even more money. So it's *at least* a $500,000 project that you're working on, with this job-hunt of yours as the doorway.

JOB-HUNTING
WHILE YOU ARE STILL
EMPLOYED

Many job-hunting books assume that you are unemployed, and hence have complete freedom as to how you allot your time. But what do you do about the job-hunt or career-change, if you are presently holding down a full-time job?

Good question. That is the case in which many find themselves. How many? Well, the government, bless its heart, did a study of job-hunting among employed workers about eight years ago, and discovered that in a typical month — it was May of 1976 —4.2% of all employed workers, or one out of every twenty, went looking for another job sometime during that month. In actual numbers, that represented 3,269,000 people who were job-hunting while still employed. If the same percentage obtains today, it means 4,500,000 are currently employed but job-hunting.

I would like to point out two things about this finding. First of all, it means that one-third of *all* job-hunters are conducting the search while they are still employed.

Secondly, they *must* be successful. There's a lot of movement going on, in the world of work. The *average* nonagricultural firm in this country has to hire — in a typical year — as many new people as it has employees. In other words, a firm with three employees will probably have to hire two or three employees each year. A firm with 100 employees will probably have to hire 90 new employees each year. That's on the average. If you want a more detailed breakdown, this is what the study turned up: the average retail firm with say 100 employees may have to hire 136 new people each year; the average firm dealing in services and having say 100 employees may have to hire 111 new employees each year; the average financial institution, 74; the average manufacturing firm, 65; the average transportation or public utilities company, 32; and the average construction company, a whopping 202 new employees for every 100 it currently has.

It is this job-hunting behavior on the part of employed workers which helps to create so many vacancies — thus increasing *every* job-hunter's chance of success so dramatically.

How do employed job-hunters go about their search? You guessed it: the same way unemployed job-hunters do. According to the government's study, 70% of all employed job-hunters contacted an employer directly. But, back to our original question: how do you find time to do the job-hunt if you are presently holding down a full-time job? We have asked employed job-hunters how they did it, and the sum of their advice to you — based on their experience — is:

(1) Determine to keep at it, with every spare hour you can find. Press evenings, weekends, lunch hours and the like, into the service of your job-hunt.

(2) Use evenings and weekends to do the original homework, figuring out what your skills are and what it is you want to do, as well as where you want to do it. Later on in your job-search, use evenings and the weekend also to write thank you notes, send out letters, and the like.

(3) For the actual calling upon potential employers, if they are in the city where you presently work, press your lunch hours into service. If you "brown-bag it," you will have time to

make and keep one appointment, particularly if your intent is to make the interview no longer than twenty minutes — a good idea, in any case, for the exploratory or information interview. People take lunch hours at all different times: 11:15 a.m., 11:45, 12 noon, 12:30, 1 p.m. While you are on your lunch hour, somebody you want to see hasn't gone to lunch yet, or has just come back. Sometimes you can move your lunch hour — if the place where you are presently working is flexible about that — to the 11 a.m.-12 noon time slot.

(4) Press late afternoons into service. Many people you will want to see are on an executive or management level, and they often do not get away from their offices promptly at 5. It is appropriate to estimate how long it will take you to get across town to them, and ask them if they could see you that long after your quitting time, on a particular day.

(5) Press holidays into service. Holidays fall into two classes: those which everyone observes, like Christmas and New Year's Day; and those which some people observe, like Washington's Birthday, etc. In the case of the latter kind of holiday, if you have it off, you will sometimes be able to visit the people you want to see, because they do not have it off.

(6) Press Saturdays into service. Sometimes the people you want to see work on Saturday, or are occasionally willing to set up appointments for Saturday.

(7) Press your sickleave into service. In some organizations, workers accumulate sickleave, and have the right to take it as time off. If that is the case with you, use such days off judiciously, to visit potential employers who interest you.

(8) Press your vacations into service. If you are dead-serious about the importance of your job-hunt or career-change, it is not too great a sacrifice to devote one year's vacation time to your job-hunt. This is especially important if you are trying to secure employment in a distant city. Schedule your vacation in that city, and make arrangements and appointments, by letter and phone, ahead of time (see chapter 6, on how to research a place at a distance).

(9) If you have sufficient savings, the following strategem may be one you would like to consider in addition to all the above: If you have a whole list of people and places you need to visit, and you require a concentrated period of time in which to do this, and cannot wait until your vacation time, you have the

right to ask your present employer if you can have a leave of absence without pay. So long as the time requested is no longer than a week or so, and so long as it is scheduled at the convenience of the employer (i.e., not in the week that they need you the most), this request will often be honored. You can give, as the reason, the simple truth: Personal Business.

Should you feel guilty about job-hunting while you are still employed? Well, sure, if you want to. But there is no need. One-third of all job-hunters are doing the same thing: it is a common practice in our economy. Nothing oddball about it. Moreover, remember these simple truths: Your employer has certain rights, including the right to fire you at any time, for sufficient cause; moreover, they have the right to prepare for this act of firing ahead of time, laying the groundwork, transferring part of your work to other colleagues, etc. You, as employee, likewise have certain rights, including the right to quit at any time, for sufficient cause; moreover, you have the right to prepare for this act of quitting ahead of time, laying the groundwork through interviewing and job-searching.

"Same career, change of career, same career... change of..."

© Copyright, 1980, King Features Syndicate, Inc. Used by special permission.

In planning one's life, there is always dreaming in the reality, and reality in the dreaming.

(The Tortoise, after
he beat The Hare)

CHAPTER FIVE

Only *You* Can Decide:

What Do You Want To Do?

THE FIRST KEY
TO CAREER PLANNING
AND JOB-HUNTING

We come now to the homework that you MUST do on your-self, as an essential prelude to your job-hunt. That homework begins with your getting at the issue of what it is that you want to do.

> *You have got to know what it is you want, or someone is going to sell you a bill of goods somewhere along the line that can do irreparable damage to your self-esteem, your sense of worth, and your stewardship of the talents that God gave you.*

You live half your life at your job, nine to five. God's world already has *more* than enough people who can't wait for five o'clock to come, so that they can go and do what they really want to do. It doesn't need us to swell that crowd. Us ... or anyone else. It needs people who know what they really want to do, and who do it *at* their place of work, *as* their work.

© 1980 United Feature Syndicate, Inc. Used by permission

Can you really sit down and figure out a career — or an alternative career — for yourself, based on what you really enjoy doing — without first going back to school for a million years of re-training? You bet you can. You can, and you must.

We're not just talking about your job. We're talking about your life.

YOUR JOB OR YOUR LIFE

Some people have been given the gift of rare wisdom. David Maister is one of those. He is an associate professor at the Harvard Business School, where of course he gives advice to its students. He has developed a bunch of "Laws" as a summary of his advice. Here are some of them:

Maister's Laws of The Job Search*

1. You can't decide what you want from a job until you're clear on what you want from life.

2. Some people have been too busy "succeeding" to figure out what success means to them. Don't look for a job until you've thought it through.

3. First figure out what you want in life. Then go look for it.

4. It's easy to fool yourself as to what you really want from life.

5. There are a lot of people around who will tell you what you should want from life: Parents, teachers, friends. You don't have to accept their answers. Don't get stampeded.

6. Ban the word "should" from your job search.

7. We all want to impress people. The tough part is figuring out precisely who we want to impress and why.

8. You can't impress everyone simultaneously. Different people are impressed by different things: money, status, intellect, character, contribution to society, and so on forever. What do you want to be admired for? By whom? We all want respect and prestige. But in whose eyes?

9. The keys to what you *really* want are the things you don't like to admit. "I don't like to admit it, but I need to be the center of attention": Okay, find a job that will let you show off. "I don't like to admit it, but I really want to be rich": Fine, go out and get rich. "I don't like to admit it, but I'm a snob." That's alright, so work with "upper class" people.

10. Don't worry about whether you'll be good at it: if it turns you on, you'll be good enough. If it doesn't you won't.

*Adapted from an article in Bob Adams's *Careers and the MBA*. Used by permission.

Now, on to our career/life planning.

WHAT YOU ARE LOOKING FOR

Any career and life planning that is worth its salt should help you to do the following things:

Goals
1. To become more aware of your goals in life. What is unique about you? What do you want to accomplish before you die? What is your life's "mission," as you perceive it?

"CATHY" by Cathy Guisewite
(c) Copyright 1981. Reprinted with permission of Universal Press Syndicate. All rights reserved.

You may revise this list ten times, as life goes on — *career and life planning is ideally an ongoing continuous process — not a single event, done once and for all;* but as you perceive it now, what are you trying to accomplish, what are you trying to become?

Skills
2. To inventory what skills you presently have — things you do well and enjoy. This inventory needs to be taken in terms of basic units — *building blocks, if you will* — so that as time goes on, these building blocks can be arranged in different constellations. This is the very heart of your planning for various careers.

Time Lines
3. To consider and identify what Peter Drucker calls the *futurity of present decisions.* Considering where you would like to go, and what you would like to do, what time spans are built into your present decisions (e.g., if school seems required, how many years before you will finish?), and what risks are built into present decisions? The purpose of your planning is not to eliminate risks — there can be no sure movement forward without them — but to be certain that the risks you take are the right ones, based on careful thought.

4. To basically decide who (or what) is controlling your career planning: accident, circumstance, the stars, the system, Providence, God (how?), your family, other people or — forgive us for mentioning this possibility — You. You see, ultimately this comes down to a question of how passive you want to be about it all. Your life, your career, where you work, the whole bag. You will improve your effectiveness and your sense of yourself as a person 300% if you can learn to think of yourself as *an active agent* helping to mould your own present environment and your own future, rather than a passive agent, waiting for your environment to mould you.

Who's in Control

HOW YOU BEGIN

How do you begin to improve your sense that you are in control, you are the steward or stewardess of your own life? You begin it by inventorying your skills. Call them your gifts, your assets, your talents, or whatever. You need to inventory them, and then put them into some kind of prioritized *order*.

You are aiming at ultimately being able to fill in this chart:

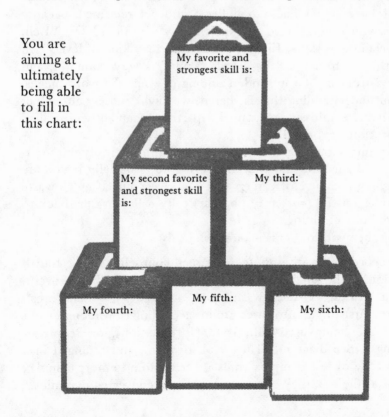

My favorite and strongest skill is:

My second favorite and strongest skill is:

My third:

My fourth:

My fifth:

My sixth:

THAT BOGEY-WORD – Skills

Now, many people just "freeze" when they hear the word "skills." It begins with high school job-hunters: "I haven't really got any skills," they say. It continues with college students: "I've spent four years in college. I haven't had time to pick up any skills." And it lasts through the middle years, especially when a person is thinking of changing his or her career: "I'll have to go back to college, and get retrained, because otherwise I won't have any skills in my new field." Or: "Well, if I claim any skills, I'll start at a very entry kind of level." All of this fright about the word "skills" is very common, and stems from a total misunderstanding of what the word means. A misunderstanding that is shared, we might add, by altogether too many employers, personnel departments, and other so-called "vocational experts."

By understanding the word, you will automatically put yourself way ahead of most job-hunters. And, especially if you are weighing a change of career, you can save yourself much waste of time on the (currently popular) folly called "going back to school for retraining."

So, herewith our crash-course on skills:

According to the *Bible* of career counseling – the fourth edition of the *Dictionary of Occupational Titles* (U.S. Government Printing Office, Washington, DC, 1977), – skills break down, first of all, into three groups according to whether or not they are being used with Data (Information), or People or Things. (See diagram.) Thus broken down, and arranged in a hierarchy of less complex skills at the bottom to more complex skills at the top, they come out looking like inverted pyramids.

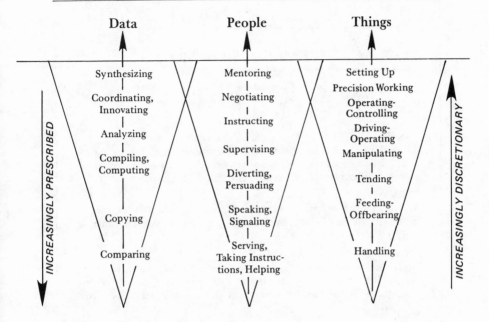

Before we explain these skills in more detail, let us look at the *most startling fact about all these skills.* It is, simply, this:

If you graded all these skills in terms of how many of their duties are prescribed in detail, i.e., by a boss, vs. how many are discretionary, i.e., left to the discretion of the employee, you would discover that the lower the skill, the *more* its duties are prescribed, with comparatively little discretion left to the employee; but, the higher the skill, the less its duties are prescribed, and the more that is left to the discretion of the employee.

This almost paradoxical meaning of the word "skill" can be easily illustrated from any, or all, of the three hierarchies on the diagram above. For the sake of comparative brevity, we will take just one, namely that which deals with people. Note, as we progress to higher levels of skills, *how it becomes harder and harder for a prospective employer (say) to draw up a job description for this skill.*

THE PEOPLE FUNCTIONS SCALE which follows, is from the *third* edition (1965) of the *Dictionary of Occupational Titles,* Vol. II, pp. 649-50, as modified and adapted by Dr. Sidney A. Fine. Thus, its skills list differs slightly from the one in the previous pictorial. Remember, as you read, each higher skill level usually or typically involves *all* those which preceded it.

WORKING WITH PEOPLE
Increasing Levels of Skill
Beginning With
The Most Elementary Definition

TAKING INSTRUCTIONS — HELPING
Attends to the work assignment, instructions, or orders of supervisor. No immediate response or verbal exchange is required unless clarification of instruction is needed.

SERVING
Attends to the needs or requests of people or animals, or to the expressed or implicit wishes of people. Immediate response is involved.

EXCHANGING INFORMATION
Talks to, converses with, and/or signals people to convey or obtain information, or to clarify and work out details of an assignment, within the framework of well-established procedures.

COACHING
Befriends and encourages individuals on a personal, caring basis by approximating a peer- or family-type relationship either in a one-to-one or small group situation, and gives instruction, advice, and personal assistance concerning activities of daily living, the use of various institutional services, and participation in groups.

PERSUADING
Influences others in favor of a product, service, or point of view by talks or demonstrations.

DIVERTING   Amuses others.

CONSULTING
Serves as a source of technical information and gives such information or provides ideas to define, clarify, enlarge upon, or sharpen procedures, capabilities, or product specifications.

INSTRUCTING
Teaches subject matter to others, or trains others, including animals, through explanation, demonstration, practice, and test.

TREATING
Acts on or interacts with individuals or small groups of people or animals who need help (as in sickness) to carry out specialized therapeutic or adjustment procedures. Systematically observes results of treatment within the framework of total personal behavior because unique individual reactions to prescriptions (chemical, behavioral, physician's) may not fall within the range of prediction. Motivates, supports, and instructs individuals to accept or cooperate with therapeutic adjustment procedures, when necessary.

continued next page

INCREASING LEVELS OF SKILL continued

SUPERVISING
Determines and/or interprets work procedure for a group of
workers, assigns specific duties to them (particularly those which
are prescribed), maintains harmonious relations among them,
evaluates performance (both prescribed and discretionary), and
promotes efficiency and other organizational values. Makes decisions on procedural and technical levels.

NEGOTIATING
Exchanges ideas, information, and opinions with others on a
formal basis to formulate policies and programs on an initiating
basis (e.g., contracts) and/or arrives at resolutions of problems
growing out of administration of existing policies and programs,
usually after a bargaining process.

MENTORING
Deals with individuals in terms of their overall life adjustment
behavior in order to advise, counsel, and/or guide them with
regard to problems that may be resolved by legal, scientific,
clinical, spiritual and/or other professional principles. Advises
clients on implications of diagnostic or similar categories, courses
of action open to deal with a problem, and merits of one strategy
over another.

At your public library, on pp. 1369-1371, in the 1977 edition
of the D.O.T., as the *Dictionary of Occupational Titles* is called,
you can find similar lists for Data and Things, if you think that
you prefer to work primarily with them, rather than with
people.

The point of all this for you, the career-changer/job-hunter, is:
1. The lower the level of skills that you think you should
claim, the more the skills can be prescribed and measured and
demanded of you. In other words, you'll have to fit in. Conversely, the higher the level of skills that you can honestly
claim, the less these skills can be prescribed and measured, and
the more you will be free to carve out the job in the shape of
you — making the fullest use of the special constellation of
abilities that are yours.
2. The higher the level of skills that you can honestly and
legitimately claim either with people, or data or things (or, in

varying degree, with all three) the less likely it is that the kinds of jobs you are thus qualified for will be advertised or known through normal channels; the more you'll have to find other ways of unearthing them — which is what the next chapter is all about.

3. Just because the opportunities for such higher level jobs or careers are harder to uncover, the higher you aim the fewer people you will have to compete with — for that job. In fact, if you uncover a need which your skills can help solve, that organization may well create a brand new job for you. This means you will be competing with no one, since you will be the sole applicant.

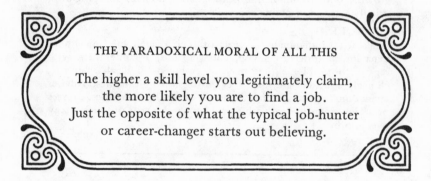

THE PARADOXICAL MORAL OF ALL THIS

The higher a skill level you legitimately claim,
the more likely you are to find a job.
Just the opposite of what the typical job-hunter
or career-changer starts out believing.

So, now that you know you are looking for your *highest* level of skills, on with the homework:

- **TOOLS & INSTRUMENTS TO HELP YOU:
  MEMORIES, FEELINGS, AND VISIONS**

What you need, at this point, are some practical — some very practical — tools or instruments. So, we are going to list a number of them. You may want to try every one. Or you may want to treat them as a kind of smorgasbord, picking and choosing a few from among all those that are offered. Your problem, in that case: how to know which ones to choose?

If you have a reflective-type mind, it will have struck you already that long-range planning must include some elements of your past, your present and your future.

The kinds of exercises which are available to you correspond to these three divisions of time.

To be sure, there is overlapping, but in terms of their major emphasis, we can categorize the following exercises in these terms:

YOUR MEMORIES (OF THE PAST):
Exercises No. 1, 2, 3 and 4.

YOUR FEELINGS (ABOUT THE PRESENT)
Exercises No. 5 and 6.

YOUR VISIONS (OF THE FUTURE):
Exercise No. 7

You'll know which ones can best help YOU, by taking into account the following considerations:

If, because of pell-melling change or great stress, your memory has just taken a holiday, then we suggest you forget about the exercises that deal with your *past*. If you are deep in apathy (literally, *lack* of feelings; lack of *consciousness* of feelings would be a better description), the exercises dealing with the *present* aren't likely to be of too much help. If you have what the Johnson O'Connor people call "low foresight," then the exercise that deals with the *future* isn't likely to be too helpful for you.

If, on the other hand, your whole mind is having trouble, then we suggest you go get a *good* rest before you tackle *any* of these exercises. It may be, of course, that even with a good rest, your mind balks at the thought of doing a whole bunch of exercises. This sort of activity *always* turned you off in school, and — *like that.*

I need to point out too that what may be surfacing here is the fact that your mind does better with pictures, and visualization, than it does with words and written exercises. Or, to use psychological jargon, the right-side of your brain (which thrives on pictures) may take precedence over the left-side of your brain (which thrives on words). If so, draw, cut and paste, doodle, take pictures, rather than writing words, words, words.

Exercises 1, 2, 3 and 4 — involving
YOUR MEMORIES OF THE PAST

The Keystone of career and life planning is The Past. Your Past. The reason for this is that the drives which will dictate your future course have not been inactive up until now, but have been continually manifesting themselves in what you have done best, and enjoyed doing the most.

Your life is a continuum, with a constant continuing core, no matter how the basic units or building blocks may be rearranged. The change lies in *the varying constellation* that these basic units are rearranged into (see page 85); but everything you enjoy most and do best will *basically* use the same building blocks that your past activities did.

In the light of all this, you need to look back and see when you were most enjoying life — precisely what activities you were doing at that moment, what skills or talents you were employing, what kinds of tasks you were dealing with, what kinds of accomplishments were being done, and precisely what it was that was "turning you on."

Here, then, are some exercises and instruments designed to assist you in doing this. Don't just read them as you go — *do* them!

PRACTICAL EXERCISE NUMBER 1

Most of us have had little or no experience at identifying our skills. A list, of sorts, would help. Also a kind of map, as to how to go at it. Such a list, and map, will be found in Appendix A, at the back of this book. It is called *The New Quick Job-Hunting Map.* "Quick" means a weekend devoted to this task alone. Compared to the average length of unemployment in this country — which stands at 16.4 weeks currently — this *is* Quick. This will probably help you identify your skills faster than any other method.

PRACTICAL EXERCISE NUMBER 2

If you don't like so structured a thing as a list, there is a more informal way of searching for your skills. It involves writing a diary of your life and your accomplishments, whether at work or play. The exercise is fully described in the companion book to this one, *Where Do I Go From Here With My Life?* by John Crystal and a friend of his.

For now, it may be sufficient to sketch the method. It has the following steps:

A. Write a diary of your entire life. An informal essay of where you've been, what you've done. Where you were working,

(c) Copyright 1980, Universal Press Syndicate.
All rights reserved. Used by special permission.

what you did there (not in terms of job titles — forget them —
but in terms of what you feel you achieved).

B. Boast a little. Boast a lot. Who's going to see this docu-
ment, besides you, God, and any twenty people that you
choose to show it to? Back up your elation and sense of pride
with concrete examples, and figures.

C. Describe your spare time, in each place where you lived.
What did you do? What did you most enjoy doing? Any hobbies? Avocations? Great. What skills did they use? Were there
any activities in your work that paralleled the kinds of things
you enjoyed doing in your leisure?

D. Concentrate both on the things you have done, and also
on the particular characteristics of your surroundings that were
important to you, and that you really enjoyed: green grass, the
theater, golfing, warm climate, skiing, or whatever.

E. Keep your eye constantly on that "divine radar": *enjoyable*. It's by no means *always* a guide to what you should be
doing, but it sure is more reliable than any other key that
people have come up with. Sift later. For now, put down anything that helped you to enjoy a particular moment or period
of your life.

F. Don't try to make this diary very structured. You can
bounce back and forth in time, if that's more helpful; go back
later, and use the questions above to check yourself out.

G. When your diary is all done, you may have a small book
— it can run 30-200 pages. (My, you've done a lot of living,

haven't you?) Now to go back over it, take a separate sheet of
paper, and put two columns on it:

Things Which, On The Basis of Past Experience, I Want To Have or Use In My Future Career(s) (With Particular Attention To Skills)	Things Which, On The Basis of Past Experience, I Want To Avoid In My Future Career(s)

As you go back over the diary, each time you come to something you feel fits in the first column, put it there. Each time
you come to something negative in your past that you feel fits
in the second column, put that there.

H. When you come to a skill that you a) *enjoyed* AND b)
did well (in *your* opinion), put it down in the first column *and
underline it twice.*

I. When this is all done, go back over column one, looking
primarily for skills. Choose the most important ones (*to you* —
again, only your opinion counts) — choose 10, 9, 8, 7, 6, 5, but
not less than five. Underline these three times.

J. Now rank them in order of decreasing importance to you.
You can use the chart on page 85. Fill it in. Now you have your
basic units.

K. What this exercise has left you with (hopefully) are: a)
five or more building blocks that when woven together will form
one coherent job description for you; b) a couple of lists which
list (for your own private thinking, at the moment) some other
things you want to have, or avoid, in your future employment.

Incidentally, in the two previous exercises, you may be
"hung up" over the idea of bragging — bragging about your
achievements, accomplishments, successes, and the like. The
Puritan in each of us dies hard, so it is time for —

"A SPECIAL WORD FOR PURITANS"

Puritans come in all sizes, shapes, genders, ages, and colors.
Puritans allegedly believe in God; but, what a god! A Puritan
believes that God didn't intend us to enjoy anything. And that
if you enjoy it, it's probably wrong for you. Let us illustrate:

Two girls do babysitting. One hates it. One enjoys it thoroughly. Which is more virtuous in God's sight? According to the Puritan, the one who hates it is more virtuous.

Two Puritans met on the street. "Isn't this a beautiful day?" said one. "Aye," said the other, "but we'll pay for it."

Puritans will talk about their failures, but hardly ever about their successes — and even then, always with a feeling that "God is going to get me, for such boasting." It's too enjoyable!

Given the Puritan's belief in God, what the Puritan fails to recognize is that enjoyment, in human life, isn't a fluke. It's part of God's plan. God wants us to eat; therefore God designs us so that eating is enjoyable. God wants us to sleep; therefore God designs us so that sleeping is enjoyable. God wants to have us procreate, love, and make love; therefore God designs us so that sex is enjoyable, and love even more so. *God gives us unique (or at least unusual) skills and talents; therefore God designs us so that, when we use them, they are enjoyable.*

That is, we gain a sense of achievement from them.

So, Puritans arise; if you believe in God, believe in One who believes in you. Downgrading yourself is out — for the duration.

"FRANKLY, IT'S NOT EASY BEING A PURITAN IN THIS 'HEDONISTIC SOCIETY!'"

(c) Copyright Chronicle Features, 1979, cartoon by Mal. Used by special permission.

PRACTICAL EXERCISE NUMBER 3

If you are relatively new to "the world of work out there" — if you are a high school or college student, a homemaker turning to work outside the home for the first time — you may feel that you don't have enough work experience to do either of the previous two exercises. Dismiss that thought! Just fill out the exercises on the basis of what you *have* done already, whether in the home, or at school, or at play. Don't overlook skills used in your leisure time, whatever you do! As an informal kind of warm-up for this, try this meandering exercise:

List all the hobbies you have done over the years, and then organize them in terms of greatest enjoyment, on down, to see what you were doing, what skills you were using, and what results you were accomplishing. This may give you a clue to what skills you enjoy using the most when no one is telling you what to do.

You can do this same exercise, of course, with your courses in school, etc.

If you want a more formal sort of warm-up, try the "I CAN" lists. They are described more fully in sections 2 and 9 of Appendix B, on pages 279 and 286.

PRACTICAL EXERCISE NUMBER 4

You may have been reading down this list of practical exercises hoping to find some kind of testing instrument.

People *love* instruments: you know, those written test-type things that tell you everything you wanted to know about yourself. They love the Strong-Campbell, and the Myers-Briggs, and that sort of thing. Unfortunately, I don't. I don't trust any instrument *that somebody else has to mark and interpret for you.* I know a man who took the Strong-Campbell back in the days when it was just "The Strong." Even then, the thing only measured interests, not skills. But the test-administrator didn't know that. So, in interpreting the test afterwards to the man, he told him, "You have no skills with mechanical things." We'll let the man tell the rest of the story. "For twenty years," he said, "I didn't even dare pick up a hammer, for fear I would permanently maim myself — after what that test-man said. Then, one year I needed to put siding on my house, but I couldn't afford to pay anyone to do it. I *had* to do it myself.

To my utter astonishment, I not only did a fine job of putting the siding up, I had the time of my life doing it. When I think of how many years I was deprived of that pleasure by that idiot test-administrator, if I met up with him tomorrow I would probably strangle him."

Anyway, on that account I don't like any instrument that you can't mark for yourself. There are such. The one I like best is John Holland's *Self-Directed Search*. It takes about an hour. A specimen set costs $3.75 (Catalog No. 3700) and can be ordered from Consulting Psychologists Press, 577 College Ave., Palo Alto, CA 94306. I've given some hints about the best way to use it, on the first page of Appendix B, at the back of this book.

Exercises 5 and 6 – involving
YOUR FEELINGS ABOUT THE PRESENT

It is possible that none of the previous exercises may strike your fancy. You want to know what other ways there are, of getting at your skills. This next family of exercises turns from the past to the present. It relies less on memory, and more on feelings.

But what use, you may ask, are feelings, in trying to determine what kind of work one should do? Aren't we interested only in skills, talents, and all that? Well, not exactly. You see, studies have revealed that:

1. Your interests, wishes and happiness determine what you actually do well, more than your intelligence, aptitudes, or skills do. This is the conclusion of numerous vocational psychologists and personnel people. Strength of desire outweighs everything else, they say.

Maybe the word "feelings" or "wishes" sounds just too "fantasy-like" to your ears. OK then, borrowing a word from biology, let's speak instead of "tropisms": things which living creatures instinctively go toward, or away from. The human animal is no exception, and we each have our own personal, unique tropisms. So, ask yourself: what do you feel drawn toward, what do you instinctively go away from? Make some lists. Your own personal tropisms may be determinative for your future career.

2. If you do work that you really feel a lot of enthusiasm for, you are bound to do an outstanding job, and be of greater

help to others as well as attracting greater recognition and reward for your work.

3. No tests or other instruments have been devised yet, that so effectively measure what you want, as just *asking you*, or having you *ask yourself* what you most like to do. As John Holland says: "Despite several decades of research, the most efficient way to predict vocational choice is simply to ask the person what he wants to be; our best devices do not exceed the predictive value of that method."[1]

Our first exercise in this section, naturally enough, simply takes Holland at his word:

PRACTICAL EXERCISE NUMBER 5

This exercise consists of a very simple question indeed. Write out your answer to the question: If you could have any kind of job, what would it be? Invent your own, if need be; or ask yourself the question: among all the people you know or have seen or read about, whose job would you most like to have? Forget for the moment what you think you *can* do. What do you *want* to do?

One woman I know declined to do any of the exercises in this chapter. *But* she did ask herself this question. She decided the person she most admired, whose job she most coveted, was a woman who appeared as hostess on a television program for children. Accordingly, our job-hunter went to the local TV station in her community with a well-thought-out, carefully written proposal for a similar children's television program. They not only bought the idea, they asked her to be the hostess. Thus did she find her ideal job. You like this story? Try the same question on yourself, then.

You may prefer to put the question to yourself in other forms, or with time sequences: a year from now, ten years from now, twenty years from now? Try them all.

This exercise, of course, presumes that you know what makes you happy. Maybe, however, you have a much clearer idea of what makes you unhappy (a list, as it were, of "negative tropisms" — things you instinctively want to avoid). Okay, the next exercise thrives on that awareness:

---

1. Reprinted, by permission of the publisher, from Holland, John L. *The Psychology of Vocational Choice*, now out of print (Ginn and Company, Waltham, MA. 1966.)

PRACTICAL EXERCISE NUMBER 6

Write a detailed answer to the question: "What are the things which make me unhappy?" When you are done, analyze what you've written into columns, with the first one subdivided:

THINGS THAT LIE WITHIN THE CONTROL OF MYSELF		THINGS THAT LIE WITHIN THE CONTROL OF OTHERS, OR FATE, OR CIRCUMSTANCE
Things which I could change thru a change in my external environment (my job, or the place where I live)	Things which I could change thru working on my interior life (what's going on inside me)	

Check these columns over, when you are done, reviewing the second list to be sure the things listed there *really* are beyond your control or power to alter. Then go over the first list and decide whether the priority for you is to work on your *external* furniture or your *internal* furniture, or *both*. List concrete resolutions for yourself, with time goals beside them. Paste the list on your bathroom mirror. Read it each morning.

Choosing a job is primarily a question of choosing your external furniture. Your surrounding environment, broadly speaking. Jobs are environments, mostly "people environments," and the issue is how well these are compatible with your internal furniture. In the past, our society has insisted that when your external furniture and your internal got "out of sync," that you should go get your internal furniture "rearranged," as it were. The increased interest in second careers these days, among those who served "honorably" in their first — clergy, doctors, aerospace engineers, physicists, executives, etc. — may be traced in large part to a new realization that where the external and internal are out of synchronization, it is easier by far, and certainly more sensible, to first try altering the external. To make the environment conform to you, rather than you to the environment.

Exercise 7 — involving
YOUR VISION OF THE FUTURE

If none of the previous exercises 'grab you,' there is still another we can suggest. It deals with the future.

As someone has said, "We ought to be interested in the future, for that is where we are going to spend the rest of our lives." We approach the future through visions and dreams.

Most of us have visions and dream dreams. It's only when we come to our job that we think our visions and dreams should be shelved. In career planning there used to be certain professionals who loved to play the game of getting you to say what you really wanted to do with the rest of your life, and then "bringing you down to earth" by saying, "All right; now, let's get realistic." What they should have asked was, "Are you *sure* this is what you really want? because if it is, chances are you will find some way to do it."

Never mind "being realistic." For every person who "over-dreams" — of doing more than their merits would justify, — there are four people who "under-dream," and sell themselves short. Remember, according to the experts, 80% of the workers in this country are "under-employed." You may end up in the same fix, if you try to keep one eye fixed on your dreams, and one eye fixed on what you *think* you know about the job market, e.g., "I'd like to be able to do this and that at my job, but I *know* there is no job in the world like that." You don't know any such thing.

"WHILE YOU'RE WAITING FOR YOUR SHIP
TO COME IN, WHY DON'T YOU DO SOME
MAINTENANCE WORK ON THE PIER ?"

(c) Copyright, 1980, King Features Syndicate, Inc.
Used by special permission.

Granted, you may not be able to find a job that has *all* that you want. But why not aim for it, and then settle for less if and when you find out that you simply have to? Don't foreclose your future prematurely. You'd be surprised what you may be able to turn up.

To be sure, dreams sometimes have to be taken in stages. If you want to be president of a particular enterprise, for example, you may have to work your way toward it through two or three steps. But it is quite likely you will eventually succeed — *if your whole heart is in your dream.*

Now, to an exercise that helps uncover what your dreams about your future truly are:

PRACTICAL EXERCISE NUMBER 8

Spend as much time as necessary writing an article entitled "Before I die, I want to . . . " (Things you would like to do, before you die.) Confess them to yourself now, and maybe you can begin to make them happen.

You may prefer to write an article on a similar topic: "On the last day of my life, what must I have done or been so that my life will have been satisfying to me?" When finished, go back over it and make two lists: Things Already Accomplished, and: Things Yet To Be Accomplished. Then make a third column, beside the one called Things Yet To Be Accomplished, listing the particular *steps* that you will have to take, in order to accomplish these things that you have listed.

1 Things already accomplished.	2 Things yet to be accomplished. *(Then number them in the order in which you would like to accomplish them.)*	3 Steps needed in order to accomplish the things in column 2

As you get involved with this exercise you may notice that it is impossible to keep your focus only on your career. You will find some dreams creeping in concerning your leisure or your life-long learning — of places you want to visit, and experiences you want to have, that are not on-the-job. *Don't omit these.* Be just as specific as possible.

Incidentally, you don't have to do this exercise just once in your life. Some career and life planning experts suggest keeping a list posted on your office or kitchen wall all year 'round, — crossing out items as you accomplish them, and adding new ones as they occur to you from month to month.

Practical Exercise (Cooling Down?)

If two weeks after putting down this chapter, you pick it up again, and realize you still haven't even begun identifying your skills through *any* of these exercises, then let's face it: you're going to *have to* pay someone to aid you. Too bad, because chances are that if you'd just try this on your own, you could do as well or better by yourself. But better this than nothing: turn to Appendix C, choose three possible counselors or places, and go ask them questions. Choose one. Pay them, and *get at this.*

CHECKING BACK

What? You say you set aside a whole weekend, locked yourself in your room, and *did* the whole *Quick Job-Hunting Map* in Appendix A? Well, *good* for you!

Here are a few questions, to check out how you did:

1. Since all transferable skills are used either with Data, or People or Things, do you now know which you most prefer working with? Is it some kind of Data, or some kind of People, or some kind of Things? What kind?

2. What's your second preference? Your third?

3. Have you got the skills to be more than one word? One word won't do. "I'm good at organizing" don't tell us *nothing.* Organizing what? People, as at a party? Nuts and bolts, as on a workbench? Or lots of information, lying in a computer? Those are three *entirely different* skills. The one word "organizing" doesn't tell us which one, at all. Sooooo, have you gone back over the skills you pulled out of the Map, and made sure that each one-word definition gets *fleshed out* with an *object* — some kind of Data/Information, or some kind of People, or some kind of Thing — and maybe also an adverb or adjective.

(c) Copyright 1980.
United Feature Syndicate, Inc.
Used by special permission.

"I'm good at analyzing people *painstakingly*," and "I'm good at analyzing people *in a flash, by intuition*," are two *entirely different skills*. The difference between them is found in the adjectival or adverbial phrase there at the end. So, have you expanded each definition as much as you can, by an object at least, and maybe an adverb or adjective? If so, great. If not, *go do it*.

4. Have you got all your skills arranged *in order of importance, or priority, for you? Anytime* you have a bunch of information about yourself, it is relatively useless to you, *until you have put it in order of priority*. "Here's what I most enjoy doing, this is next, this is next, and so on." This is *especially* true of your skills. Looking ahead to your next job or career, which skill do you *most* hope you will get to use "on the job," which next, which next? and so on.

5. Have you avoided stating your skills in the jargon or language of your past career? This is a point on which clergy, in particular, often stumble and fall. "I am good at preaching" is not a very useful skill identification. It is still cloaked in the jargon and language of *one career and one career only*. What is its *larger* form? "Teaching?" Perhaps. "Motivating people?" Perhaps. "Moving people to their depths?" Perhaps. Only you can say. But get your skills out of any jargon from your past.

6. Have you thus far steered clear of putting a job title on what you're aiming toward? Skills can point to many different jobs, which have a multitude of titles. Don't lock yourself into a box prematurely. "I'm looking for a job where I can use the following skills," is fine. But, "I'm looking for a job where I can *be* a (job title)" is a no-no, until you've done more homework and more research.

7. Are you hanging loose, willing to look at a number of alternatives, as you move through the homework and research?

Or is your desire for finishing this off *fast* leading you to push prematurely for just one way to go? Stay loose. Preserve *all* your options.

8. As you have been working on the question of your future career or future job, have you begun to get some insights into your whole life and being? Keep yourself sensitive to these things, as they pop up. Properly speaking, what you're engaged in is not merely career-planning, but *life* planning or life *designing*, if you prefer. You will become, in all likelihood, increasingly conscious of your *values* as you go along. As David Maister says, "Play to your evil secrets." They're not really so evil; you just *think* they are. But, speaking candidly and to yourself alone, what *are* your values? Truth, beauty, righteousness, ambition, compassion, security, service, popularity, status, power, friends, achievement, love, authority, freedom, glamor, giving, integrity, honesty, loyalty, sensitivity, caring,—which holds the *most* meaning and importance for you? These things will almost certainly come clearer for you, as you move on through your job-hunting or career-planning homework. Stay alert and sensitive to these. You will get much clearer about who you are willing to work with and for, and who you are not. Those who *share* your values will be on your hit parade; those who don't, won't.

9. Does all this planning, and the exercises, and the reflection seem like *just too much?* Too much work. Too much time. Just too much. Have you thought of involving your loved ones and friends with you? Too much trouble? I see. Well, if you don't want to work at all of this, then consider this one last question, here: what or who is going to rescue you, if you don't? As Ezra Pound said, *A slave is one who waits for someone else to come and free him.* I think that's an erroneous definition of slavery in historical times, to say the least. But as an insight into those who are slaves at the workplaces of today, it has the ring of truth. Who are *you* waiting for, to come and save you — from boredom at your job, from a wasted life, and years of deep regrets?

Students spend four or more years
learning how to dig data out of the library
and other sources, but it rarely occurs
to them that they should also apply some of
that same new-found research skill to their
own benefit—to looking up information
on companies, types of professions, sections
of the country that might interest them.

Professor Albert Shapero

*The William H. Davis Professor
of The American Free Enterprise System
at Ohio State University*

CHAPTER SIX

Where Do You Want To Do It?

THE SECOND KEY
TO CAREER PLANNING AND
JOB-HUNTING

It is not sufficient merely to know what your skills are. You have to know WHERE you want to use them.

Suppose, for example, your principal and favorite skill is Welding. Do you want to weld together a wheel, or the casing of a nuclear bomb? You see — it makes all the difference in the world as to WHERE you choose to use that skill.

WHERE is a matter of "what basic materials or kinds of people or forms of data/information do you want to use your skills with?" And it is a matter of "what kinds of values or goals do you want your skills to serve?" And it is a matter of "what sort of work environment, physical, emotional and spiritual, do you need for the most effective employment of your skills?" And it is a matter of "what level do you want to be working at, supervisory, or as a member of a team, or as an individual working by yourself?" And, "as working for another, or as working in your own enterprise?"

All of *that* is involved in the issue that follows hard on the heels of WHAT DO YOU WANT TO DO? — namely, WHERE DO YOU WANT TO DO IT?

So, let us begin.

Turning Skills Into Careers

● Researching your skills involves trying to discover what different kinds of careers, defined as constellations or arrangements of skills, are open to you; and then arranging these in order of priority *according to your enjoyment of them.*

PUTTING THE BUILDING BLOCKS TOGETHER

If you did *The New Quick Job-Hunting Map,* or one of the alternative exercises in the previous chapter, you now know what the basic building blocks of your skills are. Now, you want to know, of course, how you arrange them into different constellations or careers.

We begin with some basic vocabulary:

Technically *a job is a flexible combination of tasks* — which can be arranged and rearranged in a number of different tantalizing ways. *A career is a flexible combination of skills* — which can be arranged and rearranged in a number of different tantalizing ways.

WHAT KIND OF RESEARCH DO YOU NEED TO DO?

Your research from here on out will divide into two parts:

Part I. <u>Researching What Careers or Industries Interest You the Most, What Kind of Job within an Industry Interests You the Most, What Organizations Have Such Jobs, and Who There Has the Power to Hire Such a One As You.</u> During this part of your research *you* are the screener; *they* are the screenees. You are looking careers, industries, jobs, organizations over, trying to decide which of them pleases *you.* They have to meet your criteria, or they get crossed off your list. You are gathering information in order to narrow things down. It is premature for you to be thinking about getting hired anywhere yet; you don't know where you want to be. Until you've concluded this part of your research. If a job offer *accidentally* surfaces during this

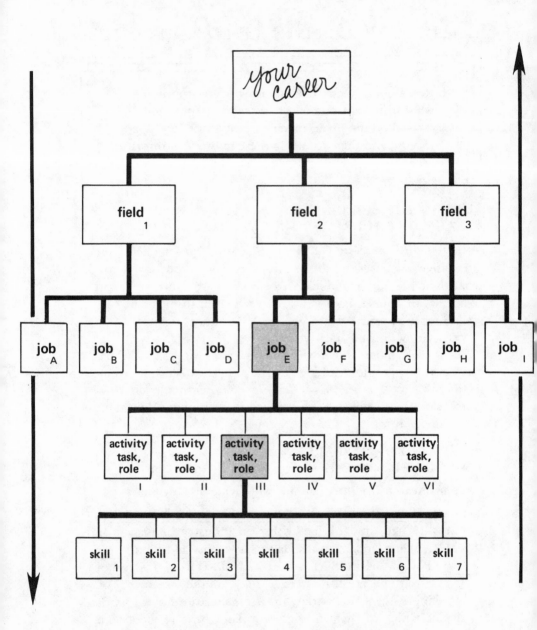

FROM SKILLS TO CAREERS

part of the process, it won't be because you were doing *anything* to encourage it. Your response, in fact, will reveal that. "Well, I'm tickled pink that you would want me to be working here. But, until I've finished my survey and am clearer about where my skills could best be used, in a way that would be most productive and give me the most satisfaction, I just can't say Yes or No to your kind invitation. But, when I've finished my personal survey, I'd sure be glad to get back to you about this, as this seems to me to be the *kind* of place I'd like to work in, and the kind of people I'd like to work with."

Over the years, I've asked job-hunters again and again what was the most valuable part of this whole process. And they have responded again and again: "I learned to not just jump at the first offer I got, but to be more patient, and . . . well . . . more picky. I knew the right opportunity would come along, if I first took the time to find out what it was that I was truly looking for."

Yes. And that is why, during this phase of your research, you are *not* open to job offers. You are not looking for job offers. You are not yet thinking about job offers. You're visiting places to find out the information you need to know, in order to turn skills into a career, and a career into a job you would love. Whether the places you hit along the way happen to have a vacancy, or happen to want you, is — for the moment — premature and irrelevant. You have to first of all decide whether or not *you* want *them*.

Part II. Interviewing for Hire. Having found the career field you like best, having found what sort of industry within that field appeals to you the most, having discovered what size organization and what kind of organization you'd like to work for, having narrowed down the possibilities to four or five that really seem to be just ideal (from your point of view), you now RESEARCH THEM THOROUGHLY (as we shall describe in the next chapter), and at those four or five places you seek an actual interview for an actual job, where you would be able to do the thing you have decided you would most like to do. At this point *and only at this point,* you now become the Screenee, and the organizations or employers become the Screeners. Though, *of course,* you are still keeping your eyes and ears open in case you see something dreadful that will put you abruptly back into the role of Screener and cause you to say, to yourself at least, "I have just learned this place really isn't for me."

In any event, the part we are talking about in this chapter is what we have called Part I, above — researching your ideal job — where you are the Screener; and is not to be confused with Part II (next chapter) where you become the screenee. If you *feel* as though you are the Screenee in this first part of the research we are describing, you're doing something wrong. Just remember, as a human being you've got rights: including the right to decide where it is you'd like to use your rich gifts, talents, skills, and the right to go look some places over and decide whether or not they interest you, and whether or not you like what they're doing, and whether or not you could do your most effective work there.

This is even true in those industries or places where hiring is "tight." Look at it from the point of view of the Employer. He or she has fewer dollars to spend, in most cases. Wants more value for what dollars they do spend. Wants people who are truly excited about working *there*, people who have taken the time to look at other places, but want most of all to work *in this place* — and know why.

Throughout this search on your part to find WHERE you'd like to use your skills, there are an amazingly large number of resources to aid you in your search. However, these resources will be useless to you unless you keep firmly in mind what kinds of questions you want the resources to help you with.

(c) Copyright 1979, United Feature Syndicate, Inc. Used by permission.

MY QUESTIONS FOR RESEARCHING MY IDEAL JOB

A. What Skills Do I Have and Enjoy
B. Where Do I Want to Use These Skills
C. What Kinds of Organizations Can I Focus On —
    in terms of Goals,
    for use of my Skills,
    in my Geographical Area of Preference
D. What Are the Names of Such Organizations
E. What Are Their Problems —
    at the Level I Want To Work
F. Who There Has The Power To Hire Me

The Basic Principles for
Turning Skills into a Career

1 BE CLEAR ABOUT THE DIFFERENT KINDS OF
   INFORMATION YOU ARE LOOKING FOR,
IN YOUR SEARCH.

You are trying to find out the following:

A. What skills do I have that I have already demonstrated; and that I enjoy?

As we saw in the previous chapter, this list must be in detail, *and* prioritized in terms of your six or so favorites. If you failed to do these steps (identify them in detail, and prioritize them) you will *dramatically* hamper your subsequent information-search.

B. Where do I want to use these skills?

As we said earlier, someone who has the skill of welding can use that skill to weld the casting for a nuclear bomb, or to make a wheel for a cart. So, what do *you* want to use *your* skills with? In the service of what? To accomplish what? And in what geographical area?

Simply to say you want to do welding (or whatever) is not sufficient, and will seriously hamper your subsequent research. You must decide *where* you want to use the skill.

C. What kinds of organizations are there, whose goals I like, that either already use people with my skills, or ought to, and

perhaps could be persuaded to, and that are in the specific
geographical area (or areas) I would consider?

The last step above is the pre-condition for answering the next
three. An overseas soldier — for example — cannot do an information-search about corporations' departments of mental hygiene back here in the States, until he or she has *first* selected
at least an area of the country, and two or three cities, there,
by name.

**D. What are the names of such organizations, in the cities
or areas I would consider?**

The more specific and detailed you have been in step C, above,
the easier this step D will be. The more general you have been,
the harder this step will be, e.g., "Corporations" is too general.
In a particular city, that will turn out to be a very long list. But
(for example) "Corporations with not more than 200 employees, which produce such and such a product" is a much shorter
list, in any particular city (or area). Likewise, "nonprofit organizations" is too general. That again will produce a long list, if
your information-search is thorough. "Nonprofit organizations
dealing with . . . " what? health services, consumer protection,
or what? *The more detailed you are, the easier it will be for you
to do this part of your research.*

**E. What are those organizations' problems, or challenges,
particularly in the departments or areas where I might be
working?**

A lot depends on the level at which you want to work. If at the
clerk or secretary level, the problems are pretty predictable:
absenteeism, too-long coffee or lunch breaks, not caring about
the subject-matter, not accepting your supervisor's priorities
about which work needs to get done first, etc. If you want to
work at a higher level, the problems are likely to be correspond-
ingly more complex. But you *can* figure them out — usually by
asking: what would a *bad* employee in this department be like?
The problems to be solved are often in the employee, rather
than in the situation.

**F. Who there has the power to hire for the level of job
I am interested in?**

It's not likely to be the Personnel Department, unless you're
talking about entry-level.

2 DETERMINE HOW MUCH TIME YOU HAVE BEFORE YOU ABSOLUTELY HAVE TO FIND A JOB.

Yes, of course it would be just dandy if you could conclude your research — successfully — within a month. And, many people do. But the average length of the job-hunt in America is currently 16.4 weeks. It is not *at all* unusual for a job-hunt to take nine months (something symbolic about *that*) or longer. Soooo, how much time *do* you have before you simply *must* have your next job? This is the place to total up your savings, your partner's income if applicable, money you could borrow, cuts you could make in your expenses, and so forth, and then divide it all by your weekly expenses. The earlier you can get started, the more lead-time you can give yourself, the better.

3 OUTLINE FOR YOURSELF A PLAN OR STRATEGY FOR FINDING THE INFORMATION YOU ARE LOOKING FOR.

Let's refer back to the questions you are seeking answers to:

MY QUESTIONS FOR RESEARCHING MY IDEAL JOB

✓ A. What Skills Do I Have and Enjoy
  B. Where Do I Want to Use These Skills
  C. What Kinds of Organizations Can I Focus On —
        in terms of Goals,
        for use of my Skills,
        in my Geographical Area of Preference
  D. What Are the Names of Such Organizations
  E. What Are Their Problems —
        at the Level I Want To Work
  F. Who There Has The Power To Hire Me

The answer to A should already be in your hand by the time you get to this point in the process. This was what the previous chapter was all about. But if you tried it, and got bogged down, so that you are still hazy about what your favorite skills are, you may then: (1) Recruit your mate, or a friend, or business acquaintance to help you work through the map; OR (2) Use a professional career expert such as your college career-planning or placement office; or a career counselor, to be found by the methods suggested in Appendix C at the back of this book.

In the course of the next step: trying to turn your skills into careers, your plan should start with your consulting one or more of the following persons. Ask them: What occupations do you know of, that would use the skills that I have?

Your *librarian* (or business librarian); *counselors* at the appropriate department of your local State Employment office; *friends* knowledgeable in the fields that interest you; *consultants* to the fields you are interested in; and the like.

You can also figure out, on your own, *who* it is that might have some ideas about possible careers for you, by the simple act of examining your skills, and *turning those skills into people* you might go see.

Suppose that you have discovered you are skilled in: counseling people, particularly in one-to-one situations; that you are well-versed in psychiatry; and that you love carpentry and plants.

How do you put all this together into one unified career? Well, begin by translating each of the skills, knowledges or interests you have, into a corresponding PERSON. Counseling = counselor, psychiatry = psychiatrist, carpentry = carpenter, plants = gardener.

Next, ask yourself which of these persons is most likely *to have the largest overview?* This is often, but not always, the same as asking: who took the longest to get their training? The particular answer here: the psychiatrist.

In the place where you presently are, then, plan to go see a psychiatrist (pay them for fifteen minutes of their time — if there is no other way) or go see the head of the psychiatry department at the nearest college or university, and ask them: Do you have any idea how to put all the above together in a job? And if *you* don't, *who* might?

If you carry out this plan, in this particular case, you will eventually be told: Yes, it can all be put together. There is a branch of psychiatry that uses plants to help heal people. You can use all your skills and interests. You can even use your carpentry to build planters for those plants.

During this particular part of your research, you're essentially working your way UP the chart on page 110. First, you're filling in your three, four, five or six favorite skills. Then you're asking, "What kinds of tasks or activities use all those skills, together?" And then: "What sorts of jobs let you do those

MY QUESTIONS FOR RESEARCHING MY IDEAL JOB
A. What Skills Do I Have and Enjoy
✓ B. Where Do I Want to Use These Skills
C. What Kinds of Organizations Can I Focus On —
      in terms of Goals,
      for use of my Skills,
      in my Geographical Area of Preference
D. What Are the Names of Such Organizations
E. What Are Their Problems —
      at the Level I Want To Work
F. Who There Has The Power To Hire Me

kinds of tasks or activities?" And, finally, "What fields or industries have such jobs?"

In laying out your plan for your research, the experience of successful job-hunters in the past suggests the following: use books, libraries, printed resources, as much as you can, until what you want to know REQUIRES you to go out and talk with people. Then, go talk to people WHO ARE USING THE SKILLS you most want to use. Talk, in other words, not to those who could eventually hire you (you're not at that point, yet), BUT TO THOSE WHO ARE DOING WHAT YOU THINK YOU MIGHT LIKE TO DO.

You are engaged in a task that is essentially like that of trying on shoes. You're trying to see what styles you like, what colors you like, and *most of all* do they fit you? — *before* you have committed yourself to a lifetime of boredom or frustration in that job or those jobs. The beauty of this research: it gives you a quick and painless way to try on jobs and see if they fit you.

PLAN TO RESEARCH THE LEVEL
AT WHICH YOU'D LIKE TO WORK

As your research progresses, as you become clearer about the kind of work you'd most enjoy doing, you will have to begin making decisions about what level you'd like to work at: entry, intermediate, senior, or what?

This isn't just a matter of how much authority you're entitled to, or how much you'd like to have. Level is related, more than anything else, to how high a level of skill you can legitimately claim. *And* to how much salary you're going to need.

This point in the process of researching your ideal job is the time you need this information. For it will determine WHAT LEVEL OF JOB you are exploring. So, time to do a little math (ugh!). Maybe you'd prefer to think of it as a:

PLAN TO RESEARCH THE
PRICE TAG ON YOUR LIFE STYLE

We're going to talk about money. For some people, that's a *big* issue; for others, it's rather insignificant – because, well, *somehow,* they always manage to survive.

But I want to emphasize that we are talking about it at this point in the process, because it will help determine at what level you should do your research on your ideal job and at what level you may end up working. In other words, leaving aside the question of what money can buy, you need to know what your minimum salary requirements are going to be, before you can adequately research a company or organization.

If you're not into 'just subsistence,' then we suggest you make up two budgets. First: the 'rock-bottom need' budget – what you *need* to just survive, if you found yourself and your loved ones between a rock and a hard place. Second: the 'I hope' budget – what you *hope* you will have to live on. The categories, for both budgets include, of course:

Food—at home; Food—out;
Housing—rent/mortgage, tax, insurance;
Housing—furnishings;
Housing—utilities and
household supplies;
Transportation—car payments,
insurance, parking, gas, other
maintenance; public transportation;
Clothing—purchases, maintenance;
Hairdos, toiletries;
Medical—insurance, physicians' visits,
other, including dental;
Education—tuition, books, loan
repayment;
Recreation;
Gifts, contributions;
Life insurance;

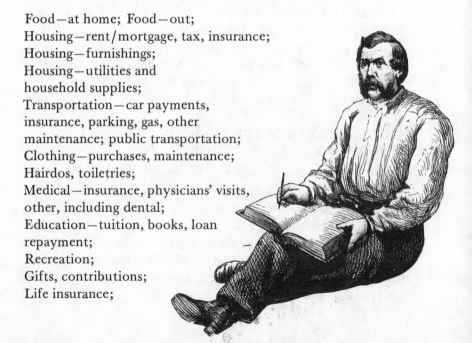

Union dues;
Savings;
Payments on debts;
Pension contribution[1];
Social Security; federal/state
income taxes;
and—

PLUS 15% . . .

To each budget add 15% more, because we all habitually underestimate our needs, and by about that much.

What you have now is your range: the amounts *between which*
you can bargain, at the conclusion of a promising job interview,
and the level at which you want to do your exploring, now.

Once you know what you need and want to be earning,
weekly or yearly, THEN when you zero in on a career that
interests you, you can ask your local librarian to help you find
out the salaries in that field. You'll know then whether or not
you're interested in working at *that* level. At this writing, the
average salary for non-supervisory workers in the U.S. (on private non-agricultural payrolls) was $8.43 hourly, $299.27
weekly, and $15,562.04 annually — in case you were wondering.

---

1. Military are advised by the creative minority not to include their retirement pay in
any way in their computations. That's extra, for emergencies. Clergy are advised that
they probably make $30,000-40,000 — on the average — although this is hard to
comprehend, until you add in all the perquisites, etc., or ask the thought-provoking
question: how much would it cost to hire skilled laypersons to do *all* my work, if I
were to leave?

Aids for Your Research

PRACTICAL AID NUMBER 1

The Dictionary of Occupational Titles (1977), or D.O.T. It is "the greatest single source of occupational information in the world" *and* "an unwieldy mishmash." But in it you can locate occupations or jobs by a) physical demands, b) individual working conditions, c) interest, d) aptitude or skills, e) educational requirements, f) vocational preparation, and so forth.

Each occupation has been given a nine-digit code number. The first three digits are called *the occupational group* and describe The World of Work. The second three digits describe skills, i.e., what workers do with data, with people, and with things. The last three digits indicate the varying titles of occupations that have in common the first six digits.

You are encouraged to go to your library, and browse in the D.O.T. for a while, to get the feel of it.

The point of this research is to *be sure that you do not get prematurely locked into one field or occupation, but that you see how many alternative options are open to you.*

Our Canadian readers (or job-hunters in the U.S.A. who want a slightly different perspective) will want to look up in their library the *Canadian Classification and Dictionary of Occupations,* 1971. Vol. I and II.

PRACTICAL AID NUMBER 2

Dictionary of Holland Occupational Codes: A comprehensive cross-index of Holland's RIASEC codes with 12,000 DOT occupations. Compiled by: Gary D. Gottfredson, John L. Holland, and Deborah Kimiko Ogawa (1982). Your library isn't likely to have this book, unless it's a large library or has a special section devoted to careers. If you want it, you may have to pop for the price — $18.50 — yourself. You can order it from its publisher, Consulting Psychologists Press, 577 College Ave., Palo Alto, CA 94306. It's immensely useful because it gives you a useful doorway into the D.O.T. Otherwise, you may be aimlessly wandering around in the D.O.T. for days, and never get out. Anyway, *with this little gem in hand,* once you've figured out your

"Holland code" — normally by taking his Self-Directed Search, as described in the previous chapter — this book tells you all the titles in the D.O.T. that match your "code." So, it leads you from skills to careers in three almost painless steps: take the SDS, look up the code in this Dictionary, and finally go read in more detail the same listings in the D.O.T. Voila! Poof! And Ta Da!

Incidentally, this is as good a place as any to mention that all expenses of a job search are allegedly tax deductible on Federal tax returns. This includes the price of the books you purchase to help you with your job-hunt — as above — cost of any professional career counseling, travel costs, postage, stationery, resume printing, and the like. Needless to say, *careful detailed* records must be kept, daily.

PRACTICAL AID NUMBER 3

Occupational Outlook Handbook, U.S. Department of Labor, Washington, D.C. Get this at your library. It gives an outline for 300 or so major occupations. For each one, it lists: what its future looks like, the nature of the work, the usual training required, employment outlook, earnings and working conditions. It's helpful if you don't just want to get into occupations that're closing out; but its prophecies should be taken with a large barrel of salt. There is incidentally an *Occupational Outlook Handbook for College Graduates.*

The very word "outlook" (occupational or employment) ought to make you beware. "A good outlook" for a particular industry only means, if you stop to think about it, that there is relatively little competition for the openings that exist; i.e., that there are more openings than there are bodies to fill them. On the other hand, "a bad outlook" for a particular field, or a prediction that it is going to be 'crowded,' is only another way of saying there is going to be a lot of competition. That doesn't mean you shouldn't go after such a job, if it appeals to you. It just means you will have to follow the techniques described in this book more faithfully, that's all. Time and again men and women have gotten positions in a career where everyone told them there was No Employment At All; and they did it by following precisely the strategies described in these chapters.

PRACTICAL AID NUMBER 4

Many, if not most, fields have professional journals. Once you begin to find a field that looks interesting to you, ask your local librarian to assist you in getting your hands on the appropriate journal or journals in that field. Follow all leads that they may suggest to you, as your reading of articles and ads uncovers these, for additional information.

Again, many if not most fields have some kind of professional, trade, or union associations. Your public library has all kinds of listings of such associations — yours for the asking.

If your library doesn't have what you are looking for, try to see what other libraries there are, in the city or town where you are: Chamber of Commerce library; university libraries; libraries at appropriate businesses, etc.

PRACTICAL AID NUMBER 5

If all the obvious sorts of occupations do not "grab you," and you decide that what you want help in researching are "alternative kinds" of work, we suggest you look at some of what used to be called "counter-culture" directories: such as Peoples'

Yellow Pages. See your local bookstore. Also see Section 1, in Appendix B (page 277).

To find further sources of information about alternative kinds of jobs in your own community, visit "new age" bookstores, food co-ops, health food stores and restaurants, laundromats, record and bicycle shops, any place organized as a collective, communes, and groups organized around issues (such as the nuclear freeze, rape-crisis centers, etc.) — not to mention the offices of such places as the American Friends Service Committee. You will find that these places attract a goodly number of people likewise committed to alternative kinds of work. So, screw up your courage to go look at bulletin boards there (if they have one) plus any literature they may be giving out. Braver still, talk to the staff there; the higher up they are, the more likely that they will know of other resources or contacts for you. And, better yet, get involved there — either as a volunteer, or as an employee. You will make lots of contacts, particularly if they put out some kind of newsletter or any other communication. You will also have a chance to do loads of talking to people there.

You will also find that browsing in such excellent books as *The Next Whole Earth Catalog, Second Edition,* just to see which subjects strike your fancy, may give you some helpful clues as to the direction your heart and mind are heading in.

PRACTICAL AID NUMBER 6

If you have no idea of where else to go to find out what you want to know, there is an immensely helpful guidebook for your further research: *Finding Facts Fast: How to Find Out What You Want and Need to Know,* by Alden Todd. 1979, second edition. If your library or bookstore doesn't have it, you can order it directly from its publisher, Ten Speed Press, Box 7123, Berkeley CA 94707. $3.95, paperback. It is subtitled: A handbook for students, political activists, civic leaders and professionals . . . based on methods used by reference librarians, scholars, investigative reporters and detectives.

Well, that completes our list of practical aids to your research.

Of course, despite this wealth of material, you cannot simply hide yourself away in the libraries all the time. (Don't you wish!) This information out of books *must* be supplemented by

talks with *insiders* — brokers, college alumni, friends, anyone you know who has friends within the particular fields, organizations or jobs that you are interested in, so that they can give you helpful insights. Use every contact you know, once names of organizations that interest you begin to surface in your notes.

In the course of researching a field we urge you particularly to consult with people who are doing the very thing you think you might like to do. You should not be hesitant about asking for their time. *If they really like their own vocation,* they should be very receptive to your desire to know more about that vocation: what they do, the various kinds of tasks and skills required, and the aspects of it that they particularly enjoy, or particularly don't enjoy.

You say you don't like what I'm saying about the importance of talking to people because YOU ARE SHY, PAINFULLY SHY? Well, me too. BUT shyness will yield, IF it's a true enthusiasm that you're talking to someone about. If you *love* computers, then you probably forget all about your shyness *when* you're talking to someone else about computers. So, just remember, during this research of your ideal job, when it is time for Shy You to go talk with people, it's your ENTHUSIASM you're exploring — the thing in this world you're dying to know more about, than any other subject.

Also, during this first stage of your research, it is *perfectly permissible to take somebody with you* — anyone, though I don't particularly recommend that it be your mother, or your dog Ralph.

Your shyness is *your* servant. You are not its servant. Make it serve you. Put on your best clothes, stand tall and straight, shoulders back, and get out there. Conduct yourself *as quietly confident that you would be an asset to any organization that you ultimately decide to serve.* You will be, indeed. The thoroughness with which you're doing this research, shows *that.*

Wherever you go, whatever you read, whoever you talk to, keep always in the forefront of your mind what it is you're trying to find out. Essentially what you are looking for, at this point, is an answer to the question: *What occupation or occupations will use as many of my strongest skills, and on as high a level, as possible?* So that — *at my work — I am doing what I enjoy most, and not just waiting until I get home from work to start enjoying myself.*

While doing this research, please remember that the *woods are alive* with people who will solemnly tell you *something that ain't true* as though they were sure of it with every fibre of their being. So, check and cross check and cross check again the information that books, people, and experts give you. Let no one build any boxes for you; and watch that you don't hand them any wood with which to build one for you. In the end, there is virtually no information you want that you cannot find. This is a *knowledge society,* and the only limits — really — lie within you, as to the commitment, diligence and perseverance you are willing to lavish on all this.

```
        MY QUESTIONS FOR RESEARCHING MY IDEAL JOB
              A. What Skills Do I Have and Enjoy
              B. Where Do I Want to Use These Skills
          √ C. What Kinds of Organizations Can I Focus On —
                  in terms of Goals,
                  for use of my Skills,
                  in my Geographical Area of Preference
              D. What Are the Names of Such Organizations
              E. What Are Their Problems —
                  at the Level I Want To Work
              F. Who There Has The Power To Hire Me
```

FOCUSING DOWN:
TO KINDS OF ORGANIZATIONS

You will eventually get to the point where you know the kind of career that interest you. *Then* your task will be to identify what kinds of organizations interest you, within that field.

Suppose you've decided, let us say, that being a consultant looks more enjoyable, and promises to use more of your top skills than anything else. The question you then face is: should I be a consultant in education, in business, in nonprofit organizations, in fund-raising, or what? It is important that you identify in what *kinds* of places you might enjoy doing this.

It is the same with any other career or occupation. You want to teach, let us say. Do you want to teach at a university, a college, a junior college, a business school, in private industry, or where? The purpose of this stage of your research is to look at *all the options,* so that you can choose the one you prefer the most — along with some 'plan Bs.'

You are looking for the organizations, colleges, associations, small businesses, institutions, agencies, etc., where you would be *happiest* working. Why? Because the more you enjoy *what* you are doing and *where* you are doing it, the better you are going to use the talents which God gave you. It is a matter of your effectiveness, or — if you will — of Productivity.

Here are *the kinds of questions* that you are (hopefully) trying to find the answers to, as you do this part of your research:

☐ 1. Do I want to work for a profit-making company, a nonprofit firm, agency, college, association, foundation, small business, the government, or what?

☐ 2. Do I want to work for an older and larger organization, or get in on the ground floor of a new and smaller one, with growth possibilities? If you're in an area where hiring is "tight," look *long and hard* at the new and smaller organizations. It's true that their failure rate is high; *but* it's also true that that's where two-thirds of all new jobs get created — in businesses with twenty or less employees.

☐ 3. Do I want to advance rapidly? If so you need an organization with solid plans for expansion — overseas or at home.

☐ 4. Do I want to work for a "going concern" or for "a problem child" type of operation? As the experts say, a company in trouble is a company in search of leadership. The same goes for foundations, agencies, etc. If that is your cup of tea (well, is it?), you can probably find such places without too much investigation. Some experts say if you go for such a challenge, give yourself a time limit, say 3 to 5 years, and then if you can't solve it, get out. The average job in this country only lasts 3.6 years, anyway.

"I used to ask myself,
'What can I do to help my fellow man?' but
I couldn't think of anything that wouldn't have put me
to considerable inconvenience."

Reproduced by special permission of Playboy Magazine; Copyright (c) 1983 by Playboy.

□ 5. Other questions: what do I want to accomplish with my skills? what working circumstances do I want? what opportunities? what responsibilities? what kinds of job-pressures am I willing to exist under, and do I feel capable of handling? what kinds of people do I want to work with? starting salary? salary five years from now? promotion opportunities?

These sorts of questions will help you identify the *kinds* of organizations. But, once your research has gotten all *that* nailed down, you need to get more specific. You will need *names* of specific organizations.

FOCUSING DOWN:
TO NAMES OF ORGANIZATIONS

Now, the first thing that's rather obvious is that you can't find the *names* of places until you've decided on a geographical area. You may have foreclosed that problem, already. "Here I live, and here I'll stay." Fine. The matter is settled. But suppose you have more flexibility. Suppose you're about to leave college. Or you've just been through a divorce, and the place where you were is the place you no longer wish to be. Or suppose you're facing retirement, and you can move *anywhere* that the two of you can agree on. In *that* case, this is the point at which you MUST decide.

In some cases *where the vacancies are* will determine where you go. There are only a very limited number of places where such work is to be found. That might be true of, say, a steelworker or an automobile worker, or an actor, or a network newscaster.

But in the case of most fields, vacancies are distributed throughout the country. So it doesn't much matter where you go. You therefore might as well choose a place where you would really *like* to be. There are a number of extremely useful books to aid you in this decision, and they are to be found in Section 25 of Appendix B on page 301 of this book.

Once you've got a particular geographical place *nailed down,* in your mind — either the place where you already are, or two or three places where you'd like to be — *then* you are ready to start researching for the names of particular organizations in the fields or industries or occupations that interest you.

MY QUESTIONS FOR RESEARCHING MY IDEAL JOB
   A. What Skills Do I Have and Enjoy
   B. Where Do I Want to Use These Skills
   C. What Kinds of Organizations Can I Focus On —
         in terms of Goals,
         for use of my Skills,
         in my Geographical Area of Preference
 ✓ D. What Are the Names of Such Organizations
   E. What Are Their Problems —
         at the Level I Want To Work
   F. Who There Has The Power To Hire Me

To help you find those names, there are books galore, in your
local library. Or the library at your nearby community college,
four-year college, or university. Tell your librarian what it is
that you're trying to find out: what field you're zeroing in on,
etc. Following is a list of directories you will find useful not
only at this point, but later, too, when you are trying to find
out names of people within organizations, problems of organizations, and the like:

American Men and Women of Science.
American Society of Training and Development Directory.
    Who's Who in Training and Development, Suite 305,
    600 Maryland Ave., SW, Washington, DC 20024.
Better Business Bureau report on the organization
    (call the BBB in the city where the organization is located).
Business Information Sources, by Lorna M. Daniels.
    University of California Press, Berkeley, CA 94720.
    Annotated guide to business books and reference sources.
Career Guide to Professional Associations, Garrett Park Press,
    Garrett Park, MD 20766.
Chamber of Commerce data on the organization
    (visit the Chamber there).
College library (especially *business school* library),
    if there is one in your chosen area.
Company/college/association/agency/foundation *Annual
    Reports.* Get these directly from the Personnel Department
    or publicity person at the company, etc., or from the
    Chamber or your local library.

*Consultants and Consulting Organizations Directory —
Sixth Edition.* Gale Research Company, Book Tower,
Detroit, MI 48226. Editors: Paul Wasserman and Janice
McLean. 1984.

Contacts Influential: Commerce and Industry Directory.
Businesses in particular market area listed by name, type
of business, key personnel, etc. (Contacts Influential,
Market Research and Development Services, 321 Bush St.,
Ste. 203, San Francisco, CA 94104, if your library doesn't
have it.)

Directory of Corporate Affiliations. (National Register
Publishing Co., Inc.)

Directory of Information Resources in the United States.
(Physical Sciences, Engineering, Biological Sciences)
Washington, DC. Library of Congress.

Dun & Bradstreet's Million Dollar Directory. Very helpful.

Dun & Bradstreet's Middle Market Directory. Very helpful.

Dun & Bradstreet's Reference Book of Corporate Managements.

Encyclopedia of Associations, Vol. I, National Organizations,
Gale Research Co. Lists organizations that are in the
business of giving out information.

Encyclopedia of Business Information Sources (2 volumes).
4th Ed. Gale Research Co.

Fitch Corporation Manuals.

F & S Indexes (recent articles on firms).

F & S Index of Corporations and Industries. Lists "published
articles" by industry and by company name. Updated weekly.

Fortune Magazine's 500.

Fortune's Plant and Product Directory.

The Foundation Directory.

How to Reach Anyone Who's Anyone, by Michael Levine.
Price/Stern/Sloan Publishers, Inc. 410 N. La Cienega Blvd.,
Los Angeles, CA 90048.

Industrial Research Laboratories of the United States,
R.R. Bowker Co., 205 E. 42nd St., New York, NY 10017.

Investor, Banker, Broker Almanac.

MacRae's Blue Book.

Moody's Industrial Manual (and other Moody manuals).

National Directory of Addresses and Telephone Numbers,
(Concord Reference Books, 240 Fenel Lane, Hillside, IL
60162.)

*National Recreational Sporting and Hobby Organizations
   of the U.S.,* Columbia Books, Inc., 777 14th St., NW,
   Washington, DC 20005.
*National Trade and Professional Associations of the United
   States and Canada and Labor Unions.* Garrett Park Press,
   Garrett Park, MD 20766.
Plan Purchasing Directory.
Register of manufacturers for your state or area
   (e.g., *California Manufacturers Register).*
Research Centers Directory, 6th ed. Gale Research Co.
   Also: *New Research Centers,* updating the original
   1979 volume.
Standard and Poor's Corporation Records.
Standard and Poor's Industrial Index.
Standard and Poor's Listed Stock Reports
   (at some brokers' offices).
*Standard and Poor's Register of Corporations, Directors
   and Executives.* Key executives in 32,000 leading companies,
   plus 75,000 directors.
Telephone Contacts for Data Users. Customer Services Branch,
   Bureau of the Census, 301-449-1600 for statistical
   information on any subject.
Thomas' Register of American Manufacturers. Thomas
   Publishing Co.
*Training and Development Organizations Directory —
   Third Edition.* Gale Research, Book Tower, Detroit, MI
   48226. Editor: Paul Wasserman. 1983.
United States Government Manual. Or call the Federal
   Information Center of the General Services Administration
   at 202-755-8660 to find the names of experts in any field.
   For help on a question no one seems to know the answer to,
   try the National Referral Center at the Library of Congress,
   202-287-5670.
Value Line Investment Survey, from Arnold Bernhard and Co.,
   5 E. 44th St., New York, NY 10017. (Most libraries have a set.)

Walker's Manual of Far Western Corporations and Securities.
Who's Who in Finance and Industry, and all the other Who's
   Who books. Useful once you have the name of someone-
   who-has-the-power-to-hire, and you want to know more
   about them.

DAZZLED?

If all of the above seems like an embarrassment of riches, and you don't know where to begin, there's even a guide to all these directories: If you don't know which directory to consult, see —

- Klein's *Guide to American Directories*
  or
- Gale Research Company's *Directory of Directories*
  or

  when you are about to throw up your hands in despair,
- remember there is a person who knows how to use *all* these books: your friendly neighborhood librarian.

Besides these directories, some other resources may also be worth perusing. Periodicals: *Business Week, Dun's Review, Forbes, Fortune,* and the *Wall Street Journal;*

Trade Associations and their periodicals; Trade journals.

There are also excellent surveys of key companies, e.g., Moskowitz, Milton; Katz, Michael; and Levering, Robert, ed., *Everybody's Business, An Almanac: The irreverent guide to corporate america.* Harper and Row, 10 E. 53rd St., New York, NY 10022.

OTHER SOURCES OF NAMES OF ORGANIZATIONS: YOUR CONTACTS

When you're looking for something the books just aren't able to turn up, you need to turn to your contacts. Someone among them will know.

Suppose you're trying to find out the name of a place that would a) let you work with your hands, b) using wood, c) making it into something useful, for the home. You try the library, but it's a total loss. Maybe you run into a librarian who's overworked and underpaid and is having *a really bad day*. And, by yourself, you can't make heads or tails out of the directories there. Well, you still have your contacts. You ask *every one of them*, "What places do you know of, where someone is working with their hands, using wood, and making something useful for the home?"

Every contact. That means all the members of your family. Your relatives. Your doctor, dentist, gas station attendant, check-out clerk at the supermarket. Everyone you meet along the way, during your job-hunting research. Everyone you meet, anywhere.

Whenever a job-hunter writes me and tells me they've run into a brick wall, as far as finding out the names or organizations is concerned, I know what the problem will turn out to be—usually. They aren't making sufficient use of their contacts.

The more people you know, the more people you meet, the more people you talk to, the more people you enlist as part of your own personal job-hunting network, the better your job-finding success is likely to be. Keep their names on 3 x 5 file cards with addresses, phone numbers, and anything about where they work or who they know that may be of use at a later date.

To do your job-hunt well, you need to be in twenty places at once, with your eyes and ears wide open. You can't be, really. But your contacts *can* be. IF they know what you are looking for, and IF you have enlisted them to keep their eyes and ears open on your very specific behalf.

Some job-hunters cultivate new contacts whenever they can. If they go to hear a speaker on some subject *that interests them,* they make it a point to join the crowd that gathers 'round the speaker at the end of the talk, and — with notebook poised — ask such questions as: "Is there anything special that people with my technical expertise can do?" And then you mention your specialty: computer scientist, health professional, chemist, writer, or whatever. Very useful information may thus be turned up. You can also ask if you can contact the speaker for further information — "and at what address?" Conventions, likewise, afford rich opportunities to make contacts. Says one college graduate: "I snuck into the Cable Advertisers Convention at the Waldorf in N.Y.C. That's how I got my job."

DON'T PAY SOMEONE TO
DO THIS RESEARCH FOR YOU,
WHATEVER YOU DO

There are a number of reasons why *no one else* can do all of this job-hunting research for you; not a job-counselor, not a friend, not anyone.

1. Only *you* really know what things you are looking for, and what things you want to avoid if possible.

2. You need the self-confidence that comes to you as you practice this researching. You need it *before* you go after the organizations that interest you.

3. The skills you use to *find* a job are close to the skills you use to *do* the job, after you get it. Therefore, by doing all this research you are increasing your qualifications for the job itself. Thus, this conclusion: the more research you do, the more qualifications you will have.

Can you do this research yourself, then?

Of course you can. As we have seen, its secret is simply a continuous blend of:

WRITTEN STUFF,
AND PEOPLE

You will be dealing *alternatively* with written material — such as books, journals, magazines, or other material which librarians and such can direct you to — *and* — with *people,* who can tell you what you need to know. So: YOU READ until you need to go talk to someone because you've run out of books; then YOU TALK TO PEOPLE until you know you need to get back and do some more reading.

In the old days I used to urge people, during this part of their job-hunting research, to give preference to TALKING TO PEO-

PLE rather than to READING. We called this phase of TALK-
ING TO PEOPLE "Informational Interviewing."

Now, however, I believe just the opposite is true. I believe
you will find it infinitely more to your advantage if you give
preference to doing as much of your job-hunting research
as possible THROUGH READING, *before* you go out, rather
than through talking to people. The reason for this is that in
many quarters,

INFORMATIONAL INTERVIEWING IS
FROWNED UPON BY SOME EMPLOYERS

Let me recount some history. When we first studied successful job-hunters *circa 1970,* we discovered that the most successful ones went out and conducted lots of talks with people
before they ever went in for a hiring interview. They were looking over particular fields, and then particular industries, and
then particular organizations, to see if those fields, industries
and organizations were of any interest *to them.*

John Crystal called this part of their job research "a personal
economic survey." Others, however, called it "informational
interviewing." That name stuck, and became very popular. Job-
hunting-book after job-hunting-book began to advise people to
do "informational interviewing," based on the discovery that
this is what successful job-hunters and career-changers *instinctively* did, without anyone telling them to.

Rules began to be formulated. If informational interviewing
was to be done at all, we all said, it must be done with integrity.
The rules for preserving that integrity:

1. You must not yet have made up your mind where you
wanted to work. You must be *genuinely* still looking for information.

2. You must be talking to "common folk," to those doing the kind of work you think you might like to do, and not just to potential employers for you.

3. You must see yourself, during *this* phase of your job-hunt, absolutely as the one who is the Screener — the one who is accepting or rejecting, for the time being.

4. You must not for a moment think of informational interviewing as really a "job interview in disguise," a clever way to get past trusting receptionists and guileless employers, before you hit them with your Real Mission: asking for a job.

Countless thousands of job-hunters and career-changers went out and did precisely what is described above. They did True Informational Interviewing, and they did it with integrity. They are still doing it, and with great benefits.

BUT — (you knew that "but" was coming, didn't you?) there were others. Others who either did not understand what they read (I'm trying to be charitable), or who had it explained to them poorly by career counselors and workshop leaders who did not understand. And there were others whose whole life style has been a graduate course in manipulation and cleverness in trying to outwit other people, who therefore were fore-ordained to see "Informational Interviewing" as one more exercise in deviousness and clever trickery.

In any event, out they went with either poor understanding or poor intent, and, claiming to be "Informational Interviewers," were really asking for a job. And fooling no one, least of all the employers in whose offices they were sitting. (With ironic justice, a number of such have "pulled" this even on me.)

They broke every rule. They *had* already made up their mind where they wanted to work. They were *not* genuinely looking for information. They went *only* to people who could potentially employ them. They did *not* see themselves as the Screeners in the process. And they *really did* think this was just a "job interview in disguise," — a clever way to get in to see someone.

As a result, in some places and with some employers, they spoiled it for everyone, particularly those trying to do "Informational Interviewing" as it was originally conceived, with honesty and integrity. Although it was, in actual fact, only a minority of all the employers in this country who were thus victimized, they were (and are) a *very vocal* minority — the kind of employers who give interviews to *The Wall Street Journal,* who get covered in surveys, and quoted in magazine articles. And so, the word has now gone out in *some* places: "Informational interviewing is a trick."

Countless *millions* of employers, of course, have not even *heard* to this day of "Informational Interviewing," much less that some job-hunters are abusing it. But enough have. Particularly those in large cities, or those in companies among the Fortune 500.

So, my counsel is that while the activity should be continued, the *term* is better abandoned. Words *do* change, become outdated, outmoded, in every field. The word *intercourse,* for example, once meant "connection or dealings between persons." If you are determined to still use that word with *that* meaning ("I went over to see him last Thursday, and we had pleasant intercourse.") I suggest you choose your audience very carefully.

Likewise, with the term *Informational Interviewing.* It is now synonymous in some employers' minds with *trick.* We may mourn the decline of it, as a useful phrase. But that's what happens to Language.

There is a larger issue than whether or not we may use the term. And that is, may we still do The Thing which the term once described? Does ALL our job-hunting research have to be done through the reading of books and magazines and reports? Is it no longer *kosher* to go talk with people, while we are trying to find out information about potential fields, or potential industries, or potential organizations that might interest us?

My own judgment about this, based on talking to countless job-hunters, is that it is still *perfectly* appropriate to go talk to people while you are doing your job-hunting research, provided —

1. provided you don't call it "Informational Interviewing." You are "researching your ideal job." Period. And it had *better* be absolutely true —

2. provided there is something you really need to know, and you can't find it in printed materials, microfiche, or on disks —

3. provided you approach, first of all, people whose business it is to give out information: librarians, public relations officers, even personnel officers, and find out all they know —

4. provided you approach no organization unless you have first gotten your hands on everything they've got, in print,

about who they are and what they do — AND HAVE READ IT thoroughly —

5. provided when you approach an organization, you talk to those with lesser authority first, to find out everything that they know, so that later if you approach someone higher up there for particular information, you are using her time or his time only to acquire information *which they alone know* —

6. provided before you approach anyone higher up, you ask that organization for everything their public relations department (or desk) has, in print, about that person (or go to your local library, and do the same, through directories, clippings, etc.) so that if part of what you need to know has already been written up, you won't waste their time needlessly on *that*. And if you are seeing senior Vice-Presidents or heads of organizations, you *will* need to call ahead, for an appointment. Don't just "drop in." The time of senior people is usually heavily scheduled, and your coming by unannounced — "I just happened to be in the neighborhood" — is almost universally perceived as "unprofessional." —

7. provided you GO TO A SMALLER AND LESS-KNOWN ORGANIZATION RATHER THAN TO A LARGER AND WELL-KNOWN ONE, whenever possible, for — in the very nature of the case — the smaller organization will have had less people approach it, with any job-hunting research questions, than the larger, better known one.

In this manner, if you follow these seven Cautions, I think you will generally be well-received, and generally be able to find out what it is you need to know. *So, do use people as part of your research.* But *do* your reading *first*.

Do mention to people you are interviewing who the other people are that you have already seen. The more research you have done, the more valuable you are to each succeeding person you talk to, in that industry or field. Your impressions, opinions, and overview may be useful for this person to hear. So, don't think of your research interviews as "one-way streets," where you are doing all the "taking." You have much to give, as well. You possess, increasingly, an overview which they may not have. You have formed, increasingly, some impressions, that they may find helpful. You have learned, increasingly, what the problems and challenges are, in that field, which the person you are talking to may be "dying to know." So, as time goes on, *remember to share.* Ask the questions you came to ask, seek the information you need to know, but tell her or him what it is *you* have learned, thus far. Information is always a two-way street. If they are valuable to you, you can also be valuable to them.

And, of course, *don't* forget to send a thank you note *that very night* to *anyone* you talked to, during the day. And, to that end, get their business card, or their name and address while you are yet talking to them, so that you will know where that thank you note should be sent.

SUMMARY: WHAT IT IS THAT YOU ARE LOOKING FOR

When You Are Reading or Talking To People About—	Among The Things You May Be Looking For Are—
your skills.	what kind of work uses *most* of these skills *together*
fields of possible work	which ones you will be happiest (and therefore most effective) in, because they fit in with your total Life Mission as you perceive it
geographical area that you have chosen . .	the kind of places that might need your skills, in the field you have chosen
places where you might want to work . . .	to find out if there is any reason why you might *not* want to work there; to find what problems they have *and* which problems are both important and ones which your skills can help solve.

If the place where you have decided to live (and work) is far away, then you will want to know how to start researching that place *before you go there.* Well, there *are* ways. Consider the questions you are trying to find answers to, during this part of your job-hunting research:

MY QUESTIONS FOR RESEARCHING MY IDEAL JOB

A. What Skills Do I Have and Enjoy
B. Where Do I Want to Use These Skills
C. What Kinds of Organizations Can I Focus On —
      in terms of Goals,
      for use of my Skills,
      in my Geographical Area of Preference
√D. What Are the Names of Such Organizations
E. What Are Their Problems —
      at the Level I Want To Work
F. Who There Has The Power To Hire Me

Now, let us see how you find their answers, even at a distance.

HOW TO SURVEY A PLACE...
FAR AWAY

If you are researching a far-away place, set down on paper which of the above information-searches you can do right where you are, and which ones you need others' help with, in the city or place of your choice.

Your two lists will *probably* come out looking like this:

Searches I Can Do Here	Searches Others Must Do There
A- (in detail:)	
B- (in detail:)	the rest of
C- some detail	C-
D-	D-
E -	E- in detail
F - some	F-

2 *Figure out if there isn't **some** way in the near future*
that you could go visit the city or cities of your choice.

You may be able to do this even if you are presently employed. Does a vacation fall within the time period you have
between now and when you must finally have that job? Could
you visit it on vacation? Could you take a summer job there?
Go there on leave? Get sent to a convention there? Get appointed
to a group or association that meets there? Think it through.
You will *have* to go there, finally (in almost all cases) for the
actual job interview(s). *If worse comes to worse,* go there a
week or so ahead of that interview. Better late than never, to
look over the scene in person, and do some on-site research.

3 *For the time being, regard the city or town where you*
presently are, as a replica of the city or town you are
interested in going to (in some respects at least) — so that
some of your research can be done where you are, and
then its learnings transferred.

You recall earlier we discussed the case of a man who loved
psychiatry, and plants, and carpentry, and discovered that there
was a branch of psychiatry which used plants in the treatment
of deeply withdrawn patients. So, our man discovered an occupation where he could use his love of plants and his love of psychiatry together (and presumably use his carpentry to build the
planters that would be needed). Suppose you were this man.
Having found this out in the place where you live, you could
then write to your target city or town to ask, What psychiatric
facilities do you have *there,* and which ones — if any — use
plants in their healing program?

Thus can you conduct your research where you are, and then
transfer its learnings to the place where you want to go.

4 *Until you can physically go there, use every resource and*
contact you have, in order to explore the answers to
C, D, E and F.

✳ **THE DAILY OR WEEKLY NEWSPAPER THERE.**
Almost all papers will mail to subscribers anywhere in the world.
So: subscribe, for a six-month period, or a year. You'd be sur-
prised at what you can learn from the paper. Some of the an-

swers to C, D, E and F will appear there. Additionally, from the ads and business news items, you will know which businesses are growing and expanding — hence, hiring — in that city.

✳ THE CHAMBER OF COMMERCE, AND CITY HALL (OR THE TOWN HALL) THERE.

These are the places whose interest it is (in most cases) to attract newcomers, and to tell them what kinds of businesses there are in town — as well as some details about them. So: write and ask them, in the beginning, what information they have about the city or town in general. Then later, don't hesitate to write back to them with more specific questions, as your target organizations become clearer in your mind.

✳ THE LOCAL LIBRARY OR REFERENCE LIBRARIAN, IF YOUR TARGET CITY/TOWN HAS ONE.

It is perfectly permissible for you to write to the library in your target city, asking for information that may be only there. If the librarian is too busy to answer, then use one of your contacts there to find out. "Bill (or Billie) I need some information that I'm afraid only the library in your town has. Specifically, I need to know about company x." Or whatever.

✳ YOUR CONTACTS.

Yes, of course, you know people in whatever city or town you're researching. For openers, write to your old high school and get the alumni list for your graduating class. If you went to college, ask for their alumni list also (for your class, at the very least). Subscribe to your college's alumni bulletin for further news, addresses, and hints. If you belong to a church or synagogue, write to the church or synagogue in your target city, and tell them that you're one of their own and you need some information. "I need to know who can tell me what nonprofit organizations there are in that city, that deal with x." "I need to know how I can find out what corporations in town have departments of mental hygiene." Or, whatever. To find further contacts, ask your family and relatives who *they* know in the target city or town of your choice. You will find, upon patient and persistent exploration, that you know or can contact far more people in that city, who might help you, than you would originally think.

✳ **THE APPROPRIATE STATE, COUNTY, AND LOCAL GOVERNMENT AGENCIES, ASSOCIATIONS, ETC.**
Ask your contacts to tell you what that appropriate agency might be, for the field or kinds of organizations (or jobs) that you are interested in.

HOW HARD SHOULD I WORK AT THIS?

We kept score with one man's job-hunt. He was researching a distant place. While still at a distance, by means of diligent research he turned up 107 places that seemed interesting to him. Over a period of some time, he sent a total of 297 letters to them. He also made a total of 126 phone calls to that city. When he was finally able to go there in person, he had narrowed the original 107 that looked interesting, down to just 45. He visited all 45, while there. Having done his homework on himself thoroughly and well, — and having obviously conducted *this* part of his search in an extremely professional manner, he received 35 job offers. When he had finished his survey, he went back to the one job he most wanted — and accepted it.

No one can argue that you should be dealing with numbers of this magnitude. But this may at least give you some idea of *how hard you may need to work* at this. Certainly, we're not just talking about five letters and two phone calls. We're talking about rolling up your sleeves, and being *very thorough*.

NOW, YOU KNOW WHERE YOU WANT TO WORK

Of course, if you have merely *read* this chapter — at this point — don't be surprised if no blinding light has come to illuminate your path. Just reading doesn't count. Nor does putting this book under your pillow at night, and hoping you can absorb it by osmosis. No, dear friend, you've got to DO THE RESEARCH! That is the only way you will truly profit from this step of the job-hunting or career-changing process.

In the absence of inspiration, try perspiration. Roll up your sleeves, and get at it!

You're a bunch of jackasses. You work your rear ends off in a trivial course that no one will ever care about again. You're not willing to spend time researching a company that you're interested in working for. Why don't you decide who you want to work for and go after them?

Professor Albert Shapero
(again) to his students

CHAPTER SEVEN

You must identify the persons who have the power to hire you and show them how your skills can help them with their problems.

THE THIRD KEY
TO CAREER PLANNING AND
JOB-HUNTING

While conducting the research described in the last chapter, the distinction between *research interviews* and *job interviews* may have gotten a little hazy in your mind. So, let us take one more look at the distinction. The part of your job-hunt that involves going to talk to people has two distinct *stages to it*; distinct, and separate.

(1) *Trying to make up your mind what kind of job(s) you want.* During this stage, it is important to go talk to everyone you can who holds down a job that you think you might be interested in. During this stage, it is *inappropriate* to ask for a job. Even if you like job C, that you are presently investigating, you do not know (yet) if job E may prove even more attractive to you, when you get to it. You may be considering being a television writer, a lumbering executive, a salesperson for computers, and a teacher in a private school. Until you have talked to all these people, it is inappropriate to say, Hey, do you have a job?

(2) *Once you've made up your mind what kind of job you want, trying to find out who has them, and trying to get hired there.* At this point, it is not only appropriate to ask if they have a job — it is absolutely necessary.

If you confuse these two stages, you will find yourself asking for a job during the first stage, when you haven't yet made up your mind as to what you really want. You won't know whether this is the best job for you. Your indecision will *show*. And many an employer will think you are *by nature* indecisive; hence they will not hire you. So, keep the stages separate and distinct in your mind. Until you know exactly what job you want, you are still doing *research interviews*.

But once you *have* made up your mind, you are ready for *job interviews*. And that's what this chapter is all about.

We begin with the $64,000 question:

HOW MANY WANT THE JOB THAT I WANT?

Job-hunters such as yourself, dear Reader, begin by thinking there are too few job markets (and therefore, too few jobs) "out there." Actually, however, the truth is far stranger: there are too many. If you try to hit them all — as so many job-hunters do — you will only diffuse your energies and your effectiveness. Better, far better, to concentrate your job-hunting energies and effectiveness as you have been doing.

In order to see why this is so, we must take a (mercifully) brief look at this whole thing that is laughingly called:

The Job Market

Upon hearing this very misleading term, one has visions — instantly — of some central place, like the Stock Exchange, say, where every job opening and every job-hunter can meet each other. Such a vision may dance, like a sugar plum, in the job-hunter's head; but the reality is quite different. And, much more jolting.

When you start into the *supposed* unified job market, to conduct your own job-search or career change, you discover sooner or later that what you actually face is *14 million or more separate job markets* (for this is how many individual businesses, organizations, agencies, and foundations there allegedly are in this country). Every business or organization has its own way of going about the process of hiring — separate, independent of, and uncoordinated with, other businesses or organizations. Hence, each is a separate job market.

THE SOURCE OF THE MYTHOLOGY

What has deluded people into speaking of the whole country as a vast single job market? Two factors are responsible for this mischief:

First of all, the term itself. *Market* is a metaphor, or analogy. By analogy with the market where we weekly shop for food, experts have come to speak — in the world of business — of four *markets* today:

a) the market for information; b) the market for goods and services; c) the market for capital, money, investment; d) the market for labor.

Whatever usefulness the metaphor may have in the hands of genuine experts, as it is commonly bandied about in everyday language it often means little more than *demand,* e.g., "How's the labor market this month?" Nonetheless, once the term (for whatever reason) becomes part of our everyday vocabulary, it

leads the naive job-hunter down a primrose path. For in point
of fact, there is no such central market. There is no one place a
job-hunter can go, to find what jobs are available.

The second factor which has deluded people into thinking of
the country (as a whole) as though it were one market is the
statistics that appear in the newspapers each month. Statistics,
indeed! You need to remember how an English professor once
declined the word "lie":

LIES, DAMN LIES, AND STATISTICS

Once a month (the first Friday of the month, usually, published in Friday afternoon's or Saturday morning's papers — if
you care) the nation is alternately comforted or terrorized by
One statistic for the whole country. It is published (naturally)
by the U.S. Government (its Bureau of Labor Statistics). And
it is, of course, The Unemployment Figure.

To understand it, let us look at how the figure is deduced. We
will take October 1984 as our example.

*1. The figure with which we begin is the number of people in
the nation who want to work. That was 115,722,000 in October of 1984.*

*2. Then we ask how many people in the nation are actually
employed that month. That was 107,291,000 that month, if
you count those in the Armed Services — 105,586,000 if you
don't.*

*3. Then the government subtracts the second figure from the
first, i.e., 107,291,000 from 115,722,000 — and this difference
is the unemployment figure for that month (October 1984).*

In reality, the first and third figures are much larger than the
government admits, because the government fails to count
those who want full-time work but have temporarily taken a
part-time job as a stop-gap; and it fails to count those who are
unemployed but have become so discouraged that they have
stopped looking.

AN INTIMIDATING FIGURE

In any event, every month prominent press coverage is always
given to *this one statistic: the unemployment figure for the entire country.* Every sensitive soul is staggered at the thought of
8,431,000 people — or more — looking for a job, and unable to

find it. You, as job-hunter, are further depressed at the thought of more than eight million people competing with you for the jobs that there are. And the fear that you might join the ranks of the *permanently* unemployed.

It would be bad enough if the unemployment statistic were all you knew. But the media very thoughtfully fleshes out the statistic with endless detailed stories of what has happened to the unemployed.

We are told industry horror stories, such as what is happening to the airline industry (currently) or to the steel industry or to the copper industry or to the auto industry. We are told individual horror stories, such as how one family has lost its home, car, and everything — or how some job-hunter, in total despair over the fact that society apparently does not value him or want him, took his own life. And if the country is in one of its periodic recessions we are bombarded almost daily in the newspapers and on television, with interviews — not with successful job-hunters who were able to find a job in spite of hard times, but with unsuccessful job-hunters who describe with bitterness how they tried everything "and I still couldn't find a job." We are given supplementary statistics until they are coming out our ears. Recently, for example, those statistics were: every second black teenager was out of work; every fourth teenager; every fourth construction worker; every fifth black worker; every seventh Hispanic; every seventh blue-collar worker.

If the contemporary situation isn't bad enough, there are always some handy, long-range predictions about the terrible things technology, automation, computers and such, will do to eliminate our jobs within the coming decade.

By the time that *You as Newspaper Reader or Television Viewer* are ready to become *Job-Hunter or Career Changer,* you are convinced that it is foolish of you to even venture out into the so-called Job Market, because there can't be a single job left out there. Surely, they all have been snapped up.

This depressing picture is, however, based upon a false assumption. Namely, that *if there are any vacancies out there, surely eight million or more job-hunters have been able to find them all and snap them all up.* Wrong! Even in the hardest times, many many vacancies go unfilled. Sometimes the jobs in question call for a peculiar constellation of skills, that do not commonly occur in the general population. And sometimes the employer just doesn't know how to get the word out to those job-hunters who might be qualified. Remember, the job-hunting 'system' of this country (and most countries of the Western world or Western culture) frustrates employers as much as it frustrates job-hunters.

HOW MANY VACANCIES ARE THERE?

It is important that you know. Not only *how many* vacancies there are, but *how they get created*. Such knowledge will buoy your spirit, and give you a firm basis for Hope (which job-hunters need more than any other commodity).

Okay, then, here is our short tour of vacancies.

Vacancies are created in two different ways:

(1) Jobs now filled fall vacant. The employed are a restless lot, excuse me, the employed are a tremendously *mobile* population. During the best of times, they change jobs at the rate of 800,000 *per month* — and during the worst of times, they still leave at the rate of at least 300,000 per month. This means, of course, that they create 300,000-800,000 vacancies *each month,* turning the employment world into essentially a game of musical chairs. The chair may be filled one minute, then empty the next. And *while it is empty, you can plunk down in it if you are alert and Janie (or Johnny) on the Spot.*

(2) New jobs get created. In fact, the ability of the U.S. economy to create new jobs is regarded with awe throughout the rest of the world. You'd like a figure? Sorry, we don't have one. No one knows how many new jobs get created each year. We only know *the net* rise — which figure is a product of *the gross* number of new jobs created, minus the number of jobs that got permanently phased out in our society due to businesses failing, or whole industries fading out of existence. We don't know either figure. And thus it is that a *net* rise of over 2 million new jobs *could* represent any of the following figures: 3 million new jobs created *in toto,* minus 1 million phased out; 5 million new jobs minus 3 million phased out; or 7 million new jobs minus 5 million phased out.

In any event, the *net* number of new jobs created has ranged between 2 and 3 million a year, except during Recessions. Add this, then, to the 800,000 jobs which fall vacant *each month,* and you can easily see why the creative minority insists that there is a *minimum* of 1 million job openings each month.

That's how many vacancies there are. And *all that the unem-ployment figures tell you is how many people might be com-peting with you* for whatever vacancies there are, or for what-ever new positions there might be.

Are eight million people, then (or whatever the unemploy-ment figure is, in a given month) competing for the job you want? Well, of course they are not. And, for the the following reasons:

1. *Stiff demands on the part of job-hunters:* If ever there were an era, once upon a time, when an unemployed worker was willing to take any kind of work, just so it brought in some money, that time is no longer. Many of the unemployed these days are extremely particular about the kind of work they are willing to do. Some want only highly skilled work. Some want only very unskilled work. Some want only jobs that will pay as well as their former job did. Some want only jobs that they can truly enjoy, and will settle for nothing else, not even something that would logically be a step toward that goal. For one and all of these, until they find such jobs, they are willing to live off savings, food stamps, welfare, or the income of whoever else in the house *is* working.

2. *Stiff demands on the part of employers:* A lot of jobs call for very special skills which just may not exist in sufficient abundance, and so the jobs stay vacant for long periods of time.

3. *Low visibility:* There are a number of vacancies for which any number of qualified applicants could be found if only the employers had some way of getting the word *out*. But, particu-larly for jobs that are responsible, many employers prefer not to advertise the vacancy, inasmuch as they are very particular about whom they hire. The consequence of all this? Just to speak of vacancies on the level of "Management," it was esti-mated not long ago that during an average year there are 750,000 management vacancies, only 250,000 of which were filled by the end of the year. Jobs at other levels of responsibil-ity exhibit the same disparity. I repeat my unending refrain: employers are as thwarted by our job-hunting system as job-hunters are.

4. *Fictitious job-hunters:* Some people who are collecting unemployment insurance (and therefore are listed by the U.S.

Government as job-hunters, which *in theory* they must be in order to collect) actually have no interest in competing for any of the 1 million vacancies that month: such persons as students between semesters, seasonal workers, production workers on temporary layoff, singers, actors and dancers awaiting a call, and people who are moonlighting (holding down full-time jobs but still collecting unemployment insurance as though they were unemployed).

When you add all this up, it does not mean that you have *no* competition for the job you want. Let's not be silly. There is competition for most good jobs; and in some cases the competition is *fierce* — as for jobs with short hours, high pay, requiring only common garden-variety skills.

BUT, the competition isn't with eight million other job-hunters. That's the point. Furthermore, you can cut the competition down even further by keeping in mind two VERY IMPORTANT secrets, which most job-hunters never think of.

1 JOB MARKET DIAGRAMS OR STATISTICS NEVER INCLUDE JOBS NOT YET BORN

The untutored job-hunter is sure that the job-hunting task consists — in one way or another — of unearthing *jobs which someone held before, and which are now vacant. So the untutored job-hunter searches classified ads, employment agencies, etc. looking for vacancies.*

It does not occur to them that if, instead, you select the organizations or companies that interest you, and do enough research to unearth their problems (and how you can help solve them), the company may be perfectly willing to create a new job, which never existed at that company before.

Certainly, a little reflection will tell you why companies may be willing to do this. Pretend, for a moment, that you are an executive of some company or organization. Your organization exists in order to get a certain job done, or product produced. And it's doing a pretty good job. But *naturally* you've also got problems; who doesn't? You don't publicly call them "problems," of course; you call them "challenges," "opportunities for growth," and that sort of thing. But privately, as you lay your head down on the pillow at night, you can call them by their real name: "problems." Some of them are relatively minor and

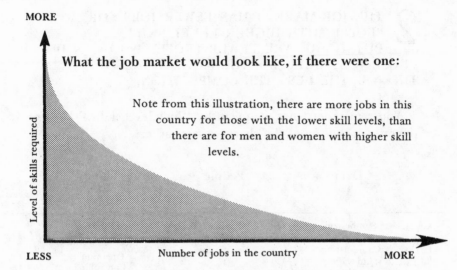

MORE

What the job market would look like, if there were one:

Note from this illustration, there are more jobs in this country for those with the lower skill levels, than there are for men and women with higher skill levels.

Level of skills required

LESS   Number of jobs in the country   MORE

perhaps of long standing — just something you've learned to live with. Others are relatively new and of major importance, maybe even in a sense *time bombs.* If you don't solve these, they're going to break your back. They're costing you money, sometimes a lot of money.

Now, naturally, your employees are aware of these problems — and some at least are trying to help you solve them. But, for one reason or another, they haven't succeeded. Then, into your office one morning comes some job-hunter who knows an amazing amount about your company or organization, including some of the major problems — excuse me, "challenges" — that you are facing. That person has analyzed them, and has skills which they believe can help solve them. Very soon, you believe they can too, but *there is no vacancy for this person to fill, in your company. Will you go and try your darnedest to create a new job, in order to get your hands on this person? Regardless of their age, background, or whatever?* Provided you have the power (and our man or woman won't be talking to you unless you do) *you bet you will.* In fact, you may have been thinking for some time that you needed this new position, anyway. You just haven't gotten around to doing anything about it — 'til now.

That's the first secret: you not only are going after vacancies, but also after jobs which haven't been born yet.

The second secret is:

2 THE JOB MARKET HAS FEWER JOBS FOR
PEOPLE WITH HIGHER LEVEL SKILLS:
BUT THERE ARE FEWER PEOPLE WHO CAN DO
THOSE JOBS WELL. SO, THE MORE SKILLED
THE JOB, THE LESS THE COMPETITION.

You remember what we mean by "high level skills." They're
the ones at the top of the chart we saw earlier:

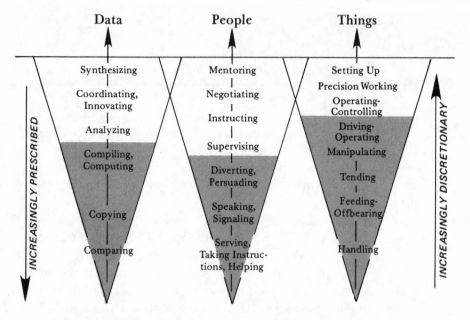

"High level skills" also refers to "complex knowledges" — the
kind you pick up after many years of schooling, or many years
of experience.

Now, the impact of these "high level" skills (if you have
them) upon your job-hunt is simply this:

a) The *higher the level* of skills that you can legitimately
claim, either with people, data or things (or, in varying degree,
with all three) the less those kinds of jobs are advertised or
known through normal channels; the more you'll have to find
your own individual ways of unearthing them — which is what
this chapter you are now reading is all about.

b) Just because the opportunities for the higher level jobs
(or careers) are harder to uncover, the higher you aim, the less
people you will have to compete with — for that job. In fact, if

you uncover, as you are very likely to, a genuine need in the organization (or organizations) you like, which you can help resolve, they are very likely to create a brand new job for you, which means — in effect — *you will be competing with practically no one, since you are virtually the sole applicant.* New jobs are always ready to be created, even in places where hiring is "tight." In a recent year, for example, when there was a record number of bankruptcies, there was also a record number of new businesses starting up. New businesses create jobs that never existed before. And you — regardless of your age, sex, race, lack of supposed credentials, or inexperience — can go after those new jobs *if* you pursue newer, smaller businesses, instead of the "Big Guys" that so many falsely pin all their hopes on.[1]

Now, let me repeat:

THE PARADOXICAL MORAL OF ALL THIS

The higher a skill level you can legitimately claim, *the more likely you are* to find a job. Just the opposite of what the typical job-hunter or career changer starts out believing.

That's why, if you skipped over the chapter on skill-identification, or you haven't yet done the *Quick Job-Hunting Map* at the end of this book (Appendix A), you MUST go do it. NOW, dear reader. If you just hazily, lazily *guess* what your skills are, you will *always* define them at too low a level — and thus increase the number of people you are up against in your search for a job. Not to mention what will happen to you even if you do find such a job. If it fails to use your highest skills, because you failed to take the time to define them, misery, m-i-s-e-r-y, lies ahead for you, in all likelihood.

Skill identification, as in the *Quick Job-Hunting Map,* is your guarantee that you are reaching for the highest skill level you can legitimately claim, *and thus increasing your chances of finding a job and job satisfaction.*

When you know your highest skills, and where you want to use them, when you have an idea of what kind of places you would like to work, then AND ONLY THEN, you are ready to consider the question of how will you sell yourself to a place that interests you? And the answer is: you sell yourself by find-

---

1. A widely-cited study by Professor David Birch of my old alma mater (M.I.T.) determined that 66% of all new jobs created during a seven-year period (which included a major Recession) were created by small firms with 0-20 employees.

ing out as much as you possibly can BEFORE YOU GO IN THERE FOR AN INTERVIEW. You lay your hands on everything you can that is in print about them. You read all their brochures, annual reports, addresses of the chairman or boss — whatever. You talk to everybody you know, to find out everything you can about them: the good and the bad. When you do go in, you want to be able to sell them on the fact that they need your skills. IF in fact they do. And you'll know *that,* before you go in, because in all of your reading and research about them you're keeping your ears and your eyes alert for whatever problems or challenges they are currently facing. *That* is what will determine whether or not they need your skills.

THE STEPS IN GETTING MY IDEAL JOB

A. What Skills Do I Have and Enjoy
B. Where Do I Want to Use These Skills
C. What Kinds of Organizations Can I Focus On —
   in terms of Goals,
   for use of my Skills,
   in my Geographical Area of Preference
D. What Are the Names of Such Organizations
✓ E. What Are Their Problems —
   at the Level I Want To Work
F. Who There Has The Power To Hire Me

AN ORGANIZATION'S PROBLEMS

All organizations have money — to one degree or another. What you are looking for are *problems* — specifically, *problems that your skills can help solve. What problems are bugging this organization? Ask; look. (If you know some people within a company or organization that looks interesting to you, ask them ever so gently:* What is the biggest challenge you are facing there?)

The problem does not have to be one that is bothering only *that* organization. You may want to ask what problem is common to the whole industry or field — low profit, obsolescence, inadequate planning, etc.? Or if there is a problem that is common to the geographic region: labor problems, minority em-

Drawing by Ed Fisher; (c) 1981 The New Yorker Magazine, Inc. Used by permission.

"... and give me good abstract-reasoning ability,
interpersonal skills, cultural perspective, linguistic comprehension,
and a high sociodynamic potential."

ployment, etc. All you really need is one major problem that you would truly delight to help solve.

If this idea is new and puzzling, still, to you: that your getting a job depends upon *your seeing and selling that job as a solution to some problem,* then consider the following. You yourself know already how *problems* affect an organization's profits. Think of five stores you have been in, where you debated whether you would ever go back. Why was that? Well, of course, because of some problem they had. What was it? You weren't waited on, when it was your proper turn? You weren't told all the information you needed to know, in order to make an intelligent purchase? The person with whom you were dealing insisted on going by the rule book, no matter what common sense and compassion would otherwise dictate? The person with whom you were dealing had some small amount of power but was misusing that power for all it was worth? The organization had installed a computer where a person used to be, and the person between you and the computer seemed to be taking orders from it, rather than vice versa? The organization had, in a word, lost the human touch? Or what? You will quickly realize, you are more aware of an organization's problems than you thought you were.

All you have to do now is polish this awareness of yours. Assuming you did the work outlined in the previous chapter and in *The Quick Job-Hunting Map*, you've got a (manageable) list of places that interest you. What you now need BEFORE YOU GO THERE (or BACK THERE) is to identify — within the area, department or tasks that interest you — what kinds of problems you could help solve, if they hired you.

Some of this you can figure out, just by thinking, and logical analysis. You may, for example, want to think how an unsatisfactory employee would behave in the job you are going to go after, and what problems such behavior would create. You of course intend to be a very competent, and enthusiastic employee, if you get that job. Therefore, you already can think of some problems you would eliminate, just by your extreme competency and enthusiasm for the work.

Beyond this, however, you want to learn as much as you can about the workings of the companies or organizations that interest you: what they are trying to accomplish, how they go about it, and — like that. There is only one name for this kind of investigation on the part of a job-hunter (You) — and that is: "intensive research."

As you go through all this intensive research concerning the places where you might like to work, two things will happen:

1. *Your list will get smaller,* as you discover some of the places that interested you *did not have the kind of problems or difficulties that your strongest skills could* a) solve; and b) let you enjoy doing so, during the process. Eliminate these places from your list. You would be unhappy there, even if they hired you. Know that now, and cross them off.

2. You will get to know *a great deal* about the remaining organizations which still interest you, including — most specifically — *their problems, and what you could do to help solve them.*

A Picture of this Part of Your Job-Hunt:

JOB MARKETS IN THE UNITED STATES
14,000,000
(that's the total number of non-farm employers)

1 You narrow this down by deciding just what area, city or county you want to work in. This leaves you with however many thousands of job markets there are in that area or city. **2** You narrow this down by identifying your Strongest Skills, on their highest level that you can legitimately claim, and then thru research deciding what field you *want* to work in, above all. This leaves you with all the hundreds of businesses/community organizations/agencies/schools/hospitals/projects/associations/foundations/institutions/firms or government agencies there are in that area and in the field you have chosen. **3** You narrow this down by getting acquainted with the economy in the area thru personal contacts; supplementing this with study of journals in your field, in order that you can pinpoint the places that interest you the most. This leaves a manageable number of markets for you to do some study on. **4** You now narrow this down through further research of those 'markets', with this question uppermost in your mind: *can I be happy in this place, and, do they have the kind of problems which my strongest skills can help solve for them?* **5** When your research is completed, you have a list of the companies or organizations which still look interesting to you; and you will now carefully plan how to approach them for a job; in your case *the*

JOB

YOU'LL LIKE THIS JOB, EXCEPT EVERY NOW
AND THEN, WHEN THEY DUMP A LOT OF
PAPER WORK ON YOU.

© 1982 NEA, Inc. Used by special permission.

RULES FOR FINDING OUT IN DETAIL
THE NEEDS OR PROBLEMS
OF AN ORGANIZATION

<u>Rule No. 1:</u> *If it's a large organization that interests you, you don't need to discover the problems of the whole organization. You only need to discover the problems that are bugging the-person-who-has-the-ultimate-responsibility (or power) -to-hire-you.* The conscientious job-hunters always bite off more than they can chew. If they're going to try for a job at the Telephone Company, or IBM or the Federal Government or General Motors or — like that — they assume they've got to find out the problems facing that whole organization. *Forget it!* Your task, fortunately, is much more manageable. Find out what problems are bugging, bothering, concerning, perplexing, gnawing at, the-person-who-has-the-power-to-hire-you. This assumes, of course, that you have first *identified* who that person is. Your contacts can probably help, here. Also the directories that are listed on pages 129-131. Once you have identified her, or him, *find out everything you can about them, professionally.* The directories, again, will help. So will the clippings, at your local library. So will any speeches they have given (ask their organization for copies, of same).

If it's a committee of sorts that actually has the responsibility (and therefore Power) to hire you, you will need to figure out who that one individual is (or two) who sways the others. You know, the one whose judgment the others respect. How do you find that out? By using your contacts, of course. Someone will know someone who knows that whole committee, and can tell you who their *real* leader is. It's not necessarily the one who got elected as Chairperson.

Rule No. 2: *Don't assume the problems have to be huge, complex and hidden. The problems bothering the-person-who-has-the-power-to-hire-you may be small, simple, and obvious.* If the job you are aiming at was previously filled by someone (i.e., the one who, if you get hired, will be referred to as "your predecessor") the problems that are bothering the-person-who-has-the-power-to-hire-you may be uncovered simply by finding out (through those among your contacts who know your prospective boss) what bugged him or her about your predecessor. Samples:

"They were never to work on time, took long lunch breaks, and were out sick too often"; OR

"They were good at typing, but had lousy skills over the telephone"; OR

"They handled older people well, but just couldn't relate to the young"; OR

"I never could get them to keep me informed about what they were doing"; etc.

Sometimes, it's as simple as that. Don't assume the problems *have to be* huge and complex. In your research you may be thinking to yourself, "Gosh, this firm has a huge public relations problem; I'll have to show them that I could put together a whole crash P.R. program." That's the huge, complex and hidden problem that you think the-person-who-has-the-power-to-hire-you *ought to be concerned about.* But, in actual fact, what they *are* concerned about is whether (unlike your predecessor) you're going to get to work on time, take assigned lunch breaks, and not be out sick too often. Don't overlook the Small, Simple and Obvious Problems which bug almost every employer.

Rule No. 3: *In most cases, your task is not that of educating your prospective employer, but of trying to read their mind.*

Now, to be sure, you may have uncovered — during your research — some problem that the-person-who-has-the-power-to-
hire-you is absolutely unaware of. And you may be convinced
that this problem is *so crucial* that for you even to mention it
will instantly win you their undying gratitude. Maybe. But
don't bet on it. Our files are filled with sad testimonies like the
following:

"I met with the V-P, Marketing in a major local bank on the
recommendation of an officer, and discussed with him a program I devised to reach the female segment of his market,
which would not require any new services, except education,
enlightenment and encouragement. His comment at the end of
the discussion was that the bank president had been after him
for three years to develop a program for women, and he wasn't
about to do it because the only reason, in his mind, for the
president's request was reputation enhancement on the president's part. . ."

Inter-office politics, as in this case, or other considerations
may prevent your prospective employer from being at all receptive to Your Bright Idea. In any
event, you're not trying to find
out what *might* motivate them to
hire you. Your research has got
to be devoted rather to finding
out what *already does* motivate
them *when they decide to hire
someone for the position you are
interested in.* In other words, you
are trying to find out What's Already Going On In Their Mind.
In this sense, your task is more
akin to a kind of mind-reading
than it is to education. (Though
some people-who-have-the-power-
to-hire are *very* open to being
educated. You have
to decide whether
you want to risk
testing this.)

Rule No. 4: *There are various ways of finding out what's going
on in their mind: don't try just one way.* We will give a kind of
outline, here, of the various ways. (You can use this as a checklist.)

A *Analyzing the Organization at a Distance and
Making Some Educated Guesses.*

1. If the organization is expanding, then they need:

   a. More of what they already have; OR
   b. More of what they already have, but with different style,
      added skills, or other pluses *that are needed;* OR
   c. Something they don't presently have: a new kind of
      person, with new skills doing a new function or service.

2. If the organization is continuing as is, then they need:

   a. To replace people who were fired (find out why; what was
      lacking?); OR
   b. To replace people who quit (find out what was prized
      about them); OR
   c. To create a new position (yes, this happens even in
      organizations that are not expanding — due to
      1) Old needs which weren't provided for, earlier, but
         now must be, even if they have to cut out some other
         function or position.
      2) Revamping assignments within their present staff.)

3. If the organization is reducing its size, staff, or product or
   service, then they

   a. Have not yet decided which staff to terminate, i.e., which
      functions to give low priority to (in which case *that* is
      their problem, and you may be able to help them identify
      which functions are "core-functions"); OR
   b. *Have* decided which functions or staff to terminate
      (in which case they may need multi-talented people
      or generalists able to do several jobs, i.e., functions,
      instead of just one, as formerly).

B *Analyzing the problems of the-person-who-has-the-power-
to-hire-you by talking to them directly.*

It may be that your paths have accidentally crossed (it happens). Perhaps you attend the same church or synagogue. Per-

haps you eat at the same restaurant. In any event, if you *do* ever have a chance to talk to her or him, listen carefully to whatever they may say about the place where they work. The greatest problem every employer faces is finding people who will listen and take them seriously. If you listen, you may find this employer discusses their problems — giving you firmer grounds to which, when it comes time to approach them for a job interview, you can relate your skills.

C   *Analyzing the problems of the person-who-has-the-power-to-hire-you by talking to their "opposite number" in another organization which is similar (not to say, almost identical) to the one that interests you.*

If, for some reason, you cannot approach — at this time — the organization that interests you (it's too far away, or you don't want to tip your hand yet, or whatever), what you can do is pick a similar organization (or individual) where you are — and go find out what kind of problems are on their mind. (If you are interested in working for, say, a senator in another state, you can talk to a senator's staff here where you are, first; the problems are likely to be similar.)

D   *Analyzing the problems of a prospective employer by talking to the person who held the job before you — OR by talking to their "opposite number" in another similar/identical organization.*

Nobody, absolutely nobody, knows the problems bugging a boss so much as someone who works, or used to work, for them. If they still work for them, they may have a huge investment in being discreet (i.e., not as candid as you need). Ex-employees are not necessarily any longer under that sort of pressure. Needless to say, if you're trying to get the organization to create a new position, there is no "previous employee." But in some identical or similar organization *which already has this sort of position,* you can still find someone to interview.

E   *Using your contacts/friends/everyone you meet, in order to find someone who:*

1. Knows the organization that interests you, or knows someone who knows;

2. Knows the-person-who-has-the-power-to-hire-you, or knows someone who knows;

3. Knows who their opposite number is in a similar/identical organization;

4. Knows your predecessor, or knows someone who knows;

5. Knows your "opposite number" in another organization, or knows someone who knows.

F *Supplementary Method: Research in the library,* on the organization, or an organization similar to it; research on the-individual-who-has-the-power-to-hire-you, or on their opposite number in another organization, etc. (Ask your friendly librarian or research librarian for help — tell them what you're trying to find out.)

See also the books listed in Appendix B on
page 290: Executives and the Business World.

ANALYZING AN ORGANIZATION'S PROBLEMS

[ ] If it's a decent-sized company, send for (or go pick up) their annual report to stockholders; granted it's a public relations piece, it still may help quite a bit. If the organization is too small to have an annual report, get whatever pamphlets they have, describing their work. Also, use your contacts to try to find people who know a lot about them. Then, after studying what you find out, you will want to weigh the following questions:

IF IT IS A LARGE COMPANY:

[ ] How does this organization rank within its field, or industry? Is this organization family owned? If so, what effect has that on promotions? Where are its plants, offices or branches? What are all its projects or services? In what ways have they grown in recent years? New lines, new products, new processes, new facilities, etc.? Existing political situations: imminent proxy fights, upcoming mergers, etc.? What is the general image of the organization in people's minds? If the organization sells stock, what has been happening to it (see an investment broker and ask).

**QUESTIONS TO BE ASKING YOURSELF
REGARDLESS OF THE COMPANY'S SIZE:**

[ ] What kind of *turnover of staff* have they had? What is the attitude of employees toward the organization? If you've been there, are their faces happy, strained, or what? Is promotion generally from within, or from outside? How long has the chief executive been with the organization?

[ ] Do they encourage their employees to further their educational training? Do they help them pay for it?

[ ] How do *communications* work within the organization? How is information collected, and by what paths does it flow? What methods are used to see that information gets results — to what authority do people respond there? Who reports to whom?

[ ] Is there a "time-bomb" — a problem that will kill the organization, or drastically reduce its effectiveness and efficiency if they don't solve it real fast?

<u>Rule No. 5</u>: *Ultimately, this is a language-translation problem. You're trying to take your language (i.e., a description of your skills), and translate it into their language (i.e., their priorities, their values, their jargon, as these surface within their concerns, problems, etc.).* You should be aware to begin with that most of the-people-who-have-the-power-to-hire-you for the position that you want DO NOT like the word "problems," as I said earlier. It reminds them that they are mortal, have hangups, haven't solved something yet, or that they overlooked something, etc. "Smartass" is the word normally reserved for someone who comes in and *shows them up.* (This isn't true of every employer or manager, but it's true of altogether too many.) Since you're trying to use *their* language, speak of "an area you probably are planning to move into" or "a concern of yours" or "a challenge currently facing you" or *anything* except: "By the way, I've uncovered a problem you have." Use the word *problems* in your own head, but don't blurt it out with your prospective employer, *unless you hear them use it first.*

Beyond this, your goal is to be able to speak of Your Skills in terms of *The Language* of Their Problems. Here are some examples, in order to bring this all home:

The person who has the power to hire you, was bugged by or concerned about:	You therefore use language which emphasizes that you:
Your predecessor had all the skills, but was too serious about *everything*.	have all the skills (name them) *plus* you have a sense of humor.
This place is expanding, and now needs a training program for its employees.	have the skills to do training, and in the area they are concerned about.
All the picayune details they have to attend to, which they would like to shovel off on someone else.	are very good with details and follow up. (That had better be true, or don't say it.)
Their magazine probably isn't covering all the subjects that it should, but that's just a gnawing feeling, and they've never had time to document it, and decide what areas to move into.	have done a complete survey of its table of contents for the last ten years, can show what they've missed, and have outlined sample articles in those missing areas.

When you finish your research, and can translate your skills into *their* language, you are ready to go see them.

How do you get in? Well, your *primary and most preferred avenue* must always be: contacts — people you know who also know them, and are willing to kick in the door for you, via a phone call, a letter, or permitting you to use their name.

Of course, *everyone* will tell you that the preferred way to get in, is by first sending them your resume. So strong is this belief, that there is a thriving industry in this country which does nothing else but prepare resumes for people. Belief in resumes' effectiveness among job-hunters, rivals fundamentalist belief in the power of prayer. So, we'd better stop for a moment and take a look at:

THAT OLD DEBBIL:
THE RESUME

Over the years I have tended to downplay the whole subject of resumes, largely because my interviews with successful job-hunters year after year have revealed that a large proportion of them never used a resume in getting their job. And never intend to. I said this once to a group of college placement people, many of whom were devoting large blocks of time to teaching students how to write a resume. When I sat down afterward, I found myself next to the personnel director for a huge public utility company, which employed thousands of people. He leaned across to me. "I listened to what you said about resumes," he began. I waited for the axe to fall. However he went on: "I've been trying to tell these counselors for years to get off this obsession they have with resumes. I'll interview anyone. But I don't read resumes. Haven't read one in five years. I can't tell a thing about a candidate from a resume. I was so glad you said what you did. Maybe they'll listen if they hear it from you."

The subject of resumes *is* loaded. So, perhaps we ought to briefly summarize what is known about resumes.

> RÉ-SU-MÉ rez-ə-mā n [F. *resume* fr. pp. of *resumer* to resume, summarize] SUMMARY *specif:* a short account of one's career and qualifications prepared typically by an applicant for a position.
>
> —Webster's

Resumes can serve four different functions: they can be a SELF-INVENTORY, preparing you before the job-hunt to recall all that you've accomplished thus far in your life; they can be an EXTENDED CALLING CARD, whose purpose is to get you invited in for an interview, by the employer(s) to whom you send that "calling card"; they can be an AGENDA FOR AN INTERVIEW, affording the interviewer a springboard from which to launch his or her inquiry about you, after you have been invited in; and, finally, resumes can be a MEMORY-JOGGER for the employer after the interview, or for a whole committee — if a group is involved in the hiring decision.

It is as EXTENDED CALLING-CARD that the resume is most often used. Indeed, as calling-card it may be sent out to hundreds of prospective employers. Its lack of effectiveness in this role is well-known. I cited the statistics in chapter 2. Only one job-offer is tendered for every 1470 resumes that the average company receives. What is not so well-known, is the tremendous damage which can be done to your self-esteem by depending upon resumes. This damage is created by the following facts:

a) *Some* job-hunters do actually get an interview, and subsequently a job, because they sent out resumes.

b) *Many, many more* job-hunters do *not* get a job by means of a resume. In fact, many do not even get one invitation to an interview, in spite of sending out 800 or 900 resumes.

c) The ones who do get a job thereby, talk a lot about it; the ones who find their resumes don't work for them, rarely say much. Consequently, there is a widespread *mythology* in our culture that "resumes usually work."

d) When resumes don't work at all for a particular job-hunter, he or she usually assumes something is drastically *wrong with them.*

The result: plummeting self-esteem. It is not that a method has been tried, and failed. It is that a method *which you think works for almost everyone else* has failed for you. Hence, depression. Emotional paralysis, etc.

HOW TO GET IN

Well, you can see why I disbelieve in resumes as extended calling cards. How then *do* I think you are going to get in for an interview? I think you are going to get in by methods we KNOW are most effective:

a) *COMMITMENT. Devoting eight hours a day, five days a week, to the job-hunt.*

b) *GOING FACE-TO-FACE. Knocking on the door, personally, at every organization that looks the least bit interesting.*

c) *USING CONTACTS. When you find a place you like, or are curious about, but you can't get an interview there, asking every person you know if they know someone who works there, and can get you an invitation to an interview.*

I believe in these three strategies because I know they work.

RESUMES

Given the fact that the resume AS EXTENDED CALLING-CARD is not very effective, what can we say about its other three roles? Well, I believe the exercises in chapters 4 and 5, plus the *Quick Job-Hunting Map,* really supplant any need for the resume as SELF-INVENTORY. And your own research about organizations that interest you really supplants any need for the resume as AGENDA FOR AN INTERVIEW. But, after talking with countless numbers of successful job-hunters, I am bound to say that a resume may be very useful *after* the interview as A MEMORY-JOGGER FOR THE EMPLOYER.

It is an ancient saying in career-counseling: "A resume is something you should never send ahead of you, but always leave behind you." I believe that. Further, I believe it is often — if not always — wise *not* to carry a resume into an interview, but to say truthfully, "I don't have one with me, but I can mail one to you tonight." Then go home, construct a resume tailored exactly to the skills needed in the job you both just discussed, type it up *very* neatly, or run it over to a professional place post-haste, and then send it, along with a thank-you note as a cover letter.

I think there is a genuine need sometimes for the resume as memory-jogger. Many hiring decisions are made by a committee, and you do not always have a chance to meet them all. Oftentimes you may be called back for three or four more interviews, before they decide who they want. The resume, left behind from the first, will remind them of who you are.

FOR THAT FARAWAY CITY, YOU MAY HAVE TO SEND A RESUME

If you're interested in leaping across the country for your next job, it may of course be impractical for you at first to go there yourself. You may need to test the waters. I already suggested, in the previous chapter, how you research a faraway city. But suppose that research is completed. You know some organizations that, at this distance, look like "possibles." You can't yet afford the money (or time, perhaps) to actually go there. What should you do?

Well of course you will begin by using every contact there, that you have developed. If a letter comes from you with the name of a mutual contact in that target city, the person to whom the letter is addressed is *always* going to pay more favorable attention to that letter, than would be the case if you were a total stranger. (Unless — the job-hunter's nightmare — your mutual friend/contact has misrepresented how close he or she is to your target person, and as a matter of fact said person can't stand the sight of your mutual friend. It is of embarrassment, to die.)

E.J. DYER   MOQ 2723   JACKSONVILLE, NC 28542   (919) 353-8390

I SPEAK
THE LANGUAGE
OF
MEN
MACHINERY
AND
MANAGEMENT
. . .

OBJECTIVE: Sales of Heavy Equipment

QUALIFICATIONS   * Knowledge of heavy equipment, its use and maintenance.

              * Ability to communicate with management and with men in the field.

              * Ability to favorably introduce change in the form of new
                 equipment or new ideas... the ability to sell.

EXPERIENCE   * Maintained, shipped, budgeted and set allocation priorities for
                 85 pieces of heavy equipment as head of a 500-man organization
Men and   (1975-1977).
Machinery

              * Constructed twelve field operation support complexes, employing
                 a 100-man crew and 19 pieces of heavy equipment (1965-1967).

              * Jack-hammer operator, heavy construction (summers 1956-1957-1958).

Should you enclose a resume? Opinions vary widely. *Everything* depends on the nature of the resume, and the nature of the person you are sending it to. Resumes, after all, are a lot like dating. There is no man who is liked by all the women he dates. There is no woman who is liked by all the men she dates. Some employers like resumes; some hate them.

Some will like your resume; others, no matter what format or style it is in, won't like it. The question that concerns you the most, will inevitably be: never mind that not all employers will like my resume—will the employers *I care about the most* like it? Ah, that is the $64,000 question.

Management	* Planned, negotiated and executed large scale equipment purchases on a nation to nation level (1972-1974).

Sales	* Achieved field customer acceptance of two major new computer-based systems:
	   - Equipment inventory control and repair parts expedite system (1968-1971)
	   - Decision makers' training system (1977-1979).
	* Proven leader ... repeatedly elected or appointed to senior posts.

EDUCATION	* B.A. Benedictine College, 1959. (Class President; Editor Yearbook; "Who's Who in American Colleges"). * Naval War College, 1975. (Class President; Graduated "With Highest Distinction"). * University of Maryland, 1973-1974. (Chinese Language). * Middle Level Management Training Course, 1967-1968 (Class Standing: 1 of 97).
PERSONAL	* Family: Sharon and our sons Jim (11), Andy (8) and Matt (5) desire to locate in a Mountain State by 1982, however, in the interim will consider a position elsewhere in or outside the United States ... Health: Excellent ... Birthdate: December 9, 1937 ... Completing Military Service with the rank of Lieutenant Colonel, U.S. Marine Corps.
SUMMARY	A seeker of challenge ... experienced, proven and confident of closing the sales for profit.

I have a hobby of occasionally collecting resumes that work. I delight in showing them to employers. Many of them don't like them at all. "That resume will never get anyone a job," they say. I delight in telling them, "Sorry, you're wrong. It already has. What you are saying is that it wouldn't get them a job *with you*."

The resume reproduced above is an example of what I mean. Jim Dyer, who had been in the Marines for twenty years, wanted a job as a salesman for heavy construction and mining equipment. He devised this resume, and had fifteen copies made. "I used," he said, "a grand total of seven before I got *the* job in *the* place I wanted!"

Like the employer who hired him, I *loved* this resume. Yet, when I've shown it to other employers, they criticized it for using a picture, for being two pages long instead of one, etc., etc. In other words, had Jim sent his resume to *them,* they wouldn't have been impressed enough to invite him in for an interview.

So, I repeat, matching your resume to the right employer is a lot like a dating game. Don't believe *anyone* who tells you there's one right format for a resume, or one way that's guaranteed to win.

If you decide you want to send your resume to a faraway place, and you want further guidance as to how to write one, I refer you to the books listed in section 24 of Appendix B, at the back of this book. The best of these, by a long shot, is Richard Lathrop's *Who's Hiring Who,* wherein he recommends (and describes) "a qualifications brief" — akin to John Crystal's idea of "a written proposal" , — instead of a resume.

My own admonitions are: above everything else, *remember not to put anything negative in your resume that would cause you to be screened out.* Save confessions and excruciating honesty for the confessional. E.g., omit "divorced," if that be your case, because it may imply "quitter" about your future in that organization. (Say "three dependents" or "single" and leave it at that.)

Never lie; but do select your truths carefully, as Bernard Haldane says. Don't volunteer something negative. Confessions are for the confessional, not the resume.

The most important quality needed in your resume, besides neatness and clarity, is that it should be a *living* resume, which it will be ONLY if YOU shine through it all. One job-hunter, for example, found this unique truthful way of describing her period of job-hunting: "Job-Hunter (Self-Employed) January 1982 - January 1983.

- Developed and executed all phases of marketing and advertising for product.
- Targeted markets and identified the needs of diverse consumers.
- Developed sales brochure
- Designed packaging, and upgraded visual appeal of product
- Scheduled and conducted oral presentations"
  So, *she* shined through it all.

If you have followed faithfully the techniques suggested by the creative minority (as outlined in these chapters), your resume will show it. Don't, whatever you do, just copy or adapt someone else's resume. It will be self-evident to the reader that you didn't go through the processes in these chapters. In the competitive game that job-hunting alas is, *that* will earn you four demerits, and a free trip to Siberia.

FOR THAT FARAWAY CITY, SEND YOURSELF

It will ultimately be *essential* for you to visit the geographical area you want to work in—if it's not where you presently live.

If going into a strange new geographical area is a totally new experience for you, and you have no friends there in your chosen area, just remember there are various ways of meeting people, making friends, and developing contacts rather quickly with people who share some interest or enthusiasm of yours. There are athletic clubs, Ys, churches, charitable and community organizations, where you can present yourself and meet people, from the moment you walk in the doors. You will soon develop many acquaintances, and some beginning friendships, and the place won't seem so lonely after all.

Also, visit or write your high school before you set out for this new town and find out what graduates live in the area that you are going to be visiting for the first time: they are your friends already, because you went to the same school. As I indicated earlier, all of these acquaintances, friends and key individuals have one common name: contacts. Contacts, CONTACTS.

Once you get there, you will want to talk to key individuals *who can suggest other people you might talk to, as you try to find out what organizations interest you.* You will want to define these key individuals in your distant city ahead of time and let them know you are coming. Your list may include: friends, college alumni (if you attended college), high school pals, church or synagogue contacts, Chamber of Commerce executives, city manager, regional planning offices, appropriate county or state offices in your area of interest, the Mayor, and high

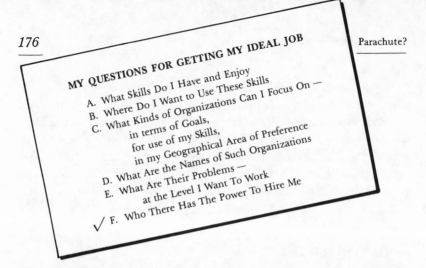

MY QUESTIONS FOR GETTING MY IDEAL JOB

A. What Skills Do I Have and Enjoy
B. Where Do I Want to Use These Skills
C. What Kinds of Organizations Can I Focus On —
   in terms of Goals,
   for use of my Skills,
   in my Geographical Area of Preference
D. What Are the Names of Such Organizations
E. What Are Their Problems —
   at the Level I Want To Work
✓ F. Who There Has The Power To Hire Me

level management in particular companies that look interesting from what you've read or heard about them.

When you "hit town," you will want to remember the City Directory, the Yellow Pages of your phone book, etc. You *may* want to put a modest-sized advertisement in the paper once you are in your chosen geographical area (or in the place where you currently live, if that is where you intend to do your job-hunting), saying you would like to meet with other people who are following the job-hunting techniques of *What Color Is Your Parachute?* That way you'll form a kind of 'job-hunters anonymous,' where you can mutually support one another in your hunt. With such help, or by yourself, you then set about the process. A job-hunter describes it:

"Suppose I arrived cold in some city, the one place in all the world I want to live — but with no idea of what that city might hold as a match and challenge for my 'personal-talent bank.' I have an economic survey to make, yes; but I also have an equally or more important personal survey to accomplish. Can this city meet my peculiarly personal needs? To find out, I meet Pastors, bankers, school principals, physicians, dentists, real estate operators, et al. I would be astonished if opportunities were not brought to my attention, together with numerous offers of personal introduction to key principals. All I would be doing is forging links (referrals) in a chain leading to my eventual targets. *The referral is the key.*"

People who haven't tried this are understandably afraid: afraid important men or women won't have time to see them, afraid they won't be able to get past the secretary or receptionist, etc. But, as was said above, referral (by one of your contacts) is the key.

Organizations, including hospitals, colleges, and everything else, love to be loved. You are going to be a very rare bird when you walk in their front door. You loved them enough to find out a lot of information about them. *You know far more than you are ever going to have to use,* at least during the hiring process. But the depth of your knowledge will pay off in your quiet sense of competence. You know they have problems — oops, "challenges" — and you know you can help solve them.

This fact will be of great interest — most of the time — to the person you go to see, provided you have taken the trouble to identify, learn about, and ask to see *the top executive whose responsibility it is to solve the particular problems that you have zeroed in on.*

That is the person you are going to need to approach, by name, by appointment: the person who has the interest, the responsibility and the motivation for hiring *this problem solver: Y-O-U. . .*

You are going to ask to see that person only, and if it's a large organization, generally you are going to avoid—

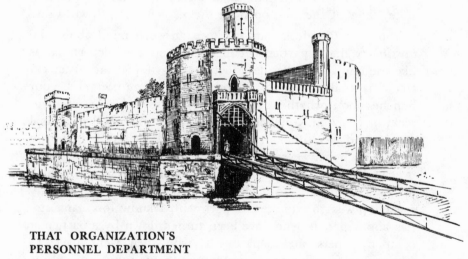

THAT ORGANIZATION'S
PERSONNEL DEPARTMENT

This advice has been given historically since job-hunting manuals were first written.

The advice has always been strongly stated by them all:

> The personnel department in most large companies,
> they say, is at the bottom of the social and executive
> totem pole; it rarely hears of middle-high level vacancies

> even within its own company; when it does know of
> the vacancies, it rarely has the power to hire except for
> entry level; in almost all other cases it can only
> screen out applicants, and refer those who survive,
> on up to higher executives; therefore it is in the
> job-hunter's interest (generally speaking) to skip
> over this extra screening-out process. In other words,
> avoid this department like the plague.

I myself first echoed the above advice some fifteen years ago, and now that it is the year of our Lord 1985, I am bound to say that I do not think things have changed much. But I do think they have changed *a little*. That is to say, *some* job-hunters who have successfully concluded their job-hunt have written to tell me of an anonymous personnel department here or there that did *not* see itself as an extra screening-out step in the job-hunting process, but was — au contraire — the very model of helpfulness to them. The personnel director sat down with them and helped them figure out just exactly where "upstairs" they might fit in, and then sent them on up with an introductory note, "kicking the door open for them" as it were. Bravo! I say.

You may therefore want to keep an open mind about the *possibility* that a particular company's personnel department is like the one I have just described, and — if you are in an extreme risk-taking mood — follow your intuition and your hunches about whether or not *this* is a personnel department to seek, or to avoid. Going in there merely to pick up their annual report, and any other printed material they have, which you should do in any event, gives you a chance to look the place over and decide. Apart from visiting it briefly, merely to pick up such literature, you will probably still find it (generally speaking) wise to avoid that department. I know too many stories about people who have been turned down by a particular company's personnel department, who then went back to square one, found out who, in that very same company, had the power to hire for the position they wanted, went to that woman or man, and got hired — ten floors up from the personnel department that had just rejected them.

If not the personnel department, what then? Well, you are going to have to do enough research — using the directories beginning on page 129 and your contacts — to figure out who has the responsibility for hiring in the division, department or whatever that you are interested in. If you can't figure out, despite all your best efforts, who that person is, there is a simple rule you would do well to remember: *when in doubt, go too high rather than too low on the organizational chart.* You will probably be referred "down"; but if you go too low, you will rarely be referred "up."

It will help you further, as I said earlier, if you learn as much as you can about that person-who-has-the-power-to-hire. Once you have their name, look them up in *Poor's Register, Who's Who in Commerce and Business,* or any other of the *Who's Who* directories, and consult your friendly neighborhood research librarian as well for any clippings or other file material they may have on your target person. Further, consult every acquaintance, friend, relative you know — i.e., all your Contacts — to see what they may know about him or her. . . before you ever go to meet them for a potential hiring interview.

(c) 1980 NEA, INC. *Contra Costa Times.*
Used by special permission.

WELL, YOU WANT TO SEE THEM, BUT DO THEY WANT TO SEE YOU?

This is the question which bothers almost everyone new to the job-hunt. We sort of just assume the answer is "No." And particularly so, if we have some very obvious job-market handicap, such as age, or a psychiatric history, or a prison record, or whatever.

You need to remember, no matter what your job-market handicap may be, this simple but profound truth:

ALL EMPLOYERS DIVIDE INTO TWO GROUPS: 1) THOSE WHO WOULD BE PUT OFF BY YOUR HANDICAP. And 2) THOSE WHO WOULD NOT BE AT ALL PUT OFF BY YOUR HANDICAP. YOUR JOB IS TO FIND THE SECOND KIND OF EMPLOYER, AND NOT PAY ANY ATTENTION TO THE FIRST.

This is true, no matter what the odds. If out of every 100 employers, 75 would be bothered by your history, but 25 wouldn't care about it in the slightest, YOUR JOB IS TO MAKE YOUR WAY QUICKLY THROUGH THE 75, AND FIND THOSE OTHER 25. THEY ARE THE ONLY ONES YOU REALLY WANT TO SEE, ANYWAY.

I can hear your objections, right now. "But, hey, I'm over 60 years old. Employers don't want someone that old."

Now, you *know* what I'm going to tell you: "All employers divide into two groups: 1) those who would be put off by your age, and 2) those who would not be at all put off by your age. Your job is to find the second kind of employer, and not pay any attention to the first."

Please! Make no generalizations about "employers." There ain't no such animal. In any and all circumstances that you can possibly come up with, there are *always* at least two kinds of employers. Your job is to find the second kind, and pay no never mind to the first. You wouldn't want to work for them anyway, now would you?

Having said that, remember this. You're not visiting an employer in order to get him or her to do something for *you* — like it was a big favor, or something. If you've done your homework so that you *know* you can be part of the solution there, and not part of the problem, then you're going in to see this employer in order to do a favor *for them*. That's not an arrogant posture for you to take. It can be stated very quietly and confidently. But, it *is* the truth.

You are coming to see this employer, in order to make an oral proposal, followed hopefully by a written proposal, of what *you* can do for *them*.

What a switch from the way *most* job-hunters approach an employer! And will he or she, in such a case, be glad to see you? You bet they will. Because:

Reproduced by Special Permission of PLAYBOY Magazine; copyright © 1979 by Playboy

"I'll tell you why I want this job. I thrive on challenges. I like being stretched to my full capacity. I like solving problems. Also, my car is about to be repossessed."

THE PERSON YOU ARE GOING TO SEE IS JUST LIKE YOU, UNDER REAL STRESS

The creative minority in this field have correctly pointed out that one of the reasons the hiring process in America today, at least beyond the $20,000 level, is so difficult, is because of the great stress involved for the executive who is interviewing.

Let's look at some of those sources of stress:

1. The odds are very great that the executive who does the interviewing was hired because of what they could contribute to the company, and not because they were such a great interviewer. In fact, their gifts in this arena may be rather miserable.

2. They can't entrust the process to someone else, because they have to live with whoever gets hired afterwards. So, hiring-interviews for above entry-level-positions have a heavy accent of "I wish I could get someone else to do this for me, but I can't afford to take that chance."

3. If the person-with-the-power-to-hire makes a mistake, they are going to have to rub shoulders with that mistake, day by day. They don't usually hire someone, and then never see that new employee again. An executive who has the responsibility of hiring for this position is given or takes that responsibility

(customarily) away from the personnel department *because this position is directly under them and they're going to have to live with whoever is hired, day by day.*

4. If they hire a mistake, it's going to make them look very bad with their superiors, board of directors, stockholders, or whoever it is that they report to.

5. If they hire a mistake and they aren't the chief executive yet, this could cost them a promotion personally — since they have proved they have bad judgment; and maybe their department is getting botched up — to boot.

6. If they hire a mistake, it's going to cost a lot of money. The costs of terminating their "mistake," going through the long hiring process for the replacement, and then training that replacement, totaled about $7000 in the case of a secretary, or over $200,000 in the case of a senior executive, in 1984. So you see, mistakes in hiring cost the employer lots of *money and time.*

Not bad. In one twenty-minute interview, or even several of same, this hapless interviewer can botch up part of the organization, cost the organization a great deal of money, lose their own promotion, be called to account, and acquire a whole new set of ulcers. No wonder hiring is such a stressful situation for the employer, not just the job-hunter.

STRESS IN THE INTERVIEW
FOR THE EMPLOYER

This all comes out clearly in the questions the employer typically asks, during the hiring interview. You as job-hunter, are sitting there perspiring and thinking of how stressful the hiring interview is for *you.* Rarely will it ever occur to you that the interview is just as stressful for this individual sitting across the desk, looking so calm, so much in command, so much at ease.

"S/he doesn't look as though they are under any stress," you whisper to me. For the purposes of this enchanting conversation we are about to launch into, pretend I am the angel on your shoulder. So, I reply, "Well, if this employer is so much at ease, how come there is fear hidden behind every question they are asking you?"

**"WHAT DO YOU MEAN?" YOU RETORT.
"I DON'T SEE ANY FEAR BEHIND THEIR QUESTIONS.
WHAT FEARS COULD AN EMPLOYER POSSIBLY HAVE?"**

That's easy. They run the gamut. For openers, the Employer
has the following fears when You, the Job-hunter, are face-to-
face with him or her:

a. That You Won't Be Able to Do the Job: That You Lack the
   Necessary Skills or Experience

b. That If Hired, You Won't Put In a Full Working Day

c. That If Hired, You'll Be Frequently "Out Sick," or Otherwise
   Absent Whole Days

d. That If Hired, You'll Only Stay Around for a Few Weeks or at
   Most a Few Months

e. That It Will Take You Too Long to Master the Job, and Thus
   Too Long Before You're Profitable to That Organization

f. That You Won't Get Along with the Other Workers There, or
   That You Will Develop a Personality Conflict with the Boss
   Himself (or Herself)

g. That You Will Do Only the Minimum That You Can Get Away
   With, Rather Than the Maximum That You Are Capable Of

h. That You Will Always Have to Be Told What to Do Next,
   Rather Than Displaying Initiative; That You Will Always Be
   in a Responding Rather Than an Initiating Mode (and Mood)

i. That You Will Have a Work-Disrupting Character Flaw, and
   Turn Out to Be:
   Dishonest, OR   a Spreader of Dissention at Work, OR
   Lazy, OR   An Embezzler, OR
   A Gossip, OR   Totally Irresponsible, OR
   A Liar, OR   Incompetent

   In a word: No Fun to Have Around

j. (If This Is a Large Organization, and Your Would-Be Boss Is
   Not the Top Person) That You Will Bring Discredit upon
   Them, upon His or Her Department/Section/Division, etc.
   for Ever Hiring You In the First Place—Possibly Costing
   Your Would-Be Boss a Raise or Promotion

"WELL, IF WHAT YOU'RE SAYING IS TRUE, THEN DURING THE JOB-INTERVIEW THE WOULD-BE EMPLOYER IS AN ABSOLUTE BUNDLE OF FEARS."

Yes, and it's not something he or she can really talk about. It's the job-hunter who is *supposed* to be afraid of the interview; *not* the employer. Moreover, employers don't usually talk with each other about this sort of thing. So, oftentimes an employer is facing the job-interview thinking that he or she is the only employer in the world with sweaty palms. They've never had a chance to check it out, and discover if other employers feel the same way.

"THAT MUST MAKE FOR LONELINESS, AS AN EMPLOYER WITH SWEATY PALMS APPROACHES THE JOB-INTERVIEW PROCESS."

Yes, he or she often feels extremely isolated and alone. That's why, in larger organizations, the hiring decision is often shared with a committee or a veritable army of his or her peers, within that organization. The rationale for this style of hiring might well be stated as: "Deliver me from my fears."

"AND MY LONELINESS."

Yes.

"WELL, SURELY AN EMPLOYER CAN'T KEEP THEIR FEARS ENTIRELY HIDDEN. THEY MUST SURFACE DURING THE INTERVIEW, IN SOME FASHION."

Absolutely. Fear is behind almost *every* question that an employer asks. Indeed, any job-hunter will be able to "field" the employer's questions, during the interview, if the job-hunter just keeps in mind that behind every question is some Fear.

"CAN YOU GIVE ME SOME EXAMPLES?"

Of course. But first let me say that the most important thing to keep in mind is that no Employer cares about your past. The only thing the employer can possibly care about is your future. Therefore, the more a question *appears* to be about your past, the more certain you may be that some Fear is behind it. And that Fear is about your future — i.e., what will you be like, *after* the employer decides to hire you. *If* he or she decides to hire you.

So, let's run down typical
employer interview questions—
see what they are, then what the
fear behind those questions is,
and perhaps some key phrases
that can be used in answering
the questions—so as to allay the
the Fear.

THE INTERVIEW QUESTION:
<u>"Tell me about yourself."</u>

• The Fear Behind the Question: The Employer is afraid they
won't ask the right questions during the interview.

The Employer is afraid there's something in your background
or in your attitude toward your work that will make you a Bad
Employee.

• The Point You Try to Get Across to Answer Their Fear: You
would make a good employee, and you have proved that by
your past.

• Ideas or Phrases You Might Use: The briefest history in the
world, of where you were born and raised, hobbies, interests, etc.

The briefest description of where you have worked or the
kind of work you have done. ANY sentence or phrase which
describes your past attitude toward your work in a positive
way:

"Hard worker"

"Came in early, left late"

"Always did more than was expected of me"

Etc.

THE INTERVIEW QUESTION:
<u>"What kind of work are you looking for?"</u>

• The Fear Behind the Question: That it isn't the same kind of
job the employer needs to fill—e.g., they are looking for a secretary, you are looking to be office manager; they are looking
for somebody who can work alone, you are looking for a job
where you would be rubbing shoulders with other people.

• The Point You Try to Get Across to Answer Their Fear: You
have picked up many skills, which are transferable from one
field to another.

- Ideas or Phrases You Might Use: You are looking for work where you can use your skills with People (specify what those skills are — that you most enjoy).

AND/OR

You are looking for work where you can use your skills with Data or Information (specify what those skills are — that you most enjoy).

AND/OR

You are looking for work where you can use your skills with Things/Machines/Tools/Plants etc. (specify what those skills are — that you most enjoy).

P.S. If you are applying for a known vacancy, you can *first* respond to this question by saying, "I'd be happy to answer that, but first it seems to me it's more important for you to tell me what kind of work this vacancy entails."

Once the employer has told you, *don't forget* to then answer their question. But now you can couch your answer in terms of the skills you genuinely have, which are *relevant* to the work the employer has described.

THE INTERVIEW QUESTION:
"Have you ever done this kind of work before?"

- The Fear Behind the Question: The Employer is afraid you can't do the work, that you don't possess the necessary experience or skills.
- The Point You Try to Get Across, to Answer This Fear: You have transferable skills.
- Ideas or Phrases You Might Use: The same ones as in the last question. Plus:

  "I pick up stuff very quickly."
  "I have quickly mastered any job I have ever done."
  "Every job is a whole new universe, but I make myself at home very quickly."

THE INTERVIEW QUESTION:
"Why did you leave your last job?"
OR
"Why did your last job end?"
OR
"How did you get along with your former boss
and co-workers?"

• The Fear Behind the Question: The Employer is afraid that
you don't get along with people. Especially Bosses.
• The Point You Try to Get Across, to Answer This Fear: That
you do get along well with people, and your *attitude* toward
your former boss(es) and co-workers proves it.
• Ideas or Phrases You Might Use:
  "My *job* was terminated" (if you were fired)
  "My boss *and I* both felt. . ."
  "I would be *happier* and *more effective* in a job where (here
describe your strong points: e.g., I would be under less supervision and have more room to use my initiative and creativity)
  Say as many positive things as you can about your boss and
co-workers (without telling lies).

THE INTERVIEW QUESTION:
"How much were you absent from work during your last job?"

• The Fear Behind the Question: The Employer is afraid that
you will be absent from work a lot, if they hire you.
• The Point You Try to Get Across, to Answer This Fear: You
Will Not Be Absent from Work.
• Ideas or Phrases You Might Use: If you *were* absent quite a
bit on a previous job, say why and stress that it is a *past* difficulty (if it is).
  If you were *not* absent on your previous job, stress your good
attendance record, and *the attitude* you have toward the
importance of always being at work.

THE INTERVIEW QUESTION:
"How is your health?"

• The Fear Behind the Question: The Employer is afraid that you will miss work because of sickness.
• The Point You Try to Get Across, to Answer This Fear: You are a hard worker, and you have no health problem that keeps you from being at work daily.
OR
(If you do) you stress your attendance average in terms of how many days *per month* you have been absent at previous jobs, and you stress how *hard* you work on the days that you *are* there.
• Ideas or Phrases You Might Use: Your productivity, compared to other workers, at your previous jobs.
   Your determination to *produce* more than other workers, if you get this job (or more than your predecessor did).

THE INTERVIEW QUESTION:
"Can you explain why you've been out of work so long?'
OR
"Can you tell me why there are these gaps in your work record or work history?" (Usually asked, after studying your resume)
OR
"How long have you been out of work?"

• The Fear Behind the Question: The Employer is afraid that you don't really like to work, and will quit the minute things aren't going "your way."
• The Point You Try to Get Across, to Answer This Fear: You like to work.
AND
You regard times when things aren't going well as Challenges.
• Ideas or Phrases You Might Use: You were working hard during the times when you weren't employed. Either: studying, doing volunteer work, sitting down to do lots of hard thinking about how you could most effectively use the talents you have been given, trying to get beyond merely "keeping busy" to finding some sense of mission for your life.

THE INTERVIEW QUESTION:
"Doesn't this work (or this job) represent a step down,
for you?"
OR
"Don't you think you would be underemployed if you took
this job?"
OR
"I think this job is way beneath your talents and experience."

• The Fear Behind the Question: The employer is afraid that you *could* command more salary and more responsibility, that you are only taking *this* job as a stopgap measure, and that you will leave him (or her) as soon as something better turns up.
• The Point You Try to Get Across, to Answer This Fear: You will stick with this job just as long as you possibly can, so long as you *and the employer* agree this is where you should be.
• Ideas or Phrases You Might Use: "This job isn't a step down for me. It's a step *up* — from being on welfare."

"I like to work, and I give my best to every job I've ever done."

"Every employer is afraid the employee will leave too soon, and every employee is afraid the employer might fire him (or her). We have mutual fears. I'll do a crackerjack job here, and I'll stay as long as we both agree this is where I should be."

THE INTERVIEW QUESTION:
"Tell me, what is your greatest weakness?"

• The Fear Behind the Question: The Employer is afraid you have some work-flaw or character-flaw — and is hopeful you will confess to it, now.
• The Point You Try to Get Across, to Answer This Fear: You have limitations just like any other person but you work constantly to improve them and make yourself into a more effective worker.
• Ideas or Phrases You Might Use: Mention some weakness of yours that has a positive aspect to it. Stress the positive aspect, e.g., "I don't respond well to being over-supervised, because I have a great deal of initiative, and I like to use it — anticipating problems before they even arise."

Well, there are many other interview questions we could look at; but I think you get the idea.

"Yes, I do. You're saying that if you <u>listen</u> hard to an Employer's interview questions, and ask yourself what fear is behind that question, you will realize all questions are questions about the future; and — realizing that — you will know how to answer them."

Precisely.

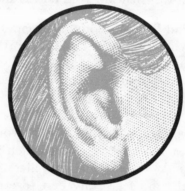

THE ESSENCE
OF THE INTERVIEW

Given this understanding — that the employer is under as much stress in the hiring interview as you are — you can see what the hiring interview really is: two fearful people sitting there, talking to each other.

It is obviously important that both of you get a chance to talk, during the interview, in order to find out what it is you need to know. It is therefore hardly surprising that in a survey done some years ago, it was discovered that successful hiring interviews were those *where both the employer and the would-be employee equally had a chance to talk, during the interview.* So, let's see what it is that each of you needs to talk about.

During the interview, as John Crystal has pointed out, the employer has got to have four main questions on his or her mind:

1. "WHY ARE YOU HERE? Why have you chosen this particular place to come to? What attracted you to us?"

2. "WHAT CAN YOU DO FOR ME? Since, as a manager or executive, I have certain tasks I need to get done, how is it that you could help me with those tasks, goals, problems, and challenges?"

3. "What KIND OF PERSON ARE YOU? If I were to hire you, would you be easy to get along with, or difficult? Will you fit in with the folks already here, or will you be an irritant? Will you and I get along, or won't we?"

4. "HOW MUCH ARE YOU GOING TO COST ME? What's the least amount of money that I could get you for, if I decide I want you?"

That's what the employer has *got* to want to know. We must add, however, that many employers are unsophisticated in conducting hiring interviews. Therefore, they often do not know precisely how to ask these questions. You may need to guide them.

WHAT QUESTIONS CAN AN EMPLOYER ASK?

	EMPLOYERS CAN DO OR ASK	EMPLOYERS CAN NOT DO OR ASK
Your sex—	Notice your appearance.	Make comments or take notes unless sex is a BFOQ.
Marital status—	Status after hiring, for insurance purposes.	Are you married? Single? Divorced? Engaged? Living with anyone? Do you see your ex-spouse?
Children—	Numbers and ages of children after hiring, for insurance purposes.	Do you have children at home? How old? Who cares for them? Do you plan more children?
Physical data—	Explain manual labor, lifting, other requirements of the job. Show how it is performed. Require physical examination.	How tall are you? How much do you weigh? Do you have any physical or mental handicaps?
Criminal record—	If security clearance is necessary, can be done prior to employment.	Have you ever been arrested, convicted or spent time in jail?
Military—	Are you a veteran? Why not? Any job-related experience?	What type of discharge do you have? What branch did you serve in?
Age—	Age after hiring. "Are you over 18?"	How old are you? Estimate age.
Housing—	If you have no phone, how can we reach you?	Do you own your home? Do you rent? Do you live in an apartment or a house?
Religion—		What is your religious background?

continued

How Do You Handle it?

As a job applicant, what can you do if you are asked one of the illegal questions? The Wall Street Journal pointed out you have three courses of action:

"1. Answer the question and ignore that fact that it is not legal.
  2. Answer the question with the statement: "I think that is not relevant to the requirements of the position.
  3. Contact the nearest Equal Employment Opportunity Commission office.

"Unless the violation is persistent, is demeaning, or you can prove it resulted in your not being employed, number three should probably be avoided. The whole area is still relatively new; many interviewers are just not totally conversant with the new code requirements.

"Answer number two is probably, in most circumstances, the best to give. There are times when it may cost you the job, but are you that interested in working for someone who is all that concerned about your personal life?"

Now, what is it that you, as job-hunter, want to cover in this same interview? Well, these have got to be the things on your mind:

1. "HELP ME TO UNDERSTAND, COMPLETELY AND THOROUGHLY, WHAT THIS JOB INVOLVES. I've done what research I could, outside this room, but now there are still many things I do not know about this job. I need your help in filling up those gaps."

2. "ONCE I UNDERSTAND IT, I MUST WEIGH WHETHER OR NOT MY SKILLS TRULY MATCH THIS JOB. If there is a mismatch, let's find it out during this hiring interview, and not later."

3. "ARE YOU THE KIND OF PEOPLE I WOULD LIKE TO WORK FOR, OR ARE YOUR VALUES SO DIFFERENT

FROM MINE, THAT WE WILL NEVER WORK OUT TO-
GETHER? [The same question as the employer has.] Beyond
all question of competency to do the job, would we get along?"

4. "IF MY SKILLS MATCH THIS JOB, AND IT LOOKS AS
THOUGH WE WOULD GET ALONG WITH EACH OTHER,
CAN I PERSUADE YOU TO HIRE ME? Can I show you that
I would bring to this job both enthusiasm and effectiveness, in
a way that would reflect favorably on your judgment for having
hired me?"

There you have it. Four things the employer wants to cover
during the interview; four things you want to cover. Eight, altogether. If a hiring interview, gently steered by you, covers these
eight points, it will ALWAYS be a successful interview. Whether
you get hired or not. For, as Richard Germann has pointed out,
a successful initial interview is one where you get invited back
for further discussion. And I would add, a successful interview
is also one where you would not want to work there, and you
find that out during the interview.

You are not there "to sell yourself" as so many career counselors may mistakenly tell you. You are there to find out more
information, upon which you may then make a decision: "Yes,
I would like to work here," or "No, I wouldn't want to work
here." Only if your decision is "Yes" do you ever go on to the
next step of trying "to sell yourself" to them. But until that
"Yes" is reached, *they* are as much on trial during the interview
(with you), as you are (with them). DON'T FORGET THAT
FOR EVEN ONE MOMENT during the hiring interview.

If you are under serious consideration, you will probably be
called back for a second interview. And perhaps a third and
fourth interview, in a large organization.

HOW SHOULD YOU CONDUCT YOURSELF
DURING THE INTERVIEW?

The object of the interview is to find out the information
you need to know; and, to help the employer find out the information he or she needs to know. To speak only of the latter,
for the moment, you will need to remember that there are three
ways in which you give them the information they want:

A. By your words. These words will deal with your past, and
your future. What you have already accomplished, and what
you want to accomplish in the time to come.

B. Your actions. These deal with the present, and what kind of person you are, as demonstrated in this interview and in your job-hunt.

C. Your written stuff — resume or proposal — which you leave behind you or send to the employer, after the interview.

The major point I wish to make, here, is that THERE MUST BE A CONSISTENCY BETWEEN THESE THREE MODES.

If you, for example, *by your words* claim that you are very good with details, but *by your actions* in the interview reveal you haven't done any detailed research on this company or organization, you will probably not get that job. *Whatever you claim* must be substantiated *by your actions* in the interview, *and in your written proposal* that you leave or send thereafter. There *must* be a consistency between all three. This employer is fearful, remember. By such consistency, you allay his or her fears about You.

ARE YOU READY FOR THIS INTERVIEW?

Well, of course you are. IF you did all the homework outlined in the previous two chapters, and in the New *Quick Job-Hunting Map* of Appendix A. With respect to the questions on *your mind*, you *know* what you want to know:

1. What does this job involve, by way of skills and tasks? *If* you did the homework, you know your chief skills. What you want to know is, does this job require such skills? They will talk about objectives, and tasks and duties. You must translate this (in your head) into *the skills required* to achieve those objectives, accomplish those tasks, and carry out those duties.

2. Do my skills match this job? *If* you have done your homework, you will know what skills you have, that you are trying to match up with this job.

3. Are you the kind of people I would like to work for? *If* you have done your homework, you will be infinitely more conscious of your values, than the average job-hunter is. You will therefore know *what values or style of operation* you are listening for, above, beneath and within all that you are hearing or seeing.

4. Can I persuade you to hire me? *If* you have done your homework, there *will* be a consistency during the interview and thereafter, between your words, your actions, and your written proposal. It is this consistency, combined with enthusiasm and

your obvious competency, that will be most persuasive in the end.

You will clearly understand, from all of this, that the success of the job interview *depends upon how well and thoroughly you did the homework on yourself, before* you ever came in for the interview.

HOW DO YOU ANSWER THEIR QUESTIONS?

Well, let's recall what their questions have *got* to be:

1. "WHY ARE YOU HERE?" *If* you did all your research, as described in the previous chapter, you'll know the answer. If you didn't, you won't. The essence of a good answer to this question is some variation on: "I have been interested in organizations which are _____ , and yours particularly attracted me because _____ "

2. "WHAT CAN YOU DO FOR ME?" *If* you did all your research, you will know that what the employer is essentially asking, here, is: "Will you help this organization to better do its work, and achieve its goals, and if so, in what way?" If you did your research, you will know what that company's work and goals are, what their problems and challenges are, and how you would be an asset toward the accomplishing of that work, the achieving of those goals, and the overcoming of those problems and challenges.

3. "WHAT KIND OF PERSON ARE YOU?" You will answer this question by *everything* you say during the interview, and everything you do during the interview. It is likely that *nothing* will escape the scrutiny of the person across the desk from you. And I mean: your haircut or hairdo; your manner of dress; your posture; your use of your hands; your body odor or perfume; your breath; your fingernails; the sound of your voice; the way in which you do or don't interrupt; the hesitant or assured manner in which you ask your questions or give your answers; your values as evidenced by the things which impress you or don't impress you; the carefulness with which you did or didn't research this company before you came in; the thoroughness with which you know your skills and strengths; your awareness of what you are willing to sell in order to get this job *and* what you aren't willing to sell in order to get this job; your enthusiasm for your work; and — that's just for openers. We can throw

in whether or not you smoke (in a race between two equally qualified people, the non-smoker will win out over the smoker 94% of the time, according to a study done by a professor of business at Seattle University); whether, if at lunch, you order a drink or not; whether you show courtesy to receptionist, secretary, waiter or waitress, or not; and — like that. Everything is grist for the mill, as the employer tries to divine "what kind of person is this?" What the employer, if he or she be an average employer, is looking for, are:

- any signs of dishonesty or lying;
- any signs of irresponsibility or tendency to goof off;
- any sign of arrogance or excessive aggressiveness;
- any sign of tardiness or failure to keep appointments and commitments on time;
- any sign of not following instructions or obeying rules;
- any sign of complaining or blaming things on others;
- any sign of laziness or lack of motivation;
- any sign of a lack of enthusiasm for this organization and what it is trying to do;
- any sign of instability, inappropriate response, and the like.

Since the employer will probably end up having to fire anyone with these signs, the employer would like to find these things out *now* rather than later.

Beyond these tangibles, there are the intangibles of *making a good impression*. Study after study has confirmed that if you are a male, you will make a better impression if:

- your hair or beard is short and neatly trimmed;
- you have freshly bathed, use a deodorant, and mouthwash and have clean fingernails;
- you have freshly laundered clothes on, and a suit rather than a sports outfit, and sit without slouching;

- your breath does not dispense gallons of garlic, onion, stale
  tobacco, or strong drink, into the enclosed office air;
- your shoes are neatly polished, and your pants have a
  sharp crease;
- you are not wafting tons of after-shave cologne fifteen feet
  ahead of you.

And, if you are a female, you will make a better impression
if:
- your hair is newly 'permed' or 'coiffed';
- you are freshly bathed, use a deodorant, mouth wash
  and have clean or nicely manicured fingernails;
- you wear a bra, freshly cleaned clothes, a suit or
  sophisticated-looking dress, and sit without slouching;
- your breath does not dispense gallons of garlic, onion, stale
  tobacco, or strong drink, into the enclosed office air;
- you wear shoes rather than sandals;
- you are not wafting tons of perfume fifteen feet ahead
  of you.

Now please, dear reader, do not send me mail telling me how
asinine you think some of these 'rules' are. I *know* that. I'm
only reporting, here, that study after study reveals these things
do affect whether or not you get hired. There are *of course* employers who care about none of these things, and will hire you
if you can do the job. Most such jobs, however, are in back
rooms, away from people, staring at little computer chips, or
such like.

You *are* on trial, in a sense, during this interview. All of the
above factors are a part of that trial.

Of course, what makes the job interview tolerable or even
fun, is that *you* are studying *everything* about this employer, at
the same time that they are studying everything about you. You
are just as much in need of making up your mind about what
kind of person *they* are, and whether or not you would like to
work with them, as they are doing with you. Two people, both
sizing each other up. Well, you know what that reminds you of.
The dating game. The job interview is indeed every bit like 'the
dating game.' *Both* of you have to like the other, before you
can get on to the question of 'going steady.' Thus the employer
is just as much 'on trial' during the job interview as you are. Realizing *that,* can take some of the stress away.

4. "HOW MUCH ARE YOU GOING TO COST ME?" Until they have said "We *want* you," *and* you have decided, "I want them," all discussion of salary tends to be inappropriate. You may think to yourself, "Yes, but what if they have a fixed salary figure in mind, and it is way below what I could accept — shouldn't I find that out as early as possible, so that I can graciously excuse myself, and go elsewhere?" That's logical, except for one minor little point: if you're the first person they've interviewed, and they haven't yet had a chance to get to know you very well, they may assume you are 'average material' and so mention merely an average kind of salary. But if they have seen a lot of people, *and* have had a chance to get to know you over two or three interviews, say. And if they are *very* impressed with you by this time and by contrast, *obviously* they are now going to be willing to do whatever they can to get a hold of you. And if *that* takes more money than they were originally prepared to offer, they may push themselves to find it. This happens *very* often.

If you allow discussion of salary to take place prematurely, you will be told *the lowest* figure they had in mind, but it will be presented as though it were *the highest* they could go. They haven't seen you yet in all your splendor. They don't know what they would be getting if they got you. Or, what they would be losing, if they let you go. Therefore, generally speaking until a firm offer has been made, postpone all discussion of salary.

As it is unlikely you will get to this point in the first interview at that particular place, this means you will probably go home not having gotten to this fourth question (or eighth, if you include your four first). All the more reason to have done your salary research as best you can, *before* you go in for that first interview.

BACK HOME AFTER THE FIRST INTERVIEW
AT THAT PLACE

That evening, you put your feet up, turn on the TV, and have a pleasant evening to yourself or with your loved one, right? Wrong. That evening *you work*. You've got to send them something in writing. At the very least, you are going to send them:

THE ABSOLUTELY CRUCIAL
THANK YOU NOTE

Each evening, you MUST take time to sit down and write (pen or typewriter) a brief thank you note to *each person that you saw that day.* That includes executives, secretaries, people who gave you helpful information, or anyone else who gave you a helping hand in any way. It should be regarded as basic to the simplest dictates of courtesy and kindness, that you write such notes. After all, you are presenting yourself as one who has skills at treating people as people. Prove it. *Your actions must be consistent with your words.*

This thank you note serves several purposes. First of all, it helps them to remember you. Even if the interview did not go well, and you have lost all interest in working there, they (executive and secretary or receptionist) may still hear of *other* openings, that might be of interest to you. In the thank you note, you can mention this, and ask them to keep you in mind.

If the interview went rather well, and you are hopeful of being invited back, then The thank you letter can reiterate your interest in further talks. You can also correct any impression you left behind you. Add anything you forgot to tell them. Underline anything that you want to emphasize from among those things discussed.

The importance of sending a thank you letter to *everyone* is one of the most essential steps in the entire job-hunt. *Yet it is the most overlooked step in the entire process.* We know of one woman who was told she was hired because she was the *only* interviewee, out of 39, who sent a thank you letter after the interview.

That's right, the thank you letter may actually get you the job. *You cannot afford to think of this as simply an optional exercise. It is critical to your getting hired.*

If you are still interested in that place, with the thank you letter you may want to include two other documents. The first, and preferred piece of paper, would be a written proposal from you as to what it is you would like to be able to do for that organization, what it is you hope you could accomplish for them. As evidence, you will want to cite *relevant* past accomplishments of yours, taking care *in each case* to cite:

a) what the problem was
b) what you did to solve it
c) what the results were, of your actions

The virtue of such a written proposal is that it looks forward rather than backward, as the resume does. And it puts into writing the essence of the hiring interview: you are not asking them merely to do something for you. More importantly, you are offering to do something for them.

The second piece of paper to be included with your thank you letter, if you are still interested in that place, is a resume — *carefully* tailored to that particular place and that particular job. Composed, and neatly typed, that very evening if necessary. Don't mention any skill, any experience, or any personal data that isn't *absolutely relevant* to that particular job.

If you have included a proposal, the resume is really unnecessary. If you haven't included a written proposal, then some kind of summary of your background and history *should* be included, to remind them of who you were in that parade of people that they interviewed.

MEANWHILE, BACK AT THE RANCH

While you are sitting there, writing out your thank you letter and proposal, the employer you saw that day is also sitting at home, reflecting on the interview. What's going on in his or her head, do you suppose? Well, you know. They are sifting through all the candidates they saw, trying to decide who stands out, so far. *Usually,* they've seen a number of candidates who — in terms of skills — are equally qualified. We will assume you are among those. But the problem the employer faces is *trying to decide who stands out, on other grounds.* How do you think they decide that? On what grounds do they give the nod to one person over seventeen others, equally qualified? The answer will vary from employer to employer, but most often, according to a survey we did, this is how the employer chooses you over other candidates, equally qualified:

1) I would ask myself, does this prospective employee *fit in* with the people who are already here? Does this person share compatible perspectives, exhibit integrity, manifest a desire to work as part of a team, and have similar values and sense of humor?

(2) I would ask myself, does this prospective employee give the feeling of great *enthusiasm for this particular job?* How much does he or she seem to *want* it?

(3) I would ask myself, does this prospective employee have an *appearance* that I like? This is an intangible thing, and I can't define it, but it has to do with my intuition about the person, their face, the way they dress, and how reliable or stable I feel them to be, beneath all the externals. I look for a quiet self-confidence.

(4) I would ask myself, does this prospective employee give me the feeling that he or she would give that *extra boost of energy* to their work that I like to see, rather than just trying "to get by." I think this is dependent on how much the prospective employee truly has their own individual goals, toward which they are striving.

(5) Finally, I would ask myself, does this prospective employee seem to have a genuine *enthusiasm for our organization* and what it is trying to do? Does he or she seem to like its goals, appreciate its style, and want to work for its success?

If you get chosen, it will probably be because you *stood out* from the other applicants, in these five areas. Therefore, in your thank you note, and in your written proposal, *anything* you can point to that demonstrates you stand out in these arenas, will be very much in your favor: particularly, your enthusiasm for that place and for that job.

WHEN YOU GET INVITED BACK

Assuming things are going favorably, you will be invited back for another interview, or interviews. If you still like them, and they increasingly like you, an offer will be made. *That's* the time to deal with the fourth question that has got to be on the employer's mind:

"How much are you going to cost me?" As I said earlier, if this matter gets raised before you have each decided you want to work together, turn the question gently aside. If the employer says, "How much salary are you looking for?" early on in the game, you can respond with gentleness and grace: "I think that's a fair question once we have both decided that this is where I should be working. First, however, there are other areas we need to explore."

But if you have explored those areas, and are agreeing 'to go steady', *then* the subject of "how much are you going to cost me?" is not only legitimately raised. It is crucial that it be raised. "The laborer is worthy of his (or her) hire," says the Scriptures. Which, roughly translated, means: "You are entitled to get what you are worth, and not a penny less."

Unhappily, you and the employer are likely at this point to be at odds with each other. Your would-be employer is interested in saving money as much as possible — therefore, in getting you for as little as possible. So you must negotiate.

There are exceptions, to be sure. Times when the employer offers you so much more than you were expecting, that your jaw drops open. This happens, but don't count on it.

Count rather on the fact that you will need to do some negotiation. Salary negotiation it is technically called, as you probably know. And few of us are born knowing how to go about this. We need some instruction in the technique. So, here is that instruction:

SALARY NEGOTIATION

A woman was once describing her very first job to me. It was at a soda fountain. I asked her what her biggest surprise at that job was. "My first paycheck," she said. I know it sounds incredible, but I was so green at all this, that during the whole interview for the job it never occurred to me to ask what my salary would be. I just took it for granted that it would be a fair and just salary, for the work that I would be doing. Did I ever get a shock, when my first paycheck came! It was so small, I could hardly believe it. Did I ever learn a lesson from that!" Yes, and so may we all.

AT ITS SIMPLEST LEVEL

To speak of salary negotiation is to speak of a matter which can be conducted on several levels. The simplest kind — as the above story reminds us — involves remembering to ask during the job-hiring interview what the salary will be. And then stating whether, for you, that amount is satisfactory or not. *That* much negotiation, everyone who is hunting for a job must be prepared to do.

© Copyright, 1980. *Saturday Review*, April 12, 1980.
Used by special permission.

"Let's talk salary. How does 'astronomical' sound to you?"

It is well to recognize that you are at a disadvantage if salary negotiation is approached on this simplest level, however. A figure may be named, and you are totally unprepared to say whether this is a fair salary for that particular job, or not. You just don't know.

AT ITS NEXT HIGHEST LEVEL

Hence, you may prefer to do a little research ahead of time. The books which will prove useful to you are listed in section 24 of Appendix B, on page 299. Try to find these, first of all, in your local library.

• If it's a non-supervisory job you are interested in, you can find out a 'ballpark figure' for that industry, by having your library unearth for you the latest monthly issue of the U.S. Department of Labor's *Employment and Earnings*.

If it's a manager's or supervisory job you are interested in, you will find many of the books listed in our previous chapter will unearth the information you want. For those graduating from college, some of this information is to be found in the "Salary Surveys" put out by the College Placement Council, from Bethlehem, Pennsylvania. See your library, or the career counseling/placement office of a nearby college.

• *The Occupational Outlook Handbook* will also give you ballpark figures for a selected list of jobs. The job you are interested in *may* be included.

In all dealings with this kind of information, you must keep in mind that there are often *serious* variations in salary from region to region. I haven't seen a good example lately, but this chart some years ago made a profound impression on me, so I will reproduce it here to give you an idea of the *kind* of thing that happens within *all* occupations.

AVERAGE WEEKLY EARNINGS
OF LEAD DRAFTSMEN

		REGION	
$ 295.00	Detroit, Michigan		
226.00	Dayton, Ohio	$213.50	North Central
215.50	Chicago, Illinois	202.00	Northeast
206.00	Houston, Texas	199.00	West
193.00	Seattle, Washington	192.00	South
189.50	Columbus, Ohio	204.00	United States
175.00	Salt Lake City, Utah		
173.00	Scranton, Pennsylvania	These figures are now outdated
172.50	Raleigh, North Carolina	but they show *comparative*
162.50	Little Rock, Arkansas	differences at least.

Such regional differences in salary reflect, of course, a variety of factors, such as differences in cost of living, differences in supply and demand, etc.

If your librarian simply cannot find for you, or help you find the salary information that you want, remember that almost every occupation has its own association or professional group, whose business it is to keep tabs on what is happening salarywise within that occupation or field. To learn the association or professional group for the field or occupation you are interested in, consult the *Encyclopedia of Associations, Vol. 1,* at your library.

WHAT DO THEY PAY?

Here are average annual salaries for selected jobs, paid in 1984 for persons in the following occupations. Unless otherwise specified, the figure is the national average for all workers.

Less than $20,000

Senior key entry operator $12,500
Bank assistant branch manager $18,000
Waiter/waitress (Las Vegas) $14,000–$17,000
Armed security guard $17,297
File clerk $10,712
College bookstore director $19,913
Police "911 Line" operator, NY $13,180
Radio news reporter $13,000
Licensed practical nurse (Washington State) $12,360
Manufacturing production worker $18,886

Secretary (high school grad) $16,000
Turkey cleaner (East) $11,270
Messenger $11,230
Typist $13,041
Roman Catholic nun (East) $6,000 + housing
Minor pro league basketball player $15,000
Accounting clerk $16,077
Correctional officer (Washington State) $17,232
Typing pool supervisor (Minnesota) $16,476
Grocery produce clerk $10,100

$20,000 to $29,000

Airline flight attendant $27,000
Bank cashier $28,000–$38,000
Federal government (all jobs) $25,354
Fire fighter $24,000
Data processing specialist $22,500
Cook (Las Vegas) $20,000–$25,000
Word processing manager $22,400
Buyer, 2-4 yrs. exp. $27,600
Association exhibits manager $28,200
Accountant, 5-8 yrs. exp. $26,500
College assistant professor $22,000
Auditor $29,005

Technical recruiter $24,300–$35,900
Registered nurse (Minnesota) $20,672
Bank branch manager $27,500
Postal service worker $23,058
Secretary (Bachelor's degree) $20,000
Publications editor, 5+ yrs. exp. $29,400
Radio news director $24,000
Painter (Minnesota) $20,484
Recruiter, managerial employees $26,460
State & local government–all employees $21,000
Vocational ed. teacher (Minnesota) $27,120

$30,000 to $49,999

Agricultural engineer $38,740
Electrical engineer $42,290
Captain, US Army $30,400
College professor $33,000
Personnel director $47,745
Senior computer systems analyst $33,000
Bank real estate lending officer $41,200
Steel mill production worker $45,023
Market research manager. $44,664

Nuclear engineer $47,640
State geological survey director $43,900
Plant manager $41,900
Recruitment manager $37,000–$42,400
Sanitary engineer $39,000
TV news director $31,200
EDP operations manager $36,500
Lawyer $49,022

$50,000 and over

Public accounting firm partner $64,500
Petroleum engineer $51,000
Judge (Cleveland) $57,000
Airline captain $95,000
Dean, engineering college $55,824
Federal civil service (top salary) $68,700
Vice-president, marketing $63,000
Investment banker $200,000

Association, top exec. (Washington) $98,500
Physician (East) $97,700
College president, large school $70,000 plus $37,000 benefits
Major league baseball player $289,194
US Cabinet officer $86,200
Chief justice, US Supreme Court $104,700

Sources: Association salary studies, *National Business Employment Weekly,* Scientific Manpower Commission, Abbott Langer and Associates, and many others. Minichart prepared by the *Career Opportunities News,* Garrett Park Press, Garrett Park, Maryland 20896. Used by permission.

In addition to the fact that salaries vary from region to region, you will want to remember that even within regions, the figure for the *average* salary there is an average among a wide range of possible salaries, as the chart on the opposite page clearly shows.

MORE SOPHISTICATED YET

Some job-hunters may want to get beyond these "ballpark figures" into more detailed salary negotiation. You may want to walk in on an interview knowing exactly what That Place pays for a job. Why? Well, for one thing, it may be too low for you — and thus you are saved the necessity of wasting your precious time on that particular place. Secondly, and more importantly, many places have — as John Crystal has so insistently pointed out — a *range* in mind. And if you know what that range is, you can negotiate for a salary that is nearer the *top* of the range, than the *bottom*.

By way of example, let's assume you did all your homework, as outlined in the previous two chapters. Let's assume you have also taken great care in filling out *The Quick Job-Hunting Map*, in Appendix A at the back of this book. You have done your research, going out and knocking on doors, as well as visiting libraries. And you have gotten your search down to three or five places that really interest you. You know in general what sort of position you are aiming at, in those particular places — and you are ready to go visit them in The Interview for Hiring — *as soon as you know what the salary range is that they probably have in mind for the position that interests you* (whether that position already exists, or is one you are going to ask them to create). How do you find out what the salary is, or should be, by way of range?

It's relatively easy to define. The rule of thumb is that you will, generally speaking, be paid more than the person who is below you on the organizational chart, and less than the person who is above you. There are — needless to say — exceptions to this rule: people who don't quite fit in the organizational chart, such as researchers financed by a grant, or consultants. But In General, the Rule of Thumb is true.

This makes the matter of salary *research* which precedes salary negotiation relatively (I said "relatively") simple. If through

EARNINGS WITHIN OCCUPATIONS VARY WIDELY

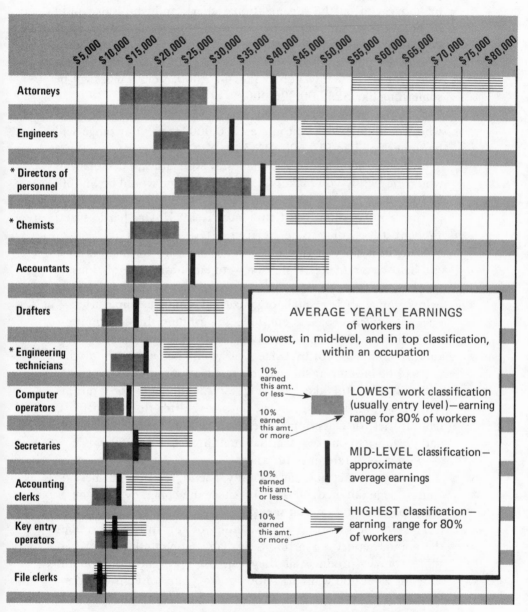

* Top earnings in these occupations are understated because an additional higher work level was surveyed but the data obtained were insufficient to warrant publication.
Source: Based upon data contained in a Bureau of Labor Statistics bulletin, *National Survey of Professional Administrative, Technical, and Clerical Pay, March 1981.*
A summary of this survey appears in BLS press release 81-326, "White-Collar Salaries, March 1981," June 26, 1981. (*Occupational Outlook Quarterly*, Fall 1981)

your own information search you can discover who is or would be above you on the organizational chart, and who is or would be below you, and what they are paid, you would know what your salary range is, or would be.

a) If the person above you makes $27,000, and the person who would be below you makes $22,000, your range will be something like $23,000-$26,000.

b) If the person above you makes $13,500, and the person who would be below you makes $10,000, then your range will be something like $10,500-$12,500.

c) If the person above you makes $7800, and the person who would be below you makes $6240, your range would be $6400-$7600.

That's not so hard to figure out, is it? Not as hard as you thought it was going to be, at any rate!

Now, how do you find out what those who would be above and below you, make? Well, first — to emphasize the obvious — you have to find out the *names* of those who would be above or below you. If it is a small organization you are going after — one with twenty or less employees — finding this information out will be duck soup. Since two-thirds of all new jobs are created by companies of that size, you would be *wise beyond your years* to be looking at such sized organizations, anyway.

But if you still like "the Big Guys," the large corporations with row upon row of cubicles, and floor after floor of offices, laboratories, or classrooms, then you need to resort with mercy and pleading to our two familiar standbys:

your local reference librarian

every contact you have (family, friend, relative, business or church acquaintance) who might know the company, and therefore, the information you seek.

You will be surprised at how much of this information *is* in the annual report, or in books available at your library. When those sources produce all they can for you, and you are still short of what you want to know, go to your contacts. You are looking for Someone Who Knows Someone who either is working, or has worked, at that particular place or organization that interests you.

If you absolutely run into a blank wall on that particular organization (everyone who works there is pledged to secrecy, and they have shipped all their ex-employees to Siberia), then seek

© Copyright, 1980. Universal Press Syndicate.
All rights reserved. Used by special permission.

out information on their nearest *competitor* in the same geographic area (e.g., if Bank of America is inscrutable, try Wells Fargo as your research base; or vice-versa).

You will be surprised at how often perseverance and legwork pay off, in this. And if your enthusiasm flags along the way, just picture yourself sitting in the interview for hiring, and now you're at the end of the interview. The prospective employer likes you, you like them, and they say: "How much salary were you expecting?" Because you have done your homework, and you know the range, you can name a figure near or at the *top* of the *range* — based on your anticipated performance in that job: i.e., "Superior."

But suppose you *didn't* do your research. Then you're Shadow-Boxing in the Dark — as they say. If you name a figure way too high, you're out of the running — and you can't backtrack, in most cases. ("Sorry, we'd like to hire you, but we just can't afford you.") If you name a figure way too low, you're also out of the running. ("Sorry, but we were hoping for someone a little more, ah, professional.") And if you're in the right range, but at the bottom of it, you've just gotten the job — *but needlessly lost as much as $2,000 a year that could have been yours.*

So, salary research/salary negotiation — no matter how much time it takes — pays off handsomely. Let's say it takes you a week to ten days to run down this sort of information on the three or four organizations that interest you. And let us say that because you've done this research, when you finally go in for the hiring interview you are able to ask for and obtain a salary that is $2,000 higher in range, than you would otherwise have known enough to ask for. In just three years, you'll have earned $6,000 extra, because of that research. Not bad pay, for ten days' work!

AT ITS MOST SOPHISTICATED LEVEL

Job-hunters with incredibly-developed bargaining needs, always ask how salary negotiation is conducted at the most sophisticated level. It is my personal conviction that Most Job-Hunters will not operate at this level, and therefore do not need this sort of information. But in case you do, or in case you are simply dying out of curiosity, it is completely described in *Where Do I Go From Here With My Life?* pages 140-142. As honed to a fine point by John Crystal, the most sophisticated salary negotiation goes like this:

You do all the steps described previously, so that you discover what the employer's range would likely be. Let us say it turns out that the range is one that varies two thousand dollars. You then "invent" a new range, for yourself, that "hooks" on the old one, in the following fashion:

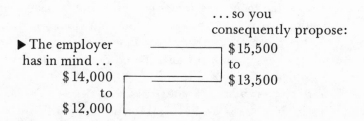

▶ The employer has in mind ...
$ 14,000
to
$ 12,000

... so you consequently propose:
$ 15,500
to
$ 13,500

And when the employer says, "What kind of a salary did you have in mind?" you respond, "I believe my productivity is such that it would justify a salary in the range of $13,500 to $15,500." This keeps you, at a minimum, near the top of their range; and, at a maximum, challenges them to go beyond the top that they had in mind, either immediately — or in terms of future raises. (Don't be afraid to ask "When?")

FRINGES

In your salary negotiation, do not forget to pay attention to so-called "fringe benefits." Such 'fringes' as life insurance, health benefits or plans, vacation or holiday plans, and retirement programs add up to 25% of many manufacturing workers' salary. E.g., if an employee receives $800 salary per month, the fringe benefits are worth another $200 per month. So, if the employee who is beneath you on the organizational chart gets $700 plus benefits, and the employee who is above you gets $1100 plus benefits, while you are offered $800 and no benefits, you are being obtained more cheaply than you had supposed. Do ask for similar benefits to those above and below you. OR, if no benefits are offered, ask for a higher salary — $1000, in this case — in order to make up.

FINALLY, THE MATTER OF A RAISE
AND OR PROMOTION

If during your salary negotiations you deal only with your initial position and salary, you will have been very shortsighted. Your initial "good salary" will annually decline in value, as inflation takes its toll. In 75 out of the last 100 years, the cost of living increased.

The urgency of protecting your initial salary against erosion, is further compounded for women by the fact that so many of you *start out* at too low a salary. You need raises and promotions even more, since the average woman would need pay raises of 70% just to bring her up to the level of a similarly qualified man.

So, you need something from this employer: some kind of assurance or guarantee that, if you do superior work, there will be raises and on some kind of a timetable. You need this, and *now* is the best time to get it. Your bargaining power inevitably diminishes once they've 'got you.'

Therefore, this question should be a part of your salary negotiation without fail: "If I accomplish this job to your satisfaction, as I fully expect to — and more — when could I expect to have my salary raised, and to what degree? Would there be a promotion in this job, and if so, on what kind of timetable?" If you have certain desires in this area, you may or may not wish to mention them at this point. But none of this discussion, as I

have repeatedly said, should take place until they have made
you a firm offer and said in no uncertain terms: "We want you."

Once this part of the salary negotiation is concluded, to your
satisfaction, do ask to have it included in any letter of agreement or employment contract that they may be sending you. It
may be you cannot get it in writing, but *do try*! The Road to
Hell is paved with Promises that went unwritten. Too many executives conveniently "forget" what they told you. Too many
executives leave the company for another position and place.
And their successor or the one over you all may disown any unwritten promises: "I don't know what caused them to say that
to you, but they clearly exceeded their authority, and of course
we can't be held to that."

Raises and promotions are something you may have to continually justify, not just during the hiring interview, but
throughout your time of work there. You will be amazed sometimes at how little attention your superiors pay to your noteworthy accomplishments. Noteworthy they may be, but no one
is taking notes. They're too absorbed with their own problems.
Accordingly, career experts such as Bernard Haldane have suggested that you should keep a weekly diary of your accomplishments, once you are on the job. Take time each Sunday to
chronicle what you accomplished that past week, or helped others to accomplish, if you were part of a team effort. That way,
when the yearly anniversary of your being hired comes around,
you can read through the diary, make up a one page summary
of its contents, and take that summary in with you when you
discuss why you deserve a raise.

SUMMARY

If you have done the *Quick Job-Hunting Map* in Appendix A,
and followed the rules for researching companies found in the
previous chapter, you will have mastered the techniques used
most often by job-hunters who wanted to find their ideal job or
new career, and succeeded.

Remember, in Candide's world it may be otherwise; but in
this world it remains true:

> The person who gets hired is not necessarily the
> one who can do that job best; but, the one who
> *knows the most about how to get hired.*

POSTSCRIPT –
DOES THIS CREATIVE METHOD
OF THE JOB-HUNT
ALWAYS WORK?

Ah, dear reader, how I wish I could assure you that it does. It would be nice if there were magic in our life. The desire to see Merlin, and unicorns, and trees that talk, lives in the child in us all.

But there is no magic in the job-hunt. There is no formula which, if you follow it scrupulously, will lead irresistibly to your finding a job. Or *the* job.

The picture of the job-hunt remains as we saw it earlier:

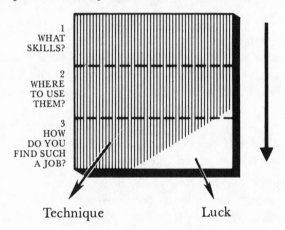

WHEN you are down in this "How" part of the process, technique – such as we have described in this chapter – is terribly important. But so is *luck*. The best technique on your part will not get you a job, if luck is not also on your side. By luck, I mean that accidental meeting with *just* the right person, to open a door for you that leads to a job.

The 'numbers game' is almost *all* luck. What this alternative method of the job-hunt does, is to try to reduce the importance of luck. But it can never eliminate its place in the job-hunt, entirely.

Follow every instruction in this book *precisely,* do every exercise *slavishly,* follow every prescription *religiously,* you still may not find the job you are looking for. Or at least not right away. Over and above everything else, *luck* must be on your side if you are to find a job.

But, we know several things about luck. We know that:

(1) *Luck favors the prepared mind.* If you've done all the homework on yourself, diligently identified your favorite skills, and *in order.* If you've gotten a pretty complete picture of the kind of job you are looking for, *you will be more sensitive and alert to luck, when it crosses your path.*

(2) *Luck favors the person who is working the hardest at the job-hunt.* In a word, the person who is devoting the most hours to getting out there and pounding the pavement, doing their research, making contacts. Luck favors the person who is putting in thirty-four hours a week on their job-hunt much more than it favors the person who is putting in five hours a week.

(3) *Luck favors the person who has told the most people clearly and precisely what he or she is looking for.* The more ears and eyes you have out there, looking on your behalf for the kind of job you want, the more likely that you will 'get lucky.' Forty eyes and ears are 'luckier' than two. Eighty, a hundred and twenty, are 'luckier' still. But before you get 'this lucky', you *must* have done your homework so carefully that you can *tell* those other eyes and ears just exactly what it is you want. Luck does *not* favor the vague.

(4) *Luck favors the person who has alternatives up his or her sleeve,* and doesn't just *bull-headedly* persist in following one method, or going after one place, or one kind of job.

(5) *Luck favors the person who WANTS WITH ALL THEIR HEART to find that job.* The ambivalent job-hunter, who is looking half-heartedly, for a job that inspires no enthusiasm in them, is rarely so 'lucky.'

(6) *Luck favors the person who is going after their dream —the thing they really want to do the most in this world.* When you want something so much that it brings tears to your eyes at the thought of getting it, you will always be 'luckier' than the person who is *settling* for 'what's realistic.'

(7) *Luck favors the person who is trying hard to be 'a special kind of person' in this world, treating others with grace and dignity and courtesy and kindness.* The person who runs rough-shod over others in their race to 'get ahead', usually is not so 'lucky.' During the job-hunt you need 'favors' from others. If you treated them cavalierly in another day and age, now is their

time to say, "Sure, I'll help you out," and then do nothing. Getting even is more popular than forgiveness, when there is a score to be settled.

So, if you would have 'luck' on your side during this phase of the job-hunt, *do* take seriously the above *ways of improving your luck.*

I am glad to have been able to hold your hand through this process. I wish you a successful job-hunt. I wish you perseverance in the hard work and time that a successful job-hunt requires. I wish you good luck.

WHAT IS SUCCESS?

To laugh often and much;

To win the respect of intelligent people
and the affection of children;

To earn the appreciation of honest critics and
endure the betrayal of false friends;

To appreciate beauty;

To find the best in others;

To leave the world a bit better, whether by
a healthy child, a garden
patch or a redeemed social condition;

To know even one life has breathed
easier because you have lived;

This is to have succeeded.

—Ralph Waldo Emerson

Appendix A

The New Quick Job-Hunting Map

A fast way to help

by Richard Nelson Bolles

Advanced Version

For information on The Beginning Version see bottom of page 271.

© Copyright 1985 by Richard Nelson Bolles

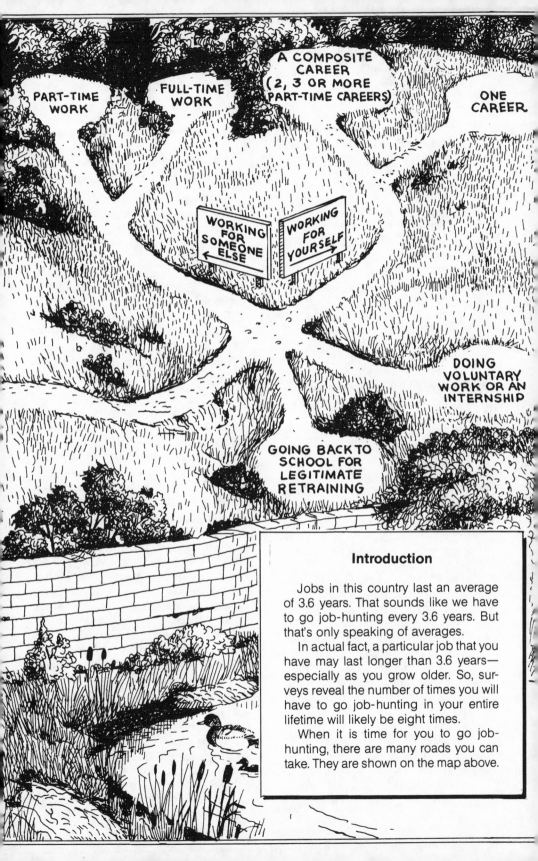

PART-TIME WORK

FULL-TIME WORK

A COMPOSITE CAREER (2, 3 OR MORE PART-TIME CAREERS)

ONE CAREER

WORKING FOR SOMEONE ELSE

WORKING FOR YOURSELF

DOING VOLUNTARY WORK OR AN INTERNSHIP

GOING BACK TO SCHOOL FOR LEGITIMATE RETRAINING

Introduction

Jobs in this country last an average of 3.6 years. That sounds like we have to go job-hunting every 3.6 years. But that's only speaking of averages.

In actual fact, a particular job that you have may last longer than 3.6 years—especially as you grow older. So, surveys reveal the number of times you will have to go job-hunting in your entire lifetime will likely be eight times.

When it is time for you to go job-hunting, there are many roads you can take. They are shown on the map above.

TO PUT THE MAP INTO WORDS

These are the choices facing You:

(1) ☐ Should I make a career change? OR
☐ Should I stay in the same field/career?

(2) If I choose to stay in the same field/career:
☐ Should I move to a different organization, though staying in the same type of job? OR
☐ Should I stay in the same organization where I am now?

(3) If the same organization:
☐ Should I stay in the very same job as I am now in? OR
☐ Should I move to a different department or different job there?

(4) If I make a career change:
☐ Should I change careers by going back to school for retraining? OR
☐ Should I change careers without going back to school?

(5) If I change careers without further schooling:
☐ Should I look for a new career in which I work for someone else? OR
☐ Should I look for a new career in which I work for myself?

(6) If I look for a new career in which I work for someone else:
☐ Should I seek a job at decent or even high pay? OR
☐ Should I seek for a volunteer job at first, or even an internship?

(7) If I look for a new career in which I work for myself:
☐ Should I seek a career made up of just one job? OR
☐ Should I seek a composite career, made up of several (2-5) different jobs/careers?

(8) And, once I have answered all the above questions, *what* is it I should do?

You need to work your way through these decisions. It may at first sight seem to you that each pair of decisions requires a different pathway. This is not true.

They are all approached by the same pathway—a basic "trunk" road that precedes them all.

This "trunk" road has three sections to it, and you MUST travel all three sections—no matter which road through Job Land you are currently leaning toward. The three sections you MUST cover, are:

1. **WHAT.** This has to do with your skills. You need to inventory and identify what skills you have that you most enjoy using. These are called transferable skills, because they are transferable to any field/career that you choose, regardless of where you first picked them up.

2. **WHERE.** This has to do with jobs as environments. Think of yourself as a flower. You know that a flower which blooms in the desert will not do well at 10,000 feet up—and vice versa. Every flower has an environment where it does best. So with you. You are like a flower. You need to decide where you want to use your skills, where you would thrive, and do your most effective work.

3. **HOW.** You need to decide how to get where you want to go. This has to do with finding out the names of the jobs you would be most interested in, AND the names of organizations (in your preferred geographical area) which have such jobs to offer, AND the names of the people or person there who actually has the power to hire you.

And, how you can best approach that person to show him or her how your skills can help them with their problems. How, if you were hired there, you would not be part of the problem, but part of the solution.

Now, to be sure, these three basic sections of your job-hunting or career-changing road will be traveled in a slightly different way, depending on your goals. If you ultimately become sure that you want to go into business for yourself, then the HOW will consist in identifying all the people who have already done something like the thing you are thinking of, so that you can go interview them and profit from their learnings and mistakes before you set out on your own. And the HOW may consist in identifying the potential customers or clients who would use your services or buy your product.

But, adaptation aside, you WILL need to travel all three sections of this basic trunk road, regardless of where you plan to end up. The only exception to this rule, is if you plan on staying at the same job and in the same organization where you presently are; and you are using this Map only to get a better picture of your strengths. In this case, you will omit the HOW picture—but will still need to travel the WHAT and WHERE sections of the road. For even if

you plan on remaining where you are—as it is already the "ideal" job for you—you will still function much better there if you know more intimately what your skills or strengths are, and where you like to use them.

(As one satisfied worker put it, "The skills inventory is something I do every two or three years. Each time I do it, I find out more specific things about what I do well. This information tells me what to watch for in the world—what kind of tasks I can volunteer for and do very well at. I know more about the *kind* of thing I want to be, do, be surrounded by. I am now sensitized and ready to recognize them when they swim by.")

THE RULE:
TAKE NO SHORTCUTS

Aside from this special case of staying right where you are, you WILL need to travel all three sections of the road, WHAT, WHERE and HOW.

If you only do the homework on the WHAT, you will be like a cart without any horse to pull it. It just stands helplessly beside the road.

"WHAT" furnishes you with the cart; "WHERE" furnishes the horse to pull it; and "HOW" furnishes the road along which your cart and horse travel, to your chosen destination.

Handicaps

Most of us think that when we go job-hunting, we need a special road, just for us. You probably think you have some special handicap in the job-hunt, that requires special handling. Here is a list of some of these handicaps—an expansion of a list originally put together by Daniel Porot, the job-hunting expert of Europe.

You may check off the ones which apply to you:

☐ I am just graduating
☐ I just graduated
☐ I graduated too long ago
☐ I am a woman
☐ I am a self-made man
☐ I am too young
☐ I am too old
☐ I have a prison record
☐ I have a psychiatric history
☐ I have never held a job before
☐ I have only had one employer
☐ I am a foreigner
☐ I have not had enough education
☐ I have had too much education
☐ I am too much of a generalist
☐ I am too much of a specialist
☐ I am a clergyperson
☐ I am Hispanic
☐ I am Black
☐ I am just coming out of the military
☐ I have a physical handicap
☐ I have a mental handicap
☐ I have only worked for large employers
☐ I have only worked for small employers
☐ I am too shy
☐ I am too assertive
☐ I come from a very different kind of background
☐ I come from another industry
☐ I come from another planet

If you checked off any of these, this makes you a handicapped job-hunter or career-changer. Most of us are so handicapped. The true meaning of the above comprehensive list is that there are about three weeks of your life when you're employable. That is, if handicaps cannot be overcome.

But of course they can be overcome. There are, after all, two kinds of employers (or clients or customers) out there:

those who will be put off by your handicap, and therefore won't hire you; AND

those who are NOT put off by your handicap, and therefore will hire you if you are qualified for the job.

You are not interested in the former kind of employer, client or customer. No matter how many of them there are. You are only looking for those employers who are NOT put off by your handicap, and therefore will hire you if you are qualified for the job.

As Tom Jackson, author of *Guerilla Tactics in the Job Market,* has well observed, the job-hunting process may best be described as NO NO NO NO NO NO NO NO NO NO NO NO NO NO NO NO NO NO NO NO NO NO NO NO NO NO NO NO NO NO NO NO NO NO NO NO NO NO NO NO NO NO NO NO NO NO NO NO NO NO NO NO NO NO NO NO NO NO NO NO NO NO NO NO NO NO NO NO NO NO NO NO NO NO NO NO NO NO NO NO NO NO NO NO NO NO NO YES.

It only takes one YES from the organization you wish most to work for, to get you the job. Every "No" that you get out of the way, as you go, will bring you that much closer to the only YES you need to hear.

The most important thing for you to know is that your best chance of bridging whatever handicap you have or think you have is CAREFUL PREPARATION ON YOUR PART.

The employers, clients, customers who will not care about your handicap will be most impressed if you approach them, not as a job-beggar, but as a resource person. Preparation such as this Map will change you from a job-beggar into A Resource Person.

In this sense, the trunk road, about which we have been talking,—the WHAT, WHERE, and HOW—is a bridge over whatever handicap you may have.

What It Takes
To Find A Job

What will it take for you to successfully get over that bridge? What will it take for you to do the WHAT, WHERE and HOW most effectively?

You want, of course, to hear that the answer is a bunch of sure-fire techniques, which we are about to teach you in this Map.

Alas, there are no techniques which will *guarantee* that you will find a job, if only you follow them faithfully.

Any true job-hunting veteran will tell you in all honesty that it takes three things to find a job:

a. Techniques. There are things others can teach you, and they will increase your effectiveness and improve your chances. You need to take these very seriously. But, by themselves, these are not enough.

b. Art. As in the phrase: "There's a real art to the way she does that." We refer here to the special stamp that each person's individuality puts on what they do. A certain amount of the job-hunt others cannot teach you. You bring your own unique art to the job-hunt, as you do to everything else you do. It's that extra pizazz, enthusiasm, energy that is uniquely yours, which must be present, before you can be successful at the job-hunt. We cannot clone you. Genuine individuality always marks every successful job-hunt.

c. Luck. Following certain techniques faithfully, and combining them with your own individual art in the way you do it, will not in and of themselves get you the job. There is always a certain amount of luck involved in any successful job-hunt. You have to be the right person in the right place at the right time.

These factors have varying importance, depending on which part of the job-hunt you are dealing with.

Your own individual way of doing things, your "art," is most important during the WHAT. This is because skill identification is more of an art, than a science. We can give you the basic rules, but a lot of it you have to do in your own individual way.

Techniques become more important during the WHERE and the HOW: those parts of the job-hunt can more easily be defined.

And Luck becomes most important during the HOW part of your job-hunt. So, if you like diagrams, your job-hunt will come out looking something like this:

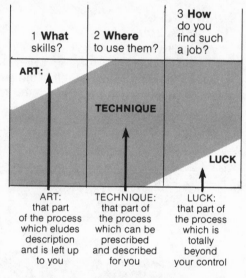

1 **What** skills?	2 **Where** to use them?	3 **How** do you find such a job?
ART: that part of the process which eludes description and is left up to you	TECHNIQUE: that part of the process which can be prescribed and described for you	LUCK: that part of the process which is totally beyond your control

What Can This Map Give You?

Obviously, this Map cannot give you good luck, or give you individuality. You must already possess that individuality, and you must have lady luck smile on you, for your job-hunt to succeed. BUT, by using the techniques in this Map and in the accompanying text book, *What Color Is Your Parachute?*, the amount of luck you will need is greatly reduced. "Luck favors the prepared mind," as someone has observed. This Map, if followed faithfully, WILL give you a thoroughly prepared mind.

Now, on to the details of the trunk road to Job Land, the bridge over handicaps: WHAT, WHERE and HOW.

What

What Skills You Have and Most Enjoy Using

The easiest way to get into the subject of your skills is to just dive in. Imagine, if you will, that this diagram below is the aerial view of a room in which a Party is taking place (the view is taken from the next floor up). At this Party, for some unknown reason, people with similar interests or skills have gathered together with one another, in the same corner of the room. As there are basically six such groups, it is fortunate the room has six corners:

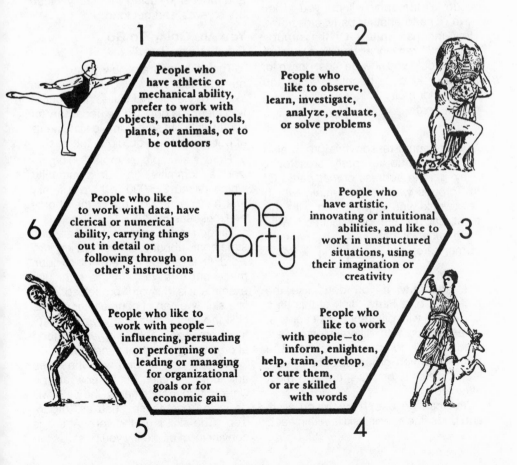

1 People who have athletic or mechanical ability, prefer to work with objects, machines, tools, plants, or animals, or to be outdoors

2 People who like to observe, learn, investigate, analyze, evaluate, or solve problems

6 People who like to work with data, have clerical or numerical ability, carrying things out in detail or following through on other's instructions

The Party

3 People who have artistic, innovating or intuitional abilities, and like to work in unstructured situations, using their imagination or creativity

5 People who like to work with people — influencing, persuading or performing or leading or managing for organizational goals or for economic gain

4 People who like to work with people — to inform, enlighten, help, train, develop, or cure them, or are skilled with words

It is a party that is to go on, all through the night. You are told that you must choose to be with one of the groups in one of the corners of the room.

a) Which corner of the room would you instinctively be drawn to, as "your kind of people"—whom you would most *enjoy* being with, for the longest time? Leave aside any question of shyness; maybe they will do all the talking, and you can just listen, with rapt attention. Write the *number* for that corner here: [4]

b) Suppose for some reason *that* group left the party, without you. (They have gone to another party, crosstown. How inconsiderate!) Of the groups which *still remain* at *this* Party, which group would you *now* be most drawn to, as "your kind of people"? Write the *number* for their corner here: [5]

c) For some reason, this group also leaves for another party crosstown. (Hey, get the address of *that* party.) Of the groups which now remain, which one would you enjoy being with the most, and for the longest time? Write the *number* of that corner here: [3]

Incidentally, if you don't like the metaphor of a Party, think of this as a bookstore, with different book sections; or a job fair, with different employers ready to talk to you, or whatever. The issue is: which group of people, subjects, interests, or skills, are you most attracted to?

You can go back now, if you wish, and underline specific skills within each

of your favorite three groups, that are the skills you like the very best.

There, you have done what we call "elementary skill identification"—and in less than three minutes. This was just to give you a quick "feel" for the exercise. The principle on which this exercise was based, is that *we are instinctively attracted to people who are doing what we would like to do. And we would like to do those things which we already do well, and enjoy.*

That's all.

Now that you've taken your first step on the bridge of WHAT skills you have and most enjoy using, let's really roll up our sleeves, and get to work.

You Are Going To Go On A 'Verb Hunt'

The skills you are now going to go hunting for, are called "transferable skills" or "functional skills." In order to find them, it is going to be necessary for you to write out some simple statements about something you did in the past.

Here is a simple example: "(I) *organized* a committee in our community, which raised $15,000 to help a family that had been burnt out of their home on Christmas Eve."

Hidden in that statement, and all such statements about your past, is a key *skill* word. It is always a verb, or a noun made out of a verb. In this particular example, it is the word "organized." That is a skill. We can of course later put the skill in various forms: *organized,* effectively *organizes,* able *to organize,* good at *organizing,* or adept at *organization.*

We can play around with the tense and form of it, later. But for now, as you write out your statements, the verb will be in the past tense, such as "organized." The skill is in the verb. And it is convincing. For, clearly you possess the

skill, since you have already demonstrated you do.

Notice that in the above example the word "I" is in parentheses. It's fine where it is, in this statement about the past. But when it comes time for you to polish and shine your skill identifications later, you will then want to wipe out the "I." It is normally *omitted* in any final definition of your skill, such as a letter or resume or 'qualifications brief.' You will be listing a number of skills at that time, and the word "I" in front of each one is totally unnecessary. After all, if it's your statement, we know who did it. You won't need to keep telling us "I."

In skill identification, first and last, it is not the noun but the *verb* that is important. That is why you may think of this part of your job-hunt—the WHAT phase —as essentially "a verb hunt."

You Need Some Stories— Seven, To Be Exact

We can't just go hunting for *verbs* by themselves. Though, you can always try that approach. You will almost certainly discover, however, that the verbs are best found in stories. So, you need to write out some stories about your past. Ultimately, you are going to need seven such stories. These stories need to be:

1. *Brief.* A paragraph or two, at most.

2. *Experiences in which You are the chief actor or actress.* Telling us a story about something done *to* you, like being given an award or something, will NOT do. It must be something YOU did. Then it's all right if there's an award, at the end.

3. *Experiences in which You accomplished something.* There must have been:

a. Some kind of problem you needed to solve.

b. Some kind of action that you took, in order to solve it.

c. Some concrete results that could be seen, or even better, measured.

4. *Experiences in which you were truly enjoying yourself.* You can dredge up Skills from anything you have ever done, anyplace. *But* what you are looking for are the Skills you used *when you were enjoying yourself, accomplishing something.*

5. *Taken from any period of your life, and from any part of your life: work OR leisure OR learning.*

6. *Told step-by-step, in detail.*

You Need Seven Sheets Of Paper

For this exercise, you will eventually need seven blank sheets of notebook paper: one sheet for each story/job/ role.

But, you start out with just one sheet, for you begin by writing just one story.

Do that NOW, please.

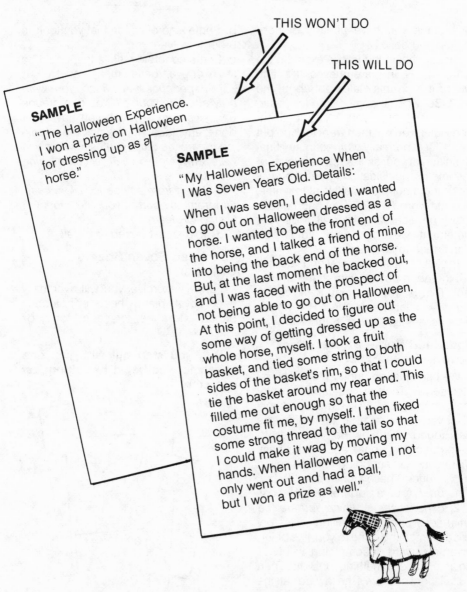

THIS WON'T DO

THIS WILL DO

SAMPLE

"The Halloween Experience.
I won a prize on Halloween
for dressing up as a
horse."

SAMPLE

"My Halloween Experience When
I Was Seven Years Old. Details:

When I was seven, I decided I wanted
to go out on Halloween dressed as a
horse. I wanted to be the front end of
the horse, and I talked a friend of mine
into being the back end of the horse.
But, at the last moment he backed out,
and I was faced with the prospect of
not being able to go out on Halloween.
At this point, I decided to figure out
some way of getting dressed up as the
whole horse, myself. I took a fruit
basket, and tied some string to both
sides of the basket's rim, so that I could
tie the basket around my rear end. This
filled me out enough so that the
costume fit me, by myself. I then fixed
some strong thread to the tail so that
I could make it wag by moving my
hands. When Halloween came I not
only went out and had a ball,
but I won a prize as well."

If you *absolutely* can't think of any experiences you've had where you enjoyed yourself, and accomplished something, then try this: Describe the seven most enjoyable *jobs* that you've had; or seven *roles* you've had so far in your life, such as: wife, mother, cook, homemaker, volunteer in the community, citizen, dressmaker, student, etc. Tell us something you did or accomplished, in each role.

Let us stop equating work with earning a living, but rather think of it as an important component of making a life.

—Ralph C. Weinrich, *Michigan Business Review*

You Need A List (Of Skills)

Once you have the story written, you will want to go back over it and identify the skills that you used in that story (in the doing of it, not the telling of it). Here we run into a problem. Not every verb is a skill. And sometimes the verb you want, is only implied in the story.

So, what are you do to? Try to name the skills, off the top of your head? Most of us have poor luck when we try to do this. We know what we did, but we run out of words to describe it. Therefore, sooner or later—usually sooner—we cry out for a list. We need a list. That's what this Map is here to give you.

You Need People, Or Data Or Things

How many skill verbs should be on the list? Well, the answer could be "thousands." After all, there are at least 12,000 different jobs in this world. There are 8,000 alternate titles for those 12,000 jobs. So, there are at least 20,000 different job titles you can choose from; and heaven only knows how many skills lie beneath those titles. *Too* many! We need some way to simplify the list. *Fortunately,* there is such a way.

All jobs deal with three things. And only three. So, ultimately all transferable skills deal with only three things, too.

Your skills are either:

skills with **People**, or

skills with **Information**,

sometimes called **Data**, or

skills with **Things**.

You have all three, in varying degrees. The question is, what are the particular skills that you have with each? *And,* which of these do you enjoy the most? That is what you now need to explore.

Basically there are only 13 things you can do with People (plus one additional group, for work with animals). And there are only 15 things you can do with Information, or Data. And there are only 11 things you can do with Things. Every other skill identification is a variation, or a sub-particle of these 40:

If you want some definitions of PEOPLE, INFORMATION/DATA, and THINGS, here goes:

• PEOPLE may mean all kinds of people, or very specific kinds of people—defined by age, culture, background, kinds of problems they face, etc. PEOPLE also includes animals, and beings from other orders of Reality.

• INFORMATION/DATA may mean information, knowledge, data, ideas, facts, figures, statistics, etc. Information is present in every job.

• THINGS may mean physical objects, instruments, tools, machinery, equipment, vehicles, materials, and desk-top items such as pencils, paper clips, telephones, stamps, etc.

14 Skills With People,
primarily, though they
also involve information
and things

/\

[14. Working With Animals]
13. Training
12. Counseling (holistic)
11. Advising, Consulting
10. Treating
9. Founding, Leading
8. Negotiating, Deciding
7. Managing, Supervising
6. Performing, Amusing
5. Persuading
4. Communicating
3. Sensing, Feeling
2. Serving
1. Taking Instructions

11 Skills With Things,
primarily, though they may
also involve information

/\

40. Repairing
39. Setting Up
38. Precision Working
37. Operating (vehicles)
36. Operating (equipment)
35. Using (tools)
34. Minding
33. Feeding, Emptying
32. Working With The Earth
     Or Nature
31. Being Athletic
30. Handling (objects)

● Using the first story we asked you to write,
above, you now need to run that story down the
list of *possible* skills with PEOPLE, INFORMA-
TION, and then THINGS. Since your possible
skills are in all three categories, the Road in this
Map now divides into three—
at least temporarily:

15 Skills With
Information or Data,
primarily, though they
also involve things

/\

29. Achieving
28. Expediting
27. Planning, Developing
26. Designing
25. Creating, Synthesizing
24. Improving, Adapting
23. Visualizing
22. Evaluating
21. Organizing
20. Analyzing
19. Researching
18. Computing
17. Copying, Storing
     & Retrieving
16. Comparing
15. Observing

- first, the road through skills with
  PEOPLE, and then
- the road through skills with
  INFORMATION/DATA, and then
- the road through skills with THINGS.

YOUR FUNCTIONAL/TRANSFERABLE SKILLS INVENTORY

I N S T R U C T I O N S

1. Get story. Take the story you have just written. It should be on a separate sheet of paper. Give the story some brief title.

2. Get list. Turn to the next page in this Map. You will see that the road flows by (on the left-hand side) a list of Skills you may have with People.

3. Read the list, one by one. Put your story's title at the bottom of the page where it says "#1." Then, read over the first People Skill, its definition, and all the skill verbs immediately under it.

4. Color in. If you feel that in the story in question you used that skill, or any of its variations, *color in* with pen or pencil the appropriate rectangle/square in column #1. For example:

1. TAKING INSTRUCTIONS		
Giving attention to instructions, and then carrying out the prescribed action.		
Representing; following through; executing; enforcing regulations; rendering support services.		

5. Copy words that apply. *If* you colored in this rectangle/square, it means you feel *some* skill verbs there, apply to you in this story. Choose the ones most meaningful to you, and copy them into the box with the heading, "I am skilled at . . ." Leave plenty of room in that box, as during the succeeding six stories that you will be analyzing eventually, you may want to copy other words for those six.

6. Adapt the words so they are yours. There is nothing sacred about the skill words on the left-hand side of the page. If you can think of a better way to say what your skill is, *do not hesitate* to put the skill into your own words. Use the *Bank* of Additional Skill-Verbs (to the right of the page) for helpful suggestions.

7. Work your way on down the page. As you read each skill in turn, do not ask yourself "Do I have this skill?" That is not the issue. The issue is: "Did I use this skill, or any of its variations, in *this* story?" If you can hardly bear to pass by a box, because you *know* you have that skill—even though it was not used in *this* story—think hard of some achievement of yours from the past, where you *did* use that skill. Jot down a reminder to yourself, to use that as your next story. You will be writing seven such stories eventually, remember. Now you know what one to write next. And maybe, before you're through going down this entire list with your first story, you'll get some terrific ideas for the other six.

8. Turn to page 238. That has to do with Skills you may have with Information. Follow the same procedure.

9. Turn to page 244. That has to do with Skills you may have with Things. Follow the same procedure.

10. You are done with your first story. You have matched it against the 40 major skills that exist in the world of work, and plucked out those that describe you *in that story.* You have also probably gotten an idea of an even better story you could have chosen. Never mind. Just make that one your next story.

11. Write your second story, now. Don't write it *until* now. You see why. As a result of running your first story all the way through this Skills List, you doubtless got a better idea of *what to write, and how* to write it. Take your second story through the same process as the first, now, beginning with writing its title down at the bottom where it says #2, on all three pages.

12. Etc. When you are done analyzing the second story, then write your third. Run it through the same process. Then your fourth. Etc. Etc. Etc. until you are done with all seven.

Skills you may have with
People

Basically thirteen skills, with one additional one that
deals with animals

	1	2	3	4	5	6	7

1. TAKING INSTRUCTIONS
Giving attention to instructions, and then carrying out the prescribed action.
Representing; following through; executing; enforcing regulations; rendering support services.

2. SERVING
Answering implicit or explicit wishes or needs of others.
Preparing (something for someone); helping; hostessing; waiting on (tables); nursing; protecting.

3. SENSING, FEELING
Apprehending through intuition, showing sensitivity to others, especially to their feelings.
Intuiting; being sensitive and responsive to the feelings of others; empathizing; showing warmth; keen ability to put self in someone else's shoes; having keen sense of taste; having keen sense of smell.

4. COMMUNICATING
Signaling, speaking or listening to others so as to convey or receive information.
Listening; receiving information; learning; questioning; interviewing; exchanging information; signaling; telling; talking; writing; informing; giving instructions; speechwriting; playwriting.

5. PERSUADING
Moving people by means of demonstration or argument toward a course of action.
Influencing; inspiring; convincing; motivating; moving; developing rapport or trust; recruiting talent or leadership; demonstrating (a product); selling tangibles or intangibles; publicizing; promoting; fund-raising; writing proposals; arranging financing.

6. PERFORMING, AMUSING
Getting up before a group of people, and performing in a manner that illuminates, gives pleasure, or both.
Exhibiting showmanship; amusing; making people laugh; acting; dramatizing; modeling; singing; dancing; playing music; giving poetry readings; making oral presentations; exceptional speaking ability; thinking quickly on one's feet; writing with humor, fun, and flair.

Your life stories/achievements ➔

1	2	3	4	5	6	7

I am skilled at	
	Additional Skill-Verbs Bank: Expert at getting things done; ability to follow detailed instructions; ability to implement decisions; unusual ability to represent others.
	Additional Skill-Verbs Bank: Attending to; rendering services to; ministering to; caring for the handicapped; skilled at public relations; dealing patiently with difficult people.
	Additional Skill-Verbs Bank: Developing warmth over the telephone; creating an atmosphere of acceptance; ability to shape atmosphere of a place so that it is warm, pleasant and comfortable; refusing to put people into slots or categories; treating others as equals, without regard to education, authority or position.
	Additional Skill-Verbs Bank: Skilled at striking up conversations with strangers; talks easily with all kinds of people; adept at gathering information from people by talking to them; listening intently and accurately; ability to hear and answer questions perceptively; adept at two-way dialogue; expressing with clarity; verbalizing cogently; responding.
	Additional Skill-Verbs Bank: Expert in reasoning persuasively; influencing the ideas and attitudes of others; making distinctive visual presentations; selling a program or course of action to decision-makers; obtaining agreement after the fact; building customer loyalty; promotional writing; creating imaginative advertising and publicity programs.
	Additional Skill-Verbs Bank: Having strong theatrical sense; understudying; addressing large or small groups confidently; very responsive to audiences' moods or ideas; distracting; diverting; provoking laughter; relating seemingly disparate ideas by means of words or actions; employing humor in describing one's experiences; exceptionally good at facial expressions or body language to express thoughts or feelings eloquently; using voice tone and rhythm as unusually effective tool of communication; giving radio or TV presentations.

Possible skills with People *(CONTINUED)*

	1	2	3	4	5	6	7	

7. MANAGING, SUPERVISING
Monitoring individual behavior and coordinating with others',
for the systematic achieving of some organizational objective.
Determining goals; interpreting goals; promoting harmonious
relations & efficiency; encouraging people; coordinating; managing;
overseeing; heading; administering; directing public affairs;
directing (production of); controlling (a project).

8. NEGOTIATING, DECIDING
Arriving at an individual or jointly agreed-upon decision,
usually through discussion and compromise.
Exchanging information; discussing; conferring; working well in
a hostile environment; treating people fairly; mediating; arbitrating;
bargaining; umpiring; adjudicating; renegotiating; compromising;
reconciling; resolving; charting mergers; making policy.

9. FOUNDING, LEADING
Enlisting and synergizing others toward a corporate objective.
Initiating; originating; founding; instituting; establishing; charting;
financing; determining goals, objectives and procedures;
recognizing and utilizing the skills of others; enlisting; displaying
charisma; inspiring trust; evoking loyalty; organizing diverse people
into a group; unifying; synergizing; team-building; sharing
responsibility; delegating authority; contracting; taking manageable
risks; conducting (music).

10. TREATING
Acting to improve a physical, mental, emotional or spiritual problem
of others, by using a specified technique or substance.
Caring for; improving; altering; rehabilitating; having true
therapeutic abilities; prescribing; counseling; praying over; curing.

11. ADVISING, CONSULTING
Giving expert advice or recommendations,
based on an area of expertise one possesses.
Reading avidly; continually gathering information with respect to
a particular problem or area of expertise; offering services; giving
expert advice; consulting; trouble-shooting; recommending;
referring.

12. (HOLISTIC) COUNSELING
Dealing with a person's problems in the context of their total self,
to identify and resolve them through self-directed action.
Advising; counseling; mentoring; facilitating personal growth and
development of others; helping people identify their problems,
needs, and solutions; interpreting dreams; solving problems;
raising people's self-esteem.

	1	2	3	4	5	6	7	

I am skilled at

Additional Skill-Verbs Bank: Devising systematic approach to goal setting; monitoring behavior through watching, critical evaluation, and feedback; adept at planning and staging ceremonies; planning, organizing and staging of theatrical productions; conducting (music).

Additional Skill-Verbs Bank: Collaborating with colleagues skillfully; handling prima donnas tactfully and well; handling super-difficult people in situations, without stress; getting diverse groups to work together; expert at liaison roles; adept at conflict management; accepting of differing opinions; arriving at jointly agreed-upon decision or policy or program or solution; promoting and bringing about major policy changes.

Additional Skill-Verbs Bank: Unusual ability to work self-directedly, without supervision; perceptive in identifying and assessing the potential of others; attracting skilled, competent, and creative people; willing to experiment with new approaches; instinctively understands political realities; recognizing when more information is needed before a decision can be reached; skilled at chairing meetings; deft at directing creative talent; adept at calling in other experts or helpers as needed.

Additional Skill-Verbs Bank: Making and using contacts effectively; finding and getting things not easy to find; acting as resource broker; giving professional advice; giving insight concerning—

Additional Skill-Verbs Bank: Helping people make their own discoveries; clarifying values and goals of others; putting things in perspective; adept at confronting others with touchy or difficult personal matters.

Possible skills with People *(CONCLUDED)*

1 2 3 4 5 6 7

13. TRAINING
Giving new information or ideas to people, through lecture, demonstration, or practice.
Knowing (something); causing an individual or group to know (something); lecturing; fostering a stimulating learning environment; instilling in people a love of the subject being taught; explaining difficult or complex concepts or ideas; giving examples; demonstrating; showing; translating; detailing; modeling desired behavior; group-facilitating; helping others to express their views; helping others to experience (something); empowering.

[14. WORKING WITH ANIMALS]
In general this involves using, with special refinement, the same skills as in the preceding thirteen categories; specifically:
Serving; sensing; communicating; persuading; performing; managing; negotiating; leading; treating; training.

1 2 3 4 5 6 7

am skilled at

Additional Skill-Verbs Bank: Designing educational events; organizing and administering in-house training events; showing others how to take advantage of a resource; explaining; instructing; enlightening; patient teaching; guiding; tutoring; coaching; using visual communications as teaching aids; interpreting; inventing down-to-earth illustrations for abstract principles or ideas; translating jargon into relevant and meaningful terms, to diverse audiences; speaking a foreign language fluently; teaching a foreign language; skilled at planning and carrying out well-run seminars, workshops or meetings; directing the production of (as, a play).

Additional Skill-Verbs Bank: Ranching; farming; animal training.

Skills you may have with
Information
Basically fifteen skills

	1	2	3	4	5	6	7

15. OBSERVING
Studying the behavior of people, animals or things,
or the details of a particular phenomenon or place.
Paying careful attention to; being very observant; studying;
concentrating; keeping track of details; focusing on minutiae.

16. COMPARING
Examining two or more people or things,
to discover similarities and dissimilarities.
Comparing; checking; making comparisons; proofreading;
discovering similarities or dissimilarities; perceiving identities
or divergences; developing a standard or model.

17. COPYING, STORING, AND RETRIEVING
Making an imitation in the mind or on various materials.
Entering (data); keeping records; addressing; posting; copying;
transcribing; recording; memorizing; classifying expertly; protecting;
keeping confidential; filing in a way to facilitate retrieval;
remembering; retrieving; extracting; reproducing; imitating;
reviewing; restoring; giving out information patiently and accurately.

18. COMPUTING
Dealing with numbers, performing simple or complex arithmetic.
Counting; taking inventory; calculating; solving statistical problems;
auditing; keeping accurate financial records; reporting; maintaining
fiscal controls; budgeting; projecting; purchasing; operating a
computer competently with spreadsheets and statistics (and, by
extension, with all computer applications: word processing, data-
bases, graphics, and telecommunications).

19. RESEARCHING
Finding and reporting on, things not easy to find.
Investigating; detecting; surveying; inventorying; interviewing;
identifying; finding; gathering; collecting; assembling; compiling;
composing; collating; tabulating; classifying; ascertaining;
determining; proving; disproving; reporting.

20. ANALYZING
Breaking a principle or thing into its constituent parts,
or basic elements.
Examining; visualizing; reasoning; finding the basic units;
dissecting; extracting; selecting; testing; evaluating; perceiving
and defining cause-and-effect relations; proving; interpreting.

Your life stories/achievements ➔

1   2   3   4   5   6   7

I am skilled at	
	Additional Skill-Verbs Bank: Being keenly aware of surroundings; being highly observant of people or data or things; studies other people's behavior perceptively.
	Additional Skill-Verbs Bank: Keeping superior minutes of meetings; having a keen and accurate memory for detail; recalling people and their preferences accurately; retentive memory for rules and procedures; expert at remembering numbers and statistics accurately, and for a long period; having exceedingly accurate melody recognition; exhibiting keen tonal memory; accurately reproducing sounds or tones (e.g., a foreign language, spoken without accent); keeping confidences; keeping secrets; encrypting.
	Additional Skill-Verbs Bank: Performing rapid and accurate manipulation of numbers, in one's head or on paper; preparing financial reports; estimating; ordering; acquiring.
	Additional Skill-Verbs Bank: Relentlessly curious; reading ceaselessly; adept at finding information by interviewing people; discovering; getting; obtaining; reporting accurately; briefing; acting as a resource broker.
	Additional Skill-Verbs Bank: Debating; figuring out; critiquing.

Possible skills with Information *(CONTINUED)*

	1	2	3	4	5	6	7
21. ORGANIZING *Giving a definite structure and working order to things.* Forming into a whole with connected and interdependent parts; collating; formulating; defining; classifying materials; arranging according to a prescribed plan or evolving schema; expertly systematizing.							
22. EVALUATING *Making judgments about people, information, or things.* Diagnosing; inspecting; checking; testing; perceiving common denominators; weighing; appraising; assessing; deciding; judging; screening out people; discriminating what is important from what is unimportant; discarding the unimportant; editing; simplifying; summarizing; consolidating.							
23. VISUALIZING *Able to conceive shapes or sounds, perceiving their patterns and structures, and to enable others to see them too.* Having form perception; imagining; able to visualize shapes; perceiving patterns and structures; skilled at symbol formation; creating poetic images; visualizing concepts; possessing accurate spatial memory; easily remembering faces; having an uncommonly fine sense of rhythm; estimating (e.g., speed); illustrating; photographing; sketching; drawing; coloring; painting; designing; drafting; mapping.							
24. IMPROVING, ADAPTING *Taking what others have developed,* *and applying it to new situations, often in a new form.* Adjusting; improvising; expanding; improving; arranging (as, music); redesigning; updating; applying.							
25. CREATING, SYNTHESIZING *Transforming apparently unrelated things or ideas,* *by forming them into a new cohesive whole.* Relating; combining; integrating; unifying; producing a clear, coherent unity; intuiting; inventing; innovating; conceptualizing; hypothesizing; discovering; conceiving new interpretations, concepts and approaches; formulating; programming; projecting; forecasting.							
26. DESIGNING *Fashioning or shaping things.* Creating (things); designing in wood or other media; experimenting; fashioning; shaping; making models; making handicrafts; sculpting; creating symbols.							

1 2 3 4 5 6 7

I am skilled at	
	Additional Skill-Verbs Bank: Bringing order out of chaos, with masses of physical things; putting into working order.
	Additional Skill-Verbs Bank: Problem-solving; making decisions; eliminating; screening applicants; reducing the size of the database; separating the wheat from the chaff; reviewing large amounts of material and extracting its essence; writing a precis; making fiscal reductions; conserving; upgrading.
	Additional Skill-Verbs Bank: Having a photographic memory; having a memory for design; ability to visualize in three dimensions; conceiving symbolic and metaphoric pictures of reality; possessing color discrimination of a very high order; possessing instinctively excellent taste in design, arrangement and color; skilled at mechanical drawing; able to read blueprints; graphing and reading graphs.
	Additional Skill-Verbs Bank: Making practical applications of theoretical ideas; deriving applications from other people's ideas; able to see the commercial possibilities in a concept, idea or product.
	Additional Skill-Verbs Bank: Having conceptual ability of a high order; being an idea man or woman; having 'ideaphoria'; demonstrating originality; continually conceiving, generating and developing innovative and creative ideas; excellent at problem-solving; creative imagining; possessed of great imagination; improvising on the spur of the moment; developing; estimating; predicting; cooking new creative recipes; composing (music).
	Additional Skill-Verbs Bank: Devising; developing; generating; skilled at symbol formation.

Possible skills with Information *(CONCLUDED)*

27. PLANNING, DEVELOPING
Determining the sequence of tasks, after reviewing pertinent data
or requirements, and often overseeing the carrying out of the plan.
Reviewing pertinent data requirements; determining the need for
revisions of goals, policies and procedures; planning on the basis
of lessons from the past; determining the sequence of operations;
making arrangements for the functioning of a system; overseeing;
establishing; executing decisions reached; developing, building
markets for ideas or products; traveling.

28. EXPEDITING
Speeding up the accomplishment of a task or series of tasks,
so as to reach an organizational objective on or ahead of time.
Dispatching; adept at finding ways to speed up a job; establishing
effective priorities among competing requirements; skilled at
allocating scarce financial resources; setting up and maintaining
on-time work schedules; coordinating operations and details;
quickly sizing up situations; anticipating people's needs; acting on
new information immediately; seeks and seizes opportunities; deals
well with the unexpected or critical event; able to make hard
decisions; bringing projects in on time and within budget.

29. ACHIEVING
Systematically accomplishing tasks in a manner that
causes objectives to be attained or surpassed.
Completing; attaining objectives; winning; meeting goals;
producing results; delivering as promised; improving performance;
making good use of feedback; increasing productivity.

1   2   3   4   5   6   7

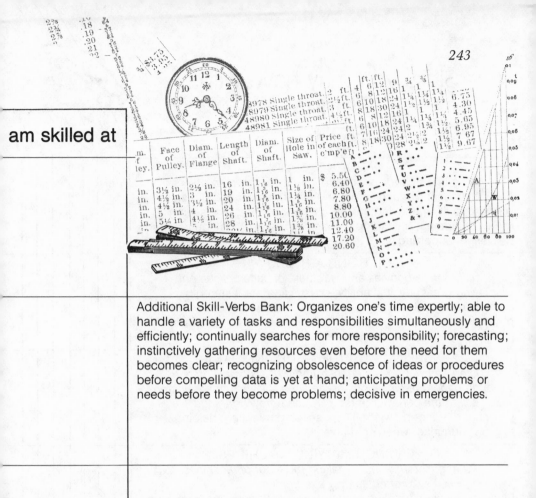

am skilled at

Additional Skill-Verbs Bank: Organizes one's time expertly; able to handle a variety of tasks and responsibilities simultaneously and efficiently; continually searches for more responsibility; forecasting; instinctively gathering resources even before the need for them becomes clear; recognizing obsolescence of ideas or procedures before compelling data is yet at hand; anticipating problems or needs before they become problems; decisive in emergencies.

Skills you may have with
Things

Basically eleven skills

	1	2	3	4	5	6	7

30. HANDLING (OBJECTS)
Using one's hands or body to identify or move an object.
Feeling; fingering; washing; raising; lifting; carrying; balancing;
pushing; pulling; moving; taking; gathering; receiving; setting
(down); shipping; unloading; separating; sorting; distributing;
delivering; supplying.

31. BEING ATHLETIC
Using one's body as an instrument of accomplishment.
Displaying great physical agility; possessing great strength;
demonstrating outstanding endurance; maintaining uncommon
physical fitness; having excellent eye-hand-foot coordination;
possessing fine motor coordination.

32. WORKING WITH THE EARTH AND NATURE
Using earth's body as an instrument of accomplishment,
though under the limitations of the special laws that are written
into the behavior of the earth and growing things.
Clearing; digging; plowing; tilling; seeding; planting; helping
to grow; nurturing; weeding; harvesting.

33. FEEDING, EMPTYING (MACHINES)
Putting materials into or taking them out of machines,
often as they are running.
Placing; stacking; loading; feeding; emptying; dumping; removing;
disposing of.

34. MINDING (MACHINES)
Monitoring, adjusting, and servicing automatic machines,
usually as they are running.
Monitoring machines or valves; watching to make sure nothing
is wrong; tending; pushing buttons; starting; flipping switches;
adjusting controls; turning knobs; stopping; making adjustments
when machine threatens to malfunction, or does.

Your life stories/achievements →

1   2   3   4   5   6   7

I am skilled at	
	Additional Skill-Verbs Bank: Having keen sense of touch; manual dexterity; good with one's hands; collecting.
	Additional Skill-Verbs Bank: Typing; printing; operating a computer; playing (a musical instrument); photographing; mastering machinery against its will.
	Additional Skill-Verbs Bank: Groundskeeping; landscaping; farming; logging; mining; drawing samples from the earth.

Possible skills with Things *(CONCLUDED)*

35. USING (TOOLS)
Manipulating hand tools (electrically-powered or not)
to accomplish that which the hands by themselves cannot.
The following skills are all accomplished with the aid of kitchen, garden or shop hand tools: using or utilizing (particular tools); manipulating (materials); working; eating; placing; guiding; moving; shaping; molding; filling; cutting; applying; pressing; binding; sewing (by hand); weaving; knitting; painting.

36. OPERATING (EQUIPMENT OR MACHINES)
Performing some or all of the following operations upon a
particular kind of (office, shop or other) machine or equipment.
You need to specify which equipment or machines you know how to perform these operations on (e.g., a computer or typewriter); and which operations: starting; operating; inputting; inserting; controlling; maintaining; monitoring; observing; checking; regulating; adjusting; changing; cleaning; refilling; producing (some kind of output, or product).

37. OPERATING (VEHICLES)
Performing some or all of the following operations
upon a particular kind of vehicle.
Driving; piloting; navigating; guiding; steering; regulating controls of; switching.

38. PRECISION WORKING
Precise attainment of set limits, tolerances or standards.
Keypunching; drilling; sandblasting; grinding; forging; fitting; tuning; adjusting; having great finger dexterity; sketching; drawing; painting; sewing minute stitches; making miniatures; skilled at working in the micro-universe.

39. SETTING UP (DISPLAYS, MACHINERY, EQUIPMENT)
Preparing; clearing; laying; constructing; building; assembling; installing; displaying.

40. REPAIRING
Putting something back into something like its original condition;
or at least into good operating condition.
You will need to say what it is that you are good at repairing or restoring: fixing; repairing; doing preventative maintenance; trouble-shooting; restoring (as, art).

1 2 3 4 5 6 7

I am skilled at

Additional Skill-Verbs Bank: Typing; printing; operating a computer; playing (a musical instrument); mastering machinery against its will.

Additional Skill-Verbs Bank: Giving continuous attention to the vehicle; offering a ready response to any emergency.

Additional Skill-Verbs Bank: Having great dexterity with small instruments (as, tweezers).

Now, You Need Priorities

Well, you did it. Seven stories all done. And analyzed for their skills. You've got a nice list called "I am skilled at..." Good going!

Now what? Well, unfortunately, this new list of your skills *will do you absolutely no good if you do not then go on to say which skill you like best, which next best, etc.*

Why? Because, until you can say *that*, you can't even begin to define "Your Ideal Job or Career." *Almost every* job demands that you have skills with People, Information and Things—in one degree or another. It's that *degree* that determines *which* job or career we're talking about.

To define your next job or career you *must* prioritize your skills. Without this essential step, you will get bogged down for sure.

This prioritizing has two levels to it:

I. What you first need to know about yourself is: "Which kinds of skills do I most enjoy using? Those with People? Or those with Information? Or those with Things? Or, if all three, which is most important to me, which is next most important, and which is least important?" What career or job you choose next, will depend upon this discovery and this decision of yours, more than any other. Don't ever underestimate the importance of the distinction between PEOPLE, INFORMATION, and THINGS. It is the key to everything.

II. Then, within the three broad families of Skills (People, Information and Things), you MUST decide *which* "People Skills," and *which* "Information Skills," and *which* "Things Skills" are most important to you.

How Do You Prioritize? You begin by just trusting your intuition. Look over your colored-in pages: People, Information, and Things. Which skills do you like most to use, of the three? People? Information? or Things? Of the three, which is next? Which is your least favorite?

Next: look at the "People Skills" pages, all by themselves. Look at the skills you wrote down, in the "I am skilled at..." sections. On a separate piece of paper, copy these with your favorite at the top, your least favorite at the bottom. Cross out (or omit) any skills *you have* but don't enjoy using. You are only looking for *enjoy* here.

You may be able to do this prioritizing just by common sense. If not, use the "Prioritizing Grid" that you will find in the next section of this Map—under "Special Knowledges"—to help you.

When you are done with your "People Skills," turn to the "Information Skills" pages, and follow the same procedure. Use a new piece of blank paper. Get all your "Information Skills"—in the "I am skilled at..." sections—written down on this blank paper, in the order of their exact priority for you. Again, omit any skills you don't truly enjoy using.

When you are done with your "Information Skills," turn to the "Things Skills" pages, and again follow the same procedure, using a new piece of blank paper. Get your "Things Skills" too, into exact priority. And, once again, omit any skills you don't truly enjoy using.

NOW you have some truly useful information.

Incidentally, on page 266 you will find a place to *summarize* your findings. There is a picture of a Tree, there. And on the left-hand side of that tree, is a place for you to write your favorite *top three* or four "People Skills," AND your favorite *top three* or four "Information Skills," AND your favorite *top three* or four "Things Skills." Do save the papers, however, on which you have written out *all* your favorite People Skills, etc. For now, the *top three* of each, will do. But later, you may want to go back and look at the rest of the list.

Where

Where You Want to Use Your Skills

14,000,000 Job Markets. Job-hunters begin by thinking there are too few job markets (and therefore, too few jobs) "out there." We argue just the opposite. There are too many. If you try to hit them all (shotgun style) you will only diffuse your energies and your effectiveness.

It is, of course, nice to 'stay loose' and be willing to use your skills any place that there is a vacancy. Unfortunately, experts say that 80% of all the vacancies which occur in this country, above entry level, are never advertised through any of the channels or avenues that job-hunters traditionally turn to.

So, you're going to have to approach any place and every place that looks attractive to you.

Thus, you can't rule out any place that looks interesting to you, because it's just possible they have a vacancy that you don't know about. Or will develop one *while you're there*. Or will decide (since they may be expanding) to create a job just for you.

You can't, of course, go visit EVERY place that looks interesting. Hence, the importance of this part of your homework. You've GOT to "cut the territory down" to some manageable size, by using:

Some Principles of Exclusion For Narrowing Down The Area You Need To Focus On

YOU START WITH
THE WHOLE JOB-MARKET IN THIS COUNTRY—

1 You narrow this down by deciding just what area, city or county you want to work in. This leaves you with however many thousands of job markets there are in that area or city. **2** You narrow this down by identifying your Strongest Skills, on their highest level that you can legitimately claim, and then thru research deciding what field you *want* to work in, above all. This leaves you with all the hundreds of businesses/community organizations/ agencies/schools/hospitals/projects/associations/ foundations/institutions/firms or government agen- cies there are in that area and in the field you have chosen. **3** You narrow this down by get- ting acquainted with the economy in the area thru personal interviews with various contacts; and supplementing this with study of journals in your field, in order that you can pinpoint the places that interest you the most. This leaves a manageable num- ber of markets for you to do some study on. **4** You now narrow this down by asking yourself: *Can I be happy in this place, and do they have the kind of problems which my strongest skills can help solve for them?* **5** This leaves you with the companies or or- ganizations which you will now care- fully plan how to approach for a job, in your case, *the* job.

Some Principles of Exclusion For Narrowing Down The Area You Need To Focus On

1 Special Knowledges. The First Principle for Narrowing Down the Organizations You Will Need to Take A Look At: WHAT SPECIAL KNOWLEDGES DO YOU WANT TO BE ABLE TO USE ON THE JOB?

Set Up A Form. Here you will need another blank sheet of paper. Divide it into four columns, and put the following headings on those columns:
1. Special Knowledges I Picked Up In School or College.
2. Special Knowledges I Picked Up On The Job, Or Just By Doing (At Home or Work).
3. Special Knowledges I Picked Up From Seminars or Workshops, Etc.
4. Special Knowledges I Picked Up Just By Reading Avidly Or Talking With People.

Down the left-hand side, you can put the Years, working back from the present, in five-year increments: e.g., 1985-1981, 1980-1976, 1975-1971, etc.

List the Knowledges You Have. Now you are ready to start filling it in. Using your memory, or borrowing that of a longstanding friend, list EVERY knowledge you have ever picked up anywhere. Examples would be as follows:

Circle the Ones You Love. When you are all done with *your* list (not mine), go back and *circle* all the knowledges you would *love* to be able to use in your next job or career.

Put Them in Priority. Then, choose your top ten, and get them into *exact order*—from most favorite, to least favorite. Use the "Prioritizing Grid" on the next page, in order to help you do this.

(You will, incidentally, need to go to a copying machine first and make several copies of this Prioritizing Grid, inasmuch as you will be using it in each of these "Where" exercises.)

Special Knowledges I Picked Up In School or College	Special Knowledges I Picked Up On The Job, Or Just By Doing (At Home or Work)	Special Knowledges I Picked Up From Seminars, or Workshops, Etc.	Special Knowledges I Picked Up Just By Reading Avidly Or Talking With People
Spanish; Psychology; Biology; Geometry; Accounting; Music appreciation; Sociology.	How to Operate a computer; How a volunteer organization works; Principles of financial planning and management.	The way the brain works; Principles of art; Speed reading; Drawing on the right side of the brain.	How computers work; Principles of comparison shopping; Principles of outdoor survival; Knowledge of antiques.

Prioritizing Grid

For Ten Items. Here is a method for taking (say) 10 items, and figuring out which one is most important to you, which is next most important, etc.:

List, Compare. Make a list of the items and number them. *In the case of Specific Knowledges, make a list of the ten subjects you know the most about, then number them 1 thru 10.* Now, look at the top line of this grid. You see a 1 and 2 there. So, compare items one and two on your list. Which one is more important to you? *State the question any way you want to: in the case of Specific Knowledges, you might ask yourself: if I was being offered two jobs, one which used knowledge #1, and one which used #2, other things being equal, which would I prefer?* Circle it. Then go on to the next pair, etc.

1 2								
1 3	2 3							
1 4	2 4	3 4						
1 5	2 5	3 5	4 5					
1 6	2 6	3 6	4 6	5 6				
1 7	2 7	3 7	4 7	5 7	6 7			
1 8	2 8	3 8	4 8	5 8	6 8	7 8		
1 9	2 9	3 9	4 9	5 9	6 9	7 9	8 9	
1 10	2 10	3 10	4 10	5 10	6 10	7 10	8 10	9 10

Circle, Count. Total Times Each Number Got Circled:

1 ___ 2 ___ 3 ___ 4 ___ 5 ___ 6 ___ 7 ___ 8 ___ 9 ___ 10 ___

When you are all done, count up the number of times each number got circled, all told. Enter these totals in the spaces just above.

Recopy. Finally, recopy your list, beginning with the item that got the most circles. This is your *new #1.* Then the item that got the next most circles. This is your *new #2.*

In case of a tie (two numbers got the same number of circles), look back on the grid to see when you were comparing those two numbers there, which one got circled. That means you prefer That One over the other; thus you break the tie.

P.S. If you need to compare any list that has more than 10 items to it, just keep adding new rows to the bottom of the grid. Thus: 1 *11*   2 *11,*   etc. Until you have all the numbers compared.

Copy this Prioritized List. When you are done, copy the 10 in their exact order of priority now on that (formerly) blank sheet of paper—one side or the other—that you have been working on.

Summarize It On The Tree Diagram. Turn to page 266 once again, if you will, and in the place provided there on the left-hand side of the Tree, put your top four or five Special Knowledges.

If You Want To Do Several Different Part-Time Jobs. If you want to have a Composite Career—combining two or three different jobs into one Career—copy the picture of the Tree onto more than one larger pieces of paper. Have a separate Tree for each separate career or job, and put different skills and different Special Knowledges (from your prioritized list) on separate Tree diagrams. Do remember, however, to save the paper that you have been copying from. It may be you will want to consult it later, to see where you might use the rest of your favorite special knowledges—in your leisure, for example.

The Second Principle For Narrowing Down The Organizations You Will Want To Take A Look At:

2 WHAT DO YOU WANT THE GOALS OF THE ORGANIZATION TO BE, WHERE YOU WILL BE WORKING?

A Product, A Service, or Information? That's the first question. Do you dodge this question by saying simply, "I want to work for a place that makes money." The response is: "Makes money doing WHAT?" We are back to the question above: Do you want to work in a place (of your own choosing or your own devising) whose goal is to produce a product? Or, would you prefer to work in a place whose goal is to render some kind of service to people? Or, would you prefer to work in a place whose business it is to get information out to people?

You have to make a decision about the goals of the organization NOW or later. You can postpone it. But you cannot evade it.

If You Choose a Product, What *Kind* **of Product?** What kind of product do you want the place to be *producing,* OR what kind of product do you want to be able to *work with, or use,* at this place? Either answer will help you narrow down the kinds of places. If, for example, you say, "I want to work at a place where I could use a drill press," that will help narrow down the places you need to take a look at, in your given city or area.

So, read over this list, and circle any products/things/whatever that interest you and that you would like to work with, *or* help produce. (Do say which, please.)

Machines	Gas turbines	Television sets	Patterns, safety	Steel, aluminum
Tools	Steam turbines	Video recorders	pins, buttons,	Rubber
Toys	Steam engines	Games	zippers	Plastics
Equipment	Fuel cells	Amusements	Dyes	Textiles
Products	Batteries	Cards	Cloths	Felt
Desk-top	Transformers,	Board games,	Sewing	Synthetics
supplies	electric motors,	checkers,	machines	Elastic
Crops, plants,	dynamos	chess, etc.	Shoes	Gym equipment
trees	Engines, gas,	Kites	Beds	Medicines
Dollies,	diesel	Gambling	Furniture	Vaccines
handtrucks	Dynamite	devices or	Sheets, blankets,	Anesthetics
Boxes	Nuclear reactors	machines	electric blankets	Thermometers
Automatic	Other things	Musical	Towels	Hearing aids
machines	belonging to	instruments	Washing	Dental drills
Paper	the field of	Money	machines,	False parts
Laundry	Energy:	Cash registers	dryers	of human body
Dishes, pots	Electronic	Financial	Wash-day	Spectacles,
and pans	devices	records	products,	glasses,
Controls,	Electronic	Roads	bleach	contacts
gauges	games	Bicycles	Cosmetics	Fishing rods,
Copying	Calculators	Motorcycles	Toiletries	fishhooks, bait
machines	Lie detectors	Mopeds	Drugs	Traps, guns
PBX switch-	Radar	Cars	Cigarettes	Beehives
boards	equipment	Parking meters	Tents	Ploughs
Valves, switches,	Clocks	Traffic lights	Plywood	Fertilizers
buttons	Telescopes	Railways	Bricks	Pesticides
Computer	Microscopes	Subways	Cement	Weed killers
Tables	X-ray machines	Canals	Concrete	Threshing
Portable power	Pens, ink, felt-tip,	Boats	Cinder-block	machines,
tools	ballpoint	Steamships	Carpenters' tools	reapers,
Kitchen and	Pencils, black,	Gliders	Chimneys	harvesters
garden tools	red or other	Airplanes	Columns	Shovels
Meats	Printing presses,	Parachutes	Domes	Picks
Typewriters	type, ink	Balloons	Paint	Lawnmowers
Mimeograph	Woodcuts,	Foods	Wallpaper	Dairy equipment
machines	engravings,	Food	Heating	Wine-making
TV camera	lithographs	preservatives	elements,	equipment
Vehicles	Paintings,	Artificial foods	furnaces	Bottles
Transparencies	drawings,	Health foods	Carpeting	Cans
Therapy center	silk-screens	Vitamins	Fire	
Cranks, wheels,	Books	Can openers	extinguishers	
gears, levers	Braille	Refrigerators	Fire alarms	
Hoists, cranes	Newspapers	Microwave ovens	Burglar alarms	
Matches	Magazines	Wells	Crafts-materials	
Candles	Teleprinters	Cisterns	Paper-mache	
Lanterns,	Telephones	Bathtubs	Hides	
oil lamps	Telegraphs	Soaps	Pottery	
Light bulbs	Radios	Umbrellas	Pewter	
Fluorescent	Records	Clothing	Paraffin, pitch	
lights	Phonographs	Spinning wheels,	Bronze, brass	
Laser beams	Stereos	looms	Cast iron,	
Windmills	Tape recorders		ironworks	
Waterwheels	Cameras			
Water turbines	Movies			

When you're done with the list, PLEASE prioritize it. Put the products in order, from your most favorite to your least favorite. Use the "Prioritizing Grid."

If You Choose A Service, What *Kind* of Service? Do you want to service or repair some kind of product? If so, review the list above, please—with that in mind. Copy down what sort of product you would like to service.

Is the kind of service you want to offer related to helping people with some kind of personal problem? If so, what kind of people, and what kind of problem? Here is a list, to get your imagination going. Circle any that enchant you.

People needing help with the following special problems:
    Life adjustment or life/work planning
    Unemployment or job-hunting
    Being fired or laid-off
    Stress
    Relationships
      Shyness
      Meeting people, starting friendships
      Complaints, grievances

Anger	Rape
Love	Abuse
Marriage	Parenting
Sex	Divorce

    Possessions
      Personal economics
      Budgeting
      Debt, bankruptcy
      Financial planning
Problems Generally Regarded As Related Primarily to the Mind
    Mental retardation
    Personal insight, therapy
    Communications, thoughts-feelings
    Illiteracy, educational needs
    Industry's in-house training
Problems Generally Regarded As Related Primarily to the 'Heart' (Beauty, Feelings, etc.)
    Expressed feelings
    Learning how to love
    Self-acceptance and acceptance of others
    Boredom
    Loneliness
    Anxiety
    Fear
    Anger
    Depression
    Mental illness
    Psychiatric hospitalization
    Death and grief

Problems Generally Regarded As Related Primarily to the 'Will" (Perfection, Ethics, Actions, Doing)
    Prescribed actions
    Competing needs
    Performance problems, appraisal
    Discipline problems, self-discipline
    Personal powerlessness
    Work satisfaction
    Values
    Ethics
    Philosophy or religion
Problems Generally Regarded As Related Primarily to the Body
    Physical handicaps
    Physical fitness
    Sexual dysfunction
    Pregnancy and childbirth
    Overweight
    Nutritional problems
    Low energy
    Allergies
    Sleep disorders
    Hypertension
    Pain
    Disease in general
    Terminal illness
    Self-healing, psychic healing
    Treatment or drug addiction
    Alcoholism
    Smoking

[*As the line between psyche and soma is very thin, many will prefer all or some of the listings immediately above to be listed under "the mind," rather than under "the body."*]

    Problems Generally Regarded As Related Primarily to the 'Spirit'
      Religion
      Stewardship
      Worship
      Psychic phenomena
      Life after death
    Problems Regarded by Some as Holistic— Embracing Body, Spirit, Mind, Heart and Will
      Any of the above may be so-regarded
      Holistic health
      Holistic medicine or healing

What Kinds of People Would You Most Like to Work With? Underline or circle any descriptions below that are a part of your answer to this question.

Individuals	People in their thirties
Groups of eight or less	The middle-aged
Groups larger than eight	The elderly
Babies	All people of all ages
School-age children	Men
Adolescents or	Women
young people	Heterosexuals
College students	Homosexuals
Young adults	All people regardless
	of sex

People of a particular cultural background

(Namely, ———————————————)

People of a particular economic background

(Namely, ———————————————)

People of a particular social background

(Namely, ———————————————)

People of a particular educational background

(Namely, ———————————————)

People of a particular philosophy or religious belief

(Namely, ———————————————)

Certain kinds of workers (blue-collar, white-collar, executives, or whatever)

(Namely, ———————————————)

People who are powerless

(Namely, ———————————————)

People who wield power (e.g., opinion-makers, etc.)

(Namely, ———————————————)

People who are easy to work with
People who are difficult to work with
("a challenge," as we say: i.e., prima donnas)
People in a particular place (the Armed Services, prison, etc.)

(Namely, ———————————————).

When you're done with the list, PLEASE prioritize it. Put the services in order, from your most favorite to your least favorite. Also, the kind of people you would like to serve. Again, don't hesitate to copy and use the "Prioritizing Grid."

If You Choose To Work For An Organization That Collects or Dispenses Information, What *Kind* of Information or Data? You may already know. Instantly. No need to work through the list below at all. On the other hand, maybe you know that you like to work with information—but you're not clear about what kind of information. If so, go over the list below, and circle the sorts of things you *love* to work with—or *would* love to work with:

Data in General

Knowledge	Words
Conceptions or	Symbols
ideas or theories	Facts
Numbers or	Information
statistics	History

Data Primarily Dealing With Things

Parameters	Designs
Boundary conditions	Blueprints
Frameworks	Wall-charts
Specifications	Time-charts
Precision requirements	Schema
Principles	Schematic analyses
Principles' applications	Techniques
Standards	Methods
Repeating requirements	Procedures
Variables	Specialized procedures

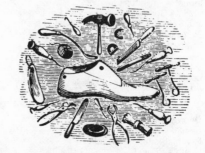

Data Primarily Dealing With People

Many of the above may be so-regarded or used. Also:

Intangibles	Objectives
Intuitions	Goals
Sequences	Project goals
Solutions	Tactical needs
New approaches	Needs
Public moods	Organizational contexts
Opinion-collection	Operations
Points of view	Systems
Sources	Work assignments
Programs	Reporting systems
Projects	Controls systems
Surveys	Performance character-
Investigations	istics
Research projects	Proficiencies
Research and develop-	Deficiencies
ment projects	Records management
Inputs	Catalogs
Outputs	Handbooks
Reports	Trade or professional
Conclusions	literature
Findings	Data analysis studies
Recommendations	Statistical analyses
Policy recommendations	Financial needs
Policy formulations	Costs
Plans	Accountings

When you're done with the list, PLEASE prioritize it. Put the types of information in order, from your most favorite to your least favorite. Again, don't hesitate to copy and use the "Prioritizing Grid."

Summarize It All, On Your Tree Diagram. Turn to page 266 once again, if you will, and in the place provided there on the left-hand side of the Tree, put your summary of 'GOALS OF THE ORGANIZATION.' It should state whether Product, Service, Information or any fourth alternative that you made up. And *which* kind, in specifics.

Combine Wherever Possible. It doesn't have to be Product OR Service OR Information. It can be any two of the above. Or any three. For example, you might decide that the kind of Information you would most like to get out to people would be a catalog. Fine, but then if that's the only thing you can say about yourself, you're going to have to cover every place in your entire 'target' geographical area, that produces a catalog of some sort. If however, you discovered that on the Product list, you liked the idea of Gym Equipment, that should be added to "catalog." It now reads "Producing catalogs of gym equipment." *That* narrows down the field in a much more satisfactory manner. You now have a *manageable* number of places to locate, investigate, and visit.

The Third Principle For Narrowing Down The Organizations You Will Want To Take A Look At:

3 AT WHAT LEVEL WITHIN THE ORGANIZATION DO YOU WANT TO BE FUNCTIONING, AND AT APPROXIMATELY WHAT SALARY?

You've GOT to make some decisions about this, at some point. For, your answer to this question will determine at what level you do your investigating, in the "HOW" section of this Map.

Here are some of the possible levels you may choose from: Volunteer • Intern • Entry-level worker • One who supervises others • One who works essentially alone •

One who works with one other, in tandem • One who works as a member of a team • The head of the organization • The founder of the organization.

The salary you desire will also influence the level at which your "HOW" investigation will proceed. See Chapter Seven in *What Color Is Your Parachute?* for guidance in stating your desires about salary.

Summarize It All, On Your Tree Diagram. Turn to page 266 once again, if you will, and in the place provided there on the left-hand side of the Tree, put your summary of "LEVEL AND SALARY DESIRED."

Good.

You now have all the basic raw materials for finding out what your ideal future job might be.

But What About The *Right* Side Of The Tree Diagram? Ah, yes. There *are* three more "principles of exclusion." *However,* these will *probably* only be useful to you *after* you have narrowed your search down to three or four places that truly interest you; and you are then trying to make up your mind between them.

At that point you will need some further principles of exclusion, to narrow down the territory. At that point, "working conditions," and "types of people you will be working with," and "preferred geography factors" will help you decide.

The Fourth Principle For Narrowing Down The Organizations, — Usually *After* You've Taken A Look At Them:

4 **WHAT KINDS OF WORKING CONDITIONS DO YOU WANT?**

Figure Out What's Important To You. *When* you are looking at, and weighing, two or more organizations, you will be able to give preference to one above the others *if* you know *under what conditions you do your best work.* This can include *anything!* Such as:

- Do you prefer work outdoors, or indoors?
- Do you want to work for an organization with 20 or less employees? 100 or more? 500 or more? 1000 or more?
- Do you want to work in a place where you know everyone, or not?
- Do you want to work in a room with windows, or don't you care?
- Do you want to be working in close physical proximity to others, or not?
- What distasteful working conditions from your past do you want to be SURE not to repeat?
- What kind of dress code, supervision, use of authority, openness to change, do you want to have—in order to do your most effective work?

Write these answers out on a separate piece of blank paper.

Prioritize The List. Then (you know by now): PRIORITIZE the list, using another copy of the "Prioritizing Grid."

Summarize It On The Tree Diagram. Turn to page 267, and enter your top five answers in the appropriate place on the right-hand side of the Tree diagram. As you stare at it, it will *of course* occur to you that *some* of the list here *may be useful to you before* you begin your search. For example, if you decide you want to work for an organization with 20 or less employees, *that* will be an important principle to have in hand *before* you begin your search—as it will determine *which* organizations you focus your attention on.

Generally speaking, however, as we said earlier, these "preferred working conditions" will be more useful to you after you have three or four particular organizations in mind.

The Fifth Principle For Narrowing Down The Organizations,—Usually *After* You've Taken A Look

5 WHAT KINDS OF PEOPLE WOULD YOU LIKE TO BE WORKING WITH?

WHAT "Kinds of People" usually means two things. *What kinds of people do you want to be dealing with as clients, customers, consumers, students, or whatever?* AND: *What kinds of people do you want to have working beside you within your organization? beside you, with you, under you, and over you?*

Who Do You Want To Serve? The answer to the first part lies in the list we saw, back when we were dealing with WHAT KINDS OF SERVICES DO YOU WANT TO OFFER, AND TO WHOM? If you need help here, now, go back and look at that list. It should give you some helpful starts toward this subject.

Who Do You Want Beside You? As for "the kinds of people you would like to have working beside you, within your organization"—all you have to do is take a blank piece of paper and make a list of all the kinds of people you have already worked with (at home or at work), and hope you will never have to work with again.

Negatives Into Positives. Then turn those "negative" factors into "positive factors"—which will often, but not always, be their opposites.

Prioritize the list (of course) and you will have a splendid list of what to look for. When at a later point in your job-hunt you have three or four places under consideration, and they look rather equally attractive to you, *this* list will separate the men from the boys, and the women from the girls. Also the sheep from the goats.

Here Come Your Values. *Most often* you will discover that "Types of People" is utterly dependent upon your "value system." You would call them your "traits." In the jargon of vocational experts, they are called "Self Management Skills." Whatever the language, we are obviously referring to all those traits (or skills) that you were missing seeing in the WHAT part of this Map. Traits/skills such as these:

Some Typical Self-Management Skills/Traits

A
Adept(ness)
Adventuresome(ness)
Alert(ness)
Assertive(ness)
Astute(ness)
Attention to details
Authentic(ity)
Authority, handles well
Aware(ness)
B
C
Calm(ness)
Candid(ness)
Challenges, thrives on
Character, has fine
Clothes, dresses well
Committed, commitment to growth
Competent (competence)
Concentration
Concerned
Conscientious(ness)
Cooperative (cooperation)
Courage(ous)
Creative, manifests creativity
Curious (curiosity)
D
Dependable (dependability)
Diplomatic (diplomacy)
Discreet
Driving (as, in ambition), drive
Dynamic(ness)
E
Easygoing(ness)
Emotional stability
Empathy (empathetic)
Enthusiastic (enthusiasm)
Exceptional
Experienced
Expert
Expressive(ness)
F
Firm(ness)
Flexible (flexibility)
G
Generous (generosity)
Gets along well with others
H
High energy level
Honest(y)
Humanly-oriented (warm)
I
Imaginative
Impulses, controls well
Initiating (initiative)
Innovative (innovation)
Insight(ful)
Integrity, displays constant
J
Judgment, has good
K
L

Loyal(ty)
M
Material world, deals well with the
N
Natural(ness)
O
Objective
Openminded(ness)
Optimistic (optimism)
Orderly (orderliness)
Outgoing(ness)
Outstanding
P
Patient (patience)
Penetrating
Perceptive(ness)
Persevering (perseverance)
Persisting (persistence)
Pioneering
Playful(ness)
Poise
Polite(ness)
Precise attainment of set goals,
   limits or standards
Punctual(ity)
Q
R
Reliable (reliability)
Resourceful(ness)
Responsible (responsibility)
Responsive(ness)
Risk-taking
S
Self-confident (confidence)
Self-control, good
Self-reliant (reliance)
Self-respect
Sense of humor, great
Sensitive (sensitivity)
Sincere (sincerity)
Sophisticated
Spontaneous (spontaneity)
Strikes balance, happy medium
Strong (as, under stress)
Successful
Sympathetic (sympathy), warm
T
Tactful(ness)
Takes nothing for granted
Thinks on his/her feet
Thorough(ness)
Tidy (tidiness)
Time, deals with well
   punctual (punctuality)
Tolerant (tolerance)
U
Uncommon
Unique
V
Versatile (versatility)
Vigor(ous)
W X Y Z

Use This List Twice: Underline.
There are two ways to approach this list.
First think of it as a list of *your own*
possible Traits. *Underline* the ones
which you think distinguish *You*.

And Then Circle. *Then* go back to
the beginning, and this time approach
the list as a list of People you would like
to be surrounded by, at work. *Circle* the
Traits that are most important to you, in
the people you work with. If you desire
different traits in your boss, from the
traits you desire in your co-workers, or
in those under you, make up three lists.

Compare. When you are done cir-
cling, do two things. First of all, compare
your Traits with those you want to find in
those around you at work. Are they the
same? Don't be surprised if they are.
Honest people usually like to be surrounded by honest people, and not by a
bunch of liars. Etc. Etc.

And Prioritize. Secondly, of course,
prioritize the list of stuff you want to
have in those who surround you at work
—unless you are going to be working
alone, in which case, this is irrelevant. It
may however have something to do
with your clients or customers, so don't
leap over this *too* quickly! Enter the
results on page 267.

**The Sixth Principle For
Narrowing Down The
Organizations,—Usually
After You've Taken A Look
At Them:**

6 WHERE DO YOU WANT TO BE, GEOGRAPHICALLY SPEAKING?

It may be that you have no choice.
Your mother lives nearby, at present,
and she is on in years, and needs you
to be near. And, you want to be near. So,
geography may not look like a very
important issue for you.

Mini-Geography. But, suppose you
find as you go on, that there are two
places which interest you. One is a 75-
minute commute, and the other is a 10-
minute commute. If you care about the
length of your daily commute, then as
you see, geography becomes a useful
tool for deciding which one to go after.
Mini-geography is operative here (one
area or another, within your county or
state). Maxi-geography might be operative at some other time of your life
(whether to move from New York to
California, or not).

Maxi-Geography. Indeed, it may be
operative now, for you. To such an extent
that you intend to go to the State of your
choice, and there conduct your job-
hunt, from the beginning. Or, to a lesser
extent—such that, if two places come to
your attention, and one is in your favorite
City in the whole country (or world),
while the other is not, the balance would
be tipped for you in favor of the one
which is in the City of your dreams.

Learn The Geography Lessons From Your Past. So, you need to think this out. If you want to move, need to move, but haven't the foggiest notion *Where,* try making a list of all the distasteful factors you have endured—geographically—since you were a small lad or lass. Conditions you hope you will never have to deal with again, as long as you live. Then turn those "negative" factors into "positives" again, prioritize them, and see what city or area it *sounds* like. Show the list to a number of your family or friends, if you have no clue.

Summarize It On The Tree Diagram. Whatever you come up with, mini-geography or maxi-, summarize it on the appropriate place, in the right side of the Tree diagram on page 267—well, you surely know it by now.

Passive vs. Active Geography. Needless to say, you may be saving this Geography consideration just to help you weigh various attractive organizations, as you get down to the wire later on. On the other hand, Geography may be what's *driving* you, right now. If so, write the name of your "target" city or area, over near the "Goals of the Organization."

Well, there you have it. The six factors which will help you decide *WHERE* you want to use your skills. Now, on to the *HOW.*

SAME CAREER BUT IN A NEW PLACE

STAYING AT YOUR PRESENT ORGANIZATION

CONTINUING IN YOUR PRESENT CAREER

STARTING A NEW CAREER

HOW
TO PUT
IT ALL TOGETHER

HUNTING FOR A JOB WHILE STILL EMPLOYED

HUNTING FOR A JOB WHILE UNEMPLOYED

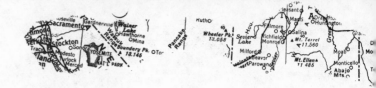

Now that you just about have the "trunk" road completed, you have the necessary information in hand, to make some intelligent choices about which of these roads you are going to follow:

So, on to the third part of your homework:

How to identify the job you have just drawn a picture of, by name or by title;

How to identify the kind of organizations which have such a job;

How to get hired there.

There are three steps to the HOW part of your homework:

The First Step
On the Road To Your Job:
PRACTICE INTERVIEWING

You need to go out and practice talking to people. Just for practice. In a non-job, low-stress, practice interview situation—just for information. You can take someone with you, if you want. If you're shy, maybe you want to take someone with you who is more at ease with people than you are; and watch how he/she does it. Anyway, by yourself, or with someone:

Your task here is to go out and talk with somebody. Somebody at *A Place That Fascinates or Interests You*—like, say, an airport (how does it get run), a toy-store, a television station, or whatever; OR somebody who has *The Same Hobby or Leisure-Activity That You Do* —like, say, skiing, gardening, painting, music, color, or whatever; OR somebody who is working on *Some Issue*

That Fascinates or Interests You—like, say, affirmative action, or ecology, or assertiveness, or lower taxes, or whatever. Use your phone book (the Yellow Pages) or friends to find the kind of person you're looking for: e.g., for skiing, try a ski-supply store, or instructor.

When you find him or her, talk about your mutual enthusiasm. If you don't know what else to ask them, here are four suggestions: *1. How did you get into this work? Or: How did you get interested in this? 2. What do you like best about doing this? 3. What do you like least about doing this? 4. Where else could I find people who share this enthusiasm, or interest, or are interested in this issue?*

Then go visit the people they suggest, and ask them (if nothing else) the same four questions. Keep at this, practice it as long as you need to, until you feel comfortable talking to people.

Then, on to the next step.

The Second Step
On the Road To Your Job:
THOROUGH RESEARCHING
TO PUT IT ALL TOGETHER

Once you feel comfortable interviewing people, you are ready to go find what kind of job, and organizations, that THE TREE Diagram points to.

Look at the factors on the left-hand side of your diagram of THE TREE. Which factor is most important to you, in your next job or career? It will probably be something that is either on your "Special Knowledges" part of the diagram, or on your "Transferable Skills" part of the diagram. Put it down under #1, below. Which factor is next? Put it down under #2, below. And so on. This will give you *the order* in which to do your research.

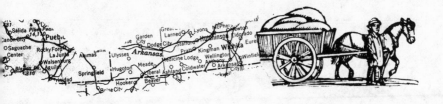
If you don't know what kinds of organizations to approach, read, mark, learn and inwardly digest chapters six and seven in *What Color Is Your Parachute?* There you will find lots of pointers and clues.

You should show your list of favorite transferable skills to your friends and family, and ask them to tell you what jobs come to mind as they read over the list. *Then,* and only then, also show them your list of top five Favorite Special Knowledges, and ask them what jobs now come to mind, that you might find worth exploring.

RESEARCHING YOUR IDEAL JOB

In the first stage of my research I'm going to identify someone whose job uses/ is characterized by

1. _____

In the second stage of my research I'm going to identify someone whose job uses/ is characterized by

1. _____ *AND*

2. _____

In the third stage of my research I'm going to identify someone whose job uses/ is characterized by

1. _____ *AND*

2. _____ *AND*

3. _____

In the fourth stage of my research I'm going to identify someone whose job uses/ is characterized by

1. _____ *AND*

2. _____ *AND*

3. _____ *AND*

4. _____

In the fifth stage of my research I'm going to…
(You can surely finish this diagram for yourself, on a separate sheet of blank paper.)

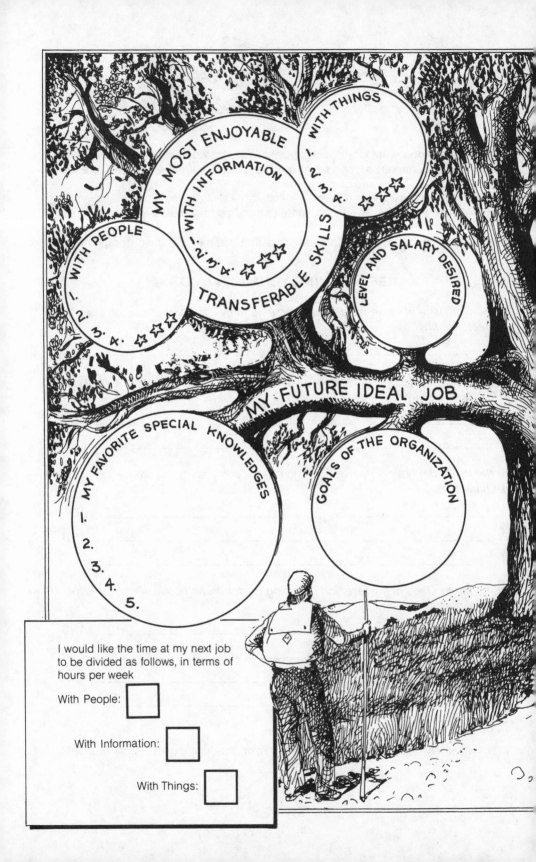

MY MOST ENJOYABLE

WITH THINGS
1.
2.
3. 4.

WITH INFORMATION
1.
2. 3. 4.

WITH PEOPLE
1.
2.
3. 4.

TRANSFERABLE SKILLS

LEVEL AND SALARY DESIRED

MY FUTURE IDEAL JOB

MY FAVORITE SPECIAL KNOWLEDGES
1.
2.
3. 4.
5.

GOALS OF THE ORGANIZATION

I would like the time at my next job
to be divided as follows, in terms of
hours per week

With People:

With Information:

With Things:

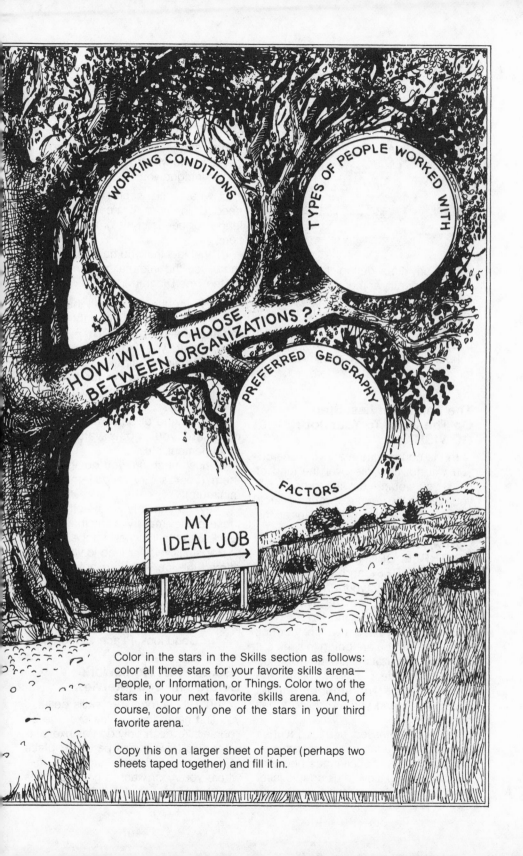

WORKING CONDITIONS

TYPES OF PEOPLE WORKED WITH

HOW WILL I CHOOSE BETWEEN ORGANIZATIONS?

PREFERRED GEOGRAPHY

FACTORS

MY IDEAL JOB

Color in the stars in the Skills section as follows: color all three stars for your favorite skills arena—People, or Information, or Things. Color two of the stars in your next favorite skills arena. And, of course, color only one of the stars in your third favorite arena.

Copy this on a larger sheet of paper (perhaps two sheets taped together) and fill it in.

If at any time during this research, you can't identify someone who actually holds the job you are interested in holding, ask your contacts for help.

Whenever you run into a stone wall, use your contacts (friends, family, school alumni, former employers, etc.) for suggestions as to where you can turn next.

The Third And Last Step On The Road To Your Job: GO VISIT

In the course of the above research, you will not only discover the kind of job(s) you would most like to have, but you will—in the course of your research —inevitably discover what organizations have such jobs.

Now, your task is GO VISIT THE TWO OR THREE ORGANIZATIONS YOU LIKED THE BEST and tell them so— together with why (your chance to discuss all the factors on The Tree Picture of the job you are looking for).

Whether they have a vacancy or not, is immaterial. You are going to seek out in each organization among your top three or so, the person who has the power to hire (not the personnel department); and you are going to tell him or her

a) what impressed you about their organization, during your research,

b) what sorts of challenges, needs or "problems" (go slow in using this latter word with sensitive employers) your

survey suggested exists in this field in general, and with this place in particular —that intrigue you.

c) what skills seem to you to be needed, in order to meet those challenges or needs in his or her organization.

d) that fact that you have these skills (here use the information summarized on the Tree Diagram).*

They, for their part, will have four basic questions they will want to know the answers to, about YOU:

a) why are you here (i.e., why did you pick out their organization)?

b) what can you do for them (i.e., what are your skills and special knowledges)?

c) what kind of person are you (i.e., what are your goals/values, self-management, etc.)?

d) how much are you going to cost them (your salary *range*—maximum, minimum)?

They may ask you directly about these, or they may try to find them out by just letting the interview happen.

Hopefully, this will lead to your being offered the job. If it does not, go on to the next place you liked the best.

For further information about any part of the above process, reread chapters 5-7 in Parachute.

Good luck, Peace, and Shalom.

*Some Final Homework Before The Job Interview

You will interpret your skills better, if you first have done a little exercise on yourself. You can only do this exercise, when you have a very particular place in mind as your "target" organization— where you *most* want to get hired. The exercise, then, goes like this:

● Make up a grid that looks like this:

I	II One of your verbs	III What? To what? To whom?	IV Problem you are going to solve	V Similarity of that company to new 'target'	VI Results: tangible facts and figures
I					

● And fill it in (Example:)

I	researched	the subject of memory	in order to help people in my company see the value of memory training	in a company which like yours, had less than 50 employees	and showed my boss that memory training would increase retention of training 400% — The Co. instituted the training & it was very successful
	I				
	I				
	I				
	I				
	I				
	I				

● and then take the following steps (next page):

Go back to the Tree diagram, and look at the skills you have listed there, under "Skills with People," "Skills with Information," and "Skills with Things." Enter them under "column II." Put them in the past tense, e.g., "organizing" becomes "organized." Thus far this grid will then read: "I organized..."

Fleshing Out The Skill. Now what you want to do at this time, is think of whatever achievement you have done, which demonstrated that you indeed have this skill. It *may be* that you will want to use one of your seven stories. On the other hand, you may think of a much more impressive achievement, now, which demonstrated that you had this skill. In the rest of this grid, you are going to describe it, under a certain form.

Filling Out The Form. In column III you say what it is you organized (or whatever the verb was)—it will always be some kind of People, or some kind of Information/Data, or some kind of Thing. In column IV you say what problem you were trying to solve.

The Bridge Between Where You Were And Where You Want To Go. In column V you say what similarities there were and are between the organization or place where you did this thing, and the organization you are now approaching for a job. This is the part of this grid that you will have to give the most thought to. What *is* it that this organization, and the place where you did this

achievement, *have in common?* Think hard. What you are trying to get across is that you know the problems of *this* organization before you, because you dealt with something similar in the past.

For example: "...in an organization which, like yours, had less than 20 employees..." OR: "I did this in an organization, which, like yours, is seeking to be the leader in its field." Etc.

Results That Can Be Seen, Or—Better—Measured. In column VI, put down the results of your action. Because you did "so and so," trying to solve "such and such" a problem, you were successful, and this is how we know it: "blah, blah."

Do The Same With Your Other Favorite Skills. Fill in the rest of the grid in the same manner, always listing your *next most favorite skill* each time you proceed on to the next line.

Oral Or Written. You should keep the results of this exercise at your fingertips or—better—at the forefront of your mind, when you go on the interview. You will then be able to truly demonstrate that you have the skills you claim to have.

If You Want Additional Help

Bernard Haldane Associates' Job and Career Building, by Richard Germann and Peter Arnold. 1981, 1980. Ten Speed Press, Box 7123, Berkeley, CA 94707. $6.95 + $.75 postage and handling.

Who's Hiring Who? by Richard C. Lathrop. 1977. At your local bookstore, or order directly from Ten Speed Press, Box 7123, Berkeley, CA 94707. $5.95 + $.75 postage and handling.

Making Vocational Choices: A Theory of Careers, by John L. Holland. 1973. Order directly from Prentice-Hall, Inc., Englewood Cliffs, NJ 07632. $15.95, paperback.

Where Do I Go From Here With My Life? by John C. Crystal and Richard N. Bolles. 1974. Ten Speed Press, Box 7123, Berkeley, CA 94707. $9.95 + $.75 postage and handling.

Job Power Now! The Young People's Job Finding Guide, by Bernard Haldane, Jean Haldane and Lowell Martin. 1976. At your local bookstore or order directly from Acropolis Books Ltd., 2400 17th St. N.W., Washington, DC 20009. $4.95, paperback.

Acknowledgements

I would like to acknowledge my debt, in this Map, to all the fine original thinkers in this field, who gave me many ideas for better helping job-hunters or career-changers:

to Sidney Fine, for thinking out the whole concept of People, Data, and Things, originally for the research on the Dictionary of Occupational Titles; I have done a kind of "rhapsody" on his work, but without his work there would be none of mine;

to John Crystal, for so very much—he was my original mentor in this field; we are particularly indebted to him in this Map for the fundamental distinction between WHAT, WHERE and HOW, as well as the concept of the Practice Field Survey;

to Daniel Porot, for so many ideas I have used particularly in this new revised version of the Map—most particularly the concepts of "job beggar," "art vs. technique," "the handicaps of the job-hunter," and "the final homework";

to John Holland, for the concepts at the base of the Party Exercise, and his whole system of RIASEC;

to Bernard Haldane, for the basic concept of doing detailed skill identification based upon past achievements.

All of us who find this Map a helpful guide are, in the end, indebted to these pioneers. And I for my part not only gratefully acknowledge their ideas, but also my gratitude for their friendship.

Those entering the job-market for the first time, and desiring a simpler skill-list than we have provided here, are referred to *The Three Boxes of Life,* in which the Beginning Version of the Quick Job-Hunting Map may be found. Or that version may be ordered separately, by writing directly to Ten Speed Press, P.O. Box 7123, Berkeley, CA 94707. $1.25 + $.50 for postage and handling.

My son, be admonished:
of making many books there is no end;
and much study is a weariness of the flesh.

Ecclesiastes

Appendix B

Special Problems and Interests
For Further Exploration:

Comments,
Books
And Other Resources

BOOKS

Every book has a different voice. That's fortunate. No one book (least of all this one) can reach every reader. If you find *Parachute* didn't give you what you needed or wanted, here are some other books that may succeed for you. Different voices.

It may also be that while *Parachute* helped you, there are still some areas where you need or want more light shed. These books should help. Different lights.

HIGHLY RECOMMENDED

Lathrop, Richard, *Who's Hiring Who?* Ten Speed Press, Box 7123, Berkeley, CA 94707. 1977. $7.95, paper. Simply excellent resource. Now back in print, revised and improved. Used more often by our readers than any other book (besides *Parachute*).

Holland, John L., *Making Vocational Choices: A Theory of Careers.* Prentice-Hall, Inc., Englewood Cliffs, N.J. 1973. $15.95, paper. Despite an incredible rise in its price recently, this book continues to be one of the most useful supplementary books for all of our readers. It is mandatory reading for anyone who is thinking of becoming a career counselor. It contains the immensely useful *Self-Directed Search*, an instrument for figuring out what occupations you might *start* your personal research with. Once you have found your "Holland code" I would recommend however that you not use the *Occupations Finder* there, which is a very limited list of possible occupations. Instead, get your hands on (from library or from the publisher, directly): Gottfredson, Gary D., and Holland, John L., and Ogawa, Deborah Kimiko, *Dictionary of Holland Occupational Codes: a comprehensive cross-index of Holland's RIASEC codes with 12,000 DOT occupations.* Consulting Psychologists Press, Inc., 577 College Avenue, Palo Alto, CA 94306. 1982. 520 pp. $18.50, paper. This invaluable book essentially does two things. 1) When you know your "Holland code", it then gives you a *comprehensive* list of occupations which may be "possibles" for you. You thus gain a better idea of where to start your research. The list is *much* broader and more comprehensive than that found in the little *Occupations Finder* at the back of *Making Vocational Choices.* 2) It gives you the DOT number for each occupation (the code number of that occupation, as found in the Dictionary of Occupational Titles); thus enabling you to go look up more comprehensive information about each possible occupation, for you, before or as you begin your own personal research.

Greiner, Peggy, et al., *Moving On: A guide for career and life planning.* Ulrich's B.B.M., Box D-1, Ann Arbor, MI 48106. 1982. $6.25, postpaid. One of the many career guidance books based on Holland's system, and one of the better ones.

Crystal, John, and Bolles, Richard N., *Where Do I Go From Here With My Life? The Crystal Life Planning Manual.* 1974. A more detailed step-by-step explanation of the process described in chapters 5-7 of *Parachute.* From: Ten Speed Press, Box 7123, Berkeley, CA 94707. $9.95, paper.

Wallach, Ellen J., and Arnold, Peter, *The Job Search Companion: The Organizer for Job Seekers.* The Harvard Common Press, 535 Albany Street, Boston, MA 02118. 1984. $5.95, paper. Primarily a book of very useful "forms" for keeping track of your job search. Intended as a supplement to other job-hunting books. If I myself were going job hunting tomorrow, I would definitely use the forms in this book to help organize my job hunt.

Jackson, Tom, *Guerrilla Tactics in the Job Market* (revised). Bantam Books, 666 Fifth Ave., New York, NY 10103. 1980. $3.95, paper. A popular and useful book.

Figler, Howard E., *The Complete Job Search Handbook: Presenting the Skills You Need to Get Any Job, And Have A Good Time Doing It.* Holt, Rinehart and Winston, 383 Madison Ave., New York, NY 10017. 1979. $5.95, paper. Tries to identify twenty skills the job-hunter needs in order to pull off a job hunt *successfully.*

Germann, Richard, and Arnold, Peter, *Bernard Haldane Associates' Job and Career Building.* Ten Speed Press, Box 7123, Berkeley, CA 94707. 1981, 1980. $6.95, paper. A detailed description of how to find a job, once you know what it is you want to do.

Billingsley, Edmond, *Career Planning & Job Hunting for Today's Student: The Nonjob Interview Approach.* Goodyear Publishing Co., Inc., Santa Monica, CA 90401. 1978. $9.50, paper. A first-rate workbook, dealing in great detail, and step-by-step, with the process described in chapters 6 and 7 of *Parachute.*

Miller, Arthur F., and Mattson, Ralph T., *The Truth About You: Discover what you should be doing with your life.* People Management Incorporated, 10 Station Street, Simsbury, CT 06070. 1977. $4.76, paper. The former publisher, Fleming H. Revell Co., lists this book as out of print, but it is still available from the authors, at the address and price listed above. A first class book, very helpful. I like it a lot.

Stanat, Kirby W., with Patrick Reardon, *Job-Hunting Secrets & Tactics.* Published by Westwind Press, A Division of Raintree Publishers Ltd. Distributed by: Follett Publishing Co., 1010 W. Washington St., Chicago, IL 60607. 1977. $4.95, paper. Points out all the strengths and weaknesses of "the numbers game." Excellent tips.

Haldane, Bernard, *How to Make a Habit of Success.* Acropolis Books, Ltd., 2400 17th St. NW, Washington, DC 20009. $4.95, paper. One of the pioneer books in this field, first published in 1960.

Haldane, Bernard, and Jean, and Martin, Lowell, *Job Power: The Young People's Job Finding Guide.* Acropolis Books Ltd., 2400 17th St. NW, Washington, DC 20009. 1980. $4.95, paper. Undoubtedly the best book available for high school students.

Haldane, Ph.D., Bernard, and Haldane, M.A., Jean M., *Job Finding Power.* Bernard Haldane, 4502 54th Avenue NE, Seattle, WA 98105. 1984. $8.75, paper.

Noer, David, *How to Beat the Employment Game.* Ten Speed Press, Berkeley, CA 94707. 1978. $4.95, paper. He tells the truth about the numbers game. Highly recommended.

Campbell, David P., *If you don't know where you're going, you'll probably end up somewhere else.* Argus Communications, Niles, IL. 1974. $1.95, paper. Useful for those who need to be convinced of the need for career planning.

Irish, Richard K., *Go Hire Yourself An Employer.* Anchor Press (Doubleday & Co., Inc.), New York, NY. 1978, 1973. $6.95, paper.

Edlund, Sidney and Mary, *Pick Your Job and Land It.* Sandollar Press, Santa Barbara, CA 93101. 1938. $4.95, paper. A classic among job-hunting books, still (mercifully) available.

If you dislike books, but like to listen to audio-cassettes, you may want to know that an overview (nothing more) of *Parachute* is available on cassette:

Bolles, Richard N., *How to Choose and Change Careers.* #20247. Psychology Today Cassettes, Box 278, Pratt Station, Brooklyn, NY 11205. $10.95, plus applicable state tax; audio-cassette.

Incidentally, they also have a cassette of:

Azrin, Nathan, *The Psychology of Job-Hunting.* #20207. Same address, same price.

ADDITIONAL RESEARCH

Some of you will find that *Parachute* gives you everything you need to successfully conduct your job-hunt. Others of you, however, may feel the need for some additional comments, help, or research, in particular areas. The areas most often mentioned by our readers, over the past ten years, have been:

1. If you want Alternative Patterns of Work
2. If you want Volunteer Opportunities or Internships
3. If you want Self-employment or Part-time Work
4. If you want Work dealing with Social Change
5. If you want to Get Work as a Writer
6. If you want to Get Work with Arts and Crafts

7. If you want Government Work
8. If you want Overseas Work
9. If you want help with the Special Problems of Women
10. If you want help with the Special Problems of Minorities
11. Help with the Special Problems of Handicapped Job-Hunters
12. Help with the Special Problems of Ex-Offenders
13. Help with the Special Problems of Executives and The Business World
14. Help with the Special Problems of Couples
15. Help with the Special Problems of Clergy and Religious
16. Help with Burnout, Lack of Promotion, Survival
17. Help with Being Fired, Riffed, Laid Off
18. Help with Mid-life, Second Careers or Retirement
19. Help with the Special Problems of Going Back to School
20. Help with the Special Problems of College Students
21. Help with the Special Problems of High School Students
22. Help with Getting a Job in Education
23. Help with Analysis of Skills
24. Help with Interviewing, Salary Negotiation, Resumes
25. Help with Job-Hunting in General, Places to Live
26. If you are a Career Counselor, or Want To Be
27. Perspectives on the World of Work Today
28. Perspectives on Creativity and the Brain

Accordingly, these are the sub-headings in the remainder of this Appendix. For the past ten years, I have tried to make this the most comprehensive career counseling bibliography to be found in any book I know of. Unhappily, this noble pursuit has run into two major obstacles:

1) There has been an explosion of books in this field. When *Parachute* was first published (1970), I had no difficulty whatsoever keeping up with the other books in the field. A good bookstore would have only about seven titles, at that time; a good library, only twenty, at best. Now, there are so many titles *no-one* can keep track. Career counseling books, in a large bookstore, have—until recently—occupied 40 feet of shelf space. (Now, a decline in their number appears to be going on. But still, the number of such books is LARGE.)

2) Some of these books have *a very short* "shelf-life". Even though we rush the newest edition of *Parachute* into print, half of the books have already disappeared (read: out of print), forever. Indeed, 90% of *all* books disappear from bookstores in less than 11 months. And, if the book is a paperback, the "shelf-life" may be much shorter. One expert claims that in computerized bookstores, the shelf-life of a paperback that

doesn't start to sell is about two weeks. It is not surprising therefore that I have been receiving a great many letters from readers trying to use this bibliography, who can't find *many* of the books listed herein. There is no point to a bibliography that is little more than a tombstone for the books that *used* to be.

Accordingly, from now on I am greatly restricting this bibliography, to:

1) Those books which have become classics, and are therefore available in most decent libraries.

2) Those books which are newly in the bookstores, and therefore deserve a hearing. A listing of a book in this section is *not* a recommendation of it. It is merely a listing of the kind of books that are available.

3) Books which are self-published, and not in any bookstore. *Parachute* is one of the few national "bulletin-boards" where such books can find their audience.

If you have a particular interest, and you don't find here any book that helps, there are two alternative routes still open to you: one is your local bookstores—go there, browse, and see what they have that is even newer than those listed in this bibliography. The other is your friendly local reference librarian. If your library has such a person, he or she can often be worth their weight in gold to you. Tell them your problem or interest, and see what they can dig up. They often know of hidden treasures, buried in books, articles and clippings, which will be an answer to your prayers.

1. IF YOU WANT ALTERNATIVE PATTERNS OF WORK

People are discovering there are all kinds of alternatives to the traditional nine to five, Monday through Friday job. Job-sharing with another worker, flex-time, where you decide which hours of the day you want to work, the four-day work week, holding down three to five small jobs rather than one full-time job, working long and hard two or three days a week, then having the other days to yourself, etc. If such alternatives appeal to you, do your informational interviewing with people who have already gone that route, first; and then with smaller employers, who are often more open than are larger employers, to new patterns of work.

Lee, Patricia, *The Complete Guide to Job Sharing*. Walker and Co., 720 Fifth Ave., New York, NY 10019. 1983. $13.95, hardcover. $6.95, paper.

Olmstead, Barney, and Smith, Suzanne, *The Job Sharing Handbook*. Ten Speed Press, Box 7123, Berkeley, CA 94707. 1983. $7.95, paper. How to share a full-time job with another person, if you don't want to work full-time.

Best, Fred, *Work Sharing: Issues, Policy Options and Prospects*. The W.E. Upjohn Institute for Employment Research, 300 W. Westnedge Ave., Kalamazoo, MI 49007. 1981. $5.00, paper.

©Copyright Mell Lazarus, Field Newspaper Syndicate. Used by special permission.

Work Times Newsletter, published by New Ways to Work, 149 Ninth St., San Francisco, CA 94103. Available from the above address for a (tax-free) donation of $25.00. An international information exchange on alternative work time.

Brown, Sydney, and Olsen, Nancy and Satten, Debby, *The People's Guide To A Community Work Center: How to start one and run it cooperatively*. New Ways to Work, 457 Kingsley Avenue, Palo Alto, CA 94301. 415-321-9675. 1982. $5.50 postpaid, paper. A step-by-step approach to setting up a community-based employment center devoted to finding cooperative work or job-sharing forms of employment, plus an apologia for the history of this particular center.

Levinson, Jay Conrad, *Earning Money Without a Job: The Economics of Freedom*. Holt, Rinehart, and Winston, 521 Fifth Ave., New York, NY 10175. 1979. $4.95, paper. The first part of this book is the best, as Jay sets forth his idea of "modular economics"— putting together several small jobs, rather than one big one—and having plenty of time left over for leisure. (One in every 20 workers, currently, holds two or more jobs.)

Meier, Gretl, *Job-Sharing: A New Pattern for Quality of Work and Life*. W.E. Upjohn Institute for Employment Research, 300 S. Westnedge Ave., Kalamazoo, MI 49007. 1979. $4.50, paper.

There are centers dedicated to helping people who want to find flexible work-time options, such as job-sharing. They often have helpful pamphlets and other publications. Among them, are:

Work/Life Options
5004 W. Tierra Buena
Glendale, AZ 85306
602-938-2351

New Ways to Work
149 Ninth St.
San Francisco, CA 94103
415-552-1000.

Flexible Career Associates
Box 6701
Santa Barbara, CA 93111
805-687-2575

Innovative Career Options
School of Business—Box 13
Metropolitan State College
1006 Eleventh St.
Denver, CO 80204
303-629-3245

Family and Career Together (FACT)
Eight N. Main St., Ste. 143
W. Hartford, CT 06107
203-521-1603

Association of Part-Time Professionals
Atlanta Chapter
c/o Debbie Weil
77 28th St. NW
Atlanta, GA 30309
404-351-6637

Division of Women's Programs
Alternative Working Arrangements Project
27000 University Ave.
Drake University
Des Moines, IA 50311
515-271-2181

Work Options for Women
1358 N. Waco
Wichita, KS 67203
316-264-6604

Work Options Limited
645 Boylston St.
Boston, MA 02116
617-247-3600

Nancy Viehmann
Pier Rd., Box 78
Cape Porpoise, ME 04014
207-967-3462

Lansing Women's Bureau
Human Resources Dept.
City of Lansing
119 N. Washington Sq.
Lansing, MI 48933
517-317-2115

Adult Career Exploration Center
Counseling Center—Memorial Hall
Glassboro State College
Glassboro, NJ 08028
609-445-5378

Workshare
311 E. 50th St.
New York, NY 10022
212-832-7061

Flexible Ways to Work
c/o YWCA
1111 SW Tenth Ave.
Portland, OR 97205
503-241-0537

Center for Flexible Employment
3060 Bristol Road
Box 404
Bensalem, PA 19020
215-757-3328

Work Time Options, Inc.
966 Summer Place
Pittsburgh, PA 15243
412-261-0846

Austin Women's Center
1505 W. 6th St.
Austin, TX 78703
512-472-3775

Phoenix Institute
383 S. 600 E.
Salt Lake City, UT 84102
801-532-5080

Association of Part-Time
Professionals
Box 3419
Alexandria, VA 22302
202-734-7975

Focus
509 Tenth Ave. E.
Seattle, WA 98102
206-329-7918

Vocations for Social Change, of Boston, Massachusetts, used to be a helpful resource to people interested in jobs dealing with social change. Unhappily, like so many other VSC's, they have now gone out of business, as have all of their publications: *No Bosses Here*; *The Boston People's Yellow Pages*, etc.

2. IF YOU WANT VOLUNTEER OPPORTUNITIES OR INTERNSHIPS

I CAN Volunteer Development Workbook. National Center for Citizen Involvement's Volunteer Readership Service, Box 1807, Boulder, CO 80306. $3.50. There is also an *I CAN Advisor's Manual* ($1.55) and *I CAN Administrative Guidelines* ($2.40), for those wishing to help recruit or train volunteers. The I CAN program, which helps volunteers identify the basic skills they are using in their volunteer work, was developed by the Council of National Organizations for Adult Education, and by the I CAN Interagency Collaboration for Volunteer Development (which included such organizations as the American Red Cross, the Girl Scouts of the U.S.A., the YWCA, the YMCA, the Junior Leagues, and the National Council of Jewish Women).

Hughes, Kathleen, ed., *Good Works: A Guide to Social Change Careers*. Center for Study of Responsive Law, Box 19367, Washington, DC 20036. 1982. Paper.

Stanton, Timothy, and Ali, Kamil, *The EXPERIENCED HAND: A Student Manual for Making the Most of an Internship*. Carroll Press, 43 Squantum St., Cranston, RI 02920-9990. 1982. $6.95, paper.

National Society for Internships and Experiential Education, *Directory of Public Service Internships: Opportunities for the Graduate, Post-Graduate, and Mid-Career Professional*. NSIEE, Suite 601, 1735 Eye Street, N.W., Washington, D.C. 20006. 1981. $12 (for non-members), paper.

Mann, Debra L., ed., *Directory of Washington Internships*. National Society for Internships and Experiential Education, 1735 Eye St. NW, Ste. 601, Washington, DC 20006. Updated yearly. $7.00, paper.

Directory of Internships, Work Experience Programs, and On-the-Job Training Opportunities. Ready Reference Press, Box 5169, Santa Monica, CA 90405. $45, hardcover. *The First Supplement to the Directory*. $37.50, hardcover.

Center for Environmental Intern Programs, 25 West Street, Boston, MA 02111, 617-426-4375.

The San Francisco Bay Area People's Yellow Pages, Box 31291, San Francisco, CA 94131. $5.95, paper. Alternative services catalog.

3. IF YOU WANT SELF-EMPLOYMENT, OR PART-TIME WORK

The self-employment route is exceedingly attractive to the unemployed, because it is a beautiful way to avoid the job-hunt. Unable to find work, we figure we have nothing to lose.

But of course you do. Your shirt (or blouse). The statistics on new businesses are depressing. You've probably heard them already, but just in case you haven't: 65% of all new businesses fail within five years. That's the bad news.

The good news, if you want the bright side of things, is that there are about 28 old businesses in this country, for every new business that starts up. This keeps the bankruptcy/failure rate *for the country* much lower than most people think. In Good Times, out of every 10,000 businesses, only 62 fail in a given year. In Hard Times out of every 10,000 businesses, 186 fail. That means 9,814 out of every 10,000 survive even during a tough Recession year. So, *if* you make it through the first few very difficult years in your new business you'll probably survive.

EVERYTHING therefore depends on how you start up. That's why you must not even for a moment think that the self-employment route is a good way to avoid the job-hunt. On the contrary, you'll have to work harder at your research, harder at setting up your business, harder at finding customers (should you be offering a service or product) than you ever would in a normal job-hunt if your experience is at all like the self-employed from whom I regularly hear. You will look back at the job-hunt as an elementary school exercise by comparison.

The ten riskiest small businesses, according to experts, are local laundries and dry cleaners, used car dealerships, gas stations, local trucking firms, restaurants, infant clothing stores, bakeries, machine shops, grocery or meat stores, and car washes.

If I could move *gradually* into self-employment, doing it as a moonlighting activity first of all, I certainly would. Test out your enterprise, as you would a floorboard in a very old run-down house, stepping on it cautiously without putting your full weight on it, at first, to see whether or not it will hold you. If you're not presently employed, and you're determined to go the self-employment or franchise route, for heaven sakes have a plan B. "I'm going to try out this self-employment, and my plan B is that if after a certain number of months it doesn't look like it's going to make it, then I'm going to . . . . . . (fill in the blank)." And give some time to the exploration of that alternative before you start your self-employment thing, so that plan B is "all in place," as they say.

No matter how inventive you are about self-employment, you're probably *not* going to create a job no-one has ever heard of; in all likelihood you're only going to create a job that *most* people have never heard of. But someone, somewhere, in this world of endless creativity, has probably already put together the kind of job you're dreaming about. Your task: to go find her, or him, and interview them to death. Why should you have to invent the wheel all over again? They've already stepped on all the landmines for you. They know where all the pitfalls are in this business you're dreaming of starting.

But suppose you can't find such a person? Well, then, figure out who is doing something that is *close* to what you're dreaming of doing, and go interview *that* person. For example, let's suppose your dream is to use computers to monitor the growth of plants at the Arctic. And you can't find anybody who's ever done such a thing. Well, then, break it down into its parts: computers, plants, and Arctic. Try combining *two* parts with each other, and you'll see what your research task is: to find someone who's used computers with plants, or computers at the Arctic, or someone who's worked with plants at the Arctic (yes, I know this is a moderately ridiculous example, but I wanted to stretch your imagination). My point is a simple one: you can ALWAYS find someone who has done something that approximates what it is you want to do, and from her or him you can learn a great deal. Better yet, they may lead you to others who have done something even closer to what it is you want to do.

How do you get funded for a new job no-one has ever heard of? Well, if it's a product or service you are offering, you get funded by convincing people to buy it. (And you ask people already offering a similar product or service how they got people to buy theirs, so you'll know what the general principles are, regarding what works and what doesn't work.)

But admittedly, this *can* be "the pits" if you have to go out and convince people, one by one, to buy your product, services, or whatever. No wonder, then, that a number of (hopefully) soon-to-be self-employed persons find the idea of a foundation grant or government grant, tremendously attractive and winsome. How, they ask—in letter after letter—can I find such a grant? Well, basically the same way you find a job. Thorough-going research. To get you started, consult your library (or else your banker) for one of the directories of grants (already) given. Such directories as:

Annual Register of Grant Support, published by Marquis Academic Media, 200 E. Ohio St., Room 5608, Chicago, IL 60611. If you have to buy it (ouch), it's $57.50, plus $2.00 for postage and handling, plus state tax (where applicable). Makes your local library look absolutely *wonderful,* doesn't it? The directory or register covers 2300 current grant programs, and has four helpful indexes. There's also the *Foundation 500,* published by the Foundation Research Service, 39 E. 51st St., New York, NY 10022. Hopefully, your local library has this only-slightly-less expensive volume, too. There is also: Lefferts, Robert, *Getting a Grant.* Prentice-Hall, Spectrum. 1979. $4.95.

The following four books are available from Public Service Materials Center, 111 N. Central Ave., Hartsdale, NY 10530: Dermer, Joseph, *New Ways to Succeed with Foundations—A Guide for the Reagan Years.* 1982. $19.50, plus $1.50 postage. *The Corporate Fund Raising Directory,* 1983–84 edition. 1982. $34, plus $1.50 postage. Guide to 550 corporations and their grant programs. Pulling, Lisa, *The KRC Desk Book for Fund Raisers/with Model Forms and Records.* 1982. $37.95, plus $1.50 postage. Describes the everyday operation of a fund-raising organization. Dermer, Joseph, and Wertheimer, Stephen, ed., *The Complete Guide to Corporate Fund Raising.* 1982. $16.75, plus $1.50 postage. Describes the entire corporate fund-raising process. If you want further help, you can get a catalog of books and materials related to fund-raising and proposal-writing by contacting the Public Service Materials Center.

The Foundation Center, 888 Seventh Ave., New York, NY 10019, is an independent, non-profit organization offering assistance in locating grants. There are four reference collections operated by the Center, in New York, Washington, DC, Cleveland, and San Francisco. There are also dozens of cooperating collections nation-wide. For information on locations nearest you, call 800-424-9836.

If you decide that applying for a grant is the way in which you would like to try to get funded, there are some rules. As Matthew Lesko (author of *Getting Yours*) points out:
1. If it is a government grant you seek, look at state and local governments as well as the Federal.
2. The money may not be where logic would suggest it should be. For example, the Department of Labor funds doctoral dissertations, the Department of Agriculture funds teenage entrepreneurs, and the like.
3. Talk to the people at the agency who are in charge of dispersing the grant funds.
4. When you have located an appropriate agency for what you want to do, ask to see a copy of a successful application (under the Freedom of Information Act).

5. If they make clear that they will not give you a large amount, ask for a small amount for a year; and let them get to know you.

Kamoroff, Bernard, *Small-Time Operator: How to Start Your Own Small Business, Keep Your Books, Pay Your Taxes & Stay Out of Trouble.* Bell Springs Publishers, P.O. Box 640, Lytonville, CA 95454. 1984. $8.95, paper.

Lant, Dr. Jeffrey L., *The Consultant's Kit.* JLA Publications, a division of Jeffrey Lant Associates, Inc., 50 Follen Street, Suite 507, Cambridge, MA 02138. 1984. $30.00, paper.

Esperti, Robert A., and Peterson, Renno L., *Incorporating Your Talents, A Guide to the One-Person Corporation.* McGraw-Hill Book Company, 1221 Avenue of the Americas, New York, NY 10020. 1984. $19.95, hardcover.

Feldman, Beverly Neuer, *Homebased Businesses.* Till Press, Box 27816, Los Angeles, CA 90027. 1983. $9.95, paper; revised.

There are, incidentally, 15 million small business enterprises in the U.S. Women own 25% of them (but only take in 9% of all small business income). That's mostly because they price goods and services too low, are not able to take risks to the same degree as men are, and often get turned down for financing because of their sex.

Lant, Dr. Jeffrey, *The Unabased Self-Promoter's Guide: What Every Man, Woman, Child And Organization In America Needs To Know About Getting Ahead By Exploiting The Media.* Premier Publishers, Inc., P.O. Box 16254, Fort Worth, TX 76133. 1983. $31.50, paper.

Hoge, Cecil C., Sr., *Mail Order Know-How.* Ten Speed Press, Box 7123, Berkeley, CA 94707. 1982. $16.95, paper.

Lesko, Matthew, *Getting Yours: The complete guide to government money.* Penguin Books, 40 W. 23rd St., New York, NY 10010. 1982. $5.95, paper.

Levinson, Jay Conrad, *Earning Money Without A Job: The Economics of Freedom.* Holt, Rinehart and Winston, 383 Madison Ave., New York, NY 10017. 1979.

Bermont, Hubert, *How To Become A Successful Consultant In Your Own Field.* The Consultant's Library, Dept. CHG, P.O. Box 309, Glenelg, MD 21737. 1978. $20.00, paper.

White, Richard M., Jr., *The Entrepreneur's Manual: Business Start-Ups, Spin-Offs and Innovative Management.* Chilton Book Company, Chilton Way, Radnor, PA 19089. 1977. $17.50, hardcover.

Mancuso, Anthony, *How To Form Your Own California Corporation.* Nolo Press, Box 544, Occidental, CA 95465. 1977. $9.95.

Hoge, Cecil C., Sr., *Mail Order Moonlighting.* Ten Speed Press, Box 7123, Berkeley, CA 94707. 1976. $7.95, paper.

Nicholas, Ted, *How to Form Your Own Corporation Without a Lawyer for Under $50.00. Complete with Tear-out Forms, Certificate of Incorporation, Minutes, By-Laws.* Enterprise Publishing Co., Inc., 1000 Oakfield Lane, Wilmington, DE 19810. 1973. $7.95 plus $.45 postage and handling.

4. IF YOU WANT WORK DEALING WITH SOCIAL CHANGE

Careers in this arena are often called "public service careers."

Public service careers may be with *government* (federal, state, or local), with *non-profit organizations*, with *agencies* (independent of state or local government, but often cooperating with them) or with *colleges* (particularly community colleges), etc.

Public service careers include such varied occupations as *Community Services Officer* at a community college, *recreation educator, city planner, social service technician* (working with any or all agencies that deliver social services), *welfare administration, gerontology specialist* (for further information, contact—among others—your State Commission on Aging), etc.

Drawing by Donald Reilly; ©1981 The New Yorker Magazine, Inc. Used by permission.

"I'm hoping to find something in a meaningful, humanist, outreach kind of bag, with flexible hours, non-sexist bosses, and fabulous fringes."

Other public service careers: *Workers with the handicapped, public health officials* (see your State Department of Public Health, or the Chief Medical Doctor at the county Public Health Agency—the Doctor often being the best informed person about *opportunities), officials dealing with the foster parent program for mentally retarded persons, workers in the child welfare program,* and so forth.

If you are interested in this general field of social service, you ought to do extensive research, including talking with national associations in the fields that interest you, state departments, county, city.

Potential employers for social or public service occupations include social welfare agencies, public health department, correctional institutions, government offices, colleges, economic opportunity offices, hospitals, rest homes, schools, parks and recreation agencies, etc.

As a research aid, there is *Human Service Organizations: A Book of Readings,* University of Michigan Press, 615 E. University, Ann Arbor, MI 48106. $7.95, paper. Deals with an analysis of the structure of schools, employment agencies, mental health clinics, correctional institutions, welfare agencies and hospitals. If you're thinking about going to work in one of these human service organizations, this could help your research.

Thorough research on your part will often reveal other ways in which *funding can be found for positions not yet created if you know exactly what it is you want to do,* and find a person who knows something about *that.*

Honigsberg, Peter Jan, Kamoroff, Bernard, and Beatty, Jim, *We Own It: Starting and Managing Coops, Collectives, & Employee Owned Ventures.* Bell Springs Publishers, P.O. Box 640, Lytonville, CA 95454. 1982. $9.00, paper.

Phillips, Michael, and Rasberry, Salli, *Honest Business.* Random House, Inc., 201 E. 50th St., New York, NY 10022. 1981. $6.00, paper.

The Briarpatch Book: experiences in right livelihood and simple living. The Briarpatch Community, New Glide Publications, 330 Ellis St., San Francisco CA 94102. 1978.

5. IF YOU WANT TO MAKE YOUR LIVING BY WRITING AND GETTING PUBLISHED

I used to live in an apartment-complex, and as I walked through the courtyard each day, I could hear typewriters going incessantly, out of every open window. They couldn't *all* be part-time secretaries, working at home. Obviously, there are a lot of budding authors and authoresses in the land. For them, some helps:

Appelbaum, Judith, and Evans, Nancy, *How to Get Happily Published: A Complete and Candid Guide*. New American Library, 1633 Broadway, New York, NY 10019. 1978. $6.95, paper.

Schemenaur, P.J., and Brady, John, eds., *Writer's Market: Where to Sell What You Write*. Writer's Digest Books, 9933 Alliance Rd., Cincinnati, OH 45242. Hardcover. Issued annually.

Mainstream Access, Inc., *The Publishing Job Finder*. Prentice-Hall, Englewood Cliffs, NJ 07632. 1981. $7.95, paper.

Mathieu, Aron, *The Book Market: How to Write, Publish and Market Your Book*. Andover Press, Inc., 516 W. 34th St., New York, NY 10001. 1981. $19.95, hardcover.

6. IF YOU WANT TO MAKE YOUR LIVING THROUGH ARTS AND CRAFTS

If your creativity is not out of the left-hemisphere of your brain (words, words, words), but out of the right-hemisphere (pictures, art, crafts, and so forth), there are books for you, too; issued annually:

Lapin, Lynne, ed., *Artist's Market*. Writer's Digest Books, 9933 Alliance Rd., Cincinnati, OH 45242.

————, ed., *Craftworker's Market*. Writer's Digest Books, 9933 Alliance Rd., Cincinnati, OH 45242.

Brohaugh, William, *Songwriter's Market*. Writer's Digest Books, 9933 Alliance Rd., Cincinnati, OH 45242.

7. IF YOU WANT TO GET A GOVERNMENT JOB

The U.S. Office of Personnel Management (formerly called the U.S. Civil Service Commission) has a *Guide to Federal Career Literature*. Order it from the Superintendent of Documents, U.S. Govt. Printing Off., Washington, DC 20402. For other information, see your nearest Office of Personnel Management (it's in all large cities), and ask them what else they've got about working for the U.S. of A.

As with any other kind of job, you've got to decide *where* it is you want to work, what skills you want to be able to use, and what it is you want to do (in other words, chapters 5 and 6 in this book apply to you as much as to non-governmental workers).

If you are new to the idea of the government as your employer, you will of course suppose that researching them won't do you any good, because you are going to have to take a Civil Service examiantion of one kind or another. Well, eventually you probably *are* going to have to take that exam. But all the principles in chapter 7 apply just as much to government managers as they do to other employers. Government managers, too, are tired of hiring people ill-suited for the job. Civil service exams don't give these managers any better clues than resumes do for non-governmental employers. So if, in the course of your research you happen to visit the government person who has the power to hire you, and if he or she takes a real liking to you, you can bet your bottom dollar they will do everything *they can* to guide you through the examination maze, so that you can end up in their office. Any government manager worth her or his salt knows how to manipulate—ah, excuse me, creatively use—standard operating procedures, so that it all works out to their best advantage.

When doing your research about salaries, once it's come down to that, it is helpful for you to know that unless you are up for an occupation for which there is an extremely limited supply of job-hunters, your government Personnel Officer will rarely have the authority to negotiate salary. If it *is* fixed, you can probably find it in the Temporary box, on a Federal SF-171. (Yes, I know you probably don't know what a Federal SF-171 is, at the moment; but you should know by the time you get to this stage of your research.)

Federal Yellow Book. 1983. An organizational directory of the top-level employees of the Federal departments and agencies. It costs $130.00, so see your library.

The publisher (Washington Monitor, Inc., 1301 Pennsylvania Ave., NW, Washington DC 20004) also publishes *Congressional Yellow Book,* an up-to-date loose-leaf directory of members of Congress, their committees and their key aides.

Federal Research Service, Inc., *Federal Career Opportunities.* Federal Research Service, Inc., 370 Maple Ave. W., Box 1059, Vienna, VA 22180 (703) 281-0200. Bi-weekly 64-page magazine. $34 for six issues. Up-to-date listing of available federal jobs plus application instructions.

Lesko, Matthew, *Information U.S.A.,* Penguin Books, 625 Madison Ave., New York, NY 10022. 1983. $19.95, paper.

Moore, Donna J., *Take Charge of Your Own Career.* Donna J. Moore, Box 723, Bainbridge Island, WA 98110. 1979. $10.00, paper, plus $.95 for postage and handling. A guide for federal employees, or would-be federal employees.

8. IF YOU WANT OVERSEAS WORK

Well, first of all, talk to everyone you possibly can who has in fact been overseas, most especially to the country or countries that interest you. A nearby large university will probably have such faculty or students (ask). Companies in your city which have overseas branches (your library should be able to tell you which they are) should be able to lead you to people also— possibly to the names and addresses of personnel who are still "over there" to whom you can write for the information you are seeking. Alternatively, try asking every single person you meet for the next week (at the supermarket checkout, at your work, at home, at church or synagogue, etc.) if they know someone who used to live overseas and now is in your city or town. By doing research with such people, you will learn a great deal.

Talking to the consulate of the country in question (should you live in or near a major city) may also be very enlightening. Books from your local library or local bookstore in the travel section, if they are recent, may also tell you much.

To supplement such research, there is Sherman, Margaret E., ed., *Whole World Handbook: A Guide to travel, study and work abroad,* 1981–82, published by Elsevier-Dutton Publishing Co., Inc., Two Park Ave., New York, NY 10016. 1981. $5.75, paper. And: Beckmann, David M., and Donnelly, Elizabeth Anne, *The Overseas List, Opportunities for Living and Working in Developing Countries,* published by the Augsburg Publishing House, 426 S. Fifth St., Minneapolis, MN 55415. 1979. $4.95, paper.

As for the general facts about living overseas, books on this subject keep getting regularly published, regularly flourish for a season, and then regularly die. But currently these are:

Casewit, Curtis W., *Foreign Jobs: The Most Popular Countries*. Monarch Press, a division of Simon and Schuster, Simon and Schuster Building, 1230 Avenue of the Americas, New York, NY 10020. 1984. $8.95, paper.

Wharton, John, *Jobs in Japan: The Complete Guide to Living and Working in the Land of Rising Opportunity*. Jobs in Japan, P.O. Box 31, Claremont, CA 91711. 1983. $9.95, paper.

Phelps, Cathy S., *The Guide to Moving Overseas*. Guide, Box 236, Lemont, PA 16851. 1978. $4.95, paper.

Shrank, Robert, ed., *American Workers Abroad*. The MIT Press, 28 Carleton St., Cambridge, MA 02142. 1979. $13.50, postpaid.

Kocher, Eric, *International Jobs: Where They Are, How to Get Them*. Addison-Wesley, Jacob Way, Reading, MA 01867. $11.45, paper, postpaid.

Your library should also have books such as Angel, Juvenal, *Dictionary of American Firms Operating in Foreign Countries*. (World Trade Academy Press.)

And to research overseas public companies which sell stock in this country, the Securities Exchange Commission will have their Form 6-K, which they filed in order to be able to sell that stock.

In general, the principles found in chapter 6, in the section on how to research cities at a distance (pp. 140–43) will apply here with equal or greater force.

9. IF YOU WANT HELP WITH THE SPECIAL PROBLEMS OF WOMEN

Now, just a (perhaps unnecessary) word of common sense—uncommon common sense, sad to say—about this whole business of job-hunting publications for women. There is a difference between *form* and *content*. In these days of liberated consciousness (or conscious liberation?) there is a great preoccupation with *form*: i.e., is the book written by a woman, or does it at least use non-sexist language? But let us not forget *content*, please. A book that does little more than outline the old numbers game (see chapter 2) is not going to do you much good, no matter how superb (i.e., non-sexist) its form may be. On the other hand, a book with helpful *content* (i.e., the creative minority's prescription) is going to help you, no matter how chauvinistic its language might be (just shut your eyes, and grit your teeth). The best of all possible worlds, of course, is to have both: a book whose form *and* content are both superb: that's the ideal women's book. But don't get hypnotized just by *form*, please.

LaRouche, Janice, and Ryan, Regina, *Strategies for Women at Work: Analyzing, Solving, and Overcoming Job Problems, Predicaments, Concerns, Complications, Obstacles, Tight Spots, Blocks, Hang-Ups, and Hazards*. Avon Books, a division of The Hearst Corporation, 1790 Broadway, New York, NY 10019. 1984. $8.95, paper.

Warschaw, Ph.D., Tessa Albert, *Rich is Better: How Women Can Bridge the Gap Between Wanting and Having It All: Financially, Emotionally, Professionally*. Doubleday and Co., Inc., 245 Park Avenue, New York, NY 10017. 1984. $15.95, paper.

Behr, Marion, and Lazar, Wendy, *Women Working Home: The Homebased Business Guide and Directory*. Women Working Home, Inc. 24 Fishel Rd., Edison, NY 08820. 1983. $12.95, paper. An estimated 5 million people work out of their home—most of them women. The authors are co-founders of the National Alliance of Homebased Businesswomen, a New Jersey based group, with 1400 members currently.

Homeworking Mothers, a quarterly newsletter for women who want to start their own business and work from their homes. Mother's Home Business Network, P.O. Box 423, East Meadow, N.Y. 11554.

Carroll, Mary Bridget, *Overworked And Underpaid: How to Go From Being a Low-Paid Secretary to Being a High-Paid Secretary to Having Your Own Secretary*. Fawcett Columbine

Books, 201 E. 50th St., New York, NY 10022. 1983. $6.95, paper. Nicely laid-out book, with amusing pictures.

Ashley, Sally, *Connecting: A Handbook for Housewives Returning to Paid Work*. Avon Books, a division of The Hearst Corporation, 959 Eighth Avenue, New York, NY 10019. 1982. $5.95, paper.

Phillips, Carole, *The Money Workbook for Women: A Step-by-Step Guide to Managing Your Personal Finances*. Arbor House, 235 E. 45th St., New York, NY 10017. 1982. $5.95, paper.

Azibo, Moni, and Unumb, Therese Crylen, *The Mature Woman's Back-to Work Book*. Contemporary Books, 180 N. Michigan Avenue, Chicago, IL 60601. 1980. $6.95, paper. Written out of the authors' experience with "displaced homemakers."

Catalyst, *What to Do with the Rest of Your Life: the Catalyst Career Guide for Women in the '80s*. Simon and Schuster, 1230 Avenue of the Americas, New York, NY 10020. 1980. $16.95, hardcover.

Kleiman, Carol, *Women's Networks*. Harper & Row, Publishers, Inc., 10 E. 53 St., New York, NY 10022. 1980. $5.95, paper.

Business & Professional Women's Foundation, *Where The Jobs Are: An Annotated Selected Bibliography*. B&PWF, 2012 Massachusetts Ave. NW, Washington, DC 20036. 1979. This foundation publishes a number of other booklets which may be of interest to women job-hunters or career-changers, including *Financial Aid: Where to Get It, How to Use It* (1978); *The Status of Clerical Workers* (1979); and some research not yet published. The foundation also runs workshops, conferences and seminars on career planning, at various places around the country, from time to time. If you are interested, you can ask them about these, when you write.

Harragan, Betty Lehan, *Games Mother Never Taught You: Corporate Gamesmanship for Women*. Warner Books, 666 Fifth Ave., New York, NY 10103. 1978, 1977. $2.50, paper. Detailing corporate politics as practiced by males, and how upwardly-mobile female executives can map their own game plan.

Ekstrom, Ruth B., Harris, Abigail M., and Lockheed, Marlaine E., *How To Get College Credit for What You Have Learned as a Homemaker and Volunteer*. 1977. Project HAVE SKILLS, Education Testing Service, Princeton, NJ 08541. $5.00, paper. They also publish the: *Have Skills Women's Workbook* ($7.95), *Have Skills Counselor's Guide* ($10.00), and the *Have Skills Employer's Guide* ($10.00). All of these include the famous "I CAN" lists, based upon the pioneering work, in the assessment of volunteer skills and knowledge, of the Council of National Organizations for Adult Education. Even for those not interested in college credit, but only in assessing the skills they picked up or sharpened as a volunteer or homemaker, this is an excellent resource. Classifies the skills under the various roles: administrator/manager, financial manager, personnel manager, trainer, advocate/change agent, public relations/communicator, problem surveyor, researcher, fund raiser, counselor, youth group leader, group leader for a serving organization, museum staff assistant (docent), tutor/teacher's aide, manager of home finances, home nutritionist, home child caretaker, home designer and maintainer, home clothing and textile specialist, and home horticulturist. *Very* helpful book, with accompanying aids.

The I CAN lists, incidentally, are also available from the National Center for Citizen Involvement's Volunteer Readership Service, Box 1807, Boulder, CO 80306. The I CAN Volunteer Development Workbook is $3.50.

Another historic resource for women is, of course:

Wider Opportunities for Women, 1325 G Street, N.W., Washington, D.C. 20005. A national nonprofit organization. Maintains a national resource and advocacy network for women's employment organizations, training programs for low-income women, and a child care counseling, information and referral program for trainee clients, monitors public policy related to jobs, affirmative action, vocational education, and training opportunities.

Books aimed at women in the world of work, appear faster than one can record them. Browse your local bookstore to see the full range of what's currently available, please.

©Copyright 1980 King Features Syndicate, Inc. Reprinted by special permission.

10. IF YOU WANT HELP WITH THE SPECIAL PROBLEMS OF MINORITIES

Davis, George and Watson, Glegg, *Black Life in Corporate America: Swimming in the Mainstream.* Anchor Press/Doubleday, 245 Park Ave., New York, NY 10167. 1983. $14.95, hardcover.

The Black Resource Guide. Black Resource Guide, Inc., 501 Oneida Pl., N. W., Suite. 500, Washington, DC 20011. 1984. $20.00, paper. A comprehensive list of black resources in the U.S.

Trower-Subira, *Black Folks' Guide to Making Big Money in America.* Very Serious Business Enterprises, Box 356, Newark, NJ 07101. 1980. $11.00, hardcover.

Johnson, Willis L., ed., *Directory of Special Programs for Minority Group Members: Career Information Services, Employment Skills Banks, Financial Aid Services*—Third Edition. Garrett Park Press, Garrett Park, MD 20766. 1980. $19.00, paper.

Wallace, Phyllis, with Datcher, Linda, and Malveaux, Julianne, *Black Women in the Labor Force.* The MIT Press, 28 Carleton St., Cambridge, MA 02142. 1980. $16.00, postpaid.

Cole, Katherine W., ed., *Minority Organizations: A National Directory.* Garrett Park Press, Garrett Park, MD 20766. 1978. $16.00, paper. An annotated directory of 2700 Black, Hispanic, Native, and Asian American organizations.

Financial Aid for Minority Students in: Allied Health, Business, Education, Engineering, Law, Mass Communications, Medicine, or Science. $3.00 per booklet, or $20.00 for all eight. Available from Garrett Park Press, Garrett Park, MD 20766.

11. HELP WITH THE SPECIAL PROBLEMS OF HANDICAPPED JOB-HUNTERS

The National Library Service for the Blind and Physically Handicapped, Library of Congress, 1291 Taylor St. NW, Washington DC 20542 has many books on career planning and job-hunting (such as *Parachute*) on tape, which they will send, with special playback equipment, to your home and back, free, if you are able to prove a "print-handicap."

Recording for the Blind, Inc., 20 Roszel Road, Princeton, New Jersey 08540 likewise has translated job-hunting books for the print-handicapped and visually-impaired.

Rabby, Rami, *Locating, Recruiting, and Hiring the Disabled.* Pilot Books, 103 Cooper St., Babylon, NY 11702. 1981. $3.95, paper. Includes over 500 sources of information covering referral agencies, media lists and other points of contact for employers.

Bruck, Dr. Lilly, Producer, *The Assertive Jobseeker: A Telecommunications Conference of nationally prominent experts.* In Touch Networks, 322 W. 48th St., New York, NY 10036. A three-cassette series, with speakers on such subjects as job-hunting and assertiveness, including *Parachute's* author. $9.00 per set.

Mitchell, Joyce Slayton, with a special section by Wallach, Ellen J., *See Me More Clearly.* Harcourt Brace Jovanovich, Inc., 757 Third Ave., New York, NY 10017. 1980. $8.95, hardcover. Particularly for handicapped youth.

Cook, Paul F.; Dahl, Peter R.; and Gale, Margaret Ann, *Vocational Opportunities: Vocational Training and Placement of the Severely Handicapped.* The American Institutes for Research in the Behavioral Sciences. Published by: Olympus Publishing Co., 1670 E. 13th S., Salt Lake City, UT 84105. 1978. $7.95, paper. *Sensational* book. Lists barriers (such as "low self-esteem," "impaired ability to read," "lack of independent living skills," etc.) then occupational clusters/divisions, jobs held by handicapped workers, and which handicaps are able to encompass particular tasks/jobs in each division.

Appleby, Judith A., et al., *Training Programs and Placement Services: Vocational Train-*

ing and Placement of the Severely Handicapped. The American Institutes for Research in the Behavioral Sciences. Published by: Olympus Publishing Co., 1670 E. 13th S., Salt Lake City, UT 84105. 1978. $16.95, hardcover. Lists, by region/state *effective* programs for helping the handicapped—152 in all. Describes each facility/program in detail. Very helpful.

Dahl, Peter R.; Appleby, Judith A.; and Lipe, Dewey, *Mainstreaming Guidebook for Vocational Educators: Teaching the Handicapped.* The American Institutes for Research in the Behavioral Sciences. Published by: Olympus Publishing Co., 1670 E. 13th S., Salt Lake City, UT 84105. 1978. $16.95, hardcover. Designed for counselors/teachers helping the handicapped—whether it be developing positive attitudes, modifying curricula, placing handicapped students in jobs, or whatever. Very useful, as are the other two books in this series, previously mentioned.

"The So-Called 'Handicapped' Job-Hunter: Strategies for Helping Him or Her in Today's Job-Market," the November-December 1978 issue of the *Newsletter about life/ work planning.* Single copies free if you send a self-addressed, stamped business envelope to: Newsletter, National Career Development Project, Box 379, Walnut Creek, CA 94596.

12. HELP WITH THE SPECIAL PROBLEMS OF EX-OFFENDERS

Federal/State Employment Offices often can be of particular assistance to ex-offenders. All offices can provide for bonding of ex-offenders, if needed to obtain employment. They also have information on tax-breaks for employers who hire ex-offenders. The larger offices even have Ex-Offender Specialists.

A general switchboard for ex-offenders is The Corrections Education Association, 1400 20th Street N.W., Washington D.C. 20036. They will know what resources are available to help the job-hunting ex-offender.

You can obtain a "Pre-Employment Curriculum" from the American Correctional Association, 4321 Hartwick Road, College Park, MD 20740. There is also: A Survival Source Book for Offenders, from Contacts, Inc., P.O. Box 81826, Lincoln, NB 68501.

Phil Young, who used to run a fine job-hunting program for offenders and ex-offenders, is now doing consultancy work in this field. You can contact him at 400 Linton, #7, Wilmington, OH 45177.

13. HELP WITH THE SPECIAL PROBLEMS OF EXECUTIVES AND THE BUSINESS WORLD

Common Body of Knowledge for Management Consultants. The American Association of Consulting Management Engineers, Inc., 230 Park Avenue, New York N.Y. 10017. If you are not at all familiar with the business world, and want a detailed breakdown of management functions and sub-functions, this is a very useful outline.

Figueroa, Oscar, and Winkler, Charles, *A Business Information Guidebook*, Amacom, 135 W. 50th St., New York, NY 10020. 1980.

Jablonski, Donna, M., ed., *How To Find Information About Companies*, Washington Researchers, 918 16th St., NW, Washington D.C. 20006.

Albert, Kenneth J., ed., *The Handbook of Business Problem Solving*. McGraw Hill Book Co., 1221 Avenue of the Americas, New York, NY 10020. 1980. $24.95, hardcover. For those who need a basic primer in understanding and solving problems in organizations.

How to Read A Financial Report. Merrill Lynch Pierce Fenner and Smith, Inc., 1 Liberty Plaza, New York, N.Y. 10080. If the organization you are interested in is large enough to have an annual financial report, that report *may* help you understand the organization better. And then again, it may not. Some (if not most) annual reports present their organizations only in *the most favorable* light possible. No warts, no pimples, no blemishes. You may also want to try: *What Else Can Financial Statements Tell You?* American Institute of Certified Public Accountants, 1211 Avenue of the Americas, New York, N.Y. 10036.

McCormack, Mark H., *What They Don't Teach You at Harvard Business School: Notes and tips of a 'street-smart executive.'* Bantam Books, 666 Fifth Avenue, New York, NY 10103. 1984. $15.95, hardcover.

Levering, Robert, Moskowitz, Milton, and Katz, Michael, *The 100 Best Companies to Work for in America.* Addison-Wesley Publishing Company, Reading, MA 01867. 1984. $17.95, hardcover. The problem is: is there any such animal as "the 100 best companies to work for," or are some companies excellent on the fifth floor, but poor down on the second floor? Nonethless, this is a fascinating book, as is everything these authors have written.

Prashker, Marti, and Valiunas, S. Peter, *Money Jobs: Training Programs Run by Banking, Accounting, Insurance, and Brokerage Firms—and How to Get Into Them.* Crown Publishers, Inc., One Park Avenue, New York, NY 10016. 1984. $7.95, paper.

Moskowitz, Milton; Katz, Michael; and Levering, Robert, eds. *Everybody's Business Scoreboard: Corporate America's Winners, Losers and Also-Rans.* Harper & Row, 10 E. 53rd St., New York, NY 10022. 1983. $5.95, paper. Who is the biggest, the best, the best-selling, the worst-selling. Who has triumphed, who's lost their shirt. Very fascinating book.

Peters, Thomas J., and Waterman, Jr., Robert H., *In Search of Excellence: Lessons from America's Best Run Companies.* Harper & Row, 10 E. 53rd St., New York, NY 10022. 1982. $19.95, hardcover. An instant classic. Well done. The title says it all.

Deal, Terrence E., and Kennedy, Allen A. *Corporate Cultures: The Rites and Rituals of Corporate Life.* Addison-Wesley Publishing Co., Inc., Jacob Way, Reading, MA 01867. 1982. $8.95, paper.

Blanchard, Kenneth, and Johnson, Spencer, *The One Minute Manager.* William Morrow and Co., Inc. 105 Madison Ave., New York, NY 10016. 1982. $15.00, hardcover. 106 pages, large print, wide margins, outrageous price, valuable content.

Behn, Robert D., and Vaupel, James W., *Quick Analysis for Busy Decision Makers.* Basic Books, Inc., 10 E. 53rd St., New York, NY 10022. 1982. $18.95, hardcover. How to make perplexing decisions, when time is short and information is limited, through the use of a decision-tree, preference-probability factors, and the like. Very useful book, with loads of helpful examples.

Herzberg, Frederick, *The Managerial Choice: To be efficient and to be human.* Olympus Publishing Company, 1670 E. 13th S., Salt Lake City, UT 84105. 1982. $19.95, hardcover. By one of the pioneers in the whole field of jobs and motivation.

Haldane, Bernard, *Bernard Haldane's Career Satisfaction and Success: How to know and manage your strengths.* Revised and enlarged. Amacom, 135 W. 50th St., New York, NY 10020. $12.95, hardcover. By one of the pioneers in the creative job-hunting process.

Wood, Jr., Orrin G., *Your Hidden Assets: The Key to Getting Executive Jobs.* Dow Jones-Irwin, 1818 Ridge Rd., Homewood, IL 60430. 1981. $15.95, hardcover.

Levinson, Harry, with the assistance of Lang, Cynthia, *Executive.* Harvard University Press, 79 Garden St., Cambridge, MA 02138. 1981. $18.50, hardcover.

Campbell, David, *If I'm in Charge Here Why is Everybody Laughing?* Argus Communications, One DLM Pk., Allen, TX 75002. 1980. $2.50, paper.

Boll, Carl R., *Executive Jobs Unlimited.* Updated edition. Macmillan Publishing Co., Inc., 866 Third Ave., New York, NY 10022. 1979, 1965. $8.95, hardcover. The classic in the executive job-hunting field.

Kanter, Rosabeth Moss, *Men and Women of the Corporation.* Basic Books, Inc., Publishers, New York, NY. 1977. $12.00, hardcover. A thoroughgoing study of how a corporation works, and how it affects the lives of the women and men in it.

Drucker, Peter, *Management: Tasks, Responsibilities, Practices.* Harper & Row, Publishers, 10 E. 53rd St., New York, NY 10022. 1973. $15.00. Should be absolutely required reading for anyone contemplating entering, changing to, or becoming a professional within the business world, or any organization.

Townsend, Robert, *Up the Organization: How to Stop the Corporation from Stifling People and Strangling Profits.* Alfred A. Knopf, New York, NY. 1970. Classic in the field.

Peter, Laurence F., and Hull, Raymond, *The Peter Principle: Why Things Always Go Wrong.* William Morrow & Co., Inc., New York, NY. 1969. $4.95, hardback. Another classic.

14. HELP WITH THE SPECIAL PROBLEMS OF COUPLES

With more and more married women in the work-force, a body of literature is beginning to appear concerning the problem of Both Partners Working:

Irish, Richard K., *How To Live Separately Together: A Guide for Working Couples.* Doubleday and Co., Inc., 245 Park Ave., New York, NY 10167. 1981. $11.95, hardcover.

Bird, Caroline, *The Two-Paycheck Marriage.* Pocket Books, 1230 Avenue of the Americas, New York, NY 10020. 1979. $2.75, paper.

Hall, Francine S., and Hall, Douglas T., *The Two-Career Couple.* Addison-Wesley, Jacob Way, Reading, MA 01867. 1979. $5.95, paper.

15. HELP WITH THE SPECIAL PROBLEMS
OF THE CLERGY AND RELIGIOUS PEOPLE

Moran, Pamela, J., *The Christian Job Hunter.* Servant Publications, 840 Airport Blvd., Box 8617, Ann Arbor, MI 48107. 1984. $6.95, paper.

Mattson, Ralph, and Miller, Arthur, *Finding A Job You Can Love.* Thomas Nelson Publishers, Nelson Place at Elm Hill Pike, Nashville TN 37214. 1982. $5.95, paperback. Very helpful and useful book, written from the Christian perspective.

Farnsworth, Kirk, and Lawhead, Wendell, *Life Planning.* InterVarsity Press, 5206 Main St., Downers Grove, IL 60515. 1981. $6.95, paper.

Olson, Richard P., *Mid-Life: A Time to Discover, A Time to Decide: A Christian Perspective on Middle Age.* Judson Press, Valley Forge, PA 19481. 1980. $5.95, paper.

Zehring, John William, *Making Your Life Count.* Judson Press, Valley Forge, PA 19481. 1980. $3.95, paper.

Rightor, Henry, *Pastoral Counseling in Work Crises.* Judson Press, Valley Forge, PA 19481. 1979. $2.95, paper.

If a book doesn't give you everything you need, there are some religious centers you can turn to. Probably no profession has developed, or had developed for it, so many resources to aid in career assessment as has the clerical profession. Many of them have broadened their services to include helping Church members, and not just clergy. Be warned however: clerical counselors are not perfect. Some are excellent, but some are not. They are, however, all sincere. Where you run into a clerical counselor who is sincere but inept, you will probably discover that the ineptness consists in an inadequate understanding of the distinction between career *assessment*—roughly comparable to taking a snapshot of people as they are in one frozen moment of time—vs. career *development*—which is roughly comparable to teaching people how to take their own motion pictures of themselves, from here on out.

Having issued this caution, however, we must go on to add that at some of these centers, listed below, are some simply excellent counselors who fully understand this distinction, and are well trained in that empowering of the client which is what career *development* is all about.

THE OFFICIAL INTERDENOMINATIONAL
CAREER DEVELOPMENT CENTERS

The Career and Personal
Counseling Service
St. Andrews Presbyterian
College, Laurinburg,
NC 28352
919-276-3162
Also at: 725 Providence Rd.
Charlotte, NC 28207
704-376-4086
Elbert R. Patton, Director

The Career and Personal
Counseling Center
Eckerd College
St. Petersburg, FL 33733
813-867-1166, Ext. 356
John R. Sims, Director

American Baptist
Center for Ministry
7804 Capwell Dr.
Oakland, CA 94621
415-635-4246
John R. Landgraf,
Director-Counselor

Clergy Career
Support System
3501 Campbell
Kansas City, MO 64109
816-931-2516
Eugene E. Timmons, Director

Lancaster Career
Development Center
561 College Ave.
Lancaster, PA 17603
717-397-7451
L. Guy Mehl, Director

North Central Career
Development Center
3000 Fifth St. NW
New Brighton, MN 55112
612-636-5120
Dr. John Davis, Director

Northeast Career
Development Center
291 Witherspoon St.
Princeton, NJ 08540
609-924-4814
Robert G. Foulkes,
Director

Career Development
Center of the Southeast
531 Kirk Rd.
Decatur, GA 30030
Robert M. Urie,
Director
404-371-0336

Midwest Career
Development Center
Box 7249
Westchester, IL 60153
312-343-6268
Ronald Brushwyler,
Associate Director

Southwest Career
Development Center
Box 5923
Arlington, TX 76011
817-265-5541
William M. Gould, Jr.,
Director-Counselor

Center for Career Development
and Ministry
70 Chase St.
Newton Centre, MA 02159
617-969-7750
Barton M. Lloyd, Associate Director
Harold D. Moore, Director

Midwest Career Development
Center, 2501 North Star Rd.,
Ste. 200
Columbus, OH 43221
614-486-0469
Frank C. Williams, Director

The centers listed above are all accredited and coordinated by the Career Development Council, Room 760, 475 Riverside Dr., New York, NY 10027. Some of them are accepting directors of Christian Education, ministers of music, and others in addition to clergy; some centers are open to all and not merely to church-related clients; some are open to high school students, as well as to adults.

ALSO DOING WORK IN THIS FIELD:

Mid-South Career Development Center, P.O. Box 120815, Acklen Station, Nashville, TN 37212. 615-327-9572. W. Scott Root, Director.

Career and Personal Counseling Center, 1904 Mt. Vernon St., Waynesboro, VA 22980, 703-943-9997. Lillian Pennell, Director.

The Episcopal Office of Pastoral Development, 116 Alhambra Circle, Ste. 210, Coral Gables, FL 33134. 305-448-8016. The Rt. Rev. David E. Richards.

Bernard Haldane, 4502 54th Ave. N.W., Seattle, WA 98105. (206) 525-8141. A pioneer in the clergy career management and assessment field, Bernard teaches (totally independently of the agency which bears his name) seminars and training of volunteers to do job-finding counseling. During 1985 he is devoting his time to starting a program in selected churches throughout the country aimed at reducing structural unemployment among blue- and white-collar workers. The ecumenical program is called Job Finding Power.

Life/Career Planning Center for Religious, 10526 W. Cermak Road, Suite 111, Westchester, IL 60153. Doing work with Roman Catholics.

16. HELP WITH BURNOUT, LACK OF PROMOTION, SURVIVAL

There is not enough said, generally, in job-hunting books about surviving after you get the job. The enemy is both within, and without. From within, the now-familiar problem of burnout. From without, various adversaries—both animate and inanimate. Marilyn Moats Kennedy has written the best overall book on this subject. Other resources follow.

Kennedy, Marilyn Moats, *Office Politics: Seizing Power, Wielding Clout.* Warner Books, 666 Fifth Ave., New York, NY 10103. 1981. $2.95, paper.

Kennedy, Marilyn Moats, *Career Knockouts: How to Battle Back.* New Century Publishers, Inc., 275 Old New Brunswick Rd., Piscataway, NJ 08854. 1980. $10.95, hardcover.

Germann, Richard; Blumenson, Diane; and Arnold, Peter, *Working & Liking It.* Fawcett Books, 201 E. 50th St., New York, NY 10022. 1984. $4.95, paper.

Brandt, Dr. David, *Is That All There Is? Overcoming Disappointment in an Age of Failed Expectations.* Poseidon Press Book, published by Pocket Books, a division of Simon and Schuster, Inc., 1230 Avenue of the Americas, New York, NY 10020. 1984. $14.95, paper.

Rogers, David J., *Fighting To Win: Samurai Techniques for Your Work and Life.* Doubleday and Co., Inc., 245 Park Avenue, New York, NY 10167. 1984. $13.95, hardcover.

Edelwich, Jerry, with Brodsky, Archie, *Burn-Out: Stages of Disillusionment in the Helping Professions.* Human Sciences Press, 72 Fifth Ave., New York, NY 10011. 1980. $19.95, hardcover.

You will also find some *very* helpful words on this subject in *Where Do I Go From Here With My Life?* (Ten Speed Press, Box 7123, Berkeley, CA 94707, 1974), pages 241–245 ("Understanding the Nature of the World of Work"), and 150–160 ("How to Survive After You Get the Job").

17. HELP WITH BEING FIRED, REJECTED, RIFFED OR LAID-OFF

Avrutis, Raymond, *How to Collect Unemployment Benefits: Complete Information for All 50 States.* Prentice-Hall, Englewood Cliffs, NJ 07632. 1983. $5.95, paper. There is much mythology about unemployment—for example, that you cannot collect if you were fired. That's only true if you were fired for misconduct. Avrutis argues that there is a trust fund set up, into which you have already contributed, from which you are now (if unemployed) entitled to collect. He tells what, where, why and how.

May, John, *The RIF Survival Handbook: How to manage your money if you're unemployed.* Tilden Press, 1737 DeSales St. NW, Suite 300, Washington, DC 20036. $4.95, plus $1.00 postage.

18. HELP WITH MID-LIFE, SECOND CAREERS, OR RETIREMENT

Boyer, Richard, and Savageau, David, *Places Rated Retirement Guide: Finding the best places in America for retirement living.* Rand McNally and Co., P.O. Box 7600, Chicago, IL 60680. 1983. $9.95, paper.

Axford, Roger W., *Successful Recareering: How To Shift Gears Before You're Over The Hill.* Media Productions and Marketing, Inc. 344 N. 27th, Lincoln, NE 68503. 1983. $12.95, paper.

Bird, Caroline, *The Good Years: Your Life in the Twenty-First Century.* E.P. Dutton, Inc., 2 Park Ave., New York, NY 10016. 1983. $15.95, hardcover. Describes coming trends on a note of optimism, amidst the pervasive trend in our society of declining hope, among the young.

Downs, Hugh, and Roll, Richard J., *The Best Years Book: How to plan for fulfillment, security, and happiness in the retirement years.* Delacorte Press, 1 Dag Hammarskjold Plaza, New York, NY 10017. 1981. $14.95, hardcover.

Sheehy, Gail, *Pathfinders.* William Morrow, 105 Madison Ave., New York, NY 10016. 1981. $15.95, hardcover.

Action for Independent Maturity, *Looking Ahead: How to Plan Your Successful Retirement.* American Association of Retired Persons, 1909 K St. NW, Washington, DC 20049. 1980. Paper.

Odell, Louise Minter and Odell, Charles E., Sr., *You and the Senior Boom: New Challenges and Opportunities for All.* Exposition Press, Inc., 900 S. Oyster Bay Rd., Hicksville, NY 11801. 1980. $12.50, hardback.

Durkin, Jon, "Mid-Life Career Changes." Johnson O'Connor Research Foundation, Human Engineering Laboratory, 701 Sutter St., San Francisco, CA 94109.

Robbins, Paula I., *Successful Midlife Career Change: Self-Understanding and Strategies for Action.* Amacom, 135 W. 50th St., New York, NY 10020. 1978. $12.95, hardcover. Very up-to-date, very thorough, very helpful. Probably the best book dealing with this problem.

19. HELP WITH THE SPECIAL PROBLEMS OF GOING BACK TO SCHOOL

To get equivalency examinations for the knowledge or experience you've already acquired out of life, write to CLEP (College-Level Examination Program), College Entrance Examination Board, Box 1822, Princeton, NJ 08541, or Box 1025, Berkeley CA 94701. It is a national standardized examination program for college credit.

Gross, Ronald, *The Independent Scholar's Handbook: How to Turn Your Interest in Any Subject into Expertise.* Addison-Wesley, General Books Division, Reading, MA 01867. 1982. $16.95, hardcover. $8.95, paper.

Graham, Lawrence, *Conquering College Life: How to Be a Winner at College.* Pocket Books, 1230 Avenue of the Americas, New York, NY 10020. 1983.

von Klemperer, Lily, *International Education: A Directory of Resource Materials on Comparative Education and Study in Another Country.* Garrett Park Press, Garrett Park, MD 20766. $5.95, if prepaid.

20. HELP WITH THE SPECIAL PROBLEMS OF COLLEGE STUDENTS

Moore, Ph.D., Richard W., *Winning the Ph.D. Game: How to Get Into and Out of Graduate School With a Ph.D. and a Job.* Dodd, Mead & Co., 79 Madison Ave., New York, NY 10016. 1985. $13.95, paper. This seems to me to be an unusually helpful and well-researched book for Ph.D. graduates.

Careers And The MBA: 1984 Edition. Bob Adams Inc., 840 Summer Street, South Boston, MA 02127. 1984. $12.95, paper.

Bemard, Susan, and Thompson, Gretchen, *Job Search Strategy for College Grads.* Bob

Adams Inc., 840 Summer Street, South Boston, MA 02127. 1984. $3.95, paper.

Gates, Anita, *90 Highest Paying Careers for the '80s.* Monarch Press, a division of Simon and Schuster, Inc., Simon and Schuster Building, 1230 Avenue of the Americas, New York, NY 10020. 1984. $8.95, paper.

Moorpark College Counseling Staff, *Exercising Your Options: A Career Fitness Plan.* Gorsuch Scarisbrick, Publishers, 576 Central Ave., Dubuque, IA 52001. 1984. $9.95, paper.

Bly, Robert W., and Blake, Gary, *Dream Jobs: A Guide to Tomorrow's Top Careers.* Wiley Press Books, John Wiley and Sons, Inc., 605 3rd Avenue, New York, NY 10158. 1983. $8.95, paper. Nine careers are herein described.

Scheele, Ph.D., Adele, *Making College Pay Off.* Ballantine Books, 201 E. 50th Street, New York, NY 10022. 1983. $2.95, paper.

Munschauer, John L., *Jobs for English Majors and Other Smart People.* Peterson's Guides, Inc., P.O. Box 2123, Princeton, NJ 08540. 1982. $6.95, paper.

"Business Week's Guide to Careers." Available on newsstands. $2.95 per issue.

Goulet, Theresa, *Sell Yourself! The career handbook for Canadian university students and prospective students.* Atgood Publications, Ltd., 401 Varsity Estates Bay NW, Calgary, Alberta, Canada T3B 2W7. 1982. $9.95, paper.

Kingstone, Brett, *The Student Entrepreneur's Guide.* Ten Speed Press, Box 7123, Berkeley, CA 94707. 1981. $4.95, paper. What college students are able to do as entrepreneurs, while still in college, has always staggered my imagination. One of them tells how it's done.

Figler, Howard E., *Path: A Career Workbook for Liberal Arts Students.* The Carroll Press Publishers, Box 8113, Cranston, RI 02920. 1979, 1975. Second edition, completely revised. Good stuff.

Malnig, Lawrence, and Morrow, Sandra L., *What Can I Do With A Major In . . .?* Garrett Park Press, Garrett Park, MD 20766. 1975. $8.95, prepaid; paper. Tells you all the career paths a major can branch out into, based on the experience of graduates at one college, at least.

Careers without Reschooling. A 12 cassette series for the liberal arts graduate. It is subtitled "The Survival Guide." ArGee Productions, 905 University Avenue, Madison WI 53715, 608-255-8480. $95. for the set, plus $3.50 for shipping and handling.

Our Canadian readers will want to know that their University and College Placement Association (43 Eglinton Ave. E., Suite 1003, Toronto, Ontario, M4P 1A2) puts out a number of publications for those related to the college scene. These include:

Career Planning Annual, 1983–1984. Published in either English or French.

McClure, Ross M., *Destiny: Career Planning Manual.* 1980. Also a counsellor's guide to go with it.

Russell, Bonita I., *Heading Out . . . . A Job Search Workbook.* 1982, 1980.

Gaymer, Rosemary, *Teach Yourself How To Find A Job.* 1980, 1974.

Finding The Right Job for You. 1982.

The Resume. 1982.

The Interview. 1982.

Books on summer jobs are listed in
the next section.

---

21. HELP WITH THE SPECIAL PROBLEMS OF HIGH SCHOOL STUDENTS

Douglas, Martha C., *Go For It: How to Get Your First Good Job.* Ten Speed Press, Box 7123, Berkeley, CA 94707. 1983. $5.95, paper. Based on Ms. Douglas' experience as coordinator of an industry training program for teenagers, at the *Contra Costa Times* newspaper in Walnut Creek, California.

O'Brien, Barbara, editor, *Summer Employment Directory of the United States.* Writer's Digest Books, 9933 Alliance Rd., Cincinnati, OH 45242. This book comes out each year. It lists 50,000 summer job openings at resorts, campuses, amusement parks, hotels, conferences and training centers, ranches, restaurants, national parks, etc. 1000 places, in all.

Woodworth, D.J., ed., *Overseas Summer Jobs: Where the jobs are and how to get them.* Writer's Digest Books, 9933 Alliance Rd., Cincinnati, OH 45242. $7.95, paper.

Bershad, Carol, and DiMella, Nancy, *The Changer and the Changed: A Working Guide to Personal Change.* Management Sciences for Health, 165 Allandale Road, Boston, MA 02130. 1983. $11.95, paper.

Henderson, Douglass, *Get Ready: Job-Hunters Kit* (for high school students). This package includes: *Get Ready, Teachers Manual; Get Ready, Students Manual; and cassette.* Get Ready, Inc., a subsidiary of Educational Motivation Inc., P.O. Box 18865, Philadelphia, PA 19119. 1980. $19.95, for the kit.

Career World—The Continuing Guide to Careers (a periodical), Joyce Lain Kennedy, Executive Editor. From $3.25 up, per subscription. Curriculum Innovations, Inc. 501 Lake Forest Ave., Highwood, IL 60040.

Reprinted with permission from *Trever's First Strike.* Brick House Publishing, 1983.

22. HELP WITH GETTING A
JOB IN EDUCATION

Teachers teach in schools. That has been the assumption that has dominated teacher-training for ages.

You would do well not to make this error. The range of places that use people with teaching skills is mind-boggling: but as just a sampling, there are—as experts like John Crystal point out—training academies (like fire and police); corporate training and education departments; local and state councils on higher education; designers and manufacturers of educational equipment; teachers associations; foundations; private research firms; regional and national associations of universities, etc.; state and congressional legislative committees on education; specialized educational publishing houses; professional and trade societies. An indication of some of the possibilities you may want to research, can be found in *Education Directory: Education Associations*. It's available in your local library, or from the Superintendent of Documents, U.S. Govt. Printing Off., Washington, DC 20402.

Moreover, the range of jobs that are done under the broad umbrella of Education is multitudinous and varied; just for openers, there is: *teaching* (of course), *counseling* (an honorable teaching profession, where it isn't just used by a school system as the repository for teachers who couldn't 'cut it'), *general administration, adult education programs, public relations, ombudsman, training, human resource development*, and the like. If the latter—i.e., training and development—is of particular interest to you, you will find there is a very useful description of the particular competencies, skills, and knowledges needed in the training and development fields. You'll find it in *Training and Development Competencies*, Patricia A. McLagan, Volunteer Study Director. Published in 1983, it is available from the American Society for Training and Development, Ste. 305, 600 Maryland Ave., S.W., Washington D.C. 20024. Our Canadian friends, namely the Ontario Society for Training and Development, have put out also a helpful guide, entitled *Competency Analysis for Trainers: A Personal Planning Guide*. It is available from O.S.T.D., Box 537, Postal Station K, Toronto, M4P 2G9, Ontario, Canada, for $5.00, plus $1.50 for postage and handling. It outlines the kinds of skills which people who are entering this field ought to possess, and provides a checklist against which one can compare one's own skills.

All of which is to say, just because you have defined your dream of life for yourself as "teacher" doesn't mean you have even begun to narrow the territory down sufficiently for you to start looking for a job. You still have more research, and information gathering to do, before you have defined exactly *what kind* of teaching, *with what* kind of *groups, in what* kind of *place*. In other words, chapters 5—7 in this manual apply to you as much as, or even more than, anyone else.

If you decide to look elsewhere than teaching, there are aids produced for various teaching specialties, that you may want to seek out, e.g., for history majors there is: *Careers for Students of History*, from the American Historical Association, 400 A St. SE, Washington, DC 20003. 1977. $3.50, paper. While, for English majors, there is: *Aside from Teaching English, What in the World Can You Do?* by Dorothy K. Bestor, available from: University of Washington Press, Seattle, WA 98105. 1982, revised. $5.95, paper.

There are other more general guides for faculty who have decided to become career-changers; new ones are produced each year, as the publishing industry has lately (very lately) become aware of the problem; these are, in reverse order of publication:

Anthony, Rebecca, and Roe, Gerald, *From Contact to Contract: A teacher's employment guide*. Carroll Press, 43 Squantum St., Cranston, RI 02920-9990. 1983. $6.95, paper.

Baldwin, Roger, et al., *Expanding Faculty Options: Career Development at Colleges and*

Universities. American Association for Higher Education, One Dupont Circle, Suite 780, Washington, DC 20036. 1981. Paper.

Furniss, W. Todd, *Reshaping Faculty Careers.* American Council on Education, One Dupont Circle, Washington, DC 20036. 1981. Paper.

Miller, Jean M., and Dickinson, Georgianna M., *When Apples Ain't Enough: Career Change Techniques for Teachers, Counselors and Librarians.* Jalmar Press, Inc., 6501 Elvas Ave., Sacramento, CA 95819. 1980. $4.95, paper.

23. HELP WITH ANALYSIS OF SKILLS

Pearson, Henry G., *Your Hidden Skills: Clues to Careers and Future Pursuits.* Mowry Press, Box 405, Wayland, MA 01778. 1981, paper.

Myers, Isabel Briggs and Peter, *Gifts Differing.* Consulting Psychologists Press, Inc., 577 College Ave., Palo Alto, CA 94306. 1980. $12.00, paper. Related to the increasingly-popular Myers-Briggs Test.

Figler, Howard E., *The Complete Job Search Handbook: Presenting the Skills You Need to Get Any Job, and Have a Good Time Doing It.* Holt, Rinehart and Winston, 521 Fifth Ave., New York, NY 10175. 1979. $5.95, paper. Deals with the skills actually used in the job-hunt process itself.

McCormick, Ernest J., *Job Analysis: Methods and Applications.* Amacom, 135 W. 50th St., New York NY 10020. 1979. $25.95, hardcover.

Scheele, Adele, *Skills For Success: A Guide to the Top for Men and Women.* Ballantine Books, 201 E. 50th St., New York, NY 10022. 1979. $2.95, paper.

Fine, Sidney A., *Functional Job Analysis Scales: A Desk Aid.* Methods for Manpower Analysis, No. 5. April 1973.

_____, and Wiley, Wretha W., *An Introduction to Functional Job Analysis: A Scaling of Selected Tasks from the Social Welfare Field.* Methods for Manpower Analysis, No. 4. September 1971.

_____, *A Systems Approach to New Careers: Two Papers.* Methods for Manpower Analysis, No. 3. November 1969.

_____, *Guidelines for the Design of New Careers.* September 1967.

(The W.E. Upjohn Institute for Employment Research's *Studies on Functional Job Analysis and Career Design.)*

The above pamphlets are available from The W.E. Upjohn Institute for Employment Research, 300 S. Westnedge Ave., Kalamazoo, MI 49007.

Fine, Sidney A., *Nature of Skill: Implication for Education and Training.* 1870 Wyoming Ave. NW, Washington, DC 20009. A superb summary of some recent thinking from the father of skills analysis in the Dictionary of Occupational Titles.

24. HELP WITH INTERVIEWING, SALARY NEGOTIATION, AND RESUMES

Zimbardo, Phillip G., *Shyness, What It Is, What To Do About It.* Jove Publications, 757 Third Avenue, New York, NY 10017. 1977. $2.25, paper.

Granovetter, Mark S., *Getting a Job: A Study of Contacts and Careers.* Harvard University Press, c/o Uniserv Inc., 525 Great Road, Rt. 119, Littleton MA 01460. 1974. $7.95, hardcover. *The* classic study of the importance of contacts for the job-hunt.

Lipnack, Jessica, and Stamps, Jeffrey, *Networking: The first report and directory—People connecting with people, linking ideas and resources.* Doubleday & Co., 245 Park Ave., New York NY 10017. 1982. $15.95, paper.

Lathrop, Richard, *Who's Hiring Who?* Ten Speed Press, Post Office Box 7123, Berkeley CA 94707. 1977, updated 1980. $7.95, paper. The very best book on how to

write a resume, or "qualifications brief," as the author prefers it be called.

Jackson, Tom, *The Perfect Resume.* Anchor Press/Doubleday. Garden City, NY 11530. 1981. $6.95, paper.

Parker, Yana, *Damn Good Resume Guide.* Ten Speed Press, P.O. Box 7123, Berkeley, CA 94707. 1983. $4.95, paper. Describes how to write a *functional* resume.

Resume Service, *Resumes That Work.* Coles Publishing Co., Ltd., Toronto, Canada. 1979. $4.95, paper.

Williams, Eugene, *Increase Your Employment Opportunities with the Audiovisual Portfolio.* Competent Associates, Box 6745, Washington, DC 20020. 1980. $12.95, paper. Focuses on teachers, but has wider application.

Molloy, John T., *Dress for Success.* Warner Books, 666 Fifth Avenue, New York NY 10103. 1975. $6.95, paper. The classic in the "personal image consultancy" field: how to make a better impression through the way you dress.

Molloy, John T., *The Women's Dress for Success Book* (same publisher, same price).

Supplement to Employment and Earnings, U.S. Department of Labor, Bureau of Labor Statistics. 1984. Order from: Superintendent of Documents, U.S. Government Printing Office, Washington, D.C. 20402. $7.50 domestic, $9.40, foreign. Tells what different occupations pay.

Wright, John W., *The American Almanac of Jobs and Salaries.* Avon Books, 1790 Broadway, New York NY 10019. 1982. $9.95, paper. A very helpful book for figuring out salaries.

Harrop, David, *World Paychecks: Who makes what, where, and why.* Facts on File Publications, 460 Park Avenue South, New York, NY 10016. 1982.

Kandel, Thelma, *What Women Earn.* The Linden Press, Simon & Schuster, 1230 Avenue of the Americas, New York, NY 10020. 1981. $6.95, paper.

Stern, Edward L., *Salary Guide and Job Outlook.* Hilary House Publishers, 1033 Channel Dr., Hewlett Harbor, NY 11557. 1981. $5.95, paper.

Harrop, David, *Paychecks: Who Makes What? The Book That Tells You What Everybody Earns.* Harper & Row, 10 E. 53rd St., New York NY 10022. 1980. $5.95, paper. While books with this old a publishing date tend to grow quickly outdated, this was the original classic in the field, and there is still much information in it which can be found nowhere else. You'll just have to add the proper inflationary adjustment, to guess what the 1985 equivalents would be.

Chastain, Sherry, *Winning the Salary Game.* John Wiley and Sons, Inc., 605 Third Avenue, New York NY 10158. 1980.

Biegeleisen, J.I., *Make Your Job Interview A Success: A Guide for the Career-Minded Jobseeker.* Arco Publishing, Inc., 215 Park Avenue South, New York, NY 10003. 1984. $6.95, paper.

Biegeleisen, J.I., *Job Resumes: How to write them, how to present them, preparing for interviews.* Grosset & Dunlap, 51 Madison Ave., New York, NY 10010. 1982, revised. $4.95, paper. A classic in the field.

Williams, Eugene, *Getting the Job You Want With the Audiovisual Portfolio*. Comptex Associates, Inc., Box 6745, Washington, DC 20020. 1982. $12.95, paper. Manual for job-seekers and career changers in professions other than teaching.

The Catalyst Staff, *Marketing Yourself: The Catalyst Guide to Successful Resumes and Interviews*. Bantam Books, 666 Fifth Ave., New York, NY 10103. 1981. $3.50, paper.

Medley, H. Anthony, *Sweaty Palms: The Neglected Art of Being Interviewed*. Ten Speed Press, Box 7123, Berkeley, CA 94707. 1978. $7.95, paper. *The* classic on interviewing.

25. HELP WITH JOB-HUNTING IN GENERAL, AND PLACES TO LIVE

At the United Nations, when Swahili is being spoken, most people from other nations do not understand—until, over the earphones, the speech is translated into their own language. So, with job-hunting. Many do not understand the language of *Parachute*. Yet the same thoughts, spoken in another's style of writing, say Howard Figler's or Tom Jackson's, may suddenly hit home to those readers. There are over 20,000,000 different job hunters out there, in an average year. No one book will ever be understood by them all. Hence, we will always need many different books on job-hunting; and the more different 'styles' or 'languages,' the better.

Bayless, Hugh, *The Best Towns in America: A Where-to-Go Guide for a Better Life*. Houghton-Mifflin Co., 2 Park St., Boston, MA 02108. 1983. $9.95, paper.

Bowman, Thomas F., and Giuliana, George A., and Minge, M. Ronald, *Finding Your Best Place to Live in America*. Red Lion Books, 609 Route 109, West Babylon, NY 11704. 1981. $9.95, paper.

Boyer, Richard, and Savageau, David, *Places Rated Almanac: Your guide to finding the best places to live in America*. Rand McNally & Co. 1981. $11.95, paper.

Ruffner, James A., and Bair, Frank E., eds., *The Weather Almanac*. Avon Books, 1790 Broadway, New York, NY 10019. 1979. $6.95, paper.

Small Town, U.S.A.: The Original Newsletter Dedicated to the Search for American Shangri-Las. Published by Woods Creek Press, P.O. Box 339, Ridgecrest, CA 93555, 619-375-1988. Subscription: $30/yr. Outside the U.S.: $36/yr. Published every other month. Usually one town is profiled in each issue. For readers who want to know about "ideal" small towns in America.

Career Paths. Bob Adams Inc., 840 Summer Street, South Boston, MA 02127. 1984. $7.95, paper.

Camden, Thomas M., *The Job Hunter's Final Exam*. Surrey Books, Inc., 500 N. Michigan Avenue, Chicago, IL 60611. 1984. $4.95, paper.

Anderson, Nancy, *Work With Passion: How to Do What You Love for a Living*. A co-publication of Carroll & Graf Publishers, Inc., 260 Fifth Avenue, New York, NY 10001, and Whatever Publishing, Inc., P.O. Box 137, Mill Valley, CA 94942. 1984. $15.95, hardcover. Good on how to establish contact with people.

Stevens, Paul, *Stop Postponing the Rest of Your Life*. Unwin Paperbacks, Sydney, London, Boston; 9 Winchester Terrace, Winchester, MA 01890. 1984.

Stevens, Paul, *Win That Job: The Australian guide to success*. Unwin Paperbacks (address above). 1984. Paper.

Stevens, Paul, *Work Satisfaction: How to Plan for, Find, and Maintain It. A comprehensive guide to planning and managing your career*. William Brooks, 723 Elizabeth Street, Waterloo, NSW 2017.

Austin, Margaret Faughnan, and Vines, Harriet Mason, *Bridges To Success: Finding Jobs and Changing Careers*. Wiley Press, a division of John Wiley & Sons, Inc., 605 Third Avenue, New York, NY 10158. 1983. $15.95, hardcover.

Truitt, John, *Telesearch: Direct Dial the Best Job of Your Life*. Facts on File, 460 Park Ave. S., New York, NY 10016. 1983. $11.95, hardback. "Telesearch" is short for "telephone job search."

Feingold, S. Norman, and Winkler, Glenda, *Nine Hundred Thousand Plus Jobs Annually: Published Sources of Employment Listings*. Garrett Park Press, Garrett Park, MD 20766. Cites periodicals which list job announcements. 1982. $9.95, paper.

Jackson, Tom, and Mayleas, Davidyne, *The Hidden Job Market for the Eighties*. Quadrangle/The New York Times Book Co., 3 Park Ave., New York, NY 10016. 1981. $9.95, paper.

Job Information and Seeking Training Program Instructor's Guide and Job Seekers Workbook. JIST, 1001 W. 10th St., Indianapolis, IN 46202. 1980. Paper.

Winston, Stephanie, *Getting Organized: The easy way to put your life in order*. Warner Books, 666 Fifth Ave., New York NY 10103. 1978. $4.95, paper. *The* classic about getting your life organized, by the founder and director of The Organizing Principle. Deals with how to better organize your time, paper, work space, closets, finances, books, clothes, tasks, etc.

26. IF YOU ARE A CAREER COUNSELOR, OR WANT TO BE

Those just getting started in the field of career counseling (within or without academia) will, of course, want to read the current edition of *Parachute* from cover to cover, and then DO all the exercises within it, before they inflict them on their helpless students or clients. *Teaching is sharing, and Sharing should only follow Experiencing*.

Among the following listings, you will find a number of workbooks designed to help you with that Sharing.

Newsletter about life/work planning. Richard N. Bolles, editor. National Career Development Project, Box 379, Walnut Creek, CA 94596. Annual subscription, January–December only, $15.00, U.S. Published six times a year, always written by the editor himself.

Career Planning & Adult Development Newsletter, published monthly by the Career Planning and Adult Development Network, 1190 South Bascom Avenue, Suite 211, San Jose, CA 95128, 408-295-5461. Membership in the Network is $24/yr. for individuals; $35/yr. for organizations. Outside the U.S., Canada and Mexico, it is $35. for individuals, $45. for organizations.

CNews: Career Opportunities News, Garrett Park Press, Garrett Park, MD 20896, 301-946-2553. $30/yr. ($25 if prepaid). Useful news for counselors (and job-hunters) about employment fields, fellowships, new books, etc.

Wallach, Ellen J., with Fulford, Nancy, *Career Management: When Preparation Meets Opportunity. Leader's Guide*. EFM Films, A Division of Education for Management, Inc., 85 Main St., Watertown, MA 02172. An excellent manual, designed to go with the film of the same title, in order to help you to use the film to serve a number of purposes: if you (as counselor) are trying to sell decision makers on the benefits of career management to their organization; or if you want to inform managers about the benefits of career management as part of an overall human resource system; or if you are working with HR professionals to assess organizational career management needs and/or to design a systems approach to career management; or if you want to give individual employees, their managers, or HR professionals an overview of career management; or if you are training personnel who are charged with career guidance responsibilities; or if you want to conduct a career management workshop; or if you are approached by an employee or manager seeking individual career counseling.

Knowdell, Richard L., and McDaniels, Carl, and Hesser, Al, and Walz, Garry R.,

Outplacement Counseling. Eric Counseling and Personnel Services Clearinghouse, School of Education, University of Michigan, Ann Arbor, MI 48109. 1983. This is the area of career development, within the world of work, that is expanding the fastest these days. For counselors interested in this as a future field of endeavor, this overview.

Maze, Marilyn, and Cummings, Roger, *How to Select a Computer Assisted Career Guidance System.* EUREKA, 5625 Sutter Ave., Richmond, CA 94804. 1982. $8.00, paper (check or purchase order must accompany your order; please add $.80 for postage and handling. California residents, please also add $.52 sales tax). For schools, organizations and agencies thinking of acquiring one of the computerized systems now available. What they can do, what they can't do.

Wegmann, Robert, *How to Find a Job in Houston.* Ten Speed Press, Box 7123, Berkeley, CA 94707. 1983. $9.95, paper. Every counselor or workshop leader who teaches a course or leads a workshop on job-hunting should find this book very helpful. Professor Wegmann has for some years, now, taught a course, for credit, on job-hunting, at the University of Houston–Clear Lake City. This book is adapted from his curriculum, with supplementary research on the city of Houston. It illustrates how to dissect *any* city or geographical area, for the purposes of the job-hunter or career-changer. It has an appendix also on "Assisting Larger Groups of Unemployed Workers to Find New Employment," by Professor Wegmann; as well as an article, "The Loss of Values in Career Counseling," by Richard N. Bolles.

Making a Living Work is an eight part television series about life/career planning. It features interviews with Richard Bolles and many others. For information, contact Elyzabeth Joffe, ITV Coordinator, Ohio University, Telecommunication Center, Athens, OH 45701. The series was produced by the Council for the Advancement of Experiential Learning (CAEL).

Mencke, Reed, and Hummel, Ronald L., *Career Planning For The 80s.* Brooks/Cole Publishing Company, a Division of Wadsworth, Inc., 555 Abrego Street, Monterey, CA 93940. 1984. $15.00, paper.

Borchard, David C., Kelly, John J., Weaver, Nancy Pat K., *Your Career: Choices, Chances, Changes.* Kendall/Hunt Publishing Company, 2460 Kerper Blvd., Dubuque, IA 52001. 1984. Paper.

Career Employment Opportunities Directory (4-Volume set). Ready Reference Press, P.O. Box 5879, Santa Monica, CA 90405. 1984. $190.00, paper.

Mirabile, Richard J., *Career Decisions: Strategies for Enrichment.* Kendall/Hunt Publishing Company, Dubuque, Iowa. 1983. $10.50, paper.

Bloomfield, William M., *The Vocational Action Plan: Targeting Job Success; a Workbook.* William Bloomfield and Associates, Inc., 90 Park St., Ste. 22, Brookline, MA 02146. 1982. $8.50, paper.

Hagberg, Janet, and Leider, Richard, *The Inventurers: Excursions in Life and Career Renewal.* Addison-Wesley Publishing Co., Jacob Way, Reading, MA 01867. 1982. $7.95, paper.

Tough, Allen, *Intentional Changes: A Fresh Approach to Helping People Change.* Follett Publishing Co./Dept. DM T82-39, 1010 W. Washington Blvd., Chicago, IL 60607. 1982. $17.95, hardcover.

Leider, Richard J., and Harding, James S., *Taking Stock: A daily self-management journal.* Taking Stock, Box 8709, Portland, OR 97208. 1981. $7.95 plus .50 postage, paper.

Crites, John O., *Career Counseling: Models, Methods, and Materials.* McGraw-Hill, 1221 Avenue of the Americas, New York, NY 10020. 1981. $14.95, hardcover.

Pilder, Richard J., and William F., *How to Find Your Life's Work.* Prentice-Hall, Englewood Cliffs, NJ 07632. 1981. $4.95, paper.

Guide for Occupational Exploration. Supt. of Documents, U.S. Govt. Printing Off., Washington, DC 20402. 1979. $11.00. Occupations organized by interest and job title.

Tiedeman, David V., *Career Development: Designing Our Career Machines*. The Carroll Press, 43 Squantum St., Cranston, RI 02920. 1979. $9.95, paper. How to use computers to design a career-decision-and-development system.

Basso, Janice L.; Kendall, Nancy P.; and Miller, Donna S.M., *Creating a Canadian Career Information Centre*. University and College Placement Association, 43 Eglinton Ave. E., Suite 1003, Toronto, Ontario M4P 1A2. 1979.

Feldman, Beverly Neuer, *Jobs/Careers serving children and youth* (including Supplement: Appendix C and Index—inserted into the book, but separate). Till Press, Box 27816, Los Angeles, CA 90027. 1978. $10.95, paper. Groups the jobs and careers according to how much education the job-hunter has had. For all those who want to work with youth or children.

Shepard, Herbert A., *The Career Management System: Life Planning*. Management Decision Systems, Inc., Box 35, Darien, CT 06820. 1976. Cassettes and workbook.

McClure, Larry, *Career Education Survival Manual: A Guidebook for Career Educators and Their Friends*. Olympus Publishing Co., 1670 E. 13th S., Salt Lake City, UT 84105. 1975. An absolutely superb little handbook for everyone who wants to understand more about how to relate education to the world of work (and vice versa). Imaginatively laid out, and written by one of the experts in this field.

Hoyt, Kenneth, et al., *Career Education: What It Is and How to Do It*. Second edition. Olympus Publishing Co., 1670 E. 13th S., Salt Lake City, UT 84105. 1974. $6.95.

Cosgrave, Gerald, *Career Planning: Search for a Future*. Guidance Centre/Faculty of Education/University of Toronto. 1973. Available from Customer Service, Teacher's College Press, 1234 Amsterdam Ave., New York, NY 10027. $4.45; or from Consulting Psychologist's Press, 577 College Ave., Palo Alto, CA 94306. It relates to John L. Holland's six people-environments.

Hoppock, Robert, *Occupational Information: Where to Get It and How to Use It in Counseling and in Teaching*. Third edition. McGraw Hill, New York, NY. 1967. A pioneer in this field.

Super, Donald E., et al., *Career Development: Self-Concept Theory. Essays in Vocational Development*. College Board Publication Orders, Box 2815, Princeton, NJ 08540. 1963. $4.50, paper. Another pioneer in the field.

27. PERSPECTIVES ON THE WORLD OF WORK TODAY

Cornish, Ed., editor, *Careers Tomorrow: The Outlook for Work in a Changing World*. World Future Society, 4916 St. Elmo Ave., Bethesda, MD 20814. 1983. $6.95, paper.

Feingold, S. Norman, and Miller, Norma Reno, *Emerging Careers: New Occupations for the Year 2000 and Beyond. Vol. I. The Newest of the New*. Garrett Park Press, Garrett Park, MD 20896. 1983. $11.95, paper ($10.95 if prepaid).

Raines, John C.; Berson, Lenora E.; and Gracie, David McI., ed., *Community and Capital in Conflict: Plant Closings and Job Loss*. Temple University Press, Broad and Oxford Sts., Philadelphia, PA 19122. 1982, hardcover.

Raelin, Joseph A., *Building a Career: The effect of initial job experiences and related work attitudes on later employment*. W.E. Upjohn Institute for Employment Research, 300 S. Westnedge Ave., Kalamazoo, MI 49007. 1980. $4.50, paper.

U.S. Dept. of Labor, Bureau of Labor Statistics, *Handbook of Labor Statistics*. Supt. of Documents, U.S. Govt. Printing Off., Washington, DC 20402. $9.95, paper.

U.S. Dept. of Labor, Employment and Training Admin., *Selected Characteristics of Occupations Defined in the Dictionary of Occupational Titles*. Supt. of Documents, U.S. Govt. Printing Off., Washington, DC 20402. 1981. Paper.

U.S. Dept. of Labor, Employment and Training Administration, *Guide for Occupational Exploration*. Supt. of Documents, U.S. Govt. Printing Off., Washington, DC 20402. Stock #029-013-0080-2. 1979. Paper.

Bureau of Labor Statistics, *Occupational Outlook Handbook*, Supt. of Documents, U.S. Govt. Printing Off., Washington, DC 20402. $9, paper. 670-page encyclopedia of careers, covering hundreds of occupations and 35 major industries.

Best, Fred, *Flexible Life Scheduling: Breaking the Education-Work-Retirement Lockstep.* Praeger Publishers, 521 Fifth Ave., New York, NY 10017. 1979. $8.95, paper.

Miller, Ann R., et al., eds., *Work, Jobs, and Occupations: A Critical Review of the Dictionary of Occupational Titles.* National Academy Press, 2101 Constitution Ave. NW, Washington, DC 20418. 1980. Paper.

U.S. Dept. of Labor and the U.S. Dept. of Health and Human Services, *Employment and Training Report of the President.* Superintendent of Documents, U.S. Govt. Printing Off., Washington, DC 20402. Paper.

Edwards, Patsy B., *Leisure Counseling Techniques.* Constructive Leisure, 511 N. La Cienega Blvd., Los Angeles, CA 90048. $11.95 per copy, postpaid (add 6% sales tax in California), paper.

Lathrop, Richard, *The Job Market.* The National Center for Job-Market Studies, Box 3651, Washington, DC 20007. $4.85, paper. What would happen if we decreased the length of the job-hunt in America, and other iconoclastic ideas which are also eminently sensible.

Terkel, Studs, *Working.* Avon Paperback, New York, 1975. $3.50, paper. A classic.

Herzberg, Frederick, *Work and the Nature of Man.* New American Library, 1633 Broadway, New York, NY 10019. 1973, 1966. $1.50, paper. A classic on motivation.

28. PERSPECTIVES ON CREATIVITY AND THE BRAIN

Our whole vocational system is oriented toward people with verbal skills, rather than intuitive; and toward achievement, rather than relationship goals. Those wishing to correct this imbalance, in themselves or in those they are trying to help, will find it extremely helpful to know more about the brain, how it is divided, and how it works. So constant are the new findings in this field, that one almost needs a newsletter to keep up. Fortunately, there are two such, which for those who can afford them, admirably serve that purpose:

Brain and Strategy. Published by Brain Technologies Corporation, 414 Buckeye Street, Fort Collins, CO 80524. 303-493-9210. Published ten times yearly. Editor: Dudley Lynch. Subscription: $29/yr.

Brain/Mind Bulletin. Marilyn Ferguson, editor. Interface Press, Box 42211, Los Angeles, CA 90042. Published every three weeks; $20.00/year.

Following are some books that I think are very helpful, though most books in the very nature of things lag behind newsletters, in their up-to-dateness:

Wonder, Jacquelyn, and Donovan, Priscilla, *Whole-Brain Thinking: Working from Both Sides of the Brain to Achieve Peak Job Performance.* William Morrow and Co., 105 Madison Avenue, New York, NY 10016. 1984. $13.95, hardcover.

Von Oech, Roger, *A Whack on the Side of the Head: How to Unlock Your Mind for Innovation.* Warner Books, 666 Fifth Ave., New York, NY 10103. 1983. $8.95, paper. A very interesting and extremely popular book.

Segalowitz, Sid J., *Two Sides of the Brain: Brain Lateralization Explored.* Prentice-Hall, Englewood Cliffs, NJ 07632. 1983. $6.95, paper. One of the latest, and one of the best, on up-to-date findings concerning the two sides of the brain.

Durden-Smith, Jo, and DeSimone, Diane, *Sex and the Brain.* Arbor House, 235 E. 45th St., New York, NY 10017. 1983. $16.95, hardcover. Answers all those questions you have been just dying to ask, about how differences in the way the two sides of our brain actually function are related to sex differences between male and female.

Springer, Sally P., and Deutsch, Georg, *Left Brain, Right Brain*. W.H. Freeman and Co., 660 Market St., San Francisco, CA 94104. 1981. $15.95, hardcover; $7.95, paper.

Edwards, Betty, *Drawing on the Right Side of the Brain: A Course in Enhancing Creativity and Artistic Confidence*. J.P. Tarcher, Inc., 9110 Sunset Blvd., Los Angeles, CA 90069. 1979. $8.95, paper. Absolutely top-notch. On the surface, a book about drawing. Actually, a book about creativity in all its facets. Splendid.

Viscott, David, *Risking*. Simon and Schuster, 1230 Avenue of the Americas, New York, NY 10020. 1977. Paper. The classic book on this subject. See if your library has it.

Two are better than one;
    for if they fall,
the one will lift up his fellow;

but woe to him that is alone when he falleth,
and hath not another to lift him up.

Ecclesiastes

Appendix C

When Books Are Not Enough
and
You Want a Live Person
to Guide You:
Counselors and Other Resources

REQUIRED READING:
If You're Thinking of Hiring a Career Counselor to Help You

Okay, you're back here in this section either because you're just curious to know what it says, or because you're ready to admit you've just got to hire *somebody* to help you, with all this.

And you've decided you've got to find somebody to help you because either:

a) you *tried* doing the exercises in the book, and you just aren't getting anywhere; or

b) you've read the book—sections of it anyway—and without even trying the exercises, you know yourself well enough to know you need someone who will explain it all to you, step by step. You're an "ear" person, more than an "eye" person, and you do better when a human being is explaining something to you, than when you're trying to read it for yourself; OR

c) you've not read the book, nor tried any of the exercises, but you *have* counted the number of pages in the book, and the very thickness of it all was so intimidating, that you've decided to toss in the towel before you even begin. ("Help!")

You've turned to this section because you figure that back here must be some sort of "authorized list" of names: people who understand this whole job-hunting process thoroughly, know how to do all the exercises in this book, have been through some kind of careful credentialing process, and received the Parachute Seal of Approval.

Ah, dear reader, how I wish it were so. But, unhappily, there is no such list. First of all, while I do train people once a year, I haven't trained all that many, over the years. Moreover, I can't guarantee that simply because they've been through my hands, they truly understand. So, publishing a list of their names wouldn't necessarily give you the information you want.

Secondly, there are lots of people "out there" who understand the whole job-hunting process thoroughly and well, even though they've never been trained by me and may not even (necessarily) have read this book. In most cases, of course, I've never met them, and consequently I don't know who they are or where they are. I simply know *that* they are.

What this all adds up to, you've already guessed. Hunting for a decent person or place to help you is just like hunting for a job. You've got to do your own research, and your own interviewing, in your own area. Getting some-body else's opinion, in effect letting them do your research for you, isn't very effective. First of all, their information is often somewhat outdated, and therefore questionable. Maybe the counselor or place they're telling you about is one they ran into a year ago. The counselor was excellent, at that time. But since then (unbeknownst to your friend) that counselor has been through a really rough time, personally: divorce, burnout, overwhelming fatigue—the works. It's affected their counseling, to say the least; they're no longer functioning at the top level they were a year ago. Your friend's recommendation is outdated—at least for the present. And, of course, it can be just the other way around. Your friend tells you someone is terrible, as a counselor, because when your friend ran into them, two or three years ago, it was true. But, that counselor has had dozens and dozens of clients since then, and learned a lot (most career counselors are trained by their clients, you know). That counselor is now very good. Your friend's "dis-recommen-dation" is now outdated.

Secondly, the three things you absolutely want from anyone you're paying good money to, are:

a) a firm grasp of the whole job-hunting process, at its most creative and effective level;

b) the ability to communicate that information lucidly and clearly to others;

c) rapport with you.

This last is a very difficult thing to pin down. Maybe this counselor is simply wonderful on the first two counts, but he reminds you of your Uncle Harry. You've always *hated* your Uncle Harry. No go. But how could anyone have known that, except you?

I repeat: no one can do this research about which job counselor is best, except you. Because the real question is not "Who is best?" but "Who is best for you?" Those last two words change everything.

What I want to do for you is:

1. Give you a brief crash course about this whole field of career counseling.

2. Tell you where to find some names with which *to start* your search for "who is best for you."

3. Give you some questions, that will help you separate the sheep from the goats, and make an intelligent decision.

Okay, here we go:

1. A CRASH COURSE ABOUT THIS WHOLE FIELD OF CAREER COUNSELING

In the whole big field of The Job Hunt, all professional help divides (one regrets to say) into the following three categories, so far as the job-hunter is concerned:

1. Professionals who are sincere and skilled.

2. Professionals who are sincere but inept.

3. Professionals who are insincere and inept.

The problem we all face when we decide to seek help with our job-hunt, is: which is which. Or, who is who. We want a career counselor who falls into category No. 1; if he or she falls into the other two categories, which of the other two they fall into is really irrelevant: ineptness is ineptness, whether it is sincere or not.

The various clues which may at first occur to us, for identifying good career counselors, are upon more serious examination not terribly fruitful. Let us tick off some of them, and see why:

★ <u>Clue No. 1</u>: Perhaps we can tell who is sincere and skilled, by the name of the specialist or their agency. Difficulty: names vary greatly from one operation to another, even when the operations are similar. Among the names which some counselors or agencies bear, you will find: executive career counselors, executive career consultants, career management teams, vocational psychologists, executive consulting counselors, career guidance counselors, executive advisors, executive development specialists, executive job counselors, manpower experts, career advisors, employment specialists, executive recruitment consultants, professional career counselors, management consultants, placement specialists, executive search specialists, vocational counselors, life/work planners, etc. If, tomorrow, some legitimate counselor who is sincere and skilled takes on a new name, the day after that some counselor who is insincere and inept will copy the name directly. What it all comes down to, is this: Wolves need sheep's clothing. Names are sheep's clothing. Trouble is, hidden in there are some genuinely helpful people. We need another clue.

★ <u>Clue No. 2</u>: Perhaps we can tell who is sincere and skilled by reading everything that the agency or counselor has written. Difficulty: both good and bad counselors know the areas where the job-hunter feels exceedingly vulnerable. Consequently, there are "turn on" words which occur in almost everybody's advertisements, brochures, and books: we will give you help, say they, with evaluating your career history, in-depth analysis of your background, establishment of your job objective, in-depth analysis of your capabilities, writing an effective resume, names of companies, preparing the covering letter, background materials on companies, interviewing techniques, salary negotiations, filling out forms, answering ads, aptitude tests, special problems—unemployment, age, too broad a background, too narrow a background, too many job changes, too few job changes, poor references, etc. We will, say they, open doors for you, tell you which companies are

©Copyright 1969 King Features Syndicate, Inc., World rights reserved. Used by special permission.

hiring, and so forth. Both the counselors who are skilled and those who are inept will never get anyone in their doors if they don't mention the areas that have put the job-hunter in Desperation City. So how they describe their services (real or alleged) doesn't separate the sheep from the goats, unfortunately. Next clue?

★ Clue No. 3: Perhaps we can tell who is sincere and skilled by the fee they charge? I mean, they wouldn't charge a high fee, would they, if they weren't skilled? Difficulty: as insiders say, low fees may mean well-intentioned but amateurish help. However, the reverse of this is *not* true. As we have already mentioned, the vacuum created by the chaotic condition of our job-hunting process has attracted both competent people *and* people who are determined to prey upon the acute state of anxiety that job-hunters are often in. And when the latter say "Let us prey" they *really* prey. And they *thrive*. They can charge anywhere between $2,000 and $10,000 (it's solely dependent on your previous salary) *up front*, before they've given you *any* services or help at all. And if you are later dissatisfied, your chances of getting your money back are remote, indeed—no matter what the contract said. (They've fashioned every legal loophole in the book, in order to keep your money.) P.T. Barnum knew what he was talking about.[1] Next.

★ Clue No. 4: Perhaps we can tell which professionals are both sincere and skilled, by talking to satisfied clients—or asking our friends to tell us who was helpful to them. If you stop to think about it, you will realize this most crucial truth: *all your friends can possibly speak to you about is the particular counselor or counselors that they worked with, at that agency, in that particular city.* Should you go to the same place, and get a different counselor, you might have a very different experience. One bad counselor in an agency that has say, six good ones, can cost you much money, time, and self-esteem, if *you* get that bad one as *your* counselor. The six good ones might as well be in Timbuktu, for all the good they'll do you. So should any of your friends offer (or should you solicit from them) advice about a place they went to, be sure to find out the counselor (or counselors) they worked with, there, *by name* so you will know who to ask for, if you decide to investigate or follow their lead.

Before we leave this clue, let us also observe that while most professional career counselors will show you letters from satisfied customers, or even give you (in some cases) their names to check out, it is impossible to find out what percentage of their total clientele these satisfied persons represent: 100%? 10? 1? .1? a fluke? If you want a clue, you may make what you will out of the fact that the top officers of the largest executive counseling firm, which allegedly did over 50% of the business in the industry before it declared bankruptcy in the fall of 1974, (namely, Frederick Chusid & Co.) gave testimony during a civil suit in a New York Federal district court which indicated that only three or four out of every ten clients had been successful in getting a new job, during a previous six-month period. More recently, another prominent executive counseling firm was reported by the Attorney

---

1. A sucker is born every minute. Or as the post office has updated it: "A sucker is shorn every minute."

General's Office of New York State to have placed only 38 out of 550 clients.[1] Are these figures average for the industry? Better than average? Worse? Nobody knows.

In any event, virtually no career counselor or career counseling firm will EVER show you letters from DISsatisfied clients. Were you to be given access to such letters (the files of many Better Business Bureaus, the Consumer Fraud division of your state or city Attorney-General's office, not to mention the Federal Trade Commission, are loaded with such letters) you would find the complaints have certain recurrent themes: the career counseling firm being complained about, they say, did not do what they *verbally* promised to do, have the exclusive lists of job openings they claimed to have, nor the access to executive suites they claimed to have, nor the success rate they claimed, nor did they give the amount of time to the client they *verbally* promised in advance (sometimes it turned out to be as few as six hours). 'Job campaigns' for the clients were slow to start, usually not until the full advance fee was paid, promised lists were slow in being provided and often were outdated and full of errors, the friendly 'intake counselor' was actually a salesperson, and is never seen again once the contract is signed, the actual counselor was often difficult (or impossible) to get ahold of after a certain period of time (sometimes coinciding with the final payment by the client of the advance fee), the 'plan' was often no news at all to the client, the promised contact with employers on the client's behalf was not forthcoming, phone calls or letters of complaint were ignored, and the fee was not refunded in whole or in part, when the client was dissatisfied, despite implicit (or explicit) promises to the contrary. Whew!

Well, that's enough of a crash course on career counseling, and the pitfalls that await the unwary or the innocent. If you are dying to know more, and your local library has back files of magazines and newspapers (on microfiche, or otherwise), you can look up:

"Career-Counseling Industry Accused of Misrepresentation," *New York Times*, Sept. 30, 1982, p. C1.

"Consumer Law: Career Counselors and Employment Agencies" by Reed Brody, *New York Law Journal*, Feb. 26, 1982, p. 1. Reed was Assistant Attorney General of the State of New York, and more recently Deputy Chief of the Labor Bureau within that State's Department of Law; in this capacity he became the leading legal expert in the country, on career counseling malpractices. He has now, however, left this work, for a job in Central America, so he is not available for the kind of helpful information he gave so many in the past.

"Career Counselors: Will They Lead You Down The Primrose Path?" by Lee Guthrie. *Savvy Magazine*, Dec., 1981, p. 60ff.

"Franklin Career Search Is Accused of Fraud In New York State Suit," *Wall Street Journal*, Jan. 29, 1981, p. 50.

"Job Counseling Firms Under Fire For Promising Much, Giving Little," *Wall Street Journal*, Jan. 27, 1981, p. 33.

---

1. "Career Counselors: Will They Lead You Down The Primrose Path?" by Lee Guthrie, in the December 1981 issue of *Savvy Magazine*, p. 60 ff.

Stuart Alan Rado has been waging a sort of "one man crusade" against career counseling firms which take advantage of the job-hunter. *His* advice, as the result of counseling many victims, is: don't go to *any* firm which requires the fee all in advance. If you are reading this too late, did pay some firm's fee all in advance, and feel you were ripped off, if you will send Mr. Rado a self-addressed stamped envelope, he will send you a one page sheet of some actions you can take. His address is: 1500 23rd St., Sunset Island #3, Miami Beach, FL 33140. 305-532-2607. He is working to help bring about new state laws, which will make it more difficult for unconscionable career counseling firms to take advantage of the hapless job-hunter or career-changer.

2. WHERE TO FIND SOME NAMES TO START YOUR SEARCH FOR WHO IS BEST FOR YOU

You start, of course, by asking everyone you know—family, friends, and people you've just met—if they know any really helpful career counselors.

You supplement this by looking in the Yellow Pages of your local telephone book. Possible headings to check out (they vary from phone book to phone book) are: vocational counselors, executive career counselors, career counselors, job counseling, guidance counselors, career consultants, employment counselors. Also any cross references that these lead you to.

I am printing in this Appendix a Sampler (only) of some of the kinds of places to be found around the country, including a number of private counselors who aren't very easy to stumble across. This is not a complete directory of anything. Countless good people, agencies and places exist, which will not be found in this Sampler. Also, countless bad people, places and agencies. To list all such, would require an encyclopedia.

The listing of an organization, agency or person in this Sampler is NOT a recommendation or endorsement of that organization, agency or person: Likewise, the failure to list a particular organization, agency or person in this Sampler is NOT a condemnation of that organization, agency or person. You MUST do your own comparison shopping, and ask some sharp questions. If you don't comparison shop, you will deserve whatever you get (or don't get).

Places fold, almost weekly in this field. Places move. The staff changes. Their phone numbers and hours change. There is *no way* this Sampler can stay up-to-date and accurate, for more than about two days. I apologize for any information or listing that proves to be inaccurate. You could be of great service by dropping us a line, if you find a place is no longer in existence, or impossible to get a hold of, or is—in your opinion—totally unhelpful. (Box 379, Walnut Creek, CA 94597)

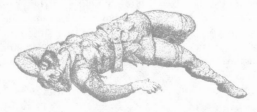

3. SOME QUESTIONS, BY MEANS OF
WHICH YOU MAY BE ABLE TO SEPARATE
THE SHEEP FROM THE GOATS

Choose, from your friends' recommendations, from the phone book, from the Sampler attached hereto, at least THREE PLACES OR COUNSELORS.

VISIT IN PERSON EACH OF THE THREE PLACES YOU HAVE CHOSEN. These are exploratory visits only. Leave your wallet and your checkbook home, please! You are only comparison shopping at this point, not decision reaching!!

Make this unmistakably clear, when you are setting up the appointment for the interview.

You will need a notebook. In this notebook, *before* you go to see each career counselor (or firm), you will need to write out the following questions. And, as you ask the questions at each place, take time to write down some notes (or direct quotes) of their answers. DON'T trust your memory.

You may prefer to make four columns across your notebook, so that it will be easier to compare the places, after you have visited all three:

At each place, with each counselor, ask every one of these questions—omitting none.

● *What is their program?* When all their gimmicks are set aside (and some have great ones, like rehearsing for interviews on closed circuit TV, or using video-tape or cassettes to record your skills or your resume, etc.) what are they offering: is it basically "the numbers game," *or* is it basically some variation of the creative minority's prescription?

● *Who will be doing it?* Do you get the feeling that you must do most of it, with their basically assuming the role of coach? (if so, three cheers); or do you get the feeling that everything (including decision making about what you do, where you do it, etc.) will be done for you (if so, three warning bells should go off in your head)?

● *What guarantee is there that it will work?* If they make it clear that they have had a good success rate, but if you fail to work hard at the whole process, then there is no guarantee you are going to find a job, give them three stars. On the other hand, if they practically guarantee you a job, and say they have never had a client that failed to find a job, no matter what, *watch out.* Pulmotor job-counseling is very suspect; lifeless bodies make poor employees.

● *Are you face-to-face, and talking, with the actual persons who will be working with you, should you decide to become a client?* It might help you to be aware that some job-hunting or career counseling firms have professional salesmen who introduce you to the company, convince you of their 100% integrity and charm, secure your decision, get you to sign the contract—and then you never see them again. You work with someone entirely different (or a whole team). *Ask the person you are talking to, if they are the one (and the only one) you will be working with, should you eventually decide to become a client.* If they say No, ask

MY SEARCH FOR A GOOD CAREER COUNSELOR

Questions	Answer from Counselor #1	Answer from Counselor #2	Answer from Counselor #3
1. What is their program?			
2. Who will be doing it?			
3. Guarantee?			
4. Who is the actual counselor?			

to meet those who would be actually working with you—even if it's a whole battery of people. When you actually meet them, there are three considerations you should weigh:

(1) *Do you like the counselor?* Bad vibes can cause great difficulties, even if this person is extremely competent. Don't dismiss this factor!

(2) *How long has this counselor been doing this?* Ask them! And what training did they have for it? (Legitimate questions; if they get huffy, politely thank them for their time, and take your leave gently *but firmly.*) Some agencies hire former clients as new staff. Such new staff are sometimes given only "on the job training." Since you're paying for Expertise already acquired, you have a *right* to ask about this before making up your mind. Incidentally, beware of such phrases as "I've had eighteen years experience in the business and career counseling world." What that may mean is: seventeen and a half years as a fertilizer salesman, and one half year doing career counseling. Persist. "How long have you been doing formal career counseling, as you are now?"

(3) *How much time will they give you?* As a minimum? As a maximum? (There's got to be a maximum, no matter what they may at first claim. Every career counselor runs into extremely dependent types as clients, who would be there all day every day if the counselor or the firm didn't have some policy

about time limits. *Press* to find out what it is, just so you'll know.) Over how long a period can you use their services? And, *will they put this in writing?* (That's the question that separates the men from the boys, and the women from the girls).

● *What is the cost of their services? Is it paid hourly, as you go along, or must it all be paid "up front" before you even start?* You will discover that there are some career counselors or agencies that charge you an hourly rate, just as a therapist might. The fee normally ranges between $50–$85 an hour. Each time you keep an appointment, you pay them at the end of that hour (or hours) for their help. There is no written contract. You signed nothing. You can stop seeing them at any time, if you feel you are not getting the help you wish. Obviously, this sort of arrangement is very much to the advantage of the job-hunter. *However,* you will also discover that there are some career counselors or agencies that, by contrast, have a policy of requiring you to pay for the entire "program" before you start, —or shortly after you start. There is *always* a written contract. You *must* sign it. (If you are married, your spouse will usually be invited to come in, before the contract is signed; you may suspect this is to help "sell" them on the idea of the contract, so they then can sell you. You may be right.) The fee normally ranges between $600–$8,000.

The contract sometimes allows it to be paid in installments, but you *are* obligated to pay it, one way or the other. You are sometimes *verbally* told that you can get your money back, or a portion of it, at any time, should you be dissatisfied with the career counselor's services. This is often *not* in the written contract. (Verbal promises, without witnesses, are difficult if not impossible to enforce. The written contract takes precedence.) Sometimes the written contract will provide for a partial refund, up to a certain cut-off point in the program. (There is *always* a cut-off point; and many times it is calculated by the counselor or agency in a manner other than the way *you* are calculating it. Consequently you are beyond the cut-off point, and the possibility of any refund, before you know it. Or, you reach the cut-off point and allow it to pass because you are, up to that point, satisfied with their services, and you have been led to believe there is much more to come. Only, there isn't. Once the cut-off point is passed, the career counselor's time becomes harder and harder to get.)

Clearly this second financial arrangement (as opposed to the hourly) is to the advantage of the career counselor or agency, more than it is to the advantage of the job-hunter. There's nothing inherently meritorious about paying someone a whole lot of money before he (or she) has performed any of the services they say they are going to perform. If you should become increasingly dissatisfied with the counseling or "program" as it progresses, you may be "out" a lot of dough. With no legal recourse. And so, the moral of this tale:

Don't pay any fee that you can't afford to lose.

While you are still doing your information gathering on the three places, find out which of these two financial arrangements the counselor or agency requires. If a contract will be involved, ask for a copy of it, take it home, and show it to a good lawyer.

Having gotten the information *you* want, and therefore having accomplished *your* purpose for this particular visit, you politely thank them for their time and trouble, and depart. You then go on to two other places, and ask the very same questions, please! There ought to be no charges involved for such comparison-shopping visits as this, and if they subsequently bill you, inquire politely whether or not a mistake has been made by their accounting department (good thinking). If they persist in billing you, pay a visit to your local friendly Better Business Bureau, and lodge a nice unfriendly complaint against the firm in question. You'd be surprised at how many firms experience *instant repentance* when the Better Business Bureau phones them. They don't want a complaint on their BBB record.

BACK HOME NOW, after visiting the three places you chose for your comparison shopping, you have to decide: a) whether you want none of the three, or b) one of the three and if so, which one.

Look over your notes on all three places. Compare those places. Time for thought, maybe using some others as a sounding board: business friend, consultant friend, placement center, buddy, mate, or anyone whose judgment you trust.

Remember, you don't have to choose *any* of the three counselors. If you didn't really care for any of them, listen to your intuition. Choose three new counselors, dust off the notebook, and go out again. It may take a few more hours to find what you want. But, remember: the wallet or purse you will be saving is your own.

A Sampler

This Sampler Has Several Sections:
I. Places Which Counsel Anyone
II.Help for Women (Many of These Also Serve Men)
III. Group Support for Those Who Are Unemployed
IV. Directories of Career Counseling Services in Various Cities/States

If you are looking for a counselor in a particular state, check under all four categories, please. Even if a particular resource listed here is not what you are looking for, they may know of other places, not listed here.

The listing of a place here is NOT a recommendation of it. Many of these places are listed at their own request. On the other hand, we never *knowingly* list a place we know to be unhelpful.

If you have had a bad experience with any of them, you will help other readers by letting us know that (our address is in the rear of this book, on the UPDATE form). However, it is CRUCIAL that you read the preceding section two or three times, BEFORE you approach any of these sections. Often you could easily have discovered whether a particular counselor is competent or not, simply by asking the right questions. The just response to many a complaint is—as the Scots would say—"Ya dinna do your homework."

I. PLACES WHICH COUNSEL ANYONE

ARIZONA

Phyllis Harper-Rispoli, 1845 So. Dobson Road, Suite 202, Mesa, AZ 85202, 602-820-0638.

Southwest Institute of Life Management, Theodore Donald Risch, Director, 2500 N. Pantano Rd., Ste. 120, Tucson, AZ 85715, 602-296-4764.

ARKANSAS

Donald D. McKinney, Ed.D., Cossatot Vocational Technical School, P.O. Box 746, De-Queen, AR 71832, 501-584-4471.

CALIFORNIA

Aware Advisory Center, YWCA, Second Floor, 2019 14th St. (near Pico Blvd.), Santa Monica, CA 90405, 213-452-3883.

Judy Kaplan Baron Associates, 7730 Herschel Avenue, Suite B, La Jolla, CA 92037, 619-456-1700. Judy Kaplan Baron, Director.

Branham & Associates, 2117 E. Brentford Ave., Orange, CA 92667, 714-637-4694.

Career Development Center, Moorpark College, 7075 Campus Rd., Moorpark, CA 93021, 805-529-2321.

Career Development Institute, 690 Market St., Ste. 404, San Francisco, CA 94104, 415-982-2636.

Career Dimensions, 1231 W. Robinhood Dr., Ste. D-1, Stockton, CA 95207, 209-473-8255. Fran Abbott.

Career Renewal, 40 Museum Way, San Francisco, CA 94114. 415-626-2741. Kal Edwards, Director.

Constructive Leisure, Patsy B. Edwards, 511 N. La Cienega Blvd., Los Angeles, CA 90048, 213-652-7389.

Criket Consultants, Box 323, Rancho Cordova, CA 95670, 916-363-4545.

De Lara & Associates, Inc., Citicorp Building, 1990 North California Boulevard, Suite 830, Walnut Creek, CA 94596, 415-932-5822. Joy De Lara, Director.

Experience Unlimited, Mr. Herman L. Leopold, Coordinator, Employment Development Department, 1225 4th Avenue, Oakland, CA 94606, 415-464-1259/464-0659.

Beverly Neuer Feldman, Ed.D., 2656 Aberdeen Ave., Los Angeles, CA 90027. 213-665-7007.

Life/Career Development, 4035 El Macero Dr., Davis, CA 95616, 916-756-8637. Russell A. Bruch, Director, Career consultant.

National University Career Center, 4007 Camino Del Rio S., San Diego, CA 92108, 619-563-7250.

New Ways to Work, 149 Ninth St., San Francisco, CA 94103. 415-552-1000. Monday–Friday, 10 a.m.–4 p.m. Free orientation session every Tuesday, 12 n–1 p.m.

Project Joy (Job Opportunities for Youth). East Oakland Youth Development Center, 8200 East 14th Street, Oakland, CA 94621. 415-569-8088. Kathleen Sullivan, Director.

Fran Schwartz, 13219 Dobbins Pl., Los Angeles, CA 90049, 213-451-2755/778-1772.

Turning Point Career Center, University YWCA, 2600 Bancroft Way, Berkeley, CA 94704, 415-848-6370. Marjorie Sywak, Ph.D., Director.

Joanne Young, Box 19273, Irvine, CA 92714, 714-552-7384.

COLORADO

Colorado Growth Center, Inc., 965 Humboldt St., Ste. 105, Denver, CO 80218, 303-831-9578. Arthur F. Smith, Jr., Counselor.

Samuel Kirk and Associates, Central Office, 1418 S. Race, Denver, CO 80210, 303-722-0717.

CONNECTICUT

Career Evaluation Services, 94 Rambling Rd., Vernon, CT 06066, 203-871-7832.

The Counseling Service of the Metropolitan Hartford YMCA, Inc., 160 Jewell St., Third Floor, Hartford, CT 06103, 203-522-4183.

Dauphinais & Gaughran, Post Office Box 174, Guilford, CT 06437, 203-453-0522. Doris Dauphinais, and Kathleen Gaughran, Directors.

People Management Inc., 10 Station St., Simsbury, CT 06070, 203-651-3581. Arthur F. Miller, Jr., President.

DISTRICT OF COLUMBIA

Georgetown University, School for Summer and Continuing Education, 37th and O. Sts. NW, Washington, DC 20057, 202-625-3003.

FLORIDA

Ellen O. Jonassen, Ph.D. 901 Hercules Ave., Ste. G, Clearwater, FL 33575, 813-441-4579.

Life Designs, Inc. Life/Work Planning Consultants, 7400 S.W. 57 Court, South Miami, FL 33143. 305-665-3212. Dulce I. Miccio and Deborah Tyson, Co-founders.

Shea Yablonsky Associates, Inc., 2530 W. Oakland Park Blvd., Fort Lauderdale, FL 33311, 305-486-1800.

GEORGIA

The Career Planning Center, of Grace United Methodist Church, 458 Ponce de Leon Avenue, Atlanta GA 30308. Mark Canfield, Director.

Charles W. Cates, Ph.D., Life Work Associates, Box 52, Decatur, GA 30030, 404-373-0336.

Judith L. Cole, M.Ed., Lenox Towers, 3390 Peachtree Rd., Atlanta, GA 30326, 404-233-0946.

Educational Information and Referral Service, Lenox Square Professional Concourse, 3393 Peachtree Road, N.E., Atlanta, GA 30326, 404-233-7497. Christine G. Free, Executive Director.

IDAHO

Life/Work Planning Services, 1955 Wilmington Dr., Boise, ID 83704, 208-375-0742. Janet Atkinson Lawrence, M.Ed.

ILLINOIS

Career Path, 3033 Ogden Ave., Suite 203, Lisle, IL 60532, 312-369-3390. Hours by appt. Kristin Trom, Counselor.

Career Potential, 1318 E. State St., Rockford, IL 61108, 815-962-7666. Mary-Stuart Carruthers.

David Helfand, University Counseling Center, Northeastern Illinois University, 5500 N. St. Louis Ave., Chicago, IL 60625. 312-583-4050.

National Office of Program Development, Inc., 103 S. Washington, Bening Square, Ste. 202, Carbondale, IL 62901, 618-529-1910; 220 S. State, Consumers Building, Ste. 1308, Chicago, IL 60604, 312-987-1171.

Occupational Consultants, Paul J. Reibman, 1030 Indian Rd., Glenview, IL 60025, 312-729-2117.

INDIANA

Career Consultants, 107 N. Pennsylvania St., Ste. 404, Indianapolis, IN 46204, 317-639-5601. Mike Kenney, Senior Partner.

IOWA

Christian Business Support Center, 6102 1st Ave. NW, Cedar Rapids, IA 52405. 319-396-1963. Rob Robinson, Director.

KENTUCKY

P. Ronniger Associates, 101 North Seventh Street, Louisville, KY 40202, 502-583-4115. Phillip Ronniger, President.

MAINE

Sojourn, Inc: Career Evaluation and Planning, Route 2, Box 5, Fairfield, ME 04937. 207-453-9756.

MARYLAND

Careerscope, Harriet Tubman Center, 8045 Route 32, Columbia, MD 21044, 301-531-6655.

Prince George's Community College, Center for Career Development, 301 Largo Road, MD 20772, 301-336-6000. David C. Borchard, Director.

D. Evan Wallick Associates, 1600 Angus Court, Crofton, MD 21114, 301-261-6945. David Wallick, President. Sliding fee scale, hourly basis.

MASSACHUSETTS

Career Change Consultant, Jane Hynes, 51 Highland St., W. Newton, MA 02165, 617-369-1686.

Career Development Consultant, Ellen J. Wallach, 8 Sherburne Rd., Lexington, MA 02173, 617-862-0997.

Changes, Carl Schneider, 7 Woodbridge St., Cambridge, MA 02140, 617-876-5085.

David J. Giber, Ph.D., Career Counselor. 8 Westland Rd., Watertown, MA 02172. 617-924-2537.

New England Career Center, 70 Chase St., Newton Centre, MA 02159. Barton M. Lloyd, Associate Director.

Westford Psychological Services, The Gateway Building, 288 Littleton Road, Westford, MA 01886, 617-692-6834. John W. Ried, Th.D., Director.

Widening Horizons, 120 Meriam Rd., Concord, MA 01742, 617-369-1626. Barbara SanClemente, M.Ed., Director.

MICHIGAN

Career Planning Services, 2777 Colony Rd., Ann Arbor, MI 48104, 313-973-9286. Catherine Schwarz.

Thibaudeaux Personnel of Grand Rapids, 820 Commerce Building, Grand Rapids, MI 49503, 616-459-8396. Donald D. Fink, Ed.D., Director of Career Counseling.

MINNESOTA

Assessment and Vocational Services, Incorporated, 6135 Kellogg Avenue South, Suite 224, Edina, MN 55424, 612-922-4397. Robert D. Haskin, Director.

Leider, Inc., 7101 York Ave. South, Minneapolis, MN 55435. 612-921-3334. Richard J. Leider, Career Development Specialist.

MISSISSIPPI

University of Southern Mississippi, Career Development Center and Adult Services Program, Southern Station, Box 5112, Hattiesburg, MS 39406-5112, 601-266-4848. Charlotte E. Tullos, Director.

MISSOURI

Career Planning and Placement Center, Adult Evening Program, 110 Noyes Hall, University of Missouri, Columbia, MO 65211, 314-882-6803.

NEBRASKA

Career Information Center, Central Community College, Hastings Campus, P.O. Box 1024, Hastings, NE 68901. 402-463-9811. Monday–Friday, 8 a.m.–4:30 p.m. No fees.

NEW JERSEY

Arista Concepts Career Development Service. 41 Wittmer Court, Princeton, NJ 08540. 609-921-0308. Kera Green Herzog, Counseling Psychologist.

Simeon J. Touretzky, M.S. Career Counselor. 160 Evergreen Rd., 8-B, Edison, NJ 08837. 201-494-8291.

NEW YORK

The John C. Crystal Center, 111 E. 31st St., New York, NY 10016. Phone 212-889-8500. Our good friend, John Crystal, devotes himself exclusively to the work of the Crystal Center, of which he is Chairman (Nella G. Barkley is president), offering programs in New York and elsewhere in the country.

Life/Work Planning, Inc. 932 Genesee Park Blvd., Rochester, NY 14619. 716-328-4912. Randall E. Davis, Career Development Specialist.

On-Track, 342 Madison Ave., Ste. 2001, New York, NY 10017. 212-953-6445. Russell P. Bosworth, President.

NORTH CAROLINA

Thomas S. Baldwin, Ph.D., Licensed Practicing Psychologist, 87 S. Elliott Rd., Ste. 200, Chapel Hill, NC 27514, 919-929-0496.

OHIO

Adult Resource Center, The University of Akron, Buckingham Center for Continuing Education, Akron, OH 44325. 216-375-7448. Also has sites at: Akron-Summit County Public Library, 55 South Main Street, Akron, OH, and: Women's Network, People's Federal Building, 39 East Market St., Akron, OH.

Bowling Green State University, College of Continuing Education, McFall Center, Bowling Green, OH 43403, 419-372-0181.

Career Resources, Third National Bank Building, 32 N. Main St., Ste. 1245, Dayton, OH 45402, 513-223-8000.

Career Shaping. 2801 Far Hills Ave., Dayton, OH 45419. 513-293-9675. Nancy Cook Cherry, Director.

New Career, 931 Chelsea Drive, Dover, OH 44622, 216-343-8464. Marshall Karp, M.A., Owner/Operator.

Pathfinders, A Division of Special Edition, 3497 E. Livingston Avenue, Columbus, OH 43227, 614-231-4088. Y. Hayon, Ph.D., Director.

Womonways, Inc., 503 McAlpin Avenue, P.O. Box 20145, Cincinnati, OH 45220, 513-221-0579, 513-221-3358. Linda Keegan, Office Manager.

OREGON

Sylvan Psychological and Counseling Services, 1012 S.W. King Avenue, Portland, OR 97205, 503-224-3600. Joe DuBay, Founder.

PENNSYLVANIA

Barbara Bell, 450 Warick Rd., Wynnewood, PA 19096. 215-642-2183.

Center for the Study of Adult Development, 3910 Chestnut St., Philadelphia, PA 19104. 215-662-4080. Joy Matkowski, M.S.C., Staff Counselor, Career Planning and Outplacement Services Division. Also located in King of Prussia, Allentown, Pennsylvania as well as in Cherry Hill, New Jersey.

LaRoche College Career Center, 9000 Babcock Blvd., Pittsburgh, PA 15237, 412-367-9300, ext. 144, 145 & 146. Kris Rosenberg, Director.

Options, Inc., 215 South Broad Street, Philadelphia, PA 19107, 215-735-2202. Marcia P. Kleiman, Director.

Pennsburg Outreach Center, 643 Main St., Pennsburg, PA 18073, 215-679-5511. Sponsored by Montgomery County Community College, Blue Bell, PA 19422.

David C. Rich, United Ministries in Higher Education, Pennsylvania Commission, 61 Cassatt Ave., Berwyn, PA 19312. 215-647-8096. David C. Rich, Director.

TENNESSEE

Resume Resources, Parkview Tower, 210 25th Ave. N., Ste. 517, Nashville, TN 37203. 615-327-0101. Jane C. Hardy, Director.

TEXAS

Adult Career Exploration Services (ACES), 300 E. Fifth St., Austin, TX 78768, 512-476-2716. ACES is an open-door community service provided by Austin Community College.

Catalyst Career Consultants, 3906 N. Lamar Blvd., Austin, TX 78756. 512-452-1229. Joia Jitahidi, Senior Consultant.

Cochran Chapel United Methodist Church, Life/Work Planning Workshop, 9027 Midway Rd., Dallas, TX 75209. Rev. Wallace Chappell and Rev. Bill Johnson.

Creative Careers, Jon Patrick Bourg. 34 Cromwell Drive, San Antonio, TX 78201, 512-735-7287

Counseling Services of Houston, Rosemary C. Vienot, P.C., 1950 West Gray, Suite 1, Houston, TX 77019, 713-521-9391.

East Texas State University at Texarkana, Career Planning & Placement Center, 2600 N. Robison Road, Texarkana, TX 75501, 214-838-6514. Tom Dart, Coordinator of Placement and Career Counseling.

Life/Work Design, 3906 North Lamar Blvd., Ste. 202, Austin, TX 78756, 512-458-2807. Jeanne Quereau, M.A.

UTAH

University of Utah, Center for Adult Learning and Career Change, 1199 Annex Bldg., Salt Lake City, UT 84112, 801-581-3228.

VERMONT

Career Crossroads, 10 Linden Street, Brattleboro, VT 05301, 802-257-7497, 802-254-5114. Donald T. Baggs, Director.

VIRGINIA

Endependence Center of Northern Virginia, 4214 9th St. N., Arlington, VA 22203, 703-525-3268.

Hollins College, Career Counseling Center, Hollins, VA 24020, 703-362-6364. Peggy-Ann Neumann, Director.

Life Management Services, Inc., 6825 Redmond Drive, McLean, VA 22101, 703-356-2630. Hal and Marilyn Shook, President and Vice President.

Psychological Consultants, Inc., 6724 Patterson Ave., Richmond, VA 23226, 804-288-4125.

Swenholt Associates, Inc., 3414 Barger Dr., Falls Church, VA 22044, 703-256-2383. Frankie P. Swenholt, President.

WASHINGTON

The Individual Development Center, Inc., 1020 East John, Seattle, WA 98102, 206-329-0600. Mary Lou Hunt, Co-director.

WISCONSIN

David Swanson, Career Seminars and Workshops, Inc., 11621 W. Blue Mound Rd., Milwaukee, WI 53226, 414-259-0265.

Madison Campus Ministry, 731 State St., Madison, WI 53706, 608-257-1039.

WYOMING

University of Wyoming, Counseling Center, Box 3708, University Station, Laramie, WY 82071, 307-766-2187.

CANADA

Ambassador Consultants Ltd., Suite 403, 602-11 Avenue, S.W., Calgary, Alberta T2R 1J8, Canada, 403-265-7148. Wayne Chaulk, Manager.

John Hamilton, Ed.D., 2161 Yonge St., Toronto, Ontario M45 3A6, Canada, 416-489-1221.

FOREIGN

Robert J. Bisdee & Associates, 22 Allenby Ave., Malvern East, Victoria, Australia 3145, 613-025-4716.

II. HELP FOR WOMEN
(MANY OF THESE ALSO SERVE MEN)

Resource centers for women are springing up all over the country, faster than we can record them. We are listing here *only a sampling* of same. If you have a favorite, not listed here, send us the pertinent information—in format similar to the next pages—and we'll list it in the next edition. (Don't, however, bother to send us college services which are available only to the students and alumnae of that college. We try not to list such places, since such a listing only frustrates non-alumnae. If, inadvertently, any such place thus restricted is already listed here, please let us know, and we'll gently remove it from the next edition.) Incidentally, the centers which are listed here will know (in all probability) what other centers or resources there are in your geographical area. Also, try your telephone book's yellow pages: "Women's Organizations and Services," or "Vocational Consultants."

In all of this you will remember won't you, our earlier description (page 311) of all career counseling professionals, as falling into one of three groups: (1) Sincere and skilled; (2) Sincere but inept; and (3) Insincere and inept? Well, dear friend, groups or organizations or centers which have been organized specifically to help women job-hunters or career-changers are not—by that act—made immune of the above distinctions. Think about it, before you agree to put your (vocational) life into somebody eles's hands. Remember: the numbers game (chapter 2), even if it is expressed in beautifully non-sexist language, is still the numbers game.

RESOURCES FOR WOMEN

ALABAMA

Enterprise State Junior College, Women's Center, Career Development Center, Highway 84 E., Box 1300, Enterprise, AL 36330, 205-347-7881 or 5431. Monday–Friday, 8 am–4:30 pm.

University of Alabama, Career Planning and Placement, 1300 8th Avenue S., Bldg. 5, Rm. 110, Birmingham, AL 35294, 205-934-4324 or 4470. Monday–Friday, 8:30 am–5 pm.

ALASKA

University of Alaska, Anchorage Education Opportunity Center, 3211 Providence Ave., Library Bldg., Rm. 103, Anchorage, AK 99504, 907-263-1525. Monday–Friday, 8am–5 pm.

ARIZONA

University of Arizona, Student Counseling Service, Old Main, Tucson, AZ 85721, 602-626-2316. Monday–Friday, 8 am–noon and 1–5 pm; Tuesday and Wednesday, 5 pm–7 pm. Official college office. Educational and career counseling, and personal and marital counseling, continuing education courses. No fees.

CALIFORNIA

Advocates for Women, 414 Mason St., 4th Fl., San Francisco, CA 94102, 415-391-4870. Monday–Thursday, 9 am–4:30 pm; Tuesday, 9 am–7:30 pm. Independent nonprofit agency. Career counseling, job referral, placement. Offices also in Berkeley and Hayward.

Alumnae Resources, 660 Mission St., San Francisco, CA 94105, 415-546-7220. Emphasis on Liberal Arts graduates. Offers workshops, seminars, individual counseling, and special events. Fees vary. Appointments necessary. Orientation Fridays at noon.

American River College, Student Services Bldg., 4700 College Oak Dr., Sacramento, CA 95841, 916-484-8391. Monday–Friday, 8 am–6 pm.

Career Design, An Affiliate of Ranny Riley & Associates, 2462 Broadway, San Francisco, CA 94115. 415-346-0733. Offers a variety of comprehensive workshops and intensive seminars, dealing with all aspects of the world of work. Fees vary.

Career Planning Center/Business Action Center, 1623 So. La Cienega Blvd., Los Angeles, CA 90813. 213-273-6633. Independent, non-profit agency. Offers career counseling, testing, workshops, and job information. Men welcome.

The Claremont Colleges, Special Academic Programs and Office for Continuing Education, Harper Hall 160, Claremont, CA 91711, 714-621-8000, ext. 8069. Monday–Friday, 9 am–5 pm. College sponsored office. Educational and career counseling, job referral, continuing education courses. Registration fee.

Crossroads Institute for Career Development, 2288 Fulton St., Berkeley, CA 94704, 415-848-0698. Monday–Friday, 9 am–5 pm.

Cypress College, Career Planning Center, 9200 Valley View St., Cypress, CA 90630, 714-826-2220, Ext. 221. Monday–Friday, 8 am–4:30 pm. Official college office. Educational and career counseling. No fees.

Information Advisory Service, UCLA Extension, 10995 Le Conte Ave., Rm. 114, Los Angeles, CA 90024, 213-206-8201. Monday–Friday, 9 am–5 pm. College sponsored office. Educational and career counseling, job referral information, continuing education courses. No fees.

Susan W. Miller, M.A., 360 N. Bedford, Ste. 312, Beverly Hills, CA 90210, 213-837-7768. Career Counselor, Educational Consultant, private practice. Career counseling for individuals using a structured, action-oriented approach.

Resource Center for Women, 445 Sherman Ave., Palo Alto, CA 94306, 415-324-1710. Monday–Friday, 9 am–5 pm; Thursday, 9 am–9 pm. Independent nonprofit agency. Educational and career counseling, adult education courses, job referral. Fees for workshops.

San Jose State University, Re-Entry Advisory Program, Old Cafeteria Bldg., San Jose, CA 95192, 408-277-2188. Monday–Friday, 9 am–5 pm; Wednesday, 9 am–7 pm. Official college program. Educational and career counseling, referral to other services. No fees.

Caroline Voorsanger, Career Counselor for Women, 2000 Broadway, No. 1108, San Francisco, CA 94115, 415-567-0890. Career counseling, assistance with skill assessment and focusing.

The Women's Opportunities Center, Univ. of California's Extension, 2801 Main St., Irvine, CA 92714, 714-856-7128. Monday–Friday, 9 am–4 pm. College sponsored office. Educational and career counseling.

Women's World International, 400 N. Tustin, Ste. 410, Santa Ana, CA 92705, 714-547-7726. Assistance with interviewing techniques, communications skills, exploring career alternatives, and achieving a professional image.

YWCA, Counseling Services, 1000 Sir Francis Drake Blvd., San Anselmo, CA 94960, 415-456-0782. Monday–Friday, 9 am–5 pm.

COLORADO

Arapahoe Community College, Career Resource Center, 5900 South Santa Fe Drive, Littleton, CO 80120, 303-794-1550. Monday–Friday, 8 am–5 pm. Educational, career, and personal counseling; variety of workshops and seminars; job search skills; community resources files; support groups; library; job referral and placement.

Career Development Center, 1650 Washington Street, Denver, CO 80203, 303-861-7254. Monday-Friday, 9 am-5 pm; evening services available. Independent nonprofit agency. A comprehensive combination of group and individual sessions for career counseling. Fees vary.

Women's Resource Agency, 2340 Robinson St., Ste. 216, Colorado Springs, CO 80904, 303-471-3170. Monday–Friday, 8 am–5 pm.

CONNECTICUT

Fairfield University, Fairfield Adult Career & Educational Services (FACES), North Benson Rd., Julie Hall, Fairfield, CT 06430, 203-255-5411. Monday–Friday, 9 am–4 pm.

Norwalk Community College, Counseling Center, 333 Wilson Ave., Norwalk, CT 06854, 203-853-2040. Monday–Thursday, 9 am–7:30 pm, Friday 9 am–4 pm.

Vocational and Academic Counseling for Adults (VOCA), 115 Berrian Road, Stamford, CT 06905, 203-329-1955. Monday–Friday, 9 am–5 pm; weekends and evenings by arrangement.

DELAWARE

Delaware Displaced Homemakers Center, Vocational Rehabilitation Building, 1715 West 4th St., Wilmington, DE 19805. 302-571-2714. Offices also in Dover, and Georgetown. Serving divorced, separated and widowed persons who have had 'homemaking' as their primary career up until now. Monday–Friday, 8:30 a.m.–4:30 p.m.

University of Delaware, The Women's Center, State Office Bldg., 5th Floor, Wilmington, DE 19801, 302-571-2088. Monday–Friday, 8:15 am–2:15 pm. Official college office. Educational and career counseling, continuing education courses. No registration fee. Other fees vary.

DISTRICT OF COLUMBIA

George Washington University, Continuing Education for Women, 801 22nd St. NW, Ste. T409, Washington, DC 20052, 202-676-7036. Monday–Friday, 9 am–5 pm. College sponsored. Educational and career counseling, continuing education courses, job referral. Fees vary.

FLORIDA

The Career Development Program, The Center for Climacteric Studies, University of Florida, The Professional Center, 901 NW 8th Ave., Ste. B-1, Gainesville, FL 32601. 904-392-3184 (3185). Monday–Friday, 8 a.m.–5 p.m. Evenings and Saturdays by appt. Help with the physical, psychological, and occupational concerns of women in their middle years (35–65 years of age). Fee.

Council for Continuing Education for Women of Central Florida, Inc., Valencia Community College, 190 S. Orange Ave., 1st Floor, Box 3028, Orlando, FL 32802, 305-423-4813. Monday–Friday, 9 am–5 pm. Independent nonprofit agency. Educational and career counseling, adult education courses, testing.

Face Learning Center, Inc., 12945 Seminole Blvd., Bldg. 2, Ste. 8, Largo, FL 33544, 813-586-1110/585-8155. Monday–Friday, 9 am–5 pm and by appointment.

The Center for the Continuing Education of Women, Miami-Dade Community College, 300 NE Second Ave., Miami FL 33132, 305-577-6840. Monday–Friday, 8:30 am–5 pm. College sponsored office. Educational and career counseling, limited job referral, continuing education courses. Fees vary.

Stetson University Counseling Center, Campus Box 1365, North Woodland Blvd., De Land, FL 32720, 904-734-4121, Ext. 215. Monday–Friday, 8:30 am–4:30 pm.

ILLINOIS

Applied Potential, Box 585, Highland Park, IL 60035, 312-234-2310. Monday–Friday, 9 am–5 pm; evenings and Saturdays by arrangement. Nonprofit educational corporation. Professional counselors. Educational, career and personal counseling. No registration fee. Other fees vary.

Harper College Community Counseling Center, Palatine, IL 60067, 312-397-3000. Monday–Thursday, 8:30 am–4:30 pm and 6–10 pm; Friday, 8:30 am–4:30 pm. College sponsored office. Educational and career counseling. No registration fee. Other fees vary.

Jean Davis, Career Counseling, 500 Davis Center, Ste. 600, Evanston, IL 60201, 312-492-1002. Offers career assessment/design, resume and marketing strategies, job interview preparation, individual consultation and workshops.

Moraine Valley Community College, Career/Life Planning and Counseling, 10900 S. 88th Ave., Palos Hills, IL 60465, 312-974-4300. Monday–Thursday, 9 am–9 pm; Friday, 9 am–5 pm. Official college office. Fees vary.

Northwestern Illinois Career Guidance Center, 1515 S. 4th St., Dekalb, IL 60115, 815-758-7431. Monday–Friday, 8 am–4 pm.

Southern Illinois University, General Studies Division, Office of Continuing Education, Campus Box 48, Edwardsville, IL 62026, 618-692-3210. Monday–Friday, 8 am–5 pm. Official college office. Educational and career counseling, continuing education courses. No fees.

Southern Illinois University, Women's Programs Office, Woody Hall, B-244/245, Carbondale, IL 62901, 618-453-3655. Monday–Friday, 8 am–5 pm. Individual advising, group discussions. No appointment needed.

Thornton Community College, Counseling Center, 15800 S. State Street, South Holland, IL 60473, 312-596-2000, Ext. 306. Monday–Thursday, 8 am–8:30 pm; Friday, 8 am–5 pm. Career Information Center.

University of Illinois Urbana-Champaign, Student Services Office for Married Students and Continuing Education for Women, 610 East John St., Champaign, IL 61820, 217-333-3137. Monday–Friday, 8 am–5 pm. Official college office. Educational and career counseling. No fees.

INDIANA

Ball State University, Career Information Services,. Muncie, IN 47306, 317-285-8290. Monday-Friday, 8 am-5 pm.

Continuing Education Center for Women, Indiana University/Purdue University at Indianapolis, 1317 W. Mich River, Indianapolis, IN 46223, 317-264-4784. Monday–Friday, 8 am–5 pm. Official college office. Educational and career counseling, continuing education courses. Fees vary.

Fort Wayne Women's Bureau, Inc., 203 W. Wayne St., Fort Wayne, IN 46802, 219-424-7977/426-0023. Peer counseling, Monday–Friday, 10 am–2 pm. Not-for-profit agency. Career counseling, job search skills training, job opportunity book.

Indiana University, Continuing Education for Women, Owen Hall 201, Bloomington, IN 47405, 812-335-0225. Monday–Friday, 8 am–5 pm. Official college office. Educational and career counseling, continuing education courses. Fees vary.

University Center for Women, Counseling and Academic Development Division, Purdue University, 2101 Coliseum Blvd. East, Fort Wayne, IN 46805, 219-482-5393. Monday–Friday, 8 am–noon, 1 pm–5 pm. College sponsored office. Educational and career counseling, continuing education courses, job referral. Fees vary.

Women's Resource Center, YWCA, 802 N. Lafayette Boulevard, South Bend, IN 46601, 219-233-9491. Monday–Friday, 9 am–5 pm.

IOWA

Drake University, Community Career Planning Center for Women, 1158 27th St., Des Moines, IA 50311, 515-271-2916. Monday–Friday, 8 am–4:30 pm. Official college office. Educational and career counseling, continuing education courses. No fee for individual counseling. Fee for group sessions.

University Counseling Service, Iowa Memorial Union, University of Iowa, Iowa City, IA 52242, 319-353-4484. Monday–Friday, 8 am–5 pm. College sponsored office. Educational, vocational and personal counseling.

University of Iowa, Office of Career Planning and Placement, Iowa City, IA 52242, 319-353-3147. Monday–Friday, 8 am–5 pm. Official college office. Educational and career counseling, job referral, placement. Fee for job placement only.

KANSAS

University of Kansas, Adult Life Resource Center, Division of Continuing Education, 1246 Mississippi St., Annex A, Lawrence, KS 66045, 913-864-4794 or 800-532-6772 (toll free in Kansas). Monday–Friday, 8 am–noon and 1–5 pm. College sponsored. Educational and career counseling, continuing education, program for displaced homemakers. No registration fee. Other fees vary.

MAINE

The Women's Center, Westbrook College, Stevens Ave., Portland, ME 04103. 207-797-7261. Monday–Friday, mornings; and by appointment. Educational and career information resource, vocational testing, and workshops.

MARYLAND

Baltimore New Directions for Women, 2511 N. Charles St., Baltimore, MD 21218, 301-235-8800. Monday–Friday, 9 am–4:30 pm. Educational and career counseling, continuing education courses, job referral, placement. Information center.

College of Notre Dame of Maryland, Continuing Education Center, 4701 N. Charles St., Baltimore, MD 21210, 301-435-0100. Monday–Friday, 8:30 am–4:30 pm. College sponsored. Educational and career counseling, continuing education courses. Fees vary.

Goucher College, Goucher Center for Educational Resources, Towson, Baltimore, MD 21204, 301-337-6200. Monday–Friday, 9 am–4:30 pm. College sponsored. Counseling to women considering a return to school. Noncredit and credit courses for adults. Referrals for career and volunteer work.

MASSACHUSETTS

Career & Volunteer Advisory Service, Project Re-Entry, 14 Beacon St., Boston, MA 02108, 617-227-1762. Monday–Friday, 10 am–4 pm. Independent nonprofit agency. Career counseling, job information. Fee for consultation.

Continuum, Inc., 785 Centre St., Newton, MA 02158, 617-964-3322. Monday–Friday, 9 am–5 pm. A private, licensed school of career education. Internship programs for adults changing, advancing, or entering careers. Career counseling for men and women of all ages and for relocated spouses. Vocational testing available. Fees vary.

Radcliffe Career Services, 77 Brattle Street, Cambridge MA 02138. Fee for counseling session. M-F 9 to 5, evenings by appointment. Open to general public as well as Harvard and Radcliffe students and alumnae. Fees vary.

Resources Center for Educational Opportunities, 19 Fort Hill St., Hingham, MA 02043, 617-749-7445. Monday–Friday, 9:30 am–11:30 am and by appointment. Branch action project of American Association of University Women.

Smith College, Career Development Office, Pierce Hall, Northampton, MA 01063, 413-584-2700. Monday–Friday, 8:30 am–4:30 pm. Official college office. Educational and career counseling. No fees.

Widening Opportunity Research Center, Middlesex Community College, Box T, Bedford, MA 01730, 617-275-8910, Ext. 291. Monday–Friday, 9 am–2 pm. College sponsored office. Educational and career counseling, continuing education courses. Fees vary.

Women's Educational & Industrial Union, Career Services, 356 Boylston St., Boston, MA 02116, 617-536-5651. Monday–Friday, 9 am–5 pm. Independent nonprofit agency. Career counseling, job referral and placement. No registration fee. Placement fees vary.

Why Not? Program, YWCA, 1 Salem Sq., Worcester, MA 01608, 617-791-3181. Monday–Friday, 9 am–5 pm; evenings by appointment. Fees vary.

MICHIGAN

Every Woman's Place, 1433 Clinton, Muskegon, MI 49442, 616-726-4493. Monday–Friday, 9 am–5 pm.

Michigan Technological University, Division of Education and Public Services, Youth Programs, Rm 208 Academic Offices Bldg., Houghton, MI 49931, 906/487-2219, Mon-Fri, 8am-5pm. Official College Office. Three, one-week, Women in Engineering Workshops. Career education and counseling.

Macomb County Community College, Community Resource Center, 14500 Twelve Mile Road, K-332, Warren, MI 48093, 313-445-7417. Monday–Friday, 8:30 am–5 pm.

Montcalm Community College, Student Services Office, Sidney, MI 48885, 517-328-2111. Monday–Friday, 8 am–5 pm; evenings by appointment. College sponsored office. Education and career counseling. No fees.

C.S. Mott Community College, Guidance Services and Counseling Division, 1401 East Court St., Flint, MI 48503, 313-762-0356. Monday–Thursday, 8 am–7 pm; Friday, 8 am–4:30 pm. Health counseling and vocational testing.

Northern Michigan University, Women's Center for Continuing Education, Marquette, MI 49855, 906-227-2101. Monday–Friday, 8:30 am–4:30 pm. Official college office. Educational and career counseling, job referral, continuing education courses. Fees vary.

Oakland University, Continuum Center for Adult Counseling and Leadership Training, Rochester, MI 48063, 313-377-3033. Monday–Friday, 8 am–5 pm. College affiliated. Personal, educational and career counseling, continuing education courses. Fees vary.

Schoolcraft College, Women's Resource Center, 18600 Haggerty Road, Livonia, MI 48152, 313-591-6400, Ext. 430. Monday–Friday, 9 am–3 pm. Continuing Education Community Services; Educational and career counseling courses, workshops, referral to other agencies, and peer counseling. For widowed, displaced homemakers and re-entry women and men. Fees for courses and workshops only.

University of Michigan, Center for Continuing Education of Women, 350 S. Thayer St., Ann Arbor, MI 48109, 313-764-6555.

Western Michigan University, Center for Women's Services, Kalamazoo, MI 49008, 616-383-6097. Monday–Friday, 8 am–5 pm. Official college office. Educational and career counseling. Fees vary.

Women's Center, University of Michigan-Dearborn, Office of Student Affairs, 4901 Evergreen Rd., Dearborn, MI 48128, 313-593-5147. Discussions and information about employment trends, study skills, childcare, re-entry, scholarships, career planning, social interactions, marriage and divorce, legal issues, rape prevention, and health care. Fees vary.

Women's Resource Center, 252 State St., Grand Rapids, MI 49503, 616-458-5443. Monday and Wednesday, 9 am–8 pm; Tuesday and Thursday, 9 am–5 pm. Independent nonprofit agency. Educational and career counseling, job referral. Fees vary.

MINNESOTA

Chart, Wesley Temple Bldg., 123 East Grant Street, Minneapolis, MN 55403, 612-871-9100. By appointment. Career development and employment services to individuals and organizations. Fees vary.

Minnesota Women's Center, University of Minnesota, 5 Eddy Hall, Minneapolis, MN 55455, 612-373-3850. Monday–Friday, 8 am–4:30 pm. Official college office. Informal advising and referral. No fees.

Southwest State University, Women's Resource Center, Marshall, MN 56258, 507-537-7160, September–May. Monday–Friday, 8 am–4:30 pm; evening schedule varies. Official college office. Educational and career counseling, job referral and placement, continuing education courses. Placement fee only.

Working Opportunities for Women, 2233 University Ave., Ste. 340, St. Paul, MN 55114, 612-647-9961. Monday–Friday, 8:30 am–5 pm. Complete career planning services for women.

MISSISSIPPI

Mississippi State University, Placement and Career Information Center, Drawer P, Mississippi State, MS 39762, 601-325-3344. Monday–Friday, 8 am–5 pm.

MISSOURI

New Directions Center, 806 N. Providence Rd., Columbia, MO 65201, 314-443-2421. Monday–Friday, 9 am–4 pm. Career planning, education referral and job placement center for women. Workshops and individual career counseling.

University of Missouri, St. Louis, Continuing Education-Extension, 313 Education Office Bldg., 8001 Natural Bridge Rd., St. Louis, MO 63121, 314-553-5511. Monday–Friday, 8 am–5 pm. Official college office. Educational and career counseling, adult education courses, limited job referral. Fees vary.

The Women's Center, University of Missouri, Kansas City, 5204 Rockhill Rd., Kansas City, MO 64110, 816-276-1638. Monday–Friday, 8 am–5 pm. Official college office. Educational and career counseling, job referral, continuing education courses. No fees.

MONTANA

Focus on Women, 9 Hamilton Hall, Montana State University, Bozeman, MT 59717, 406-994-4541. Monday–Friday, 8 am–5 pm. Workshops, seminars. Fee varies.

Women's Resource Center, Non-traditional Job Counselor, University of Montana, Missoula, MT 59801, 406-453-6691. Monday–Friday, 8 am–5 pm. Non-traditional career counseling, and job referral. No fee.

Women in Transition, Missoula YWCA, 1130 W. Broadway, Missoula, MT 59801, 406-543-6768. Monday–Friday, 8 am–5 pm. Job counseling, career counseling, job referral, resume preparation. Works with displaced homemakers.

NEW JERSEY

Adult Service Center, 112 Main Rd., Montville, NJ 07045, 201-575-0855, 335-4420. Monday, Tuesday, Thursday, Friday, 9 am–1 pm; Wednesday, 7 pm–10 pm.

Bergen Community College, Division of Community Services, 400 Paramus Rd., Paramus, NJ 07652, 201-447-1940. Monday–Friday, 9 am–5 pm. College sponsored office. Educational and career counseling, adult education courses. No fees.

Caldwell College, Career Development Center, Caldwell, NJ 07006, 201-228-4424, Ext. 307. Monday–Friday, 8:30 am–4:30 pm. College sponsored office. Educational and career counseling, limited job referral. No fees.

College Counseling and Education Center, 369 Forest Ave., Paramus, NJ 07652, 201-265-7729. Monday–Saturday, 9 am–9 pm.

Douglass College, Douglass Advisory Services for Women, Rutgers Women's Center, 132 George St., New Brunswick, NJ 08903, 201-932-9603. Monday–Friday, 9 am–2 pm. Educational and career counseling. No fees.

Fairleigh Dickinson University, Center for Women, Madison Ave., Madison, NJ 07940, 201-377-4700, Ext. 320. Monday–Friday, 9 am–5 pm. Official college office. Educational and career counseling, continuing education courses, job referral and placement. No fees.

Eve Adult Advisory Services, Kean College of New Jersey, Administration Bldg., Union, NJ 07083, 201-527-2210. Monday–Friday, 9 am–4:30 pm. College sponsored. Educational and career counseling. No registration fee. Other fees vary.

Jersey City State College, The Women's Center, 94 Audubon, Jersey City, NJ 07305, 201-547-3189. Monday–Friday, 9 am–4:30 pm. Official college office. Educational and career counseling, continuing education courses. No fees.

Jewish Vocational Service, 111 Prospect St., East Orange, NJ 07017, 201-674-6330. Five days, thirty-seven hours. Independent, nonprofit office. Educational and career counseling, job referral and placement. Fees vary.

Middlesex County College, Women's Career Information Center, Woodbridge Ave., West Hall Annex, Edison, NJ 08818, 201-548-6000, Ext. 411. Monday–Friday, 10 am–4 pm.

Montclair State College, Women's Center, Valley Rd., Upper Montclair, NJ 07043, 201-893-5106. Monday–Friday, 8:30 am–4:30 pm; evenings by appointment. College sponsored office. Educational and career counseling. No fees.

The Professional Roster, 171 Broadmead, Princeton, NJ 08609, 609-921-9561. Monday–Friday, 10 am–1 pm. Independent, nonprofit organization. Career counseling, job referral.

Reach, Inc., College of St. Elizabeth, O'Connor Hall, NJ 07961, 201-267-2530. Monday–Friday, 9:30 am–3 pm. Independent nonprofit office, Educational and career counseling, job referral. Fees vary.

NEW MEXICO

Young Women's Christian Association, Women's Resource Center, 316 Fourth St. SW, Albuquerque, NM 87102, 505-247-8841. Monday–Friday, 8 am–5 pm. Career counseling on a group basis. Classes, workshops, support groups, library. Fees on sliding scale: no one turned away for inability to pay.

NEW YORK

Academic Advisory Center for Adults, Turf Ave., Rye, NY 10580, 914-967-1653. Monday–Thursday, 9am–4 pm, some evenings.

Hofstra University, Counseling Center, 240 Student Center, Hempstead, NY 11550, 516-560-6788. Monday–Friday, 9 am–5 pm; Monday, Thursday, 6–10 pm. Official college office. Educational and vocational counseling, testing, continuing education courses. Fees vary.

Kingsborough Community College, Office of Career Counseling and Placement, 2001 Oriental Blvd., Rm. C102, Brooklyn, NY 11235, 212-934-5115. Monday–Friday, 8 am–5 pm.

Janice La Rouche Assoc., Workshops for Women, 333 Central Park West, New York, NY 10025, 212-663-0970. Monday–Friday, 9 am–6 pm. Independent private agency. Career strategies counseling. Assertiveness training. No registration fee. Other fees vary.

Mercy College, Career Counseling and Placement Office, 555 Broadway, Dobbs Ferry, NY 10522, 914-693-4500, Ext. 215. Monday–Friday, 9 am–5 pm. Evenings by appointment. Official college office. Career counseling. Fees vary.

More for Women, 1435 Lexington Ave., New York, NY 10028, 212-534-0852. Monday–Friday, 9 am–9 pm; Saturday, 9 am–4 pm. Independent private agency. Educational and career counseling, workshops. Fees vary.

New Options, 960 Park Ave., New York, NY 10028, 212-535-1444. Monday–Friday, 9 am–5 pm. Evenings by appointment.

Orange County Community College, Office of Community Services, 115 South St., Middletown, NY 10940, 914-343-1121. Monday–Friday, 9 am–5 pm. Official college office. Educational counseling, continuing education courses. Fees vary.

Personnel Sciences Center, 341 Madison Ave., New York, NY 10017, 212-661-1870. Monday–Saturday, 9 am–5 pm. Independent private agency. Educational and career counseling. Fees vary.

Professional Skills Roster, 512 E. State St., Ithaca, NY 14850, 607-272-5533. Monday–Friday, 9:30 am–12:30 pm. Independent nonprofit agency. Job referral, limited educational and career counseling. No fees. Suggested donation.

Regional Learning Service of Central New York, 405 Oak St., Syracuse, NY 13203, 315-425-5252. Monday–Friday, 8:30 am–4:30 pm. Independent nonprofit agency. Educational and career counseling. Registration fees vary.

Ruth Shapiro Associates, 200 E. 30th St., New York, NY 10016, 212-889-4284, 212-679-9858. Monday-Saturday, 9:30 am–6 pm and evenings. By appointment only. Private agency. Career/assertiveness counseling, resume/letter writing. Fees vary.

SUNY at Buffalo, Career Planning Office, 252 Capen Hall, Buffalo, NY 14260, 716-636-2231. Monday–Friday, 8:30 am–5 pm. Official college office. Educational and career counseling, job referral and placement. No fees.

Women's Center for Continuing Education, Syracuse University College, 610 E. Fayette Street, Syracuse, New York, 13202, 315-423-4116. Phyllis R. Chase, Director., M-F 9-5. Career and educational counseling. No fees.

Vistas for Women, YWCA, 515 North St., White Plains, NY 10605, 914-949-6227. Monday–Thursday, 9 am–5 pm.

Women's Career Center, Inc., 30 N. Clinton Ave., Rochester, NY 14604, 716-325-2274. Monday, Tuesday, Wednesday, Friday, 9 am–4 pm; Monday, Tuesday, 4:30 pm–8:30 pm.

NORTH CAROLINA

Duke University, Office of Continuing Education, 107 Bivins Bldg., Durham, NC 27708, 919-684-6259. Monday–Friday, 8:30 am–5 pm. Official college office. Educational and career counseling, continuing education courses, for men as well as women. Fees vary.

Fayetteville Family Life Center, 114 Highland Ave., Fayetteville, NC 28305. Monday–Thursday, 8:30 am–5 pm. Friday, 8:30 am–12 pm. Tuesdays and Thursdays in evening.

Salem College, Lifespan Center, Lehman Hall, Box 10548, Salem Station, Winston-Salem, NC 27108, 919-721-2807. Monday–Friday, 9 am–5 pm. College sponsored office. Lifespan planning, educational and vocational counseling. Fees vary.

OHIO

Baldwin-Wallace College, Experience CUE, Developmental Services, Administration Bldg. - No. 118, Berea, OH 44017, 216-826-2188. Monday–Friday, 8:30 am–5 pm; Tuesday and Thursday, 5:30 pm–9 pm.

Cleveland Jewish Vocational Service, 13878 Cedar Rd., University Heights, OH 44118, 216-321-1381. Monday–Friday, 8:30 am–5 pm; Thursday, 8:30 am–6 pm. Independent nonprofit agency. Educational and career counseling, job referral, placement.

Lifelong Learning/Women's Programs, Cuyahoga Community College, 2900 Community College Ave., Cleveland, OH 44115, 216-241-5966. Monday–Friday, 9 am–5 pm. Community service. College sponsored office. Individual educational and career counseling, no fee. Group series and programs, fees vary.

Ohio State University, Adult Career Services, Office of Continuing Education, 210 Sullivant Hall, 1813 North High St., Columbus, OH 43210, 614-422-8860. Monday–Thursday, 8 am–7:30 pm; Friday, 8 am–5 pm; Saturday, 8 am–12 pm. Career services, continuing education for adults. Individual counseling, no fee. Career planning courses, special programs and workshops, fees vary.

Pyramid, Inc., 1642 Cleveland Ave. NW, Canton, OH 44703, 216-453-3767. Monday–Friday, 8:30 am–4:30 pm.

Resource: Careers, 1258 Euclid Ave., Ste. 204, Cleveland, OH 44115, 216-579-1414. For professional development of women with one year of college or more. By appointment only. Fees vary.

University of Toledo, Center for Women, 2801 West Bancroft Street, Toledo, OH 43606. 419-537-2058. Monday–Friday, 8 am–5 pm. Specialists in helping homemakers to enter the job market. Career counseling, workshops, seminars available. Fees based on ability to pay.

Wright State University, Women's Career Development Center, 140 East Monument Ave., Dayton, OH 45402, 513-223-6041. Monday–Friday, 8:30 am–5 pm.

University of Akron, Adult Resource Center, Akron, OH 44325, 216-375-7448. Monday–Friday, 8 am–5 pm. Educational and career counseling, adult education courses, job referral, placement. No registration fee.

OREGON

Women's Programs, Division of Continuing Education, Oregon State System of Higher Education, 1633 SW Park Ave., (mail) Box 1491, Portland, OR 97207, 503-448-2219. Monday–Friday, 8:30 am–4:30 pm. Official college office. Educational and career counseling, continuing education courses. No registration fee. Other fees vary.

PENNSYLVANIA

Cedar Crest College, Women's Center, Allentown, PA 18104, 215-437-4471. Monday–Friday, 8:30 am–4:30 pm. Educational and career counseling, continuing education courses, career interest testing. Fees vary.

Indiana University of Pennsylvania, Transition Center, Uhler Hall, Indiana, PA 15705, 412-357-2227, Ext. 18. Monday–Friday, 8:30 am–4:30 pm. Educational counseling, workshops, continuing education. No fees.

Institute of Awareness, 401 S. Broad St., Philadelphia, PA 19147, 215-545-4400. Monday–Friday, 9 am–5 pm. Independent and nonprofit agency. Adult education courses, special workshops, training programs. Fees vary.

Job Advisory Service, 300 South Craig St., Pittsburgh, PA 15213. 412-621-0940. Monday–Friday 9 a.m.–4:30 p.m. Saturday, 9 a.m.–1 p.m. Independent non-profit career counseling center. Job counseling, vocational testing, resume writing, workshops. Second career internship program for re-entry women and teachers.

Lehigh County Community College, Alternatives for Women, 2370 Main St., Schnecksville, PA 18078, 215-799-2121, Ext. 177. Sponsored by college community service office. Workshops. Fees vary.

Temple University, Career Services, Mitten Hall, Philadelphia, PA 19122; or 1619 Walnut St., Philadelphia, PA, 215-787-1503. Monday–Friday, 9 am–5 pm. College sponsored offices: 215-787-7981. No registration fee.

University of Pennsylvania, Resources for Women, 1208 Blockley Hall/ sl, Philadelphia, PA 19104, 215-898-5537. Monday–Friday, 10 am–3 pm. University sponsored, continuing supportive career services, career and resume counseling, workshops, job referral and placement. Fees vary.

Villa Maria College, Counseling Services for Women, 2551 West Lake Rd., Erie, PA 16505, 814-838-1966. Monday–Friday, 9 am–4 pm. Official college office. Educational and career counseling, job referral, placement, adult education courses. No fees.

Wilson College, Office of Career Services, Chambersburg, PA 17201, 717-264-4141. Monday–Friday, 8 am–5 pm. Official college office. Educational and career counseling, job referral and placement. No fees.

SOUTH CAROLINA

Converse College, Women's Center, Spartanburg, SC 29301, 803-585-6421, Ext. 340. Monday–Friday, 8 am–5 pm. Free to students and alumnae.

Greenville Technical College, Center for Continuing Education for Women, Greenville, SC 29606, 803-242-3170. Monday–Thursday, 8 am–8:30 pm; Friday, 8 am–4:30 pm.

SOUTH DAKOTA

Sioux Falls College, The Center for Women, Glidden Hall, Sioux Falls, SD 57101, 605-331-6697. Educational, personal and career counseling.

TENNESSEE

YWCA of Nashville, Career/Life Planning Center, 1608 Woodmont Blvd., Nashville, TN 37215, 615-385-3952. Monday–Friday, 8:30 am–4:30 pm.

TEXAS

Amarillo College, Women's Programs, Box 447, Amarillo, TX 79178, 806-376-5111, Ext. 2683. Monday–Friday, 8 am–5 pm.

Austin Women's Center, 2700 South 1st Street, Austin, TX 78704, 512-447-9666. Job search workshops, Tuesdays 9:30 am and 5:30 pm. No income eligibility requirements.

Community Counseling, Everywoman Program, Richland College, 12800 Abrams Rd., Dallas, TX 75243, 214-238-6034. College-individual career and personal counseling, displaced homemakers center. No fee.

Vocational Guidance Service, Inc., 2525 San Jacinto, Houston, TX 77002, 713-659-1800. Monday–Thursday, 8:30 am–7 pm; Friday, 8:30 am–5 pm. Nonprofit organization. Educational and career counseling, job referral and placement. Fees based on sliding scale.

Women's Counseling Service, 1950 W. Gray, Ste. 1, Houston, TX 77019, 713-521-9391. Career development. Individual vocational, divorce adjustment and educational counseling.

The Women's Employment Network, Inc., 109 Lexington, Ste. 300, San Antonio, TX 78205. 512-224-3002. Group job search for women, with an "alumnae association" for graduates, to aid their job retention. Free to women on welfare and to single mothers.

Women's Resource Center, YWCA, 4621 Ross Ave., Dallas, TX 75204. 214-827-5600. Monday–Friday, 9 a.m.–4 p.m. Vocational testing, individual and group career counseling. Fees vary.

UTAH

The Phoenix Institute, 352 Denver St., Salt Lake City, UT 84111, 801-532-5080. Monday–Friday, 8 am–8 pm. Saturdays by appointment.

Women's Resource Center, 293 Union Bldg., University of Utah, Salt Lake City, UT 84112, 801-581-8030. Monday–Friday, 8 am–5 pm. Evening groups. Conferences, discussion programs, groups, personal and career counseling and referral information open to the community.

VIRGINIA

Educational Opportunity Center, 3830 Virginia Beach Blvd., Virginia Beach, VA 23452, 804-463-4810. Monday–Friday, 8 am–4:30 pm. Nonprofit agency. Educational, career, and financial aid counseling. No fees.

Hollins College, Career Counseling Center, Rose Hill House, Hollins College, VA 24020, 703-362-6364. Monday–Friday, 9 am–4:30 pm.

Mary Baldwin College, Offices of Career Services and Internships, Staunton, VA 24401, 703-887-7030. M–F, 8:30–4:30. College affiliated office. Educational and career counseling. No fee.

University of Richmond, Women's Resource Center, University College, VA 23173, 804-285-6319. Call for appointment.

Virginia Commonwealth University, University Advising Center, Room 114, 901 W. Franklin St., Richmond, VA 23284, 804-257-0200. M–Th, 8–7:30; Fr, 8–4:30; Sa, 9–1 pm. Nancy B. Miller, Director. Official university office. Educational counseling, referral to university career and personal counseling services, continuing education courses.

Old Dominion University, Women's Center, 1521 W. 49th St., Norfolk, VA 23508. 804-440-4109. Monday–Friday, 8 a.m.–5 p.m. Call for appt. Continuing education courses and career counseling.

WASHINGTON

Individual Development Center, Inc. (I.D. Center), Career and Life Planning, 1020 E. John St., Seattle, WA 98102, 206-329-0600. Monday–Friday, 9 am–4 pm. Evening counseling and appointments. Independent private agency. Career and life decision counseling, career development workshops for company and government agency employees, outplacement services and employee assistance programs. Partial scholarships available.

University of Washington, Office of Career Planning, Continuing Education DW-25, Seattle, WA 98195, 206-543-4262. Monday–Friday, 9 am–4 pm. Individual counseling by appointment; evening and Saturday groups and workshops. University sponsored office. Educational and career counseling and testing, career assessment groups, career change workshops. Fees vary.

WEST VIRGINIA

West Virginia University, Placement Service, Mountain Lair, Morgantown, WV 26506, 304-293-2221. Monday–Thursday, 8 am–8 pm; Friday, 8 am–5 pm. Official college office. Restricted to alumnae. Educational and career counseling, job referral. Registration fee.

WISCONSIN

Employment Options, 2095 Winnebago St., Madison, WI 53704, 608-244-5181. Monday–Friday, 9–5 pm. Evening and weekend appointments arranged.

Waukesha County Technical Institute, Women's Development Center, 800 Main St.,

Pewaukee, WI 53072, 414-691-5400. Career and vocational counseling; free seminars and workshops on decision making, coping, career planning and job seeking skills. Special emphasis on nontraditional employment. All services free. Appointments and reservations advised. All services open to men also.

WYOMING

University of Wyoming, Placement Service, Box 3195, University Station, Laramie, WY 82071, 307-766-2398. Monday–Friday, 8 am–5 pm. Official college office, restricted to students and alumnae. Educational and career consulting, job referral. No fees.

III. GROUP-SUPPORT FOR THOSE WHO ARE UNEMPLOYED

Forty Plus Clubs. Not a national organization, but a nationwide network of voluntary, autonomous non-profit clubs, manned by its unemployed members, paying no salaries, supported by initiation fees and monthly dues. Generally speaking (requirements vary from club to club), open only to those who are forty years of age or older, unemployed currently, seeking active employment, having made an average of between $25,000–$30,000 minimum annual salary previously. The minimum varies from club to club and has been lowered lately, so as not to discriminate against women (who are notoriously underpaid for their talents). The screening procedures again vary from club to club, and the process may take up to six weeks. It involves (usually) a personal interview, the checking out of your business references, and an informal meeting with representative active members. Insiders claim at least one-tenth leave without ever finding placement (sometimes due to their own lack of motivation), some try to hang around just for the sense of community (hence stays are often limited to six months, in some locations), and it takes the average successful member up to six months to find placement. While active in the club members must agree to give typically about sixteen hours a week, or two and one-half days to club work. Fees and monthly dues vary from club to club. There have been clubs in the following cities: Toronto, Oakland, California, Los Angeles, Chicago, Denver, Honolulu, Philadelphia, Washington D.C., New York, Cleveland, and Winston-Salem. You will need to check if the club nearest you is still operating. The white pages of your phone book will have their address and phone number (they are all listed under the title of FORTY PLUS).

Changes. 7 Woodbridge St., Cambridge, MA 02140. 617-876-5085. A group for unemployed professionals. Registration $6. Sessions $3. for unemployed, and $6. for the employed. Initial interview with the counselor is encouraged. Free. (Neither he nor the 100 or more fellow members of the Cambridge Psychotherapy Institute charge for the initial interview.) Carl J. Schneider, Counselor.

Talent Bank Associates, 475 Calkins Rd., Henrietta (near Rochester), NY 14467, (716) 334-9676. An organized form of the "Job-Hunters Anonymous" idea. A nonprofit organization comprised of unemployed persons of various professions and skills working together on a volunteer basis to find themselves meaningful, permanent employment. Free of charge. During a recent year, it served 350 people, 79% of whom found long-term employment through this program.

St. Jude's Job Network Club, a non-denominational self-help support group meets every Monday at 7:30 p.m. at St. Jude's Catholic Church, 7171 Glenridge Drive, Sandy Springs, Georgia (near northern Atlanta).

Operation Job Search, 2844 South Calhoun St., Fort Wayne, IN 46807. 219-456-3542. A community-wide career assessment program, sponsored by the city; the only such program of its kind in the country, at this writing. For all residents of the city of Fort Wayne, who are unemployed or underemployed.

Chicago Career Clubs. Meets every other Tuesday evening (at this writing) from 6-8 p.m. at Three Arts Club, 1300 N. Dearborn, Chicago. $10. per session, payable at the door. Clubs also meet in Northbrook, Evanston, Oak Park and Gwen Ellyn. Reservations are required: call 312-274-3169.

The Employment Connection (a non-profit organization), located in Terwilliger School, 6318 S.W. Corbett, Portland, OR 97201, 503-244-1055. A two week program followed up by a weekly job support group. Based on the Azrin model of the Job Club. It is run by businesses, organizations and churches in the Portland area, to help Portland area people find work. Fee.

Career Planning and Placement Center, Adult Evening Program, 110 Noyes Hall, University of Missouri, Columbia, MO 65201, (314) 882-6803. Tuesday and Thursday, 5–9 pm. Open to the public. Free. Drop-in for research. Schedule individual appointment. Help with goal clarification, resumes, interviews, job-seeking strategies, training opportunities. Job-seeking group.

Experience Unlimited. An organization for unemployed professionals, based in California. Contact: Mr. Herman L. Leopold, Experience Unlimited Coordinator, Employment Development Dept., 1111 Jackson St., Room 1009, Oakland, CA 94607. Mailing address: 1225 4th Ave., Oakland, CA 94606. 415-464-0659, 415-464-1259.

Civic Center Volunteers. Marin County Personnel Office, Administration Bldg., Civic Center, San Rafael, CA 94903, (415) 499-6104. Placement in county jobs of volunteer re-entry women, career-experimenters and students wishing to gain experience. Volunteers sign a contract for each specific job, and receive supervision and evaluation. The purpose of this program is to give work experience in various jobs and provide a place to gain confidence in one's skills, new self-esteem, etc.

T-I-E (Together in Employment). Offered in the Seattle-Tacoma area. Five individualized group sessions over two weeks. $25.00 fee. Sponsored by the Episcopal Diocese of Olympia, the specially-trained volunteers offer their programs through neighborhood churches. The seminars are however ecumenical, open to all. To register: (206) 325-4200. Steve Faust is chairman of TIE's advisory board.

Additional groups spring up, monthly, including job clubs and other group activities. Many of these are listed in *National Business Employment Weekly,* on its pages called "Calendar of Events." Available on newsstands, $3 per issue; or, order directly from: National Business Employment Weekly, 420 Lexington Avenue, New York, NY 10170. 212-808-6792. You will have to pick and choose carefully.

If you can't find any job club or support-group in your area, and therefore decide to help set one up yourself, there is a manual which will give you rather complete instructions. It is called *The Job Counselor's Manual,* by Nathan Azrin, and is available for $14.95 from University Park Press, 300 N. Charles St., Baltimore MD 21201.

IV. Directories of Career Counseling Services in Various Cities/States

Enterprising souls are now putting together listings of counselors, agencies, resources and potential employers for individual cities or metropolitan areas. While such books, unless they are revised annually, are bound to become outdated rapidly (ah, how well I know) due to places moving, folding, or rising Phoenixlike from their own ashes in a different form, nonetheless these books offer at least a starting place if you are looking for help:

NATIONAL

The National Job Bank, ed., Adams, Robert Lang. Bob Adams, Inc., 840 Summer Street, South Boston, MA 02127. 1983. $79.95, hardcover (add $1.75 for postage and handling, if ordering by mail). Lists employers, hospitals, universities, government agencies, as well as private employment agencies and services, for Metro New York, Boston, Chicago, D.C. and Baltimore, Atlanta, Texas, California, Pennsylvania, Colorado, Arizona, New Mexico and Utah. 10,000 entries, 1600 pages.

CALIFORNIA

Beach, Janet L., *How To Get A Job in the San Francisco Bay Area.* Contemporary Books, Inc., 180 North Michigan Ave., Chicago, IL 60601. 1983. $9.95, paper. An extremely well-done resource guide, describing the nature of the Bay Area, each major industry in that Area, the nature of that industry and key resources, salary titles and salary ranges, insiders' advice, key companies or organizations, together with the name of the principal contact therein.

The Northern California Job Bank, ed., Adams, Robert Lang. Bob Adams, Inc., 840 Summer Street, South Boston, MA 02127. 1982. $9.95, paper (add $1.75 for postage and handling, if ordering by mail). Lists employers, hospitals, universities, government agencies, as well as private employment agencies and services.

Visconti, Ron, *1983–1984 Bay Area Career Resource Directory.* Institute for Educational Improvement, 231 E. Millbrae Ave., Ste. 114, Millbrae, CA 94030. 1983. $6.50, paper (plus $1.25 postage and handling; California residents add $.42 tax). All orders must be prepaid.

Looking for Work . . . . A Bay Area Guide To Employment Resources. New Ways to Work, 149 Ninth St., San Francisco, CA 94103. 1983. $4.45, paper. Regular updates published, and included.

The Southern California Job Bank, ed., Adams, Robert Lang. Bob Adams, Inc., 840 Summer Street, South Boston, MA 02127. 1981. $9.95, paper (add $1.75 for postage and handling, if ordering by mail). Lists employers, hospitals, universities, government agencies, as well as private employment agencies and services.

DISTRICT OF COLUMBIA

The Metropolitan Washington Job Bank, ed., Adams, Robert Lang. Bob Adams, Inc., 840 Summer Street, South Boston, MA 02127. 1983. $9.95, paper (add $1.75 for postage and handling, if ordering by mail). Lists employers, hospitals, universities, government agencies, as well as private employment agencies and services.

ILLINOIS

The Greater Chicago Job Bank, ed., Adams, Robert Lang. Bob Adams, Inc., 840 Summer Street, South Boston, MA 02127. 1982. $9.95, paper (add $1.75 for postage and handling, if ordering by mail). Lists employers, hospitals, universities, government agencies, as well as private employment agencies and services.

MASSACHUSETTS

Boyd, Kathleen, and Ramsauer, Constance Arnold, and Senft, Ruth, *Career Connections: A Guide to Career Planning Services in Massachusetts*. Bob Adams, Inc., 840 Summer Street, South Boston, MA 02127. 1983. $9.95, paper.

The Boston Job Bank, ed., Adams, Robert Lang. Bob Adams, Inc., 840 Summer Street, South Boston, MA 02127. 1983, 1980 (all new second edition). $9.95, paper (add $1.75 for postage and handling, if ordering by mail). Lists employers, hospitals, universities, government agencies, as well as private employment agencies and services. Also has ads, of various services.

NEW YORK

The Metropolitan New York Job Bank, ed., Adams, Robert Lang. Bob Adams, Inc., 840 Summer Street, South Boston, MA 02127. 1983 (all new second edition) $9.95, paper (add $1.75 for postage and handling, if ordering by mail). Lists employers, hospitals, universities, government agencies, as well as private employment agencies and services.

PENNSYLVANIA

The Pennsylvania Job Bank, ed., Adams, Robert Lang. Bob Adams, Inc., 840 Summer Street, South Boston, MA 02127. 1982. $9.95, paper (add $1.75 for postage and handling, if ordering by mail). Lists employers, hospitals, universities, government agencies, as well as private employment agencies and services.

THE SOUTHWEST

The Southwest Job Bank, ed., Adams, Robert Lang. Bob Adams, Inc., 840 Summer Street, South Boston, MA 02127. 1983. $9.95, paper (add $1.75 for postage and handling, if ordering by mail). In addition to primary employer listings, describes those positions with strong hiring outlooks, plus the basics of job-winning, as Adams sees it.

TEXAS

The Texas Job Bank, ed., Adams, Robert Lang. Bob Adams, Inc., 840 Summer Street, South Boston, MA 02127. 1982. $9.95, paper (add $1.75 for postage and handling, if ordering by mail). Lists employers, hospitals, universities, government agencies, as well as private employment agencies and services.

Camden, Thomas M., and Bishop, Nancy, *How to Get a Job in Dallas/Ft. Worth-The Insider's Guide*. Surrey Books, Inc., 500 N. Michigan Avenue, Suite 1940, Chicago, IL 60611. 1984. $13.95.

Wegmann, Robert, *How To Find A Job In Houston*. Ten Speed Press, P.O. Box 7123, Berkeley, CA 94707. 1983. $9.95, paper. Foreword and Appendix ("The Loss of Values in Career Counseling") by Richard N. Bolles. Appendix by the author on the subject "Assisting Larger Groups of Unemployed Workers To Find New Employment." Professor Wegmann teaches a class, for credit, on job choice, at the University of Houston-Clear Lake City. A large portion of this book, consequently, is devoted to the basic steps in the job-hunt process, as he teaches them in his excellent course.

Author Index

Update for 1986

To: PARACHUTE
P.O. Box 379
Walnut Creek, CA 94597

☐ I think that the information in the '85 edition needs to be changed, in your next revision, regarding (or, the following resource should be added):

_____

_____

_____

_____

_____

☐ I cannot find the following resource, listed on page _____ :

_____

_____

_____

_____

_____

_____

_____
Name

_____
Address

_____

(Please submit this before August 1, 1985. Thank You.)

Please Read This
Before Writing To Hotline

Inasmuch as people buy *Parachute* at the rate of about 24,000 copies per month, we receive a lot of HOTLINES from readers, as you may imagine.

We answer them as rapidly as possible, but sometimes it can take up to three weeks. Added to the time it takes your letter to get to us, and our letter to get back to you, this can cause a great delay in your job-hunt. I think we can save you a lot of time — you may not even need to mail us your HOTLINE — if we tell you the most common answers that we have to send out. So, please study this checklist, *before* deciding if you still need to send us your HOTLINE:

1. Are you devoting at least six hours a day, five days a week to your job-hunt?
   IF NOT, *THAT* IS YOUR DIFFICULTY. GO DO IT.

2. If you're having trouble in getting going, are you recruiting some other job-hunters to meet with you regularly, in a group as described in Chapter 4?
   IF NOT, *THAT* IS YOUR DIFFICULTY. GO DO IT.

3. Are you clear exactly what your skills are (having used the Quick Job-Hunting Map in Appendix A)?
   IF NOT, *THAT* IS YOUR DIFFICULTY. GO DO IT.

4. Have you put your skills in their order of priority for you (as we described in Appendix A)?
   IF NOT, *THAT* IS YOUR DIFFICULTY. GO DO IT.

5. Have you got your skills described with more than one word – e.g., not just "organizing" but, say, "organizing data into meaningful groups" or "organizing people into motivated small groups"?
   IF NOT, *THAT* IS YOUR DIFFICULTY. GO DO IT.

6. Have you decided just exactly where it is you want to use your skills, in terms of factors (see Appendix A, again)?
   IF NOT, *THAT* IS YOUR DIFFICULTY. GO DO IT.

7. Have you gone out and done intensive research as described in Chapter Six, devoting at least two or three hours a day to it, for 20 days?
   IF NOT, *THAT* IS YOUR DIFFICULTY. GO DO IT.

8. Are you looking for exceptions, rather than the rule (e.g., most employers may be prejudiced against someone over 40, but are you looking for those who *aren't*)?
   IF NOT, *THAT* IS YOUR DIFFICULTY. GO DO IT.

9. If you're getting in to be interviewed for hire, after finishing your research, and getting turned down, are you going back to ask them for helpful feedback as to how you could improve the way in which you are presenting yourself?
   IF NOT, *THAT* IS YOUR DIFFICULTY. GO DO IT.

10. Are you really determined to find that job that fits you, no matter what, rather than just giving this an idle push, so you can say, Well, I knew it wouldn't work?
    IF NOT, *THAT* IS YOUR DIFFICULTY. GO DO IT.

Now you know what to work on, without even sending in the HOTLINE. If however your answer to all ten was emphatically "Yes," or if you have determined already that you just want the name of a good counselor in your area, then by all means send that HOTLINE in.

Hotline '85

 Please read, mark, learn, and inwardly digest the page to the left before you send us this Hotline page!

To: PARACHUTE
P.O. Box 379
Walnut Creek, CA 94597

(1) I HAVE READ YOUR ENTIRE BOOK AND HAVE COMPLETELY FILLED IN *THE QUICK JOB-HUNTING MAP* EXERCISE IN APPENDIX A (page 217), but I am still having trouble with the following part of the career-change/job-hunting process:

_____

_____

_____

_____

_____

_____

_____

_____

(2) I feel I need help. I have studied all the resources in Appendix C, but I need additional names or suggestions for my geographical area. If there are additional counselors you could suggest, from whom I might get help, please let me know.

Name _____

Address _____

City, State, Zip _____

Mailing List & Newsletter '85

The author of *Parachute,* Richard Bolles, is the Director of the National Career Development Project headquartered in Walnut Creek, California (26 minutes due East of San Francisco).

The Project maintains a mailing list. If you wish to be on the mailing list, please fill out the form below, and enclose a check for $15., payable to "National Career Development Project." People on the mailing list receive notification of new books or other creations from the pen of Richard Bolles, as well as of the workshops which he conducts twice a year, in various parts of the U.S. or Canada.

You will also receive a Newsletter, published randomly six times during the year, written and edited by him, containing his latest thoughts on various subjects. It contains articles about special problems that job-hunters or career changers are encountering; plus descriptions of new research or publications; plus more of Bolles' philosophy; plus news of the Project, and what we are up to lately (three new books are currently wending their way toward 1986-1988 publication dates).

Subscriptions *must* run from January through December, for a given year. So, if you send us a check in, say, June, we will send you all the issues that have already come out in the period January-June of this year, and then continue your subscription through the end of December, only. Then you have to re-subscribe, if you wish the Newsletter for the next year.

TO: Mailing List & Newsletter '85
     NCDP
     P.O. Box 379
     Walnut Creek, CA 94597

Dear Folks:

Please add me to your mailing list for the period January-December [   ] 1985 [   ] 1986, so that I may receive periodic announcements of your newly-published works, your workshops, etc., and your six Newsletters for that period. My check for $15., U.S., is enclosed, payable to: "National Career Development Project." ($30., U.S., if this is for both years.)

Name _____

Address _____

City, State, Zip _____

Organization (optional) _____

Other Books by Richard N. Bolles

THE THREE BOXES OF LIFE
And How To Get Out Of Them

"Parachute" has reshaped the way people think about jobs and how to find them. *The Three Boxes of Life* calls for as much change in the way we think about school, work, and retirement.

" . . . a rich and rewarding guidebook that provides literally hundreds of resources and opportunities for growth." — *Library Journal.* "Why aren't learning, working, and playing, lifelong — simultaneous — activities rather than boxes or blocks of time as we traditionally have been taught they must be?" — *American School Board Journal.* " . . . truly a monumental work which provides a wealth of information." — *Journal of College Placement.* " . . . an eloquent plea for the restructuring of our work lives." — *Career Planning and Adult Development Newsletter.*

Contains hundreds of resources, exercises, charts, illustrations and the complete *Beginning Quick Job-Hunting Map.* 6 x 9 inches, 480 pages, $9.95 paper. $14.95 cloth

WHERE DO I GO FROM HERE WITH MY LIFE?
by John C. Crystal and Richard N. Bolles

Here is *the workbook* for the self-motivated individual, student, professional or anyone who has an interest in a systematic approach to job-hunting and career mobility, bringing together two of the leading people in the field. "A master work in career literature." — *Washington Star-News.* 9 x 7 inches, 272 pages, $9.95 paper

THE QUICK JOB-HUNTING MAP
Advanced Version

A practical book of exercises designed to give job seekers detailed help in analyzing their skills, finding the right career field, and

Over, please

Other Books by Richard N. Bolles *continued*

knowing how to find job openings and get hired. This is a 32-page version, 8½ x 11 inches, of the *Map* printed in previous editions of this book. $1.25 paper

There will be a NEW JOB MAP based on pages 217 to 271 of this book available this summer, probable price about $2.00. Please write for details.

THE QUICK JOB-HUNTING MAP
FOR BEGINNERS
Offers special help to new job seekers and others looking for their first jobs. 8½ x 11 inches, 32 pages, $1.25 paper

TEA LEAVES: A New Look At Resumes
Richard Bolles describes how well resumes work, or don't work, and why. Also what you can do about it. 6 x 9 inches, 24 pages, $.50

Available at your local book store, or when ordering direct from the publisher please include $.75 additional per clothbound copy for postage and handling, or $.50 additional per paperback copy for postage and handling.

TEN SPEED PRESS • Box 7123, Berkeley, California 94707

May we introduce other Ten Speed Books you may find useful . . .
over three million people have already.

Who's Hiring Who by Richard Lathrop
Bernard Haldane Associates' Job & Career Building
by Richard Germann and Peter Arnold
Finding a Job by Nathan H. Azrin, Ph.D., and Victoria Besalel
Finding Facts Fast by Alden Todd
Mail Order Moonlighting by Cecil Hoge
How to Get the Degree You Want by John Bear, Ph.D.
Computer Wimp by John Bear, Ph.D.
The Moosewood Cookbook by Mollie Katzen
The Enchanted Broccoli Forest and other timeless delicacies
by Mollie Katzen
Sailing the Farm by Ken Neumeyer
Write Right! by Jan Venolia
The Wellness Workbook
by Regina Sara Ryan and John W. Travis, M.D.
How to Grow More Vegetables by John Jeavons
Anybody's Bike Book by Tom Cuthbertson
Pleasure Packing by Robert S. Wood
Sweaty Palms by H. Anthony Medley
Finding Money For College by John Bear, Ph.D.

You will find them in your bookstore or library,
or you can send for our *free* catalog:

TEN SPEED PRESS
BOX 7123 • BERKELEY, CALIFORNIA 94707

Reprinted with permission from *Trevor's First Strike*, Brick House Publishing, 1983.